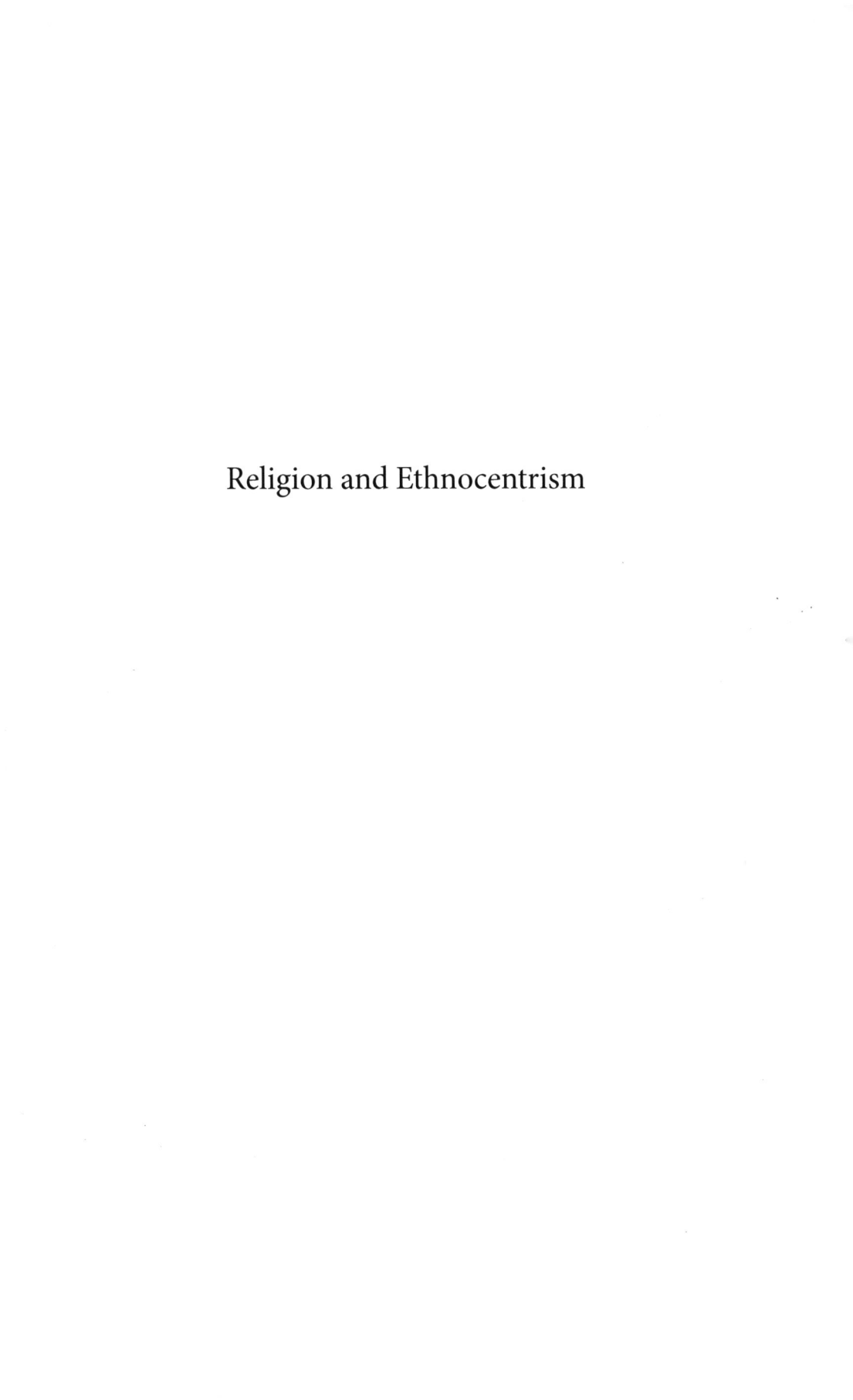

Religion and Ethnocentrism

Empirical Studies in Theology

Editor

Johannes A. Van der Ven

VOLUME 19

Religion and Ethnocentrism

An Empirical-theological Study

By

Dave Dean Capucao

BRILL

LEIDEN • BOSTON
2010

This book is printed on acid-free paper.

Library of Congress Cataloging-in-Publication Data

Capucao, Dave Dean, 1965-
  Religion and ethnocentrism : an empirical-theological study / by Dave Dean Capucao.
    p. cm. — (Empirical studies in theology ; v. 19)
  Includes bibliographical references (p.   ) and index.
  ISBN 978-90-04-18470-1 (hardback : alk. paper) 1. Catholic Church—Netherlands—Doctrines. 2. Ethnocentrism—Religious aspects—Catholic Church. 3. Ethnocentrism—Netherlands. I. Title. II. Series.

  BX1551.2.C37 2010
  282'.492089001–dc22

2010007552

ISSN 1389-1189
ISBN 978 90 04 18470 1

Copyright 2010 by Koninklijke Brill NV, Leiden, The Netherlands.
Koninklijke Brill NV incorporates the imprints Brill, Hotei Publishing, IDC Publishers, Martinus Nijhoff Publishers and VSP.

All rights reserved. No part of this publication may be reproduced, translated, stored in a retrieval system, or transmitted in any form or by any means, electronic, mechanical, photocopying, recording or otherwise, without prior written permission from the publisher.

Brill has made all reasonable efforts to trace all right holders to any copyrighted material used in this work. In cases where these efforts have not been successful the publisher welcomes communications from copyright holders, so that the appropriate acknowledgements can be made in future editions, and to settle other permission matters.

Authorization to photocopy items for internal or personal use is granted by Koninklijke Brill NV provided that the appropriate fees are paid directly to The Copyright Clearance Center, 222 Rosewood Drive, Suite 910, Danvers, MA 01923, USA.
Fees are subject to change.

Printed and bound in Great Britain by
CPI Antony Rowe, Chippenham and Eastbourne

CONTENTS

Acknowledgement	vii
Chapter One Introduction	1
1.1. Research problem	2
1.2. Research questions and aims	10
1.3. Conceptual model	14
1.4. Research Methods	18
1.5. Sampling method and data collection	20
1.6. Description of Research Population	23
1.7. Structure of the Book	25
Chapter Two Attitudes toward God	27
2.1. Images of God from a theoretical perspective	28
2.2. Images of God from an empirical perspective	44
2.3. Social location of the attitudes toward God	45
Chapter Three Attitudes toward Jesus	49
3.1. Images of Jesus from a theoretical perspective	50
3.2. Images of Jesus from an empirical perspective	79
3.3. Social location of the attitudes toward Jesus	81
Chapter Four Attitudes toward the Spirit	85
4.1. Images of the Spirit from a theoretical perspective	86
4.2. Images of the Spirit from an empirical perspective	100
4.3. Social location of the attitudes toward the Spirit	101
Chapter Five Attitudes toward Salvation	105
5.1. Images of salvation from a theoretical perspective	106
5.2. Images of salvation from an empirical perspective	128
5.3. Social location of the attitudes towards salvation	131
Chapter Six Attitudes toward the Church	135
6.1. Images of the church from a theoretical perspective	135
6.2. Images of the church from an empirical perspective	158
6.3. Social location of the attitudes toward the church	159

Chapter Seven   Attitudes toward Minorities 163
  7.1. Theoretical structure of the attitudes toward
       minorities 163
  7.2. Attitudes toward minorities from an empirical
       perspective 175
  7.3. Social location of the attitudes toward minorities 176

Chapter Eight   Religion and Ethnocentrism 179
  8.1. Characteristics of Civil Religion in the Netherlands 179
  8.2. Reactions to civil religion among Dutch Catholics 192
  8.3. Expected impact of religious attitudes on
       ethnocentrism 206
  8.4. Empirical impact of religious attitudes on
       ethnocentrism 219

Chapter Nine   Conclusion 229
  9.1. Summary of findings 229
  9.2. Theological evaluations, reflections, and statement of
       hypotheses 237
  9.3. Recommendations for future research 248

Appendices & Tables 251
Bibliography 297
Index 317

ACKNOWLEDGEMENT

It is a pleasure to acknowledge with great gratitude those persons who have assisted me in the writing of this book. I wish to thank Prof. Dr. J. van der Ven, whose influence on my intellectual and personal growth has been exceptionally valuable. I am grateful not only for his scholarly guidance but also for his personal friendship. I extend my thanks to Dr. Carl Sterkens whose assistance on every step of the writing of this book goes beyond measure. A special thanks to Prof. Dr. D. Pollefeyt for all the cordial support. I want to thank Ms. Berdine Biemans, for rendering her dedicated assistance especially on the statistical part of my work; to my Filipino colleagues, Rico, Nam, Marlon, and Gary for lending me their compassionate heart and generous support; to the Rombouts family for bestowing me countless assistance; to all the Filipino communities in the Netherlands who welcomed me in their homes and in their lives; to the Dutch parishes who allowed me access to the list of addresses of my respondents, and to all the parish members who participated in my research. I want to give my heartfelt gratitude to Cardinal Simonis for welcoming me in the Archdiocese of Utrecht in order to engage in some pastoral work while writing this book, and for lending me all kinds of assistance; to Msgr. Piet Rentinck who epitomizes the 'Father of Perpetual Succor'; and to many others who lent me their help during the completion of this book, I cannot thank you more than enough. I also want to thank in a very special way, Bishop Julio Xavier Labayen, OCD, whose life and works have been a great inspiration in my ministry and studies. It is also truly a great blessing to have a very supportive bishop, Bishop Rolly Tirona, OCD, who, together with my fellow priests of the Prelature of Infanta, have been so understanding in giving me this chance to take a study leave in order to finish this work. I also wish to acknowledge the great support and inspiration of some of my departed friends, namely: Ernst and Joy Jenis from Austria, Fr. Cha Collendres and Fr. Edwin Agapay. I want to thank the struggling poor of my country—for giving me inspiration and courage to overcome all struggles in life. To the 'church of the poor', I owe you my life and my love. I owe my profound debt of gratitude to my parents, Domingo and Teresita, to whom I dedicate this work. I also thank my brother and sisters, who constantly supplied me with care and love. And lastly yet most importantly, I want to thank the Lord for all that I am and all that I will be...*Ad maiorem Dei Gloriam!*

CHAPTER ONE

INTRODUCTION

In the beginning of 1960's, a sizeable number of immigrants came to the Netherlands as guest workers, refugees, etcetera. They eventually settled in this country and grew in number. Their fast increase in number led to a changed socio-demographic contour of the Dutch society which then inspired its leaders to shift its ideological vision of society from a mono-cultural to a multi-cultural state. Multiculturalism became then a 'consensus ideology' among its political leaders.[1] This ideological vision also influenced several of their official policies until the end of the 20th century. At the turn of the millennium, however, this multicultural vision has generated the feeling of 'disillusionment' among its populace. This was triggered by the escalating tension between the native Dutch inhabitants and the migrants. Conflicts built up in the community and the vision of multicultural society, as one author suggests, has been "relegated to the dunghill of political history" (Doomernik 2005). The repercussions of this to government's policies have been reflected for instance by the way it dealt recently with migrants by imposing stringent policies which is described by international observers as the toughest in Europe (Buruma 2006). The feeling of aversion towards immigrants is mounting, not only among the policy makers but generally among the native Dutch population. Studies show that this aversive feeling towards minorities is coupled with the mounting nationalistic feeling among its native constituents. This complex feeling of negative attitude towards minorities and a positive attitude towards the in-group is identified by sociologists as 'ethnocentrism' (Scheepers and Eisinga 1989). Studies reveal that there are several factors that account for this ethnocentric attitude. One of

---

[1] The phrase "*Integratie met behoud van eigen taal en cultuur*", i.e. social integration while retaining the language and culture of the immigrant groups, reflects this type of concensus policy on multiculturalism in the 70's. Immigrants were treated as members of a monolithic cultural bloc, on the basis of nationality—their religion only became an issue in the 1990s. Cf. http://en.wikipedia.org/wiki/Multiculturalism#_note-7 [Accessed 5 January 2004].

its major contributors is religion. A number of studies reveal that religion, far from its positive ideal of brotherhood/sisterhood, hospitality, and compassion, has been the primary origin of bigotry, ethnocentrism, and other forms of unfavourable attitude towards minorities. Other studies however, contest this sweeping claim saying that religion per se is not the cause of the problem. While it is true that there is something about religion that makes for prejudice, there is also about religion that unmakes it (Allport 1966:447). Thus, in this empirical-theological study, we intend to investigate this vexing relationship between religion and ethnocentrism. We would like to examine the rich theological resources of the Judeo-Christian tradition based on a choice of themes like God, Jesus, Spirit, Salvation, and the church, and demonstrate whether these religious attitudes contribute to an ethnocentric attitude among the believing Dutch population. By using the methods of empirical research, we intend to examine thoroughly this complex relation.

This introductory chapter is divided into seven sections. In section 1.1., the research problem is presented. First, the problems related to the in-group and the out-group in the Netherlands are examined. The problematic relationship between religion and ethnocentrism are also discussed in this section. Next, in section 1.2., the research questions and aims of this study are presented. In section 1.3., the conceptual model is introduced. In section 1.4., the research methods used are described. In section 1.5., the sampling method and data collection of this study are discussed. In section 1.6., the research population is described. Finally, in section 1.7., the structure of the whole book is presented.

1.1. Research problem

The research problem is explained in two sub-sections. First, the tension between the in-group and out-group is discussed (1.1.1.), and then an examination of the problematic relationship between religion and ethnocentrism is explored (1.1.2.).

1.1.1. Tension between in-group and out-group

In the past decades, this territorially small and yet densely populated country, the Netherlands, had been hosting immigrants coming from several parts of the globe. It ranked 24th among all countries that has stock of migrants, numbering around 1.6 million in the year 2000, which is 0.9% of the world's migrant stock (United Nations 2003). The increasing rate of immigration in this country created a dramatic change in the demographic make-up of its society in recent years. An important phenomenon brought by this influx of immigrants is the growth in number of ethnic minorities living and are still coming to this country. At this juncture, it should be noted that notwithstanding the varying definitions of the term ethnic minorities in several literatures and institutions, we shall be using a description of 'ethnic minority' that aptly fits the purpose of this study within the Dutch context. We shall understand ethnic minorities to refer to the non-western population living in the Netherlands who are mainly coming from Turkey, Morocco, Surinam, Dutch Antilles, and other parts of Africa, Asia, and Latin America.[2] Included in this group are the locally resident Moluccans, refugees (official status), caravan dwellers, gypsies, and children of such parents who are resident in the Netherlands.[3] Ethnic minorities are considered 'target groups' of the government's integration policy. Their social position is considered weak, and most of them are suffering from unemployment, occupational disability or are otherwise dependent on social security benefits. They generally thrive in the cities, and within those cities (Tesser et al. 1995).

The first wave of immigrants coming from former Dutch colonies arrived in the Netherlands during the early second half of the 20th century. In the 1960's and 1970's, non-western labourers coming from Southern Europe, Turkey and North Africa also came. Later, these migrant workers were joined by their families. Majority of these families stayed and grew in numbers. In the early 1980's, the government

---

[2] Not all groups with a foreign background are considered ethnic minority. For instance, a German living in the Netherlands has a foreign background but is not considered as ethnic minorities. Thus ethnic minorities are also referred to as *non-western* populations. The Dutch phrase allochtoon which is usually used to refer to the population with a foreign background in the Netherlands is difficult to translate in english. Broadly speaking, allochtoon refers to people whose native country or that of at least one parent is not the Netherlands. Its narrow definition refers to people born outside the Netherlands of non-Dutch parents or born in the Netherlands of two foreign parents (Aalders 2003).

[3] Persons with a foreign background are classified as western and non-western, according to their country of birth. If they are born in the Netherlands (the second generation), the classification is based on the mother's country of birth. If the mother is also born in the Netherlands, the background is determined by the father's country of birth (Aalders 2003).

recognized these 'guest workers' from Mediterranean countries and fellow citizens (*rijksgenoten*) from former colonial territories as immigrants and not as temporary visitors anymore (Rath 2001:137–159). The second wave of immigrants came during the 80's and 90's. Most of them were assylum seekers or refugees coming from different countries, e.g. Bosnia, Iraq, Afghanistan, etcetera. who fled their country for political and other reasons. Naturally, these immigrants carry with them diverse religious and cultural backgrounds. With the expanding number of ethnic minorities and their visible cultural diversity, often having distinct languages, religions and customs, a multicultural image of Dutch society emerged. Aside from the increasing influx of immigrants, it is also noted that the birth rate of ethnic minorities living inside the country is higher than that of the majority population. In 2002, for instance, two-thirds of the increase in Dutch population is attributed to non-western foreigners, about half of which is caused by newly-arrived immigrants, and the other half by births to immigrants already settled in the Netherlands. In Rotterdam itself, the Dutch Bureau of Statistics forecasts that by 2017, almost 60 percent of its 600,000 population will be members of ethnic minorities (CBS 2003; Hello 2003). Because of the historical and the recent social circumstances, one can validly conjecture that the growth in numbers of ethnic minorities is inevitable. Indeed, as long as immigration continues, the proportion of ethnic minorities will likely increase.

These profound changes in the socio-demographic make up of the Dutch society generated disquieting reactions among the Dutch population which came along with unsettling social consequences. Researches show that many people belonging to the majority group are unhappy about the presence of ethnic minorities in their neighbourhoods.[4] Inevitably, some social problems crop up, like outburst of aggression or violence, segregation, extreme right voting, etcetera. (Hello 2003:2). Previous studies indicate that these negative attitudes of native Dutch population towards minorities are intimately linked to their positive attitude towards their fellow native Dutch. This com-

---

[4] This problematic situation triggered a lot of studies, particularly in sociology, in the past decades which astoundingly reaches about 6,000–7,000 academic articles published in these two decades, averaging about one article daily. These so-called 'minority research' during the 80's and 90's were mostly aimed at developing a coherent "*minorities' policy*" which would give direction to the government's policy towards the integration of ethnic minorities in the Dutch society (Rath 2001).

plex of attitude is called *ethnocentrism* (Eisinga & Scheepers 1989). It consists of a favourable feeling towards members of the in-group and an unfavourable or negative feeling towards the out-group. The tension that arises in the present Dutch society will likely intensify unless a comprehensive understanding of the ethnocentric attitudes is fully grasped. This necessarily involves a study of several factors that generate this intricate feeling of favourable attitude towards one's fellow Dutch and the aversive feeling towards the minorities. One of the factors is religion.

1.1.2. Religion and Ethnocentrism—a Problematic Relationship

As we will show in more details below, religion is considered by earlier studies as one of the major 'culprits' behind the ethnocentric attitudes of many Dutch in-group members. However, this 'outlandish' claim seems to trigger uncomfortable feelings among church members because at the very heart of Christian teachings, the opposite has been professed. The Judeo-Christian tradition is awash with instructions to believers to care for the strangers, to treat them justly, and to accord them hospitality (Gk. *philoxenia* or love of strangers). In the Old Testament, the Israelites were directed to demonstrate hospitality to strangers because they themselves were once strangers in Egypt (Ex. 22:21–24). For this reason, molesting strangers was condemned because strangers had no protection (Ex. 22:21; Lev. 19:33–34). Hospitality in the biblical sense also includes righteous or just actions. In order to address the need to link hospitality with justice, Israel created laws in order to help and protect strangers, widows and orphans—the most vulnerable sectors of society.[5] In the New Testament, hospitality was perceived to be of great spiritual importance.[6] Jesus embodied in his person, his life, and his works the unconditional acceptance and becoming whole of all humanity through God. Through his actions, Jesus was deeply concerned with the universal reconciliation of the

---

[5] Although, one should note that there are passages in the Old Testament which are blatantly exclusivistic against strangers from foreign land (e.g. Ex. 23:20–28). There are also some texts (e.g. Deut. 14:21, 15:1–3, 17:15, 23:19–20) that show some particularistic orientation by prohibiting or excluding other nations but are actually meant to help build Israel's identity (cf. Van der Ven 2004:192–193; Schwienhorst-Schönberger 1995).

[6] See, for instance: Mt. 25:44–46; Heb. 13:2; Rom. 12:13; 1 Tim. 3:2; 1 Pet. 4:9; etc. (Koenig 1985:15).

kingdom of God. As we have seen, the scriptures reveal that offering hospitality is a significant aspect of faithful living. It is one of the core values that is preached by the Christian faith to its constituents where salvation is at stake (Mt. 25:31–40). It is interesting to note however how Christians in several periods in history have drifted from this ideal. In the recent turn of events in the Netherlands, one may question whether this religious ideal is in harmony with the actual attitudes of many Christians with regards the growing ethnic minorities in the land.

Since the beginning of the Second World War, many social scientists endeavored to comprehend this vexing relationship between religion and ethnocentrism.[7] Most of the results of these studies have indicated in one way or the other that one of the main factors that contribute to ethnic prejudice is religion. In a research undertaken by Allport and Kramer in 1946, it was demonstrated that there is a positive relationship between religious commitment and racial prejudice. Recent studies have also demonstrated that religion is a key factor that has an effect on ethnic or racial prejudice. They claim that the more religious an individual is, the more prejudiced he/she is (Hood, Spilka, Hunsberger & Gorsuch 1996). Yet, some ambivalent insights have also been obtained, noting that "there is something about religion that *makes* for prejudice and something that *unmakes* prejudice" (Allport 1966:447). This finding contends that the real issue is not whether one is a believer or not, but rather the sort of things that a person believes in is what makes him or her ethnocentric. It is not that you believe but *what* and *how* you believe which makes you ethnocentric. Some authors observed that in many studies in the past, there is always only one dimension of religiosity that has been explored in relation to ethnocentrism, for example, church membership, or religious activity or religious beliefs (Gorsuch & Aleshire 1974; Batson & Ventis 1982). Thus, some attempts to explore other dimensions of religiosity like religious practice, religious beliefs, religious experience, religious saliency, etcetera, have been included in later investigations. Subse-

---

[7] Batson summarized 47 findings based on 38 studies conducted between 1940 & 1990. He classified these findings using three indices, namely: church membership or attendance, positive attitude towards religion, orthodoxy or conservatism. He identified also 4 types of intolerance, i.e. ethnocentrism, racial prejudice, anti-Semitism, and other prejudices. He found out that 37 of 47 findings point to the existence of a positive relationship, while the other two point to the opposite.

quent studies illustrate that variety of dimensions of religiosity may have quite differential effects on prejudice against minorities (Glock & Stark 1965; 1968).[8] In terms of church attendance, various positions have also been obtained. Some claim for a curvilinear relationship, that is, non-attenders and frequent attenders are less prejudiced than infrequent to moderately frequent church attenders (Eisinga 1990; Adorno et al. 1950; Allport and Ross 1967). The moderately frequent church attenders are likely to conform to a dominant culture in which strong sentiments about white supremacy prevail, thereby inducing ethnic prejudice (Lenski 1961:533ff; Gorsuch & Aleshire 1974:281ff); conversely, non-attenders and frequent church attenders tend to evaluate these predominant societal issues critically and therefore reject prejudice. According to Eisinga et al. (1990:54–75), this curvilinear relationship can be explained by the following reasons: first, core members are possibly guided more by the religious teaching of brotherly love; second, religion may have a different meaning for core members, who would be less eager to submit themselves to external agents and would be more concerned about the social and humanistic side of religion; and lastly, modal and marginal members are more likely to be racially prejudiced because they are more conventional (since strong religious involvement is certainly no longer the norm in Dutch society, it could be argued that core church members have a less conformist identity). Some however, downplayed the curvilinear relationship by saying that it is in fact very limited (Hood et al. 1996:360). It has been pointed out that some beliefs may encourage intolerance like the doctrines of revelation and election. The doctrine of election, for instance tend to discriminate between the 'ins' from the 'outs' (Allport 1966:450). This has been re-echoed by Batson, Schoenrade & Ventis (1993:295) claiming that there appears to be a tragic, unintended effect to knowing that one is among God's elect. If some are the 'elect', then others are the 'damned', the outcasts. Some studies, however, acknowledge that some of the prominent doctrines of the past have undergone relaxation or

---

[8] Glock & Stark (1965) spell out some dimensions of religiosity, namely: *religious practice, belief, experience, and consequences. Religious practice* refers to church membership and church attendance; *belief* indicates doctrinal beliefs and religious particularism; *Experience* refers to occasions defined by those undergoing them as an encounter…between themselves and some supernatural consciousness; or any experience that is identified as religious within faith traditions (Hood et al., 1996); and, *consequences* refer to the effects of religiosity on people's daily lives (Glock & Stark 1969).

re-interpretation. Eisinga et al. (1990:54–75; 1990a:417–433) argue that another dimension of religion which is 'religious particularism' also plays a strong contributing factor to generate ethnic prejudice. According to these authors, religious particularism predisposes religious people to a religio-centric stance: when people consider their religion to be the only true religion, they tend to have an unfavourable attitude toward other religious out-groups, in fact to all religious groups not exempting the traditional Christian teachings". Another area of research goes deeper into the person's religious experiences. Results showed that people with experiences of spiritual, supernatural or other-worldly nature, may put inner-worldly tensions between in-groups and religious ethnic out-groups into another perspective, i.e. one of mutual tolerance (Scheepers et al. 2002:235–261). It is also argued that spiritual experiences ease down prejudice against ethnic minorities. Further studies on the relationship between religion and ethnocentrism showed that intrinsic religious people tended to be less prejudiced, less racist, and less anti-Semitic than extrinsic religious people (Allport 1966:447–457).[9] This argument explains why frequent church attenders in particular tend to dissociate themselves from prejudice. People who take religion seriously are able to make critical stances on predominant inter-group sentiments (Batson et al. 1993:165ff).

1.1.3. *Civil religion, reactions, and ethnocentrism*

While the abovementioned studies provide significant indicators or hunches as to how the intricate relationships between religion and ethnocentrism can be addressed and understood, this study intends to raise a new question in this whole debate by bringing into this discussion the phenomenon of the Dutch civil religion and the various reactions to it by contemporary Christian believers. In this study,

---

[9] *Intrinsic* religious orientation regards "faith as a supreme value in its own right...A religious sentiment of this sort floods the whole life motivation and meaning. Religion is no longer limited to single segments of self interest." In contrast, *extrinsic* religious orientation refers to a type of "religion that is strictly utilitarian: useful for the self in granting safety, social standing, solace, and endorsement for one's chosen way of life" (Allport 1966:455). Batson & Ventis (1982:149) suggests another type, 'religion as *quest*', which is described as an "approach that involves honestly facing existential questions in all their complexity while resisting clear-cut pat answers.... There may not be a clear belief in a transcendent reality, but there is a transcendent, religious dimension to the individual's life...[It is an] open-ended, questioning orientation."

we argue that the problem surrounding the debate concerning the relationship between religion and ethnocentrism can be explicated through an investigation of the religious attitudes within the context of the Dutch civil religion and the various reactions by the Christian believers towards it, which may or may not have an effect on their ethnocentric attitudes.

The notion of civil religion was introduced in the 18th century by the Swiss philosopher Jean-Jacques Rousseau. In the 1960's, Robert Bellah tried to reinstate the usage of this concept in contemporary studies, particularly in his investigation of the American society. He argues that the existence of civil religion is premised on the sociological idea that all politically organized societies have some sort of civil religion. According to him, civil religion overarches conventional religions in order to legitimate the system or the nation.[10] Scholars of civil religion believe that there are varieties of civil religions depending on their historical and structural conditions (Bellah & Hammond 1980; Pierard & Linder 1988). As we shall discuss extensively in chapter 8 of this book, civil religion in the Netherlands takes on a peculiar configuration.[11] Earlier studies reveal that civil religion permeates the religious attitudes of the present-day Dutch believers on a collective and broad scale (Laeyendecker 1982:346–365; 1992; Ter Borg 1990; Van der Ven 1998b). These studies point out that civil religion is manifested through common values which have an underlying 'religious core' which links people to their past tradition, their present identity and their perceived mission for the rest of the world. These common values are said to be generally present among all its population. For this reason, we choose the notion of civil religion as the basis of our assumption to describe the religious attitudes of our respondents. We assume that 'civil religion' is a phenomenon that permeates all of the Dutch society and shapes the religious landscape of the Dutch believers

---

[10] We cannot fully delve into the various definitions of 'civil religion' due to limitation of the scope and interest of this study. For a thorough discussion of the debate surrounding the definition of civil religion, one may refer to Bellah 1974; Richey and Jones 1974:14; Gehrig 1981, among others.

[11] Unlike in the United States where denominationalism sets up as a cultural and structural condition, it is seen that 'societalization' will be an important mark to view the presence of civil religion in the Netherlands. Laeyendecker (1982) predicts that there will be a decline of public religion in the pillarized period. He believes that after the Netherlands attained independent statehood, there were some shared ultimate values and symbols that seved as civil religion.

in general. We indicate that the Dutch civil religion may be characterized, among others, by the following four *ethoses*, namely: 'enlightenment' ethos, 'democratic' ethos, 'moral' ethos, and 'hidden' religious ethos.[12] We assume that the existence of civil religion in the Netherlands may account extensively for the way Christian believers interpret the diverse religious beliefs that confront them. Given the polymorphic religious images in the Judeo-Christian tradition, particularly on a number of salient Christian themes like God, Jesus, Spirit, Salvation, and Church, one can expect that there are also diverse reactions towards civil religion that are elicited among the present-day believers. In this study, we have identified three types of reactions towards the Dutch civil religion, namely: *traditional, contextual,* and *humanistic* reactions. The traditional reaction may be characterized by a negative response to civil religion which tends to reject or refuse to dialogue with it. The contextual reaction is characterized by a positive response to civil religion through a genuine effort to interpret civil religion critically and constructively in the light of the Christian tradition and vice versa. And finally, the humanistic reaction is a type of response which manifests total agreement to civil religion but at the same time tends to write off the importance of the Christian faith. Our research intends to situate the investigation of the relationship between religion and ethnocentrism within the phenomenon of the Dutch civil religion and the diverse reactions to it by the present-day Christian believers. This will be the newfangled contribution of this study in comprehending the vexing relationship between religion and ethnocentrism.

1.2. *Research questions and aims*

1.2.1. *Research questions*

The general question that we raise in this research is: what are the effects of religious attitudes, to be distinguished into traditional, contextual, and humanistic reactions to civil religion, on ethnocentrism among church members, while controlling for some relevant population characteristics? We hoist this question in this study from the point of view

---

[12] Some authors argue that because of secularization, people would prefer to speak of fundamental values (*grondwaarden*) and basic convictions (*basisovertuigingen*), or a public ethos, which do not imply automatically some reference on a transcendent being (cf. Thung 1980, Vellenga and Seldenthuis 1992).

of theology. Thus, this key question can be expounded using themes that are culled from the sources of theological concerns. The themes that we are interested to investigate in this study are the five major themes in the Christian tradition, namely: God, Jesus, Spirit, Salvation, and Church. These five themes constitute the core beliefs of Christianity: belief in *God* marks the Christian theistic tradition; belief in *Jesus* moulds a specific Christian identity; belief in the *Holy Spirit* brings out the picture of the presence of the Spirit of God and Spirit of Jesus in Christian tradition; belief in *salvation* renders a fundamental faith on the promise of God's presence in his Spirit made by Jesus; and the *church* constitutes belongingness to a community of believers whose belief refer to God, Jesus Christ, Spirit, and salvation. All these themes are also enshrined in the Creed (both Apostle & Nicene), thereby adding credence to the fact that these beliefs are indeed fundamental to Christianity. However, while these themes are considered to be essential to Christianity, it should be noted that a single definition *cannot* be ascribed to any of them. The Christian tradition is so profound and yet so diverse that it is important not to fixate one's understanding of any of these themes to a single definition. We start with theological conceptualizations in order to take account of, on the one hand, the plurality in the Christian tradition of approaches to God, Jesus, Spirit, salvation and church, and on the other hand, the rich experiences, fresh imageries, and religious wisdom which are dialectically implied in them. Furthermore, it is crucial to understand the diverse reactions of believers to these religious images in the context of the Dutch civil religion, which takes the form of either a traditional, contextual, or humanistic response. This is a vital consideration to keep in mind as the empirical-theological investigations for each of these topics are explored. Moreover, from an empirical-theological perspective, it is necessary to chart these images and to see certain patterns as they occur among people. It is likewise the interest of this work to see how these images relate with other social phenomena, like for instance ethnocentrism, being the interest of this study. We would like to know the extent to which the religious attitudes of our respondents towards these five religious themes (God, Jesus, Spirit, Salvation, and the Church) will have predictive value in relation to ethnocentrism. In this study, we shall mean by the term attitude a "learned predisposition to respond in a consistently favourable or unfavourable manner with respect to a given object" (Fishbein & Ajzen 1975:6). It involves an evaluation of a specific object based on a set of beliefs about this object with some degree of favour or disfavour. These ideas are supposed to guide the orientation to one's behaviour, or at least one's behavioural intentions (Schuman et al. 1997:1–8).

The general question will be elaborated through a number of specific research questions that we raise in this study. We bring up five specific questions related to the five themes that we mentioned earlier, which means that we will be examining the attitudes of our respondents towards each of these themes. We also raise one question that relates to the ethnocentric attitudes of our respondents. The last question is concerned about the effects of religious attitudes on ethnocentrism, and the effects of these attitudes while some relevant population characteristics are being controlled for. In summary, we shall wrestle with these seven specific questions in this study:

1. What are the attitudes of church members toward God, and what is the social location of these attitudes? (Chapter 2)
2. What are the attitudes of church members toward Jesus, and what is the social location of these attitudes? (Chapter 3)
3. What are the attitudes of church members toward the Spirit, and what is the social location of these attitudes? (Chapter 4)
4. What are the attitudes of church members toward salvation, and what is the social location of these attitudes? (Chapter 5)
5. What are the attitudes of church members towards the church, and what is the social location of these attitudes? (Chapter 6)
6. What are the ethnocentric attitudes of the church members, and what is the social location of these attitudes? (Chapter 7)
7. What are the effects of these religious attitudes, to be distinguished into traditional, contextual, and humanistic reactions to civil religion, on ethnocentrism, while controlling for some relevant population characteristics? (Chapter 8)

1.2.2. *Research aims*

This study has a two-fold aim, namely: a descriptive, and an explorative aim. First, let us explain the descriptive aim. This study intends to describe both the religious attitudes of our respondents related to the five religious themes mentioned earlier, and their ethnocentric attitudes. Based on the results of our empirical findings, we shall describe these attitudes from an empirical-theological point of view. The quantitative method employed by this study will give us a broad spectrum of empirically based description of the religious and ethnocentric attitudes of our respondents.

Second, this research has also an explorative aim. This study aims at clarifying the relationship between religious attitudes and ethnocentrism from an empirical-theological approach and hope to come up with hypotheses based on the empirical outcomes of this research. We will attempt to examine more closely the religious attitudes, which we distinguished into traditional, contextual, and humanistic reactions to the Dutch civil religion, that have an effect on the positive attitude of church members towards their in-group and their negative attitude towards minorities. This research therefore is intended to be an explorative study regarding this relationship. We do not intend to test hypotheses in this study because as far as previous studies are concerned, there are no substantive theories from which strong and reliable hypotheses have yet been generated to demonstrate this relationship, especially not in regard to the relationship between the three reactions to civil religion and their effect on ethnocentrism. Notwithstanding copious evidence of all kinds of relations between religion and ethnocentrism, no empirical-theological investigation has theoretically elucidated the link between religious attitudes and ethnocentrism. One cannot find any literature that examines the perplexing influences of these variables demonstrating the link between religious attitudes on God, Jesus, Spirit, Salvation, and Church on the one hand, and the positive in-group and negative out-group attitudes on the other, especially the absence of literature with regards the relationships between the three reactions to civil religion and ethnocentrism. Even though there are studies that were undertaken to demonstrate the link of some aspects of religion to ethnocentrism, the aim of this study is to document this relationship as thoroughly as possible, not restricting our description to those topics that have been documented already in earlier studies. Thus, as a result of this explorative study, we intend to deliver some hypotheses and recommendations for future research regarding this subject.

For reasons of the special aims of this study, being descriptive and explorative, we conducted specifically theological research in relation to the five religious themes, i.e. God, Jesus, Spirit, salvation, and church. In chapters 2 to 6, we summarise actual systematic theological studies in as much as they are needed from the general research question as formulated in 1.2: "what are the effects of religious attitudes (…) on ethnocentrism among church members". We do not only summarise relevant studies in the domain of systematic reflections on God, Jesus, the Spirit, Salvation and the church, but we structure the insights out of these studies from the general question just quoted. In other words, the theological chapters 2 through 6 are not systematic-theological of character in themselves, but the insights in them are used in order to contribute to approaching and ultimately answering the general empirical-theological question just mentioned, as it is divided into seven research questions in 1.2 The aim of these chapters is not systematic-theological *per se* but the concepts in them are used to contribute to the two-fold aim of this empirical-theological study, oriented at a descriptive and explorative aim.

1.3. *Conceptual model*

In this conceptual model, we describe the components which are included in our search for the relationships between religion and ethnocentrism. Below (see: Scheme 1.1), we see an illustration of the causal relations between religious attitudes and ethnocentrism.

On Scheme 1.1 above, the box which contains the two components of ethnocentric attitudes, namely, positive in-group and negative out-group attitudes, comprises the dependent variable. As gleaned from the social identity theory (Tajfel & Turner 1979:40ff; Gijsberts et al. 2004:8–10), the notion of ethnocentrism involves mental processes that consist of both social identification, i.e. a selective perception of predominantly favourable characteristics among members of the in-

Scheme 1.1. Conceptual model of the relations between religious attitudes and ethnocentric attitudes

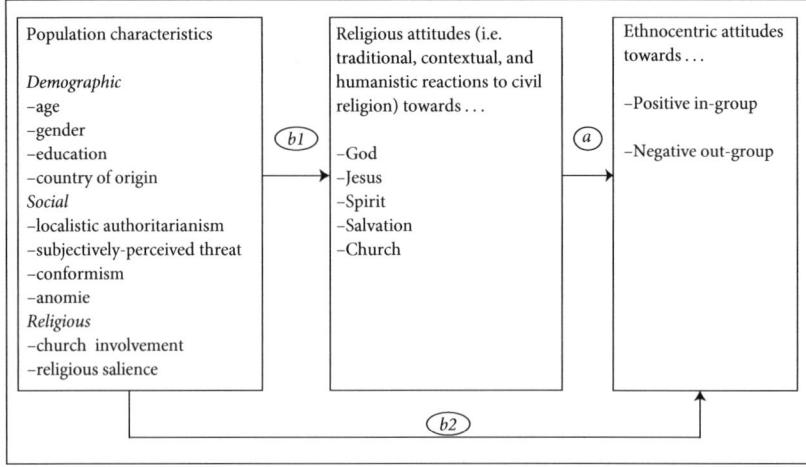

group, and social contra-identification, i.e. a selective perception of predominantly unfavourable characteristics among members of out-groups. The outcome of these complex mental processes is called ethnocentrism, which generally includes the two components of a positive in-group attitude and negative out-group attitude (Eisinga & Scheeper 1989). We shall investigate these ethnocentric attitudes in chapter 7.

The box containing the attitudes in regard to five religious themes, namely, God, Jesus, Spirit, Salvation, and church, constitutes the independent variable. In the subsequent chapters (chapters 2–6), we shall elaborate on these themes by gathering several religious images of the present-day Dutch believers. We begin with the theoretical descriptions of these religious images which takes into account, on the one hand, the reflections on the plurality in the Christian tradition of approaches to God, Jesus, Spirit, salvation and church, and on the other hand, the abundant experiences, new imageries, and religious wisdom which are dialectically implied in them. In chapter 8, we will distinguish these religious images according to their reactions to civil religion, namely: traditional, contextual, and humanistic attitudes.

We have also identified a number of population characteristics, which we distinguish into three main categories, namely: demographic (age, gender, education, and country of origin), social (localistic authoritarianism, subjectively-perceived threat, conformism, and anomie), and religious (church involvement, religious salience).[13] These population characteristics are deliberately taken in order to control for their effect on the relationship between religious attitudes and ethnocentrism.

A word of caution may, perhaps unnecessarily, be mentioned here with regards to the fact that the conceptual model refers two times to the word 'church', albeit in different combinations, i.e. in the column of religious attitudes with independent variables, which contains among others 'attitudes towards the church', and in the column of population characteristics functioning as control variables, which contains among others 'church involvement'. The ultimate question 7 (see 1.2) of the research project is about the effect of the various religious attitudes (independent variables), among which the attitudes towards

---

[13] Age: 1 = 57 years and younger; 2 = 58 to 68 years old; 3 = 69 years & older; Gender: 1 = male; 2 = female; Education = 1 = primary education; 2 = lower secondary education; 3 = higher secondary education; 4 = tertiary education; Country of origin = 1 = The Netherlands; 00 = others (non-Dutch).

church, on the ethnocentric attitudes (dependent variables), controlled for the population characteristics, among which church involvement. The position of the two variables, the independent variables 'attitudes towards church' and the control variable 'church involvement' fulfil a methodologically fundamental different function. The dependent and independent variables, among which attitudes towards the church, can be considered endogenous variables, because they belong to the core of the conceptual model, which refers to the effects relation between them, whereas the control variables, among which church involvement, can be considered exogenous variables, because they do not belong to the core of the conceptual model but only control the effects relation just mentioned.

The population characteristics mentioned have been established by previous studies to have certain influence on the ethnocentric attitudes of church members.[14] Age has often played a significant factor in social and religious research in general. In the Netherlands and in most western countries, age is shown to be correlated with ethnocentrism. Earlier studies reveal that the higher the age of the respondents, the stronger the ethnocentric attitudes (Scheepers et al. 1992:43–60; Sniderman et al. 2002:83, 123). Gender is also noted to be one of the most important predictors of several societal issues (Haleh & Maynard 1994; Weber & Dillaway 2001). Studies show that gender is significantly correlated to ethnocentrism. Coenders (2003:332) found that males demonstrate more patriotism and chauvinism but are less exclusionistic towards immigrants than females. Aside from age and gender, several studies have also indicated that education has an effect on ethnocentrism. They claim that higher educated people are less prejudiced than lower educated individuals (Hello 2003). Finally, we also included the country of origin of the respondents because of its supposed effects on people's ethnocentric attitudes as previous studies reveal. Authors like Hooghe et al. (2006) and Soroka et al. (2005) have established that immigrants tend to have lower feelings of ethnocentrism than the native-born citizens. We'll find out whether this holds true to our respondents here in the Netherlands.

---

[14] Political preference, which has often been used as population characteristic in previous studies, is not chosen as one of our population characteristic due to the 'floating' or unfixed preferences of voters in the last decennium in the Netherlands.

We also include some social characteristics which, according to earlier studies, have certain degree of influence on the ethnocentric attitudes of church members, namely: localistic authoritarianism, subjectively-perceived threat, conformism, and anomie. The localistic-authoritarian characteristic combines two important concepts in the study of ethnocentrism, namely, localism and authoritarianism. Localism refers to the extent to which the individual identifies him/herself with the local residential community (Gabennesch 1972:857–875). The localistic attitude entails a 'constriction of the mind' and a 'constriction of relationships'. Individuals with a localistic outlook has a narrow breadth of perspective and think in terms of insiders and outsiders: they are so attached to the community and wish to protect it against influences from the outside world (Gijsberts et al. 2004:34). Authoritarianism is often attributed to the work of Adorno et al. (1950) who explain that authoritarianism is a personality characteristic which consists of a cluster of nine 'sub-syndromes'. Some of these sub-syndromes accounts for the tendency of authoritarian people to define themselves in sharp contrast to other social or ethnic groups (contra-identification). We combined these two variables on the basis of a factor analysis, as shown on Appendix 1, Table 3. The subjectively-perceived threat plays an important role in ethnocentric attitudes. Because of their perception of threat, some people tend to blame minorities for the problems in society. They perceive minorities as an economic, social and cultural threat to them (Verberk 1999:145). Conformism, which refers to an uncritical attitude towards one's own social group and a rigid adherence to conventional norms and values, is also correlated to ethnocentrism (Adorno et al. 1950). We also identify anomie as an important social characteristic that can be assumed to influence the ethnocentric attitude of our respondents (cf. Eisinga & Scheepers 1989:30). Durkheim (1953;1972:184) describes the condition of anomie as the absence or diminution of standards or values, and an associated feeling of alienation and purposelessness. Srole (1956:709–716) explains that anomie is associated with a rejective orientation toward out-groups in general and toward minority in particular.

It is generally known that religious characteristics of a person influence his/her attitudes towards various social issues. We identify two significant religious characteristics, namely, church involvement and religious salience. Results of previous studies demonstrate that there is a differential effect of the type of church involvement and ethnocentrism (Lenski 1963:533–544; Gorsuch and Aleshire 1974:281–307).

Religious saliency relates to the extent to which religion plays a vital and vigorous role in the life of an individual. A person who thinks that religion is important shows positive effect on ethnocentric attitudes (Batson et al. 1993).

As can be observed on Scheme 1 above, the direction of the arrow coming from the box containing the religious attitudes (a) points toward the box containing the two components of ethnocentric attitudes which are the positive in-group and the negative out-group attitudes. This implies that we are going to examine the impacts of these five religious attitudes on the two components of ethnocentrism. This constitutes the proper themes of our study. One may also observe on Scheme 1 the direction of the arrows coming from the population characteristics. These arrows point to two directions: one is directed towards the religious attitudes (b1), and the second arrow is directed towards the ethnocentric attitudes (b2). The first arrow (b1) indicates that these population characteristics are assumed to influence the religious attitudes in terms of their social location. For this reason, we are investigating the social location of the religious attitudes in each chapter related to the five themes (chapters 2–6). The second arrow (b2) implies that these population characteristics may also influence the effect of religious attitudes on ethnocentrism. Therefore in chapter 8, we will examine the impact of these religious attitudes on ethnocentrism while controlling for these population characteristics.

1.4. *Research Methods*

The research method used in this study is the quantitative method. We utilize questionnaires to gather our data. The design of the questionnaire has been drawn from the study of literatures, existing instruments, and instruments devised specifically for this project. Several consultations and meetings were held with theologians, social scientists, and ordinary church members during the drafting of this questionnaire. The questionnaire was tried out among a number of church members in Nijmegen. Their comments were considered in the final revision of the questionnaire.

The questionnaire is composed of three main parts. One part deals with the measuring scales for ethnocentrism. Another part contains several sets of instruments to measure religious attitudes. A last part includes the population characteristics of the respondents. An introduction page, which gives a brief explanation about the subject matter and the aims of this study, is also included in the questionnaire.

1.4.1. *Measuring instruments*

The items of all the measuring instruments that are used in this study can be found on Appendix 1, Table 3, Parts 1–3. The validated scales from SOCON 2000 is used to measure ethnocentrism. This includes four items on positive attitude towards in-groups, six items on the negative attitudes towards minorities in general, and five items on negative attitudes toward specific out-groups. The measuring scales for the God images consist of a selection and adaptation of the instrument of Van der Ven (1998:156–169). The measuring scales of the Jesus images are taken from Van der Ven/Biemans (1994:204–205), to which is added items on the Spirit-motivated Christology. The 24-item instrument for the images of the Spirit is newly created for this research and entered into the questionnaire after having been tried-out among church members. The 9-item scale that is used to operationalize the soteriological dimension of transcendence is a modification of Jeurissen's instrument (1993:305–306). The 9-item scales of the temporal dimension is also a reworking of Jeurissen's instrument. The measuring instruments for the scope of salvation and the realms of salvation are both developed by the author for the purpose of this study. The instrument that is used to measure the images of the church is a selection and adaption from Jeurissen (1993:306–307). The SOCON instrument (2000) is also the main instrument we use to measure the demographic characteristics, specifically for age, gender, education, and country of origin. For the social characteristics, we employ the SOCON (2000) scales to measure authoritarianism, anomie, and subjectively-perceived threat. We use the measuring scales of Eisinga & Scheepers (1989) to operationalize conformism, and localism. Because the factor analysis on authoritarianism, anomie, subjectively-perceived threat, conformism, and localism resulted into four factors, while combining localism and authoritarianism, we considered 'localistic authoritarianism' one scale (see: Appendix 1, Tables 4 and 5). We utilize the battery of scales from SOCON to measure church involvement. These involve questions related to their membership in the church, participation in church tasks or functions, and attendance in church services. With the help of these questions we constructed, as we indicate further on, two groups of church members, i.e. active and non-active church members (see: 1.6). We also operationalize religious saliency using the 5 items from SOCON. A five-point Likert scale (1 = I totally disagree, 2 = I disagree, 3 = I partly disagree, partly agree, 4 = I agree, 5 = I fully agree) is provided to answer the questions related to ethnocentrism and the various religious attitudes (see: Appendix 1, Tables 6 and 7).

1.4.2. *Statistical methods*

The data from the completed questionnaires were subjected to a number of statistical analyses by means of the SPSS statistical program. We performed frequency analysis,[15] factor analysis,[16] reliability of scales (Cronbach's Alpha),[17] variance analysis, Scheffé test, Pearson correlation, and hierarchical regression analysis.[18] Detailed reports of these analyses are provided in their respective chapters and in the appendix.

1.5. *Sampling method and data collection*

The research population of this study is composed of the Dutch Roman Catholic church members who are living in areas where a big number of ethnic minorities live. According to the demographic data provided by the Netherlands Central Bureau of Statistics (CBS 2003b), most ethnic minorities in the country live in the four main cities, namely: Amsterdam, Rotterdam, The Hague, and Utrecht. We presume that it is on these areas where church members do have the highest frequency of encounters with the minority groups. In order

---

[15] The interpretation of the mean scores of a five-point Likert scale is as follows: 1.00–1.79=I totally disagree; 1.80–2.59= I disagree; 2.60–3.39= I feel ambivalent (2.60–2.99= I feel negatively ambivalent; 3.00–3.39= I feel positively ambivalent); 3.40–4.19= I agree; and 4.20–5.00= I totally agree.

[16] The following criteria were applied in the factor analyses: communality of items > .20, factor loading > .40, explained variance > .40; difference between factor loading of items > .15. Items that do not meet these criteria will be eliminated as this is indicated by an asterisk preceding the items in the Appendix; oblimin rotation if correlation between between factors > .30. I principally use the free factor analysis, and I only use forced factor analysis when, in cases of measurements frequently used in previous studies, the theoretic interpretability of the empirical factors from these forced analysis, is sufficiently near to the theoretical domain.

[17] Cronbach's reliability coefficient > .60.

[18] Criteria for regression analysis: Collinearity: tolerance > .10; VIF (variance inflation factor) < 10.

to contact these church members, we needed a viable and convenient channel by which we can get the addresses of our would-be respondents. The most convenient channel is through the deaneries and the parishes that are located in these four cities. Therefore, we first contacted the deaneries so as to get information concerning the names of the parishes which are situated in areas with the largest groups of ethnic minorities. The four deaneries contacted were the deaneries of Utrecht-Oudenrijn (Utrecht), Amsterdam (Amsterdam), Vliethaghe (The Hague), and Rijnmond (Rotterdam). Each of these deaneries named four parishes from their respective territory. After getting the names of the parishes from the deaneries, we contacted the pastors of each parish by telephone informing them about the research project and inviting them to participate in the study. A letter of information about the research, together with a brief description of the research project was also sent. In this first letter, the parishes are requested to allow us access to their address files from which an a-select sample of survey population could be drawn.

After two to three weeks, a series of follow-up calls were again undertaken in order to ask the pastors whether they were willing to participate. It took some time (2–3 months) to receive the responses from the pastors because most of them needed to consult and get the approval of their parish councils. Of the 16 parishes contacted, nine declared their willingness to participate.[19] Some wanted to participate on a later date due to reorganization in the clustering of parishes, while others simply did not want to cooperate for other reasons. It is important to note that one of the main considerations mentioned by most of the parishes was the issue of privacy. This issue was answered by assuring the parishes that this scientific study is bound by strict confidentiality and anonymity in reference to the names and addresses of their constituencies. Several parishes also took the initiative of informing their respective parishioners about this project through their parish bulletin or through the announcements during the Eucharistic celebrations or parish gatherings.

---

[19] There were two parishes that positively responded from the cities of Rotterdam, Amsterdam, and The Hague. In the city of Utrecht, however, there were at first two parishes that positively responded to participate. After gathering the addresses from these two parishes, we receive the information that another parish from Utrecht would want to participate in this project. Thus, we have three parishes from Utrecht.

To the nine parishes that signify willingness to participate after the second round of telephone barrage, a second letter was sent including a form wherein information concerning the name of the contact person, the total number of parishioners, and several technicalities like the possibility of printing the labels were asked. The information gathered from this form was the basis for the proportion of a-select samples from the list of members of their respective parish. After that, appointments with the contact persons were made. Then, visits to the parish ensued.

The lists of members from each parish appeared to be based on different sources. Some parishes are involved in the centralization process of the registered members under the SILA organization, while other parishes have not yet participated; some say that they are reluctant to join SILA or simply refused to participate in this institution.[20] Those parishes who were not using the SILA system employed a more distilled and a rather diminutive list of church members, while those using SILA have a more extended yet quite diluted list of members (see: Appendix 1, Table 1). From the 9 parishes, two are non-SILA program users while seven are SILA users. From the non-SILA users, we employ all the addresses from their files. These two parishes, i.e. Kanaleneiland Parochie in Utrecht and Pax Christi Parochie in Rotterdam, have less than 300 members from their list. We were told by the pastors, however, that some of these members on the list consist of the names of both active and inactive members. A random sampling took place from the files of all the participating parishes. From the parishes that use the SILA, we draw an a-select sample of 500 church members from the list of parishioners. In order to discover statistically significant differences between the different types of church members, the number of cases in each type must not, however be too small. If we have a relatively large number of samples (at least around 350–400), it will not be necessary, statistically speaking, to arrive at an equal size of sample size for each type of church members (Moser & Kalton 1971). In the SILA system, we set the pre-selection of the population with the following criteria: Age limit (18 to 85 yrs. old), head of the family, all members within the territory of the parish.

---

[20] The abbreviation SILA stands for *Stichting Interkerkelijke Ledenadministratie*. This foundation was organized for the support of the administrations of the participating churches especially in keeping up civil data of its members (cf. http://www.sila.nl).

The distribution of the questionnaires was done by mailing the questionnaires directly to the addresses of the respondents. However, two of the participating parishes required the researcher to bring the questionnaires to the parishes so that they themselves would select and mail the questionnaires to their members. The reason for this was that these two parishes could not give their lists of addresses to the researcher in view of the 'privacy' issue. Both of these parishes were given 500 questionnaires each for distribution. It was however, explained to them how an a-select sampling could be done from their list. A total of 4000 questionnaires had been distributed to all the nine participating parishes. The exact number of distributed questionnaires for every parish is mentioned in the Appendix 1, Table 1. The distribution of the questionnaires took place from January until March 2004.

The total number of returned questionnaires is 611. From these returned questionnaires, we discard those which indicate their non-membership to the catholic church. We remove those who do not reside in the 4 cities mentioned. We also do not include those questionnaires that are only partially completed. The return of the questionnaires reveal that although systematization of the profiles from the Roman Catholic parishes through the SILA system is a viable source of broad membership which is the target group of this research, some inconsistencies and contamination are also disclosed. For instance, while we seek only members of the Catholic church from the files, still a number of respondents indicate that they belong to another church group or do not belong to any at all. Most questionnaires that are not completed are due to change of addresses, death, unknown addressees, etcetera. After cancelling out these invalid questionnaires, we finally gather 451 valid respondents. A summary of the results of the data collection is reported in the Appendix 1, Table 2.

1.6. *Description of Research Population*

The research population in this study is composed of members of the Dutch Catholic church who are living in the four big cities in the Netherlands (Amsterdam, The Hague, Rotterdam, and Utrecht). We shall describe our research population according to the three main categories which we mentioned in the conceptual model on section 1.3, namely: the demographic, social, and religious characteristics.

1.6.1. Demographic characteristics

Our 451 respondents reveal the following demographic characteristics. In terms of age-group, 164 respondents (36.6%) are 57 years old or younger, 94 (20.8%) are between 58 and 68 years old, and 190 (42.1%) are 69 or older.[21] There are 217 men (48.1%) and 231 women (51.2%) in our sample. 30 respondents (6.8%) indicate primary education as their highest level of education, 195 (43.9%) lower secondary education, 56 (12.6%) higher secondary education, and 167 (36.7%) tertiary education. There are 361 (81.8%) respondents whose country of origin is the Netherlands, and 81 (18%) respondents whose country of origin is not the Netherlands.

1.6.2. Social characteristics

Our respondents display different characteristics with regards to localistic authoritarianism: 23 (5.3%) totally agree; 79 (18.1%) agree; 163 (37.3%) ambivalent; 141 (32.3%) do not agree; and 31 (7.1%) totally disagree. In terms of their subjectively-perceived threat character, we have the following distribution: 27 (6.2%) totally agree; 56 (12.8%) agree; 128 (28.4%) ambivalent; 177 (40.5%) do not agree; and finally, 49 (11.2%) totally disagree. For conformism, our respondents display the following attitudes: 14 (3.2%) totally agree; 79 (18.1%) agree; 97 (22.2%) ambivalent; 218 (49.9%) do not agree; and 29 (6.6%) totally disagree. Our respondents (n=435) manifest the following 'anomic' characteristics: 33 (7.6%) totally agree; 68 (15.6) agree; 190 (43.7%) ambivalent; 120 (27.6%) do not agree; and 24 (5.5%) totally disagree.

---

[21] The lowest cut-off for the age group in the first category is 18 years which marks an official age for public and adult life here in the Netherlands, and the highest cut-off is 57 years which is the age group that stands at the closing of Vatican II while they were still 18 years old (born on 1947 and after). We can assume that the conciliar reforms initiated by Vatican II had significant influence among these populations especially during their formative years. The middle age group covers a 10-year span of 58 to 68 years old (1936 up to 1946). This generation is comprised of church members who were born and lived at the time of the Second World War. Most people from this generation experienced the horrors of war in their youth and had practically witnessed the post war restoration. The last age group, 69 and older (born on or before 1935), is the most senior among the respondents. They were born and grew up before the war and most of them have some reminiscence of the impact of the pillarization process and the euphoria of the emancipation of the Catholics from the strong political influence of the protestants in the country. They lived at the time when a strong community spirit and an effective social control among Dutch Catholics was at its prime.

1.6.3. *Religious characteristics*

In this study we first tried to construct a cumulative scale of three groups of church members, i.e. marginal, modal and core members. The criteria were: marginal members go to church only few times a year or (almost) never; modal members go to church about once a month or more; core members go to church about once a month or more and fulfil a special task or function in the church or are an active member of a religious group or association in the church (Appendix 1, table 3, part 3, F). This construction failed because the three groups appeared not to form a cumulative scale, as many church members fulfil a special task or function in the church or are an active member of a religious group or association in the church, but do not go to church once a month or more. Therefore, in this study we label the marginal members inactive members and the modal and core members together active members. Active members are church members who regularly go to church (here defined as going to church services at least once a month); and/or have a special task in the church, and/or active in church organization or church-related groups (those who are active do not necessarily go to church regularly every Sunday). Inactive members are those who are irregular church goers (i.e. one who attends services less than once a month or practically never), and have no special task in the church nor are members of any church organization or church-related groups. Our data show that our sample consists of 310 (68.7%) 'active' members and 141 (31.3%) 'inactive' members. In terms of religious salience, our respondents display the following characteristics: 104 (24.2%) totally agree that religion is very important to their life; 155 (36.1%) agree, 98 (22.8%) are ambivalent, 56 (13.1%) do not agree, and 16 (3.7%) totally disagree.

1.7. *Structure of the Book*

This research study is composed of nine chapters. In this chapter, chapter 1, we presented the research problem, the research questions and aims, the conceptual model, the research methods, the sampling method and data collection, the description of the research population, and the structure of the book. The succeeding chapters (chapters 2–6) will deal with the five religious attitudes, namely: God, Jesus, Spirit, salvation, and church. In these chapters, we will be examining the religious attitudes both from the theoretical and empirical perspectives.

We will also investigate the social location of every religious attitude. In chapter 2, we will discuss the various attitudes towards God. In chapter 3, we will focus on the attitudes of our respondents to Jesus. Then, in chapter 4, we will discuss the attitudes toward the Spirit. In chapter 5, we will focus on the attitudes toward salvation. Next, in chapter 6, we will elaborate on the attitudes toward the church. In chapter 7, we will investigate the ethnocentric attitudes of our respondents. In this chapter, we will examine ethnocentrism from the theoretical and empirical vantage point. In chapter 8, we will investigate the relation between the religious attitudes on the one hand and ethnocentrism on the other hand, and differentiate the religious attitudes towards God, Jesus, Spirit, salvation, and church into attitudes belonging to the traditional, contextual, and humanistic reactions to Dutch civil religion. And finally, in chapter 9, we shall conclude this study through summarization of our findings, formulation of some hypotheses, and recommendations for future research.

CHAPTER TWO

ATTITUDES TOWARD GOD

Historically speaking, it cannot be denied that in Western Europe, particularly in the Netherlands, the Christian image of God has deeply influenced the so-called symbolic universe of its people. 'God', so to speak, occupied a significant niche in western civilization. It has become an important hermeneutical category to interpret the world, human life, visions, morality, rituals, relationships, (even) scientific theories, social behavior, economic and political ideals and systems, etcetera. God has been part of the socialization or upbringing of children in the family. But of course, the present day Europe is different. Secularization has indeed taken its toll. Given the pervasive influence of secularization in its poly-dimensional form (Dobbelaere 1981; 1984), we want to investigate whether God still has a place in this highly secularized country. Despite the growing impact of secularization, how come believers still cling to their belief in 'God'? Are they not affected by this secularization process? Does their belief in God remain 'orthodox' amidst, or even despite, this process; Or, are their images of God also affected and perhaps even transformed by secularization? What could be the God-attitudes of some Dutch believers who value their faith on the one hand, but at the same time put meaning on the inner-worldly values and are positively engaged with the modern world on the other (Norris & Inglehart 2004)? By posing these questions, we aim to bring our reflection of the images of God against the backdrop of the significant socio-cultural dynamics in contemporary Dutch society. In view of the aim of this research, we ask the question in this chapter: what are the attitudes of church members towards God, and what is the social location of these attitudes?

Let us capture now the possible images of God which might be lurking in the minds and hearts of the Catholic Dutch believers. We shall proceed by first presenting the various images of God from a theoretical vantage point in section 2.1.; then we present the results of our empirical investigation of these God attitudes in section 2.2.; and then, we will examine the social location of these God-attitudes in section 2.3.

2.1. *Images of God from a theoretical perspective*

In this section, we will have a theoretical discussion of God images based on the following categories: iconic versus aniconic (2.1.1.), anthropomorphic versus non-anthropomorphic (2.1.2.), transcendent-immanence versus immanent transcendence (2.1.3), and the three-fold God-world relations (2.1.4).

Concepts about God abound. Contemporary social scientists and theologians acknowledge the complexity and multi-faceted nature of this theme. Paul Ricoeur affirms this observation by saying that the images of God are diverse and polyphonous. However, he adds, "polyphony is important in order to develop an idea of the vanishing horizon that is God" (Ricoeur 1995:224). Indeed, the Christian image of God may be characterized by such plurality and complexity. Manifold reasons may explicate such reality. Lonergan (1971) ascribes it to several factors like communication, i.e. the use of the resources of the culture to communicate the message, the creative manner of communication, and the further development of the Christian doctrine along the lines of that culture. The plurality and diversity within the Christian discourse about God can also be attributed to the richness of tradition that can be found in the sources of Christian faith, like the scriptures and from the streams of interpretative traditions like the deposited or sedimentated traditions (*traditum*) and the living interpretative traditions (*actus tradendi*). Other sources can likewise be spelled out, for instance, from cultural history and theology, from other religious traditions, from varieties of religious experience, from diverse cultural context or situation, and from the contribution of scientific knowledge (Hodgson 1994:19–27). Moreover, the plurality in theological discourse cannot be attributed wholly to the human perceiving subject nor to the diversity of cultural articulations or context, but also to the inexhaustible nature of the divine 'object', who eludes total comprehension especially when such discourse comes only from a single vantage point or expression (Mahoney 1987:272). In other words, the plurality and diversity in theological discourse is a mix of the beliefs in the gracious influence of God's self-unfolding and the limited understanding and communication on the part of the human being. Now the question is, if we have these 'overabundance' and assortment of images, what conceptual boundary can allow us to identify meaningfully, but also to delineate expediently, this whole plethora of God images? Here, we shall be aided by a conceptual structure that can allow us to identify and to make sense of all the possible images that can be presumed to exist among our respondents.

We can assume that the 'creed-like' conceptualization as used in the past can be limiting and will therefore be inadequate to cover extensively the images of God among our research population.[1] Van der Ven criticizes previous studies that employ this credo-based conceptualization and operationalization of God images by saying that they often measure topics which are of minor or marginal importance in relation to the 'hierarchy of truth' of the church, and those topics "embedded in codes originating in a cultural and social situation that structurally and conjuncturally belongs to the past" (Van der Ven 1998:147). They tend to measure concepts that are coded in a 'fossilized or archaic' instrument. In this sense, the creed-like construction of the images of God cannot serve as an adequate methodical structure to cover the wide-ranging beliefs in God in the contemporary Dutch situation.

Hence, if the creed does not provide an adequate structure for our conceptualization, where then can we turn to in order to find a satisfactory conceptual structure? I propose to locate this structure in the context to which we shall investigate these images. We must not forget that any meaningful discussion of religious themes must take into consideration the context to which these images are studied. Discourse about God does not happen in a cultural vacuum (Ward 1974:3–8). In the context of secularization which we assume to impact our Dutch believers, we are confronted with the dialectics between the two poles of the 'sacred' and the 'secular', or the 'transcendent' and the 'immanent'. The main question being addressed in this context is: "In what way does human life with God really differ from human life without God?" And conversely, "what is the difference between God with human life and society and a God without them?" In other words, the question is how to locate the problem of God in the bipolar spectrum of transcendence and immanence. Where do these images of God lie within the range of 'transcendence' on the one end, and 'immanence', on the other?

---

[1] I use the term 'creed-like' in the sense of doctrinal statements particularly based on the neo-scholastic credal interpretation. Smart (1968:15f) distinguishes between the concepts of creed as 'doctrinal statements' and creed as 'mythical' which refers to stories about the activities of the gods or heroes who are of special concern to the religion.

Here, I would like to use the concept of panentheism to discern and appraise the various images which are purportedly present among our population. Panentheism comes from the combination of three Greek words, *pan* (everything), *en* (in) and *theos* (God); taken together, it means 'everything being in God' and 'God being in everything'. This notion puts together both the immanent and transcendent structure of God-world relation. God and the world interpenetrate or localize each other in their own being and yet hold their disparate nature. They neither exhaust nor contain each other in their own being, and hence transcend one another despite their mutual immanence. Panentheism underlines the intimate closeness of the relationship between God and man. In this way, the concept of panentheism tries to preserve both the 'identity' and 'difference' in the relationship between God and the world (Hodgson 1994:157). It may well be taken as a balance view that avoids the absolutist position of both theism (which refers to the absolute transcendence of God and his absolute separation from nature and mankind) and pantheism (which represents a belief in an absolute immanent God).

In the Netherlands, Felling, Peters and Schreuder (1986) proposed the 'five worldviews' to describe beliefs in the secularized Dutch context. These worldviews consist of the following. First is the Christian-theistic worldview which is assumed by people who subscribe to the tenets of Christian religion, as they are handed down from the churches. These people believe in a personal God who created the universe and provides answers to the existential problems mentioned. Second is the transcendent-deistic worldview which is a belief of people on a de-personalized supernatural force. It has been noted that those who believe in a personal God in the Netherlands have declined from 47% to 24% over the last thirty years, but the percentage who believe in a non-personal, higher power has grown from 31% to 39% over the same period (Dekker et al. 1997:12–18). While at first, this worldview has not been considered as a Christian '*Weltanschauung*', it was later accepted as an expression of the beliefs of the liberal wing of Christianity in the Netherlands (Felling et al. 1991; Van der Slik 1994). Third is the inner worldly worldview which is embraced by people who locate their existential concerns in a meaningful context, but explicitly without referring to an otherworldly or transcendent reality. Fourth is the sceptic or agnostic world view which tends to be cynical about the existence of an ultimate reality, the meaning of life, suffering and death. And lastly, the nihilistic philosophy of life which is assumed by people who reject the existence of a higher reality and the idea that human affairs such as life and death could possess any meaning. Previous studies that employed these categories confirm the plausibility of these worldviews (Felling et al. 1986; 1987; 1992). A shorter version of these five worldviews has been operationalized in the 1995 SOCON survey which utilized only three concepts, that is, (a) the personal God, (b) the deistic idea of an impersonal God or a 'higher power', and the (c) the immanentist notion of God. These concepts were linked to the three different periods in Western history (Felling et al. 1986; 1987). The traditional Christian faith in a personal God is described as a 'pre-modern' Christian concept which speaks of a God who shows care and concern for each individual. 'Personal', in this sense, refers both to God as a person and to every individual person who is dear to God (Van der Ven 1998:148). Van der Ven posits two criticisms on the operationalization and the use of this category. He says that some of the items used in relation to this concept are not drawn from pre-modernity but from Judeo-Christian tradition which covers about 3000 years. The use of the terms 'traditional' and 'pre-modern' is arguable. The second critique concerns the assumption that God in the Christian tradition is exclusively a personal God. In recent debates in theology, there has been a query as to whether it is right to call God a person. The word 'person' is a nuanced term which in contemporary usage connotes 'an autonomous being alongside other beings, or simply an individual being', instead of 'being', or 'depth of being', or 'ground of being'.[2] This makes the use of the term 'person' or 'personal' confusing for today's jargon. The second concept used in the SOCON survey is called deism.[3] Deism is a concept which became

---

[2] For instance, Tillich (1966a) comments, "If God is a being, he is subject to the categories of finitude, especially to space and substance" and "God cannot be called a self, because the concept 'self' implies separation from and contrast to everything which is not self". Tillich does not necessarily reject a personal God as long as it is construed as transpersonal or suprapersonal (See: Nikkel 1995; Van der Ven, 1998).

[3] The word deism comes from the Latin root *deus*, and its Greek equivalent, *theos*. Modern deism may be described by the following characteristics: (1) rejection of religious authorities. Authority is wrested away, both on the personal level from the clerics, and on the ideological level from religious dogma; (2) rejection of divine revelation.; (3) it rejects an 'interventionist' God; (4) it tries to be 'universally inclusive oecumenism'. It argues that 'all religions are particular and culturally determined, and represent a few fundamental religious concepts; (5) it tends towards cosmological models of explaining the world. The relationship between Man and God is impersonal; (6) finally, is the repulsion experienced towards the idea that a loving father

prominent in the period of modernity starting from the Enlightenment (18th c.) onwards.[4] It speaks of a distant God who is bereft of any anthropomorphic image or qualities. This God is seen as a non-personal higher power that exists without being inherently connected or engaged with anyone or anything. *Deism* declares a belief in an utterly transcendent reality that has no rapport with the world. It is a God or a 'Higher reality' who is indifferent and unperturbed by the sufferings and the problems of the earthly beings.[5] According to Ziebertz (2001), modern deism can be indicated by a non-personal conception of the absolute which supposes a boundless divine horizon of all reality. Religions attempt to identify this horizon. Although modern deism uses differing forms and content on the surface, deep down however, they all refer to the same thing. There are some authors who appraise this concept negatively, saying that deism hardly accounts for the liberating dimension of God as portrayed in the scriptures which, in fact, constitute the main stream idea of Christian religion. Moreover, this concept represents a God in a non-anthropomorphic, abstract, bleak and vague way. It may fall into the risk of an uncritical and even dangerous sort of 'civil religion' that legitimizes the societal status quo.[6] Van der Ven's rebuttal goes like saying that although it is true that deism does not fit into the main stream of the Christian religion, this however should not be a hindrance to study deism in an unprejudiced manner. Moreover, Van der Ven claims that one should not jump into a hasty conclusion to maintain that the 'abstractness' of this God is vague and will automatically lead to 'civil religion'. According to Van der Ven, "deism fits into this pattern, and it merits unprejudiced study from a historical, systematic and empirical point of view"

---

accepts the death of His son as a basis for the salvation of all mankind. (cf. Ziebertz 2002:14–15).

[4] The concept of deism is mainly known to be a result of the cultural climate of the Enlightenment in Western Europe. In Britain, however, deism is said to come out of the revolt against the clerical elite of the Anglican and Catholic church at that time. Deism is said to have taken on many forms which may no longer be readily identifiable today (Taylor 1989:245–274).

[5] The work of Spilka & Reynolds (1965) among a sample of Catholic girls showed a relationship between negative prejudiced attitudes and deistic God images, when God was characterized as distant, impersonal and uninvolved in human affairs.

[6] Cf. Layendecker (1992). For the relationship between civil religion and the apartheid system, see among others, Oosthuizen (1988) and De Cruchy/Villa-Vincencio (1983).

(Van der Ven 1998:148). Van der Ven (1998) maintains that the non-anthropomorphic images of God is also present in the Christian tradition, and should therefore not be exclusively labelled as 'deistic only' and not 'Christian also'. Immanentism, the third concept, is said to be an upshot of the cultural revolution of the 60's and 70's which was a time when religious 'horizontalism' gained significant influence than religious verticalism. The immanentist believer considers God as the unity and structure of human existence. God is present in the heart of human beings. The SOCON researchers, however, hold that immanentism has to be conceptually reduced to nothing more than a function of human existence. But it is unclear from the operationalization of this concept whether each item refers to a 'religious' immanentism or to a 'non-religious' one. It depends on how the respondents will comprehend or make up of the items as he/she reads it. Van der Ven warns that one should avoid a dualistic scheme whereby one assigns transcendence to God and conversely, immanence to worldly and 'godless' reality. This dichotomized view reflects a neo-scholastic thinking which has insidiously affected both church leaders and ordinary believers up until now. It posits a notion of competition between God and human beings, whereby belief in the transcendent God is diminished by valuing worldliness, and in contrast, worldliness is undermined by having faith in the transcendent God (Van der Ven 1998:156). In sum, Van der Ven criticizes the theoretical assumption of these three categories of SOCON saying that they tend to reduce Christian heritage by ascribing solely personal attributes to the image of God. They fail to take into account that transcendence and immanence are two dimensions of God which must be considered to be more complementary than as two extremes that exclude one another. They tend to dichotomize God/Transcendent reality and empirical reality. Furthermore, they assume that the sole and core source of Christian faith is only the ecclesiastical tradition in its neo-scholastic interpretation.

We mentioned earlier the criticism posed by Van der Ven (1998) against the SOCON instrument concerning the idea of immanentism. He pointed out that the SOCON instrument falls short of taking into account the dialectics between immanence and transcendence. Hence, the notion of panentheism was proposed. This notion avoids the absolutist position in relation to both immanence and transcendence. The idea of God according to the panentheists has been conceptually and empirically proven to plausibly capture the images of God among

Christian believers. This panentheistic model has been incorporated into the instrument which was constructed to operationalize the four-tier dimensions of the images of God, namely: iconic-aniconic, anthropomorphic-non-anthropomorphic; immanent transcendence; and the three-fold relation to the world, i.e. the individual, social, and cosmic relations (Van der Ven 1998). These dimensions are presumed to capture the questions that ordinary Dutch believers tend to wrestle with when talking about their belief in God. Moreover, these dimensions have already been empirically tested showing that they help configure the extensively copious aspects of the Christian doctrine of God. Let us now explain each of these levels of God-talk.

2.1.1. *Iconic versus aniconic God images*

The first level consists of the contrasting pairs, iconic versus aniconic faith. On this level, one deals with the tension between a type of faith that accepts the use of images or icons in order to reach or approach God (iconic), and a type of faith that refuses or defies the use of icons or images because of their alleged inaptness and inadequacy to approach the ultimate mystery [aniconic] (Van der Ven et al., in Ziebertz 2001:205). While some faiths accept that God can be represented through images, as in the case of iconic faiths, there are also some belief systems which conceive of the divine "as an omnipresent essence or principle governing all life, as impersonal, remote, and definitely not a being" (Stark 2001:9). The prefix 'an' in the term an-iconic serves as a kind of an *alpha privans* which denotes 'without'. In other words, it is a belief system that is devoid of any image-ing of God.[7] This type of faith holds that God, the 'ungraspable reality', cannot simply be captured by any humanly constructed image because God lies outside the realm of images. Therefore aniconic faith totally absconds any type of images. It therefore takes place on a meta-level in relation to God images, which can aptly be attributed as 'metatheism'. Moreover, this type of faith is not simply a negation of theism in its metaphysical or ontological sense, nor is it a kind of transitional phase from theism to atheism. It is rather an epistemic claim which

---

[7] Van der Ven argues that this construct even goes farther than the 'moderate negative theology' like that of Ricoeur (1995:217–235) who holds that "God always surpasses any god image and continually coordinates his own absence with respect to these images, thereby causing human beings to continually set off in search of new images" (Van der Ven 1998:157).

is, that God radically surpasses all forms of human knowing and naming. This idea resonates well with the post modern way of God-talk as the 'incomprehensible' and 'hidden' God, according to David Tracy. Earlier, Tracy (1975) contends that the notion of panentheism, the doctrine that all is in God but God's inclusion of the world does not exhaust the reality of God, is the best way to render the modern concepts of God's relationship to us as described in the bible. However, in his recent works, Tracy (2002:62–89) focuses more and more on the mystical and neo-platonic traditions of thought and draws heavily on postmodern thinkers. He prefers to speak of God as 'incomprehensible' (from the tradition of the 6th century mystic called pseudo-Dionysius) and 'hidden' (Martin Luther). Tracy claims that debates about God in the period of modernity deals with what is actual and possible, what is concrete and experiential. God can be understood by way of persuasion and argument by appealing to reason, to experience, or to the imagination. But in the post-modern age, Tracy argues, God-talk should be concerned more with the category of the impossible. Influenced by the ideas of Kierkegaard, Tracy (2002) contends that direct communication with God is impossible. This hidden and incomprehensible God cannot be known through persuasion and argument; one either believes in or is offended by this God. These categories of incomprehensible and hidden God cater to the postmodern man's interest, namely, to break from totalitarian and triumphalist orientation and system, and to focus intellectually and spiritually to the 'other' and not to the 'self'. According to Tracy, it is better to start one's God-talk with the categories of the 'open', the 'hidden', or the 'void'. Tracy gets inspiration from the apophatic tradition and the apocalyptic tradition in the light of Luther. He develops his theory of religious fragments which he said suits best the category of the 'impossible'. While this concept broadens the normative iconic Christian God images, it has also its dangers. Van der Ven (1998:271) states that this 'unknowable' and 'unnamable' reality can "secretly and unconsciously become filled with all conceivable pretensions and claims because there is no criterion and no measure for such a God. Thus, this unknown God can 'aniconically' sacralise every conceivable pretension and claim, from ordinary social conventions to human sacrifice; even child sacrifice, the sacrifice of Isaac, may be so justified".

Previous studies reveal that the younger generation of the Dutch population could easily relate with the aniconic images of God (Pieper & Van der Ven 1998:64–80). In a survey carried out among students in Nijmegen, the only one of the 53 items relating to faith in God that was valued positively on average was "There is a power that transcends the purely visible" (Van der Ven & Biemans 1994:85). Another is the result of the study made in 1987 among 15 to 16 year old school children in Germany, Holland, Austria and Great Britain which demonstrate that these youngsters value negatively the God in classical Christian and theological terms but were more receptive or positive on the idea of an 'indefinable' or a 'secret' God (Ziebertz 2001:13–14). But the denial of any image in reference to God should in no way be interpreted as atheistic. This research shows that "statements critical of religion and those statements with classic Christian vocabulary both tend to be rejected" (Ziebertz 2001:14). These findings clearly demonstrate that the debate on God nowadays have moved beyond the topic of contention during the 60's and 70's which delved on the contrasting notion of the Christian God versus atheism. Thus, as Ziebertz (2001:13–14) suggests, contemporary discussions on the image of God should highlight the idea of the 'anonymous' God/divine. It is interesting to probe how far our Dutch believers have embraced the aniconic images. Can we say that the more secularized people are, the more they tend towards the aniconic image of God?

2.1.2. *Anthropomorphic versus non-anthropomorphic God images*

On the second level, a distinction can be made between the anthropomorphic and non-anthropomorphic images of God. This distinction is proper only to the iconic faith and obviously not to the aniconic faith. Anthropomorphic images portray God by using symbols or descriptions that befits a person. 'God' is often described as someone who is behaving and feeling like a human being. God, in the anthropomorphic faith, is portrayed as a being like ourselves in the fundamental respect that we are both—God and ourselves—persons. God is called a 'Father', or a 'mother', a brother or sister, a 'host' or a 'stranger', etcetera. The Christian tradition abounds with such images or concepts. God is also portrayed to have a human feeling. God 'acts' and 'reacts'. He cares for his people. God's 'divine pathos', to borrow Heschel's (1953:61) words, allows Him to feel the pain and suffering of His people.[8] In several occasions in the bible, God is portrayed to

---

[8] Heschel (1953) explains that 'pathos' is not an attribute but a situation. Man's deeds do not necessitate but only occasion divine pathos. Man is not the immediate but merely the incidental cause of pathos in God. There is no nexus of causality, but

directly intervene in human affairs, although, at some instances, God simply remains 'passively present' in human history. Moreover, this anthropological image of God extends from being personal to being transpersonal. God can be located on the level of the individual person but also goes beyond (*trans*) that person, in a manner that He is also present in the other.

With the development of science in the modern era, the anthropomorphic portrayal of God has been the subject of debate and questioning. Slowly, God has been stripped off of his/her personal attributes. Dux (1973, in: Van der Ven, Dreyer & Pieterse 2002:208) calls the consequence of this development as the 'desubjectivisation of world views'. In this process, non-personal images or concepts had been attributed to God. William James (1978), for instance, calls God as the 'divine more', or the 'something beyond the self' according to Dewey, or the 'numinous' designated by the expression 'mysterium, tremendum, et fascinans' according to Rudolf Otto. There are also some theologians, like Schoonenberg, who are not comfortable with an explicit anthropomorphic characterization of God thus argue that God is not *a* person, but rather 'personal'. Hick disagrees on this idea by saying that this is a distinction without a difference. We cannot conceive of a personal being who is not a person. And we know what a person is only because we are ourselves persons. God, then, is like us—or rather we are like God—in this very basic respect. For a while, the official church became wary of this development saying that by emphasizing the non-personal image, 'God' might be deprived of his essential character which is love and power. However, it cannot be denied that non-anthropomorphic images are also part of the Christian tradition. One can find this belief especially among the teachings of the great Christian mystics. John of the Cross refers to God as the beloved wisdom, or the absolute unity according to Meister Eckhart.

The dynamics between the anthropomorphic and non-anthropomorphic images of God in the Christian tradition can be attributed to the inexhaustibility of the reality of God. God cannot simply be contained by our minds. This reality called God slips our very grasp, because, as Pseudo-Dionysius says in his work, *The Mystical Theology* (1987:141), "It is not soul or mind, nor does it possess imagination,

---

only one of contingence between divine and human attitudes, between human character and divine pathos.

conviction, speech, or understanding. It cannot be spoken of and it cannot be grasped by understanding [...] It does not live nor is it life. It is not a substance, nor is it eternity or time. It cannot be grasped by the understanding [...] It is neither one nor oneness, divinity nor goodness. It is not sonship or fatherhood. There is no speaking of it, nor name nor knowledge of it. It is beyond assertion and denial. We make assertions and denials of what is next to it, but never of it, for it is both beyond every assertion, being the perfect and unique cause of all things, and, by virtue of its preeminently simple and absolute nature, free of every limitation, beyond every limitation; it is also beyond every denial."

Previous empirical studies on God images corroborate the presence of both the anthropomorphic and non-anthropomorphic images among the Dutch believers (Janssen et al. 1994:1045–122). Some studies reveal that belief in the anthropomorphic images is modestly decreasing, both from among believers in the older and the younger generations. Studies show that a rising number of believers adhere to non-personal images (Goddijn et al. 1967; Dekker et al. 1997), or at least not decreasing compared to the personal images (Felling et al. 1992:40–41). However, as Ziebertz (2001) demonstrates, people who 'believe now but did not used to' tend to accept a personal and a caring God. This is particularly true among the younger generation more than the elderly group of converts. Nonetheless, while the anthropomorphic or personal images of God still find favour among some believers, the influence of non-anthropomorphic images continue to escalate.[9]

2.1.3. *Immanent trancendence versus transcendent immanence God images*

On the third level, a distinction can be made between immanent transcendence as opposed to transcendent immanence with regards the images of God. The differentiation between these two 'inversed' categories emerges from the basic idea of panentheism. Panentheism

---

[9] One reason for claiming that belief in anthropomorphic image is said to persist among believers is that "For the average worshipper, it is very essential that his God be a divinity who can sympathize with his human feelings and emotions...It was precisely the anthropomorphism of Yahweh which was essential to the initial success of Israel's religion" (Stark 2001:26).

portrays the 'middle ground' for the two contrasting ideas of theism and pantheism. Theism refers to the absolute transcendence of God. According to this notion, God is absolutely and totally detached from humanity and cosmos. This notion stresses that God is the first and only cause and is not influenced by the world. Traditional theism posits the idea of a God who is "a person without a body (i.e. a spirit), present everywhere, the creator and sustainer of the universe, a free agent, able to do everything (omnipotent), knowing all things (omniscient), perfectly good, a source of moral obligation, immutable, eternal, a necessary being, holy, and worthy of worship" (Swinburne 1977:2). In contrast to theism, pantheism represents a belief in an absolute immanent God. It presupposes that the world is ruled by the laws of nature. God is considered as the unity and structure of the world and therefore, exists only in relation to the world and nothing more. In the Netherlands, pantheistic believers increased from about 35% in 1985 to about 45% in 1990 (see: Felling et al. 1992; Van der Ven & Beauregard 1997). A third concept which lies in the middle of these two contrasting notions is the so-called panentheism. Panentheism claims that God is both immanent and transcendent.[10] A panentheistic image of God rejects the absolute or unipolar claims inherent in both theism and pantheism. Both of these absolutist positions are deterministic in nature and are uneasy with individual freedom and creativity. According to Tracy (1988:184), panentheism is rather more attuned with the Judeo-Christian tradition than the theistic and pantheistic beliefs. In contrast to the deterministic nature of both theism and pantheism, panentheism is rather voluntaristic in its nature. It emphasizes that God and the world do affect each other, and that God provides numerous possibilities, encouraging man to seek out self-fulfilment and to co-participate in the world as creative continuation.

Van der Ven (1998:160–161) distinguishes between immanent transcendence and transcendent immanence. The former refers to the immanent nature of God's transcendence, while the latter refers to the transcendent nature of his immanence. Immanent transcendence underscores that 'God is in everything', while transcendent-immanence stresses 'Everything is in God'. While the former looks at the

---

[10] This term is said to be coined by Krause (1781–1832), and further developed by Hartshorne. (1976). The latter made a three-fold distinction between theism, pantheism, and panentheism.

God-world relation from the perspective of God being the subject of such relationship, the latter looks at this same relationship from the perspective of the 'world'. While it sounds ideal having a balance view between immanence and transcendence, some believers tend to create a rivalry between these two, often ending up embracing one extreme pole and sacrificing or discarding the other. By stressing absolute transcendence, one ends up with a concept of a distant God (*deus remotus*), or at best, a God who comes into the world as *deus ex machina*. On the other hand, if one emphasizes absolute immanence, one ends up reducing God to 'brute' reality, or consigning 'God' to sheer corporeality. As Hodgson (1994:166) remarked: "pantheism tends to confuse all things with God and divinizes physical and human nature."

2.1.4. *A three-fold relation*

In what follows, we shall discuss the three-fold relations between God and human reality, namely: individual, social, and cosmic.

2.1.4.1. *Individual*

Christian theology teaches that God relates to human reality in a variety of ways. God connects with the world of the individual, with the social world, and with the cosmic world or nature (Van der Ven 1998:161). To the individual, God is related to him/her as the integrating force of his/her personal human existence. God is seen as the source of the fundamental 'trust' and the abiding strength within the person. God treats humanity not just in a general and anonymous way, but relates to each individual person in a specific and special manner. There is some sort of 'exclusiveness' and 'familiarity' in this relationship to which the person may exclaim: "God knows and understands me" or, "I trust God will never abandon me". Process theology asserts that the value of individual human existence is of utmost importance to God. Williams (1968:117–127), for instance, argues that since man is part of God's history, then the meaning of personal existence must be found by appropriating God's acts and purposes as the basis for human actions. This individual relationship with God is underscored by authors who view revelation as inner and personal. They argue that revelation is interior and it comes individually to particular persons (Sabatier 1897:34). It is in the individual person that the experience or the awareness of the divine is revealed. Some contemplatives like the late Thomas Merton, are convinced that the search for God can be realized through the awareness of the true self. "God transforms our hearts, in which, without knowing how, God transforms us into himself and we begin to realize obscurely yet deeply that our lives are hidden with Christ in God" (Finley 1978:117).

2.1.4.2. *Social*
Aside from being embedded in the relationship with the individual, God is also located in the interactions among individuals. This social aspect of the individual includes interaction with others in his or her environment in friendship and care. This positive social interaction serves as revelatory moment for God's presence. God is the dynamic *gestalt* of this social world; He holds it together and gives it unity; He delivers cohesion and orientation (Van der Ven & Beauregard 1997). The social interaction is seen as the locus of God's unfolding. In John 15:12-15, Jesus declared to his disciples that they are no longer to be called his servants but friends. God is unveiled in the bonding of peoples in a free and reciprocal interaction. Hence, Christians acknowledge that when people form friendships, God's love is at work, or that God's love is present whenever people live in friendship.

Contemporary authors criticize the tendency of modern culture to over-emphasize individual self in relation to God and other aspects of human life. They say that the construction of the modern self is drawn heavily around the themes of self-sufficiency, self-expression, autonomy, search for authenticity, natural development, personal creativity, individualism and emancipation. Because of this tendency, the 'modern self' fails to take into account the social dimension and the broader aspects of the integral human self. It relegates the need for solidarity and concern for other people in favour of one's individual need. Moreover, according to Charry (1998:90), this idea of the modern self "tugs at natural bonds of culture and family that once provided a strong sense of belonging". Moltmann (1997) challenges Christians to step out from creating individual relationship with an individual God as the norm of personhood and dignity. Furthermore, the idea of the modern self is challenged by the Christian belief that authentic freedom which requires self-mastery is only possible with the help of God. Hence, contemporary authors contend that, although relationship between the individual and God is central, there is a need for a doctrine of God and His working in history which will have to encompass the complex social structure and cosmic realities. The Christian experience of the divine should not be confined to the boundaries of a too intimate personal subjectivity or individual entrepreneurship with God. Boff (1997) explains that each human person has his or her irreducible uniqueness. However, this uniqueness consists of two things: that the person is unique and is consciously knows that he or she is unique. He is both irreducible being (individual) but one ever in communication (person). Boff links uniqueness to *haecceitas* which he said is a term used by Dun Scotus to mean 'this clearly defined embodiment here' or here-ness (from *haec* = this [here]). He further explains that individuality is not a question of number but "a negation of number insofar as the individual is singular and irreplaceable in a conscious manner" (Boff 1997:59–60). Despite one's irreducible individuality, human beings share the same genetic code with all living beings and share the same infrastructure with the cosmos.

2.1.4.3. *Cosmic*

One of the paradigm shifts in contemporary theology is the swing from an anthropo-centric worldview to a cosmo-centric one (Hodgson 1994). This shift brings to fore the relationship between God and nature. The ecological sensibility highlights the idea that the crisis of the environment is also the crisis of the human spirit. Furthermore, the shift from an essentialist to a relational worldview in contemporary thinking brings to our awareness that reality is a complex and a multidimensional unity, and that life is inter-connected. Reflecting theologically, Hodgson (1994:92) claims that "God acts purposively in natural and human history, but we cannot claim that God simply is cosmic energy or that God has endowed the world as a whole with a cosmic blueprint". God's relation to the cosmic world indicates the presence of God in the world or nature.[11] God interacts with nature. Dostoyevsky (1999:309), in his renowned novel, *The Brothers Karamazov*, posits this expression: "Love all God's creation, the whole and every grain of sand of it.... If you love everything, you will perceive the divine mystery in things." The Creator leaves His own mark and promise of His permanent or providential presence in the creature

---

[11] Kalbheim & Ziebertz (2001) identify three ideal typologies for the relationship between God and Nature:—The Christian (and monotheistic) faith, which views God as a pre-condition for Nature and Nature refers back to God; the mechanical world view, which sees nature as devoid if not separated from God; and the holistic world view, a view that God is immanent within Nature, i.e. God as a pre-condition of Nature.

(Boff 1997). This experience is expressed by such statements as "I experience God's goodness in the peace of nature", or, "I experience God's hand in the beauty of nature". This reciprocal relationship between God and nature is acknowledged by Paul Ricoeur saying that "our sense of radical dependence on a higher power thus may be reflected in a love for the creation" (Ricoeur 1995:297). Ricoeur argues that one cannot read only the 'book of the bible' and get rid of the 'book of nature', or the other way around. The experiences of an awesome and stupendous presence that cannot satisfactorily be expressed through human language are moments that trigger the mystical or spiritual awareness. Ricoeur reflects on how religious language is evoked by the experience in nature. He said: "The sacredness of nature shows itself in symbolically saying itself. And the showing founds the saying, not vice versa. Its sacrality is immediate or it does not exist." And he adds: "…in the sacred universe the capacity for saying is founded on the capacity of the cosmos to signify something other than itself. The logic of meaning here thus proceeds from the very structure of the sacred universe" (Ricoeur 1995:54–55).

The abiding presence of God in His creation has been time and again expressed in manifold theological treatises and mystical texts. These texts try to affirm the Divine presence in nature and the universe, and that the beauty of our natural world is a revelatory locus of the divine. Ideas regarding God's relationship with nature have been recently propagated by ecological and eco-feminist theologians. They bring to our awareness the connectivity of all things, and that God is like the mother earth that nurtures and cares for Her creation (cf. Berry & Clark 1991; Green 1994). Now, from an empirical side, previous study reveal that people who are religiously active reject the separation of God and Nature. For them, God plays a very active role in Nature. God is the creator of the world, but he is also immanently present in nature (Kalbheim and Ziebertz 2001). We want to know whether this is also true among our population.

In summary, we illustrate these various God images in the scheme below (Scheme 2.1.). The first distinction is made between the iconic and aniconic faith. We identified 'metatheism' as a concept belonging to the aniconic faith while the 'iconic' images of God consist of the anthropomorphic images and the non-anthropomorphic. The second distinction refers to the anthropomorphic and non-anthropomorphic groups which have been sub-categorized into: *theistic, panentheistic,*

Scheme 2.1. Images of God from a Theoretical Perspective

Iconic Anthropomorphic
1. theism
2. individual panentheism
3. social panentheism
4. cosmic panentheism

Iconic Non-anthropomorphic
5. deism
6. pantheism

Aniconic Non-anthropomorphic
7. metatheism

deistic, and *pantheistic* images. The sub-categorization on this level has been carried out based on the presumption that neither the deistic images nor the pantheistic images apply to the anthropomorphic group. Finally, the individual, social, and cosmic aspects of God's anthropomorphic relation to the world have been spelled out.

The next section will deal with the empirical dimension of the images of God. In what follows, we intend to provide the empirical 'grounding' of the conceptual framework that has been spelled out in the preceding section regarding the attitudes of the Dutch believers towards God. We want to find out the empirical tenability of the conceptualization of these images. Does the empirical data corroborate with the theoretical conceptualization we made about the images of God? Do these conceptual distinctions correspond with the empirical behaviour and attitudes of church members towards God?

2.2. *Images of God from an empirical perspective*

In the previous section, we discussed the seven conceptual images of God. We identified four anthropomorphic images, namely: theism, individual panentheism, social panentheism, and cosmic panentheism. For non-anthropomorphic images, we categorize three concepts, namely: deism, pantheism, and metatheism. We categorize metatheism as a representative of the aniconic image of God. These seven concepts were operationalized into two items per concept based on the shorter version of the original 24-item list of Van der Ven's instrument (2004:589–590). Eight items were presented to measure the anthropomorphic images and a separate set of six items for non-

Table 2.1. Images of God from an Empirical Perspective

Empirical Model	Mean	Standard Deviation	Pearson Correlation (r)	Reliability of Scales (*Cronbach's Alpha*)	Valid Cases
I. Theism (Theoretical model 1)	3.6	1.10	.75		422
II. Panentheism (Theoretical models 2, 3 & 4)	4.0	.88		.92	437
III. Pantheism (Theoretical model 6)	3.6	.99	.70		413
IV. Metatheism (Theoretical model 7)	3.9	.98	.47		425

anthropomorphic images. Hence there was a total of 14 items for the entire images of God (For a complete list of items, refer to Appendix 1, Table 3, Part 2).

We subjected the scores on God images all together, both anthropomorphic and non-anthropomorphic ones, to one factor analysis. The free factor solution analysis (mineigen = 1) did not result in an interpretable outcome. For that reason, we conducted a factor analysis with a forced four factor solution which resulted into the following pattern: anthropomorphic theism, anthropomorphic panentheism (items of all panentheistic images formed one factor), non-anthropomorphic pantheism, and the aniconic non-anthropomorphic metatheism (see: Appendix 2, Table 1). Items indicated by an asterisk (*) in the appendix indicate that deism was eliminated (see: Appendix 1, Table 3, Part 2). This four-factor solution explained a total of 78% of the variance. On the basis of the outcome of the factor analysis, we constructed four scales, of which we inspected their reliability. The table above (Table 2.1.) contains the summary of the empirical result for the images of God.

From the result of the analysis, one can observe that the respondents generally agree with all the God images: panentheism (mean: 4.0), metatheism (mean: 3.9), pantheism (mean: 3.6), and theism (mean: 3.6).

2.3. *Social location of the attitudes toward God*

In this section, we consider a number of demographic, social and religious characteristics of our respondents in relation to their attitudes

Table 2.2. Social location of the attitudes toward God *(eta & rho)*

	Theism	Panentheism	Pantheism	Metatheism
DEMOGRAPHIC CHARACTERISTICS				
Age *(eta)*	.27**	.13*	—	.17**
Gender *(eta)*	—	—	.12*	—
Education *(eta)*	.25**	.21**	.14*	—
Country of origin *(eta)*	—	.10*	—	—
SOCIAL CHARACTERISTICS				
Localistic authoritarianism *(rho)*	.26**	.24**	.13*	.10*
Subjectively-perceived threat *(rho)*	.15**	—	—	—
Conformism *(rho)*	.25**	.25*	.14*	.12*
Anomie *(rho)*	.23**	.17*	—	—
RELIGIOUS CHARACTERISTICS				
Church involvement *(eta)*	.29**	.38**	—	—
Religious salience *(rho)*	.42**	.62**	.18*	—

** $p < .01$; * $p < .05$ (2-tailed)

towards God. For demographic characteristics, we shall pay attention to gender, age, country of origin, and education of our respondents. We also identify some social characteristics, namely localistic authoritarianism, conformism, anomie, and subjectively-perceived threat. In terms of religious characteristics, we shall consider their church involvement and religious salience. We assume that at least some of these characteristics have a relation with their attitudes towards God.

We conducted variance analysis *(eta)* and correlation analysis *(rho)* in order to establish the social location of the God attitudes of our respondents. We use variance analysis *(eta)* to examine the association between the demographic characteristics and the different God attitudes. We use variance analysis *(eta)* to examine the relations between church involvement and God-attitudes. We employ correlation analysis *(rho)* for religious salience and for the social characteristics (localistic authoritarianism, conformism, anomie, and subjectively-perceived threat). Details of these analyses can be found on Appendix 2, Tables 3 and 4. The table above (Table 2.2.) establishes the social location of attitudes toward God from significant associations and correlations only.

From the variance analysis, the Scheffé test, and the correlation analysis, we can gather the following significant observations regarding the social location of God images among our respondents. In terms of demographic characteristics, age demonstrates significant associations to three out of four God images, namely, theism (eta .27), panentheism (eta .13), and metatheism (eta .17). The oldest age group (69 years and older) scores higher on these God images than the youngest ones (57 years and younger) (see: Appendix 2, Table 3). We notice that gender is associated to only one God image, which is the pantheistic God image (eta .12). Our female respondents accept this God image more intensely than their male fellows. Education is associated to three God images which are theism (eta .25), panentheism (eta .21), and pantheism (eta .14). The respondents with a lower education (primary education and/or lower secondary education) score higher on theism, panentheism, and metatheism than those with a higher education (higher secondary education and/or tertiary education) (see: Appendix 2, Table 3). Country of origin is only associated to anthropomorphic panentheism (eta .10). The social characteristics of our respondents also exhibit interesting correlations with God attitudes. Localistic authoritarianism is significantly correlated to theism (rho .26), panentheism (rho .24), pantheism (rho .13), and metatheism (rho .10). Subjectively-perceived threat is correlated only to theism (rho .15). Conformism is significantly correlated to theism (rho .25), panentheism (rho .25), pantheism (rho .14), and metatheism (rho .12). Anomie is correlated to two God images, namely: theism (rho .23), and panentheism (rho .17). When we examine their religious characteristics, we notice that church involvement is associated to two anthropomorphic God images, i.e. theism (eta .29) and panentheism (eta .38), but not to any non-anthropomorphic God images. Active members score higher on theism and panentheism than the inactive members (see: Appendix 2, Table 3). Religious salience is correlated to both of the anthropomorphic God images, i.e. theism (rho .42) and panentheism (rho .62), and to one non-anthropomorphic image, pantheism (rho .18).

Summary

In this chapter, we investigate the images of God as they appear among our population. The seven conceptual images that include both the anthropomorphic and non-anthropomorphic images have been submitted to empirical testing and analysis. Only four images of God appeared to be the ones that are present in our respondents' consciousness, namely: theism, panentheism, metatheism, and pantheism. We have indicated that our respondents strongly adhere to a panentheistic God image. It is interesting to note that metatheism is likewise favourably accepted by our Catholic respondents. Results of our analysis also demonstrate variances and diversity particularly if seen from the social location of our population. We found out that age, education, localistic authoritarianism, conformism, anomie, church involvement, and religious salience are significant social locators of God images. Our analysis reveals that the oldest age group scores higher on theism, panentheism, and metatheism God images than the youngest ones. We also discover that respondents with a lower education (primary education and/or lower secondary education) score higher on theism, panentheism, and metatheism than those with a higher education (higher secondary education and/or tertiary education). Localistic authoritarianism and conformism are significantly correlated to all four God images, namely: theism, panentheism, pantheism, and metatheism. Subjectively-perceived threat is correlated only to theism. Anomie is correlated to two God images, i.e. theism and panentheism. In relation to the religious characteristics, church involvement is noted to be associated only to two anthropomorphic God images, namely: theism and panentheism. Active members score higher on theism and panentheism than the inactive members. Religious salience is correlated to theism, panentheism, and pantheism. We note that theism and panentheism are clearly socially located, while the other two non-anthropomorphic God images are not.

CHAPTER THREE

ATTITUDES TOWARD JESUS

In this chapter we deal with the attitudes towards Jesus. Religious attitudes based on the Christian tradition cannot help but speak about Jesus as a significant aspect of its belief system. Christians profess that Jesus is the messiah or the saviour not only of the Christian believers but also of all humankind. However, looking at this same tradition, one may note that there are discordant claims about Jesus which already started since the time of the apostles. In Marks gospel, Jesus asked this key question to his disciples: "Who do you say that I am?" (Mk. 8:27). Since then, this same query had been unremittingly raised, discerned, debated, re-constructed, or even tussled upon throughout history. Sadly enough, the answer to such question did not always yield a positive and unifying end. History is replete with examples showing how Christians break up with believers of other religions, with advocates of non-religious convictions, and even among their fellow Christians by virtue of their belief in Jesus Christ. Dutch history is neither spared from this discordant and conflict-ridden past. Indeed, for several centuries, the claim for Jesus seems not to sow unity but rather division in the community, resonating the very words of the master himself who once said: "Do you think that I have come to bring peace to the earth? No, I tell you, but division!" (Lk. 12:51). The 'Jesus controversy' continues to haunt and divide people. In the present-day Dutch society, we may ask: Is Jesus a source of unity or division? Let us suspend our answer to this question to the later part of this work. Meanwhile, let us first deal with the main question that we set for this chapter: what are the attitudes of our respondents towards Jesus, and what is the social location of these attitudes? Given the highly secularized Dutch situation, what images of Jesus may prominently appear among our respondents? To what extent do believers identify themselves with the traditional belief in Jesus? Is it more likely that these believers are no longer fixated to the orthodox or traditional teachings but have rather transformed, modified, or perhaps transmuted their attitudes toward Jesus in order to suit the new situation? Given the plurality of religious attitudes which are made available to the contemporary Dutch believers, is it not unlikely that believers may have in mind not just a mono- but a dual or even poly- images of Jesus in the wake of Christological pluralism that may characterize the contemporary Dutch church?

Let us find some illumination to these queries in what follows. We shall proceed in this chapter by presenting a theoretical perspective of the images of Jesus in section 3.1; then we shall put forward the results of the research findings on the empirical part in section 3.2, and finally, we shall look at the social locations of our respondents' images of Jesus in section 3.3.

3.1. *Images of Jesus from a theoretical perspective*

In this section, we will discuss the theoretical images of Jesus through the distinction we made between 'tradition-bound' Jesus images (section 3.1.1.), 'hermeneutic-oriented' Jesus images (section 3.1.2.), and 'humanistic' Jesus image (section 3.1.3).

One can assume at the outset that there are varieties of attitudes towards Jesus which may be present among the contemporary Dutch Catholics. But the question is: how can we identify these attitudes in such a way that we can classify them and substantiate their existence through our empirical investigation? So as to address this problem, we shall take into account three general divisions of these attitudes towards Jesus from a theoretical perspective, namely: the tradition-bound images, the hermeneutic-oriented images, and the humanistic image. Let us describe the main characteristics of these three general strands of attitudes towards Jesus which we construct in this study.

It should be clarified at the onset that when we construct this general division for our study of the various attitudes towards Jesus, we do not intend to make a distinction based on a chronological position of these discourses in the history of theological thought. Rather, we take this broad distinction in order to underscore how each Christological discourse takes into account the two poles of doing theology, namely tradition and human experience (De Mesa & Wostyn 1990:5–18). Thus, when we speak of tradition-bound Christologies, we refer to theological assertions about Jesus which take the classical tradition *(traditum)* mainly as the source of Christian faith about Jesus while more or less putting aside today's contexts which permeate the actual belief in Jesus among ordinary Christians. In contrast to the tradition-bound Christology, hermeneutic-oriented Christologies regard human experience as a compelling source of Christian faith. In their reflections about Jesus, the hermeneutic-oriented Christologies consider tradition and context seriously. They underscore the task of contextualization of religious beliefs. The third general category, which we identify here as humanistic image of Jesus, plainly abandons the Judeo-Christian tradition as a source of reflection about Jesus. Humanistic Jesus discards any transcendental interpretation about the man Jesus whom they simply regard as a human being just like any other human beings. Our respondents may have certainly been introduced into this type of a purely humanistic attitude towards Jesus in the context of a pervasive process of secularization in the Dutch society.

We presume that our respondents are socialized into these three general strands of Christological assertions as we broadly describe them above. In what follows, we shall give a detailed presentation of the Christologies that fit into these three general strands of Christological discourses. For tradition-bound Jesus images, we shall describe two representatives namely: the well-known classical and the neo-classical Jesus images. For hermeneutic-oriented Jesus images, we name five representatives: individual-related, community-related, society-related, spirit-motivated, and a secular-worldview related Jesus images. Finally, we shall describe the sole representative of humanistic attitude towards Jesus.

3.1.1. *Tradition-bound images*

In this section, we shall describe two representatives of tradition-bound images of Jesus, namely: classical and neo-classical Christologies. We classify these two Christologies as traditional Christologies because both of them are anchored on the traditional sources of Christian faith which are the revealed Word of God and the Niceo-Chalcedonian dogma. Classical Christology goes back to the Christological teachings of the 4th and 5th centuries as the foundational source of its Christological claims. The so-called neo-classical Christology is a re-assertion of the classical authoritative texts even though it was developed at a later date by Karl Barth. Like the classical Christology, it underscores that Jesus is the Son of God who is the second person of the Trinity. These traditional Christologies start with the Second Person of the Trinity who is regarded as the pre-existing divine Word in relation to the Father and the Holy Spirit. While classical Christology tends to thrust aside any reference to the on-going revelation of God in Jesus in human history and experience, the neo-classical approach admits that God can be discerned in and through human history by God's grace in Jesus only. Whereas classical approach focuses on how God became incarnate through the humanity of Jesus, the neo-classical approach emphasizes on how the human being can be brought to perfection only through the divine nature of Jesus because of the infinite qualitative distinction between God and human being. Let us now give a detailed explanation of each of these tradition-bound Jesus images.

3.1.1.1. *Classical Jesus*
It has been established by scholars that various discourses about Jesus already existed during the early beginnings of Christianity. From the four versions of the gospel itself, one can already discover a plurality of statements about Jesus, some of which were expressed through the honorific titles that were ascribed to Him.[1] The early Christian churches used models available to them to reflect on certain aspects of Jesus' life and ministry. These models influence the way they report on the events of Jesus. St. Paul and other New Testament writers, including the Johanine and synoptic authors, presented their own versions of Jesus' event. Most of these writers however did not dwell on the question about who Jesus really was but more about what God did to men in Jesus. They reported what the New Testament witnesses have proclaimed about the salvation they received from God in Jesus ('salvation-by-God-in-Jesus'). This salvation-historical perspective gets a twist in the succeeding centuries, especially when the Christian faith was brought to the Hellenistic world. Further reflections on the life of Jesus in the Greco-Roman context necessitated appropriation of their reflection of Jesus.

The plurality of Christologies was a taken-for-granted reality during the early Christian era until it became a cause of division among Christians in the Roman Empire. It was during these divisive periods when the great ecumenical councils were convened. The Council of Nicea (325 C.E.) was assembled by Emperor Constantine in order to prevent the growing division in the Roman Empire caused by the controversy created by an Alexandrian priest named Arius (c. 256–336 C.E.)

---

[1] Some examples of these titles are Christ, messiah, Son of Man, Son of God, Word, Lord, God, prophet, etcetera. Schillebeeckx however warned that the study of honorific titles overlook the very basis from which the later kerygma flowed (cf. Schillebeeckx 1979:358–422).

and his followers. For Arius, the absolute transcendence and unknowablility of God could not be compromised. He argued that there is an essential difference in *ousia* between the Father and the Son. According to him, Jesus, the incarnate Son, was definitely divine, but he was of lesser divinity than the Father who is unoriginate. Opponents of Arius saw that this position was an outright contradiction to the very conviction of Christian faith which claims that in Jesus, Christians have ultimate and definitive encounter with the one true God. Athanasius of Alexandria (c. 295–373), a staunch antagonist of Arius, figured out his argument based on the Prologue of John's Gospel (Jn 1:1) to counter the claims of Arius. He said that before Jesus came to the earth, He was the *logos* (Word) who lived with the Father from the beginning where he shares the complete divinity of the Father (Haight 1999:247–248). This *logos* argument of Athanasius strongly influenced the council, thus declaring that the Son is 'of the same substance or being with the Father' (*homoousios*). This Christological proposition had been canonized in the Nicene creed which reads: "We believe [...] in one Lord Jesus Christ, the Son of God, begotten from the Father, only-begotten, that is, from the substance of the Father, God from God, light from light, true God from true God, begotten not made, of one substance with the Father".

The decision made by the council of Nicea did not end the controversy neither did it unify positions regarding the *ousia* between the Father and the Son. In the years that followed, two diverse directions in Christology brought the debate to a stalemate, thereby causing the council of Chalcedon to be convened in 451. This council dealt mainly with the debate between the Alexandrian and Antiochene Schools. The Alexandrian school claimed for a logos-*sarx* Christology (The Word became flesh [*sarx*])—an approach which highlights the divinity of Jesus without incorporating Christ's incarnation in a real human being. The Antiochene School advocated a kind of *logos-anthropos* Christology which claimed that Christ did not merely assume fleshly nature but also that of an *anthropos*, a real human being in the full sense. Following the Tome of Pope Leo the Great, the council of Chalcedon intervened in the debate by stressing the full, unaltered and undiluted humanity of the man Jesus. This it did in terms of the doctrine of two natures.[2] It declared that the Word incarnate is a divine person with

---

[2] The official translated text read as follows: "We should confess that our Lord Jesus Christ is one and the same Son, the same perfect in godhead and the same

two natures, a divine nature and a human nature; these two natures are united in the divine person (*hypostasis*)—thanks to the formula proposed by the Cappadocian Fathers. Needless to say that Chalcedon did not really end the division at that time. Remnants of this conflict can be proven by the presence of other Christian churches even to this day, for instance the Coptic Church in Egypt who maintains their Monophysite or 'non-Chalcedonian' position, and also the Nestorians who are still found in some Asian countries. Despite these developments in the history of the church, one can say that most of the Christian churches accepted the tenets of Chalcedon which continued to be the norm for the church's belief in the person of Jesus Christ (Macquarie 1990:165). These doctrines of Nicea and Chalcedon became the foundation of classical Christologies as we have them even today.

Classical Christology is called into question by subsequent Christologies starting from the Enlightenment up to the present. Notwithstanding these criticisms, residues and effects of classical Christology still exist in recent times. In the 19th–20th century, neo-scholasticism became a dominant theological orientation in the Catholic Church. It was supposed to teach a 'perennial' theology which should uphold all the doctrines formulated in the past, including the doctrines of Nicea and Chalcedon. For some years, neo-scholasticism was the official theology mandated by Rome to be taught in seminaries. This gives us a strong basis for the assumption that the classical approach is still deeply embedded in the minds of some members who had been socialized according to the teachings of the classical formulation of the council fathers through the agency of their pastors and church workers trained in neo-scholasticism. Moreover, the dominance of (neo-)scholasticism in the Dutch churches had been reinforced by some conservative sectors of the Catholic Church after Vatican II. The rejection of the Dutch Catechism by the Vatican authorities, for instance,

---

perfect in manhood, truly God and truly man, the same of a rational soul and body; consubstantial with the Father in Godhead, and the same consubstantial with us in manhood, like us in all things except sin; begotten from the Father before ages as regards his Godhead, and in the last days, the same, because of us and because of our salvation begotten from the virgin Mary, the *Theotokos*, as regards His manhood; one and the same Christ, Son, Lord, only-begotten, made known in two natures without confusion, without change, without division, without separation, the difference of the natures being by no means removed because of the union, but the property of each nature being preserved and coalescing in one *proposon* and one *hypostasis*" (Kelly 2000: 339–340).

elicited different reactions among church authorities and members. On the one hand, the progressive view went on with new experimentation in theology, and on the other hand, conservative members revert back to old catechism of neo-scholasticism and church tradition. This is clearly evident in the publication of the *Catechism of the Catholic Church* (*Katechismus* 1995, nn. 464–483, esp. 479–483; cf. Witte 1999), which upholds the classical formulations of Christology based on Nicea and Chalcedon. Hence, while it is true that a great deal of criticism had been posed against the classical model of Christology, it is highly probable that classical Christology is strongly present in the consciousness of many Dutch believers.[3] The impact of the teachings of these 4th & 5th century councils is undeniably pervasive. It continues to influence lots of Christians from all walks of life and from various times and places. According to Van der Ven (2004:419), the classical model "left such indelible marks on the mental architecture of successive generations that they virtually constitute a Christian archive around the world, one which has remained open over the centuries and still actively functions in Christian memory".

3.1.1.2. Neo-classical Jesus

We shall now elaborate on the neo-classical Christology which we identified as one of the representatives of the tradition-bound Christology. We shall illustrate this type of tradition-bound Christology by using the Christological ideas of Karl Barth as an example. Although, Barth developed his theological thoughts only in the 20th century, we consider his Christology as a manifest representative of the classical Christology because of his attempt to approach the Christological problem through his re-interpretation of the classical credo of the 4th & 5th century for the 20th century. Karl Barth tried to revive the Chalcedonian Christology in the modern time and defended the Christological statements of Nicea and Chalcedon against the accusation of intellectualism and metaphysical abstraction by liberal theologians (McGrath 2001:165ff). He opted to restate the classical doctrine that Jesus Christ is both God and man as proclaimed by the Council

---

[3] Gillis (1998:79) criticizes Classical Christology saying that "this type of Christology does not give full autonomy to the salvific figures of the other traditions but understands them as further incarnation of the normative *logos*". Nevertheless in much of the preaching and catechetical teaching, the classic tradition is (still) dominating (again).

of Chalcedon (Hunsinger 2000:131–147). Like classical Christology, Barth places the incarnation (*logos*) as the central content of Christology and proposes a Christology in the context of the Trinity.

The development of Karl Barth's neo-classical approach can be understood as a reaction against liberal theology. His ideas were triggered by the crisis he experienced with liberal tradition since the outbreak of the First World War. He was disillusioned to see how several proponents of liberal theology provided ethical and theological arguments in favour of policies that supported the war. His criticism to the liberal tradition led him to take a theocentric standpoint in his theological method, or more exactly, a Trinitarian approach to Christology. Barth argued that one should start from the revelation of the Word of God which is totally other than the human self. He maintains that the divine and human relationship is fundamentally dialectical in nature.[4] He claimed that human persons cannot represent God in any way properly through some human representations. Thus, he puts forward the idea that one ought to speak of Him paradoxically, which involves balancing every affirmation with a corresponding negation. For Barth, this is an important theological method because it is through this process that one can do justice to a God who infinitely transcends our finite creaturely being. In contrast to liberal theology which stresses the historical Jesus in correlation to the human condition when speaking of the uniqueness and finality of Christ, Barth claimed that there is an infinite qualitative difference between God and human beings, an expression Karl Barth borrowed from Kierkegaard. According to Barth, God is the absolute 'Other', and therefore, God is never identical with anything which we name, experience, conceive, or worship as God. According to Barth, revelation comes perpendicularly from above. The history of Jesus Christ begins not with his birth in the first century, but in eternity, with the second person of the Trinity. In contrast, human history is derived from God. The history of all beings is justified and saved by the historical occurrence of Jesus whereby our world is touched by the other world. The history of Jesus Christ can only recapitulate in time what has already happened antecedently in eternity. He is not within but rather beyond history!

---

[4] Thus, Barth's theology is usually referred to as 'dialectical theology' (based on Barth's commentary on *Romans* in 1919 where he mentioned the 'dialectic between time and eternity' and 'the dialectic between God & humanity').

Barth contends that liberal Christology is at a lost because it drops the problem of the mystery of revelation. According to Barth, God's revelation is disclosed in total freedom and surprise to human existence (Haight 1999:310). Man cannot rely on human mediation in order to locate God's revelation. He views human nature to be weak and unreliable. Thus, he rejects the liberal theology's confidence on human consciousness or human rationality and feeling. Human experience, according to him, cannot be relied upon to guarantee the salvation of human beings. He discards any tendency to make man as the measure of all things or to make a god out of man. For him, human beings can be brought to perfection only through the Word of God revealed in Jesus. Thus, Barth opted for a Christology that is centered on the doctrine of the divine and human nature of Jesus. For Barth, Jesus is absolutely perfect and sinless because God is present within Him. He is the 'Word made flesh'. Reflecting on the Epistle to the Romans, Barth admits that human nature is weak and unreliable just like Adam. Thus, he writes off liberal theology's confidence on human consciousness or human rationality and feeling. Barth breaks away from all attempts in modern theology to construct a doctrine of man by beginning from man's self-knowledge which is disconnected from revelation. Human consciousness, according to him, cannot be relied upon to guarantee the salvation of human beings. For him, human beings can be brought to perfection only through the Word of God revealed in Jesus. Jesus Christ holds the 'secret truth about the essential nature of man' (Barth 1963:64). Through the life and destiny of Jesus Christ, Barth explains, he has shown the example of being obedient to God until death. Followers of Jesus must also emulate His example. He/She must make a persistent valuation of his/her actions whether they are in consonant with that of Christ. Believers have to make a choice, either to do his/her own ways or to follow God's ways through Jesus. Conversion is therefore crucial in order to follow Jesus. This conversion entails a radical change in a person's way of life, either to be on the side of God or not. The choice to follow Jesus is a sure path because He is absolutely perfect and sinless since God is present within Him. He is the 'Word made flesh'.

For Barth, any Christological claims must be firmly rooted on the scriptures. He believes that Christology ought to be built on the foundation of revelation—God's revelation in Jesus Christ as witnessed in the Scripture. Barth believes that the revelation in the scriptures is a reality in the fulfillment of the incarnation of the Son. He believes that

God is known only by revelation and this revelation is Jesus Christ, the Word made flesh. Human salvation is possible only within the horizon of this revelation. This revelation cannot be conceived proportionally or intellectually, but must be understood as an act of God in Jesus Christ and proceeds from God to the world. God's disclosure of himself in Jesus Christ has a threefold pattern: God the Father revealing himself to us in Jesus Christ; the Son is the Word and image of the Father; and the Holy Spirit is the power who discloses that image and conveys that Word. This triadic structure as perceived by Barth is nothing other than the Trinity.

Critics say that Barth's theology cultivates negative attitudes towards other religion and tends to emasculate dialogue or positive engagement with their members. This criticism is based on his outstandingly Christocentric approach in relation to other religions. In his work *Church Dogmatics* (CD IV/3:86), he declares that "Jesus Christ is the light, the one and only light of life…in all its fullness, in perfect adequacy…[with] no other light of life outside or alongside His." For Barth, the statement that Christ is the one and only light is a necessary Christological affirmation. However, Barth explains, this affirmation has 'nothing whatever to do with the arbitrary exaltation and self-glorification of the Christian in relation to other men, of the church in relation to other institution, or of Christianity in relation to other conceptions' (CD IV/3:91). It should be clarified that when Barth declares that Christ is the one light and the one Word, it does not follow that there are no other words. Rather, what Barth is simply stating is that there are 'no other words that can be set beside the Word of Christ' (DiNoia 2000:254). Barth employs the metaphor of spheres or circles to account for the relation of the Word of God to all other words which he also named as the 'parables of the kingdom'. At the center, the innermost sphere is the Word of Christ radiating outward. From the center are three concentric circles consisting of (1) the Words of the bible, (2) the Words of the Church; (3) the words outside the church, which Barth calls as *Extra muros ecclesia* (DiNoia 2000:254). Although Barth asserts that salvation is only possible through Christ, he also admits that there is the ultimate eschatological victory of grace over unbelief which comes at the end of history. In the end, God's grace will be wholly victorious and everyone will worship Christ. Therefore, while Barth claims that Christ is the only way to salvation, he also believes that this way is effective for all through the grace of God. Barth's Christocentric approach clearly affirms the particularity of God's revelation through Christ and yet this does not contradict his admission of the universality of salvation (McGrath 1998:330). He conveys a vigorous assurance of the possibility of the salvation of persons who do not yet know or acknowledge Christ which is warranted only and entirely because of the victorious reconciliation achieved by Christ (cf. *CD* IV/3:355).

The impact of the ideas of Karl Barth spreads out not only among the Protestants but also among the Dutch Catholics. Barth's radical critique to liberal Protestantism may have articulated the sentiments of traditional Catholics who were more eager to accept the divinity of Jesus than the preoccupation and overestimation on His humanity. This is a case wherein the differences within denominations are frequently bigger than differences between denominations, albeit under different labels. Traditional Protestants and traditional Catholics may converge at this point, albeit not knowing this. Can our data indeed corroborate our expectation that this type of Jesus' attitude exist among our respondents?

3.1.2. *Hermeneutic-oriented images*

Earlier, we indicated that traditional Christologies underscore the pole of the Judeo-Christian tradition as a starting point of their discourses and reflections on Jesus Christ. In contrast to this traditional approach, hermeneutic-oriented Christologies attempt to reflect on the person of Jesus Christ starting from the pole of the human experience. Many of these so-called hermeneutic-oriented Christologies have been constructed using insights from the Enlightenment and were later elaborated theologically by Friedrich Schleiermacher in the 19th century onwards (cf. Greene 2003:97–108). Schleiermacher initiated the new direction of attempting to construct a Christology 'from below', an assumption that all doctrines of Christ must begin with his humanly historical existence. Some of the most common features of these hermeneutic-oriented Christologies as they evolved starting from Schleiermacher up until our present era are the following: the recognition of the historical process or a historical consciousness, the regard for contemporary experience or the 'relevance' of experience in theological discourse; and the importance of 'hermeneutics'. While the language and approach of tradition-bound Christologies are non-experiential and a-historical, hermeneutic-oriented Christologies are rather historical and experiential.

In this section, we shall elucidate on some of the hermeneutic-oriented Christologies which we believe to have considerable influence on the religious attitudes of the Dutch believers, at least from the theoretical point of view. We want to make clear that our focus is on 'types' of Christologies and not authors. While we use authors to exemplify some types of hermeneutic-oriented christologies, we don't assume that these authors develop their Christology restrictively to one type only. Author's christologies overlap the types. In what follows, we will explain the representatives of the hermeneutic-oriented Christologies, namely: individual-related (3.1.2.1.), community-related (3.1.2.2.), society-related (3.1.2.3.), Spirit-motivated (3.1.2.4.), and secular-worldview related Jesus (3.1.2.4.). We presume that all these hermeneutic-oriented Christologies do exist in one way or the other in the mindsets of our respondents.

3.1.2.1. *Individual-related Jesus*
Our first representative of hermeneutic-oriented Christology is what we may call here as the individual-related Christology. The most influential proponent of this model is Friedrich Schleiermacher who is also considered to be the father of modern liberal protestant theology. The cultural milieu wherein Schleiermacher developed his theological thinking may be characterized by an atmosphere where reason, human experience, and autonomy have been bestowed premium value than authority and tradition. This new consciousness was influenced by the liberal ideas set off by the Enlightenment in the 18th century. Schleiermacher considered himself as a 'child of the Enlightenment' and grew up in this environment. He took up the gauntlet to address the challenge posed by these liberal ideas to theology. As Haight (1999:304) remarks: "Schleiermacher endeavoured to re-establish the credibility of the Christian message in the wake of certain elements in the critique by the Enlightenment." The main theological problem for Schleiermacher is how to make sense of our God-talk in an age of reason. He proposes to situate the Christian discourse of God within the experiential and rational capability of the human person. He maintains that God can be located within the subjective experience of the human person and that each individual human being has the capacity to become aware of the feeling of absolute dependence on God. He is convinced that Christology must not be construed as a set of propositions that can be deduced from an abstract principle but rather as an explication of the God-consciousness of Christian believers (Schleiermacher

1960:1, 348–349). He believes that God-consciousness is intrinsic in the structure of human consciousness. We quote him saying:

> It must be asserted that even the most rigorous view of the difference between Christ and all other man does not hinder us from saying that his appearing even regarded as the incarnation of the Son of God, is a natural fact..... As certainly as Christ was a man, there must reside in human nature the possibility of taking up the divine into itself, just as did happen in Christ. So that the idea that the divine revelation in Christ must be something, in this respect absolutely supernatural, will simply not stand the test (Schleiermacher 1928:64).

This idea of Schleiermacher has also been worked out in his Christological view. He portrays Jesus as a real human being just like any other. Jesus shared the feeling of absolute dependence like all other human beings. The awareness of the existence of God in Jesus was part of his development as a human person. In *Der christliche Glaube* (1960), Schleiermacher insists that Jesus needs his whole human development to be in common with the rest of the human beings. He argues that the unique identity of Jesus rests in his personal communication to his companions of his own religious consciousness in which God himself is present: his continuous, powerful God-consciousness is the true being of God in him (*welche ein eigentliches sein Gottes in ihm war*) (Schleiermacher 1960:2,43). However, he maintains that there is within all of us a potential for uninhibited God-consciousness (*Gottesbewusstsein*), which Jesus actually tries to manifest. This implies that even the existence of God in Jesus must have evolved in Jesus' life only as a potentiality which was actualized later as he grew up. It indicates how Jesus' own subservience to the will of God, a will which he had to discern, struggle with and obey, has grown in his ordinary process of development as a human person. Schleiermacher maintains that the incarnation of Jesus is an ordinary fact of life like any other human nativity. However, he explains that the beginning of the life of Jesus was also a new implanting of the God-consciousness. He stresses the growth and development in Jesus towards absolute dependence in God. He rejects the traditional notion which claims that he was already perfect in the beginning of his existence in the womb. Instead, according to Schleiermacher, in the deeds and decisions of life, he was—in the language of Hebrews, 'perfected'—so that what is called 'sinlessness' is not a static condition but the end of a process of growing into union with God (Macquarrie 1990:208). His perfect God-consciousness which controlled all the aspects of his life makes him distinct from other human beings. Thus, for Schleiermacher, Jesus' consciousness of the immediacy of God's presence within him is what distinguishes Jesus from other human beings. It is this perfect awareness of the in-dwelling of the Supreme Being as His innermost being which characterizes the uniqueness of Jesus. The intensity and uniqueness of this awareness is the essential characteristic that separates Jesus from others who believe in and are dependent upon God (Gillis 1998:79). Through his total obedience to the will of God, Jesus is the instrument whereby salvation is won. Schleiermacher therefore regards Jesus as a unique proto-image and model of total submission to faith in God which motivates Christians to discipleship. In this light, he claims that Jesus is the *Urbild* and *Vorbild* of the love of God for humanity. If Jesus has the capability to acquire a perfect God-consciousness, ordinary human beings are also capable of approaching such level of God consciousness. Christians may imitate Jesus by following his example of loving God and other human beings. By emulating the life and works of Jesus, believers may also be touched by God and may attain a feeling of absolute dependence of God.

The influence of individual-related Christology continues to stimulate many thinkers and ordinary believers until this day. Most of them maintain that this type of Christology, being a product of the Enlightenment, should not be discarded; some of its lessons can never be unlearned. Macquarrie (1990:26) illustrates well this sentiment saying that "we cannot go back to the mythology of a former age, or to its supernaturalism, or to the spiritual authoritarianism of an infallible church or an infallible Bible." Furthermore, other authors render a positive estimation on this type of Christology saying that it is "quite compatible with the new theological paradigm of pluralism. It preserves the centrality of Christ as the salvific messenger of God to the community who followed Jesus and would eventually be called Christians, but does not make the person of Jesus the unique saviour of all humanity" (Gillis 1998:80). But first, let us see how far this type of Christology has actually filtered through the religious consciousness of our respondents.

3.1.2.2. *Community-related Jesus*

Our next representative of the hermeneutic-oriented Jesus images is the community-related Christology. We identify the theological orientation of Edward Schillebeeckx to exemplify this type of Christology. Here again, we want to clarify that our focus is on the typology of Christological categories and not on authors. This means that we do not assume nor intend to restrict the whole christological treatises of Schillebeeckx to this type only. The community-related type of Christological model highlights the vital role of the community in interpreting the life and works of Jesus. In the foreword of his book *Jesus*, Schillebeeckx (1979) expressed his main concern in his Christological treatise saying that he desires to bridge the gap between academic theology and the concrete needs of the ordinary Christian. Christology, according to him, should not remain only as a doctrine but as a living force in people's lives, to bring transformation and impact into the life of each person and the community. While the individual-related Christology accentuate on the individual's consciousness as the basis of their faith in Jesus, this community-related Christology focuses especially on the stories found in the texts of the faith-communities in the first centuries which recounted their experiences of Jesus. The community-related Christology endeavours to re-interpret the stories of the first century faith-communities in the light of the questions raised in contemporary communities. This model underscores the on-going re-appropriation of our Christological claims for the modern-day society.

Schillebeeckx maintains that it is possible to identify the historical Jesus by using available biblical exegetical methods. By using results of biblical exegesis, he tries to demonstrate that the vocation and divine character of Jesus find their echo in the interpretative-experience of his disciples which they inferred from the proclamation of the kingdom by Jesus in words and deeds. Every event that transpired in the life of Jesus reveals the power of God's salvation. His words and actions, his meeting with other people who experienced love, solidarity, forgiveness, and compassion from God in and through him, disclose the salvific power of God. In the person of Jesus, God revealed himself; in him God acquired a human face, spoke a human voice and enacted his gracious benevolence. According to Schillebeeckx, the human Jesus is the revelation of God's goodwill towards humankind and the ongoing revelation of divine benevolence. For Schillebeeckx, events like miracles, exorcisms, and the resurrection should be approached with the question: what meaning or impact did these events have to the community, rather than the modernist's question: did they really happen? He underscores the need to be keen on the interpretative moment within the community, and how this change or metanoia within the community brings about praxis of God's kingdom in the society.

The community-related Christological model argues that there is a basic continuity between the accounts of the earliest followers of Jesus and the accounts of Jesus himself. By employing the exegetical method of historical-criticism, this community-related Christology assumes that one can get some knowledge of the historical Jesus as they were recorded in the gospels of the New Testament. However, the quest for the historical Jesus is not the ultimate aim of Schillebeeckx' (1979:33) Christology, but it is a starting point for hermeneutical reflections in order to address the questions of the people in the modern society. As Schillebeeckx (1979:44–45) says: "The starting point for any Christology or Christian understanding of Jesus is not simply the Jesus of Nazareth nor Church kerygma nor creed. Rather it is the movement which Jesus Himself started in the first century. This would imply that Jesus has to be understood from the different layers of human relationships." Schillebeeckx was primarily concerned that the Christian belief in Jesus of Nazareth as Christ can be intelligible for modern men and for the 'enlightened' culture. While the tendency of modern men is to conceive of God as an abstract being, this community-related Christology of Schillebeeckx presents a God, whom the historical Jesus have expressed by his words and deeds, as a caring and loving God for people. Jesus can still serve as a model to the life of highly critical men and women of modern society by finding inspiration from the words and deeds of Jesus through the stories that can be accessed through modern scientific methods. For an enlightened culture, Jesus can still be meaningfully proclaimed as the 'parable of God' and 'paradigm of humanity'. Schillebeeckx (1979:27) remarks thus: "a lot of humanists, especially among the young people, find guidance and inspiration in Jesus of Nazareth. This is evident in the Jesus movement for instance—whose adherents are outside of any church and yet find their well being, inspiration and orientation in Jesus".

One of the key concepts introduced by Schillebeeckx in most of his Christological works is the notion of experience as the medium of God's revelation. He concentrated on the personal experience of Jesus and the experience of His presence by the disciples and the apostolic communities. According to him, the Christologizing process started when the disciples and the early Christian communities experienced being saved by what Jesus said and did. According to Schillebeeckx (1981:71), the first Christians pursued the question who this person was, because through him they had begun to experience the saving power of God. As a consequence of the salvific experience of the disciples, they began to ask: Who is he and what is his relationship to God?

Schillebeeckx's Christological orientation has often been characterized as narrative Christology because it leads readers to have a narrative faith (*vertellend geloven*) that can find expression in telling stories and in life-giving, effective, 'telling' deeds (cf. Haight 1999:18). Schillebeeckx believes that one of the main tasks of theology is to gather together "elements which may lead to a new, authentic disclosure experience or source experience" (1979:571). He says that such an experience evokes models. The model that Schillebeeckx's Jesus evokes is one of kingdom/orthopraxis in view of coming kingdom or companionship with Jesus and his brothers and sisters in the Christian community while awaiting and anticipating by their practices this gracious kingdom. A community-related model therefore maintains the need for praxis in the light of the gospel message in and for the community. It is in this concrete condition of the community where the hermeneutical cycle, i.e. the dialogical interplay between tradition and context, or the text and the contemporary human situation, takes place. Schillebeeckx argues that the interpretative praxis in the life of Jesus and his disciples can also be re-appropriated for contemporary situation. Schillebeeckx insists on the correlation between human experience and the experience of Christ. He tries to address the problem of how to present an event within history as a definitive act of God, let alone a unique human act, while denying the notion of special divine supernatural intervention. He prefers to understand divine action as a kind of depth dimension to natural and human action, which comes to the conscious expression as 'revelation' in the experience of faith (Cowdell 1996:181). Schillebeeckx (1979:605) argues that the only way to affirm the credibility of Christianity is, on the one hand, by the historical study of Jesus' life and death, and on the other hand, by showing how the Christian claim to universality is substantiated in the true humanness of 'being human', as that confronts us in Jesus of Nazareth.

Schillebeeckx tries to examine Jesus in terms of Jesus' own experience of God. He believed that the records we have, although they fall short of 'a historically exact record of events', nevertheless gives a full length picture of him. While we may not have a direct access to the personal self understanding of Jesus, his message and his way of life as they were recorded in the earliest Christian writings may lead us to understand his self-understanding. One of the most reliable facts about the life of Jesus, Schillebeeckx (1979:266) declares, "is that he broached the subject of God in and through his message of the coming rule of God; and that what this implied was made plain and foremost through his authentic parables and the issues they raised, namely: *metanoia* and the praxis of God's kingdom". In this case, Schillebeeckx affirms that there is "an extraordinarily pronounced consciousness of a prophetic role' on the part of Jesus—a conclusion evidenced by the *abba* relationship" (Cowdell 1996:175). According to Schillebeeckx, Jesus' *Abba* experience generated both his self-understanding and his understanding of the Kingdom of God which he preached in word and deed. The Kingdom of God which Jesus preached is characterized by gracious benevolence and compassion from the Father whom Jesus calls *Abba*. This intimate closeness with God and humanity in Jesus and this definitive encounter has evoked a uniquely powerful response from those who interpret Jesus. Many believed that the long awaited promise to Israel has now been fulfilled in the person of Jesus. They experienced salvation in Him through his words and deeds. He was the prophet of eschatological salvation. According to Schillebeeckx, Jesus being an 'eschatological prophet' is the first of the designations which are attached to him. It is also the understanding Jesus began to develop regarding his own mission which became evident through His life and work. This interpretative model corresponds fittingly with the self-understanding of Jesus in relation to his vocation and mission, through which he is revealed as the Christ. Schillebeeckx (1979:479) maintains that the eschatological prophet is the matrix of all other titles and creedal strands which can be verified in all four gospels. It is also the strand that held together all four creedal models (*maranatha, theios aner*, wisdom, and easter Christologies) and which antedates the New Testament.

The community-related Christological model maintains that the revelation of Jesus Christ comes not in pure uninterpreted events but rather includes the response of faith of the believers to those events. "Revelation then issues in the response of faith [...] The eschatological presence of God in Jesus and man's ultimate comprehension of reality, are correlative" (Schillebeeckx 1979:635). In explaining this community-related Christology, Schillebeeckx moves away from the distinction between Jesus of history and the Christ of faith. For him, all early Christian traditions are both 'kerygmatic' and recollection of Jesus of Nazareth. He maintains that the Christ of faith is a largely justifiable interpretation of the Jesus of history, while at the same time holds that Jesus of Nazareth is the norm and criterion of any true interpretation. He tries to reconstruct the historical Jesus with the aim of showing that in this person of Jesus, one can speak of the universal significance of the final saving activity of God in history.

It can be argued that the influence of this community-related model among the Dutch Catholic believers could be quite robust since it relates more closely to their everyday life. This type of Christological model may be more appealing to them due to its experiential, narrative, and communitarian character. Furthermore, it can also be said that this 'experiment' in Christology brought forward by Schillebeeckx may have a resounding impact among Dutch faithful since they cater to the 'intellectual culture' which characterize Christianity in western societies, including the Netherlands. It may also be argued that this type of Christology may be highly persuasive among many Dutch believers due to its heavy use of results of scientific and historical biblical methods which could be intelligible to men and women of modern societies. Let us see how far our empirical results can substantiate these premises.

3.1.2.3. *Society-related Jesus*
The society-related model highlights the image of Jesus as the liberator. This model has been compellingly advanced by the church in Latin America. Reflecting on the situation of poverty, oppression, violence and dehumanization, the Latin American church contends that the most suitable description of Jesus is that of a liberator, the one who liberates people from inhuman conditions and alienating structures. Jesus' liberating message also gives direction to the struggle of peoples and inspires them to be active agents in transforming their society. We would like to discuss the three key features of this society-related model, namely: the hermeneutical cycle, the historical Jesus, and the praxis orientation. While these features characterize most of the hermeneutic-oriented Jesus images, they have been uniquely interpreted for societal liberation in this society-related Jesus model.

The conception of Jesus as liberator is a product of an hermeneutical cycle (Sobrino 1978:17–40; Boff 1978). According to this model, the Christian understanding of Jesus cannot be done in a vacuum. One must pay attention to the concrete situation (*locus*) and the specific historical setting in which the Judeo-Christian tradition is proclaimed. In Latin America, the *locus* of Christian reflection about Jesus is the context of economic, political, cultural, and religious dependency, or in other words, the 'world of the poor'. It is within this setting that Christians begin to reflect about Jesus Christ. As Sobrino (1993:28) explains: "[while it is true that] the setting does not invent the content, but away from this setting, it will be difficult to find [Christ] and to read adequately the texts about him." A critical understanding of social realities necessitates a radical critique of the ideology of power and the systemic injustice created by these unjust societal structures. The comprehension of these realities leads to an ideological suspicion. These social realities are not to be construed in a naïve sense as given, as socially politically innocent and value-free. Hence, a hermeneutics of suspicion is brought to bear upon this 'experience' so as to make evident the politics of bias inherent in any given social situation, including the reality of the church's institutional life, which is always situated in historical time and political place. The application of ideological suspicion to the whole ideological superstructure in society is also applied to the Christian tradition. In the experience of oppression and suffering of the people, what does our faith in Jesus have to say? What interest(s) are being served by a particular teaching of the Christian faith? Then, a process of re-interpretation or re-construction of the tradition in the light of the present experience takes place. In this kind of condition, the key questions believers would ask are: how to proclaim God as Father in an inhuman world?, and how do we tell the 'non-persons' that they are the sons and daughters of God? If Jesus Christ is the saviour of humanity, what does this mean in the current situation? Who is Jesus Christ and what is the meaning of salvation that he proclaimed? Salvation, for instance, should be re-interpreted not only as a spiritual salvation but also as social and political salvation. It involves being saved from the menacing poverty and oppression, but it also consists of the struggle for social and political justice. God is proclaimed to have taken the side of the exploited peoples of the world in the manner that He delivered Israel out of Egypt in the Exodus account. It also relates to the New Testament which portrays Jesus as someone who is called "to bring good news to the poor and to proclaim release to the captives (Lk. 4:18). The hermeneutical process, according to this model, is a spiraling movement which involves a new interpretation of the Christian tradition that transforms reality, and the new reality in turn produces another change in the interpretation of the Judeo-Christian tradition, and so on in spiraling succession.

Another important feature of the society-related model is its special challenging interpretation of the historical Jesus. This model insists on beginning from a Christology from below, that is, beginning from the concrete historical ministry of Jesus, instead of starting from a

Christology 'from above' which sets off from a doctrine of Trinity and the incarnation of the eternal logos. Sobrino (1978:12-13) mentions two reasons for beginning from the historical Jesus: (a) there is similarity between the Latin American situation and the time of Jesus; not only is there resemblance between the two situation of poverty and exploitation but the themes also coincide; (b) the early Christian churches were not founded on imagined Christology but on the witness of people who claimed they had seen the Risen. The interest of this society-related model in going back to the historical Jesus is prompted not primarily by a theoretical, historical-exegetical interest but by a practical one—that is, a theological reflection from within the socio-historical context of Latin America. As Bussmann (1985:43) writes: "The passion for liberation which is surging like a wave across the whole of Latin America has become the hermeneutical key for the return to Jesus." The aim is to underscore the Christological elements that serve to constitute a paradigm of liberation. "From this central fact it revalues the whole life, action and destiny of Jesus in such a way that Christ the liberator—without any implication of ignoring the totality of Christ—is, first and foremost, Jesus of Nazareth, the so called-historical Jesus" (Sobrino 1993:12).

Our final characterization of the society-related model is the special interpretation of its praxis-orientation. This praxis orientation of the society-related model of Jesus asserts that in order to know God, one has to participate in the praxis of liberation of the poor in history. Liberating praxis implies transforming any political, economic, and cultural structure of society that oppress and alienate people. Liberation is an integral process incorporating all these aspects (Gutierrez 1974:24; cf. Boff 1980:240). According to Bussmann (1985:44-45), while the classical belief in Jesus claims that one can gain access to the resurrected Lord through some sort of direct intentional act, for instance by a profession of faith, a doxology, a prayer, etcetera, this society-related type of Jesus argues that one can gain access to him only through a specific kind of praxis which the gospels describe as the following of Jesus, or discipleship. Following the path of Jesus implies following the path of liberative action. Moreover, this society-related model also insists that the liberational praxis involves taking sides. It requires believers to take a preferential option for the poor. This preferential option for the poor however, should not be construed as a biased view or a reduction of the purportedly universal scope of God's love. As Gutierrez (1974:24) explains, "preference implies the universality of God's love, which excludes no one. It is only within the framework of this universality that we can understand the preference, that is, what comes first." Boff (1980:240) explains: "Jesus who is human salvation is also human liberator. Jesus as liberator is brought forth by his preferential option for the poor. His mission makes him the liberator of the poor and inspires them in their struggle against all forms of alienation." Following Jesus as the liberator implies that believers need to take a radical conversion in their mode of belief and bear witness in their commitment to liberate the poor which includes sacrificing their lives.

Although this society-related model originates from a continent distant away from the Netherlands, and that the contextual condition between these two places differ to a large extent, it is interesting to see how the society-related model 'flows' beyond its border and find influences among our western Dutch believers. One can contend that the reason for the persuasive influence of this society-related model among the Dutch believers has been generated by its resonance or congruence to the civil or social values like freedom and democracy which are dearly treasured by many Dutch people.

3.1.2.4. *Spirit-motivated Jesus*
In the current discussion on the uniqueness and universality of Jesus in relation to other religions and the debates surrounding cultural pluralism and diversity, emancipation and social praxis, some authors argue that the Spirit-motivated Christology is a viable concept to explain the relationship between the Christian claims on the unique role of Jesus in salvation history on the one hand and the Christian discourse on the universal scope of salvation on the other. Walter Kasper (1976:267–268), for instance, states that "a Christology in a pneumatological perspective is [...] what best enables us to combine the uniqueness and the universality of Jesus Christ. It can show how the Spirit who is operative in Christ in his fullness is at work in varying degrees everywhere in the history of humankind, and also how Jesus Christ is the goal and head of all humanity." He adds, in order to be complete, a pneumatic Christology must stress the active presence of the Spirit throughout the human story of the man Jesus on the one hand, and the sending of the Spirit to the world by the risen Christ, on the other. In order to reflect on the uniqueness and universality of Jesus and His relevance for the modern world, contemporary proponents of Spirit-motivated Christology underscore the rootedness

of this type of Christology in the historical Jesus and its experiential character.

The Spirit-motivated Christology insists that reflections about Jesus must be rooted on the historical Jesus of Nazareth whose integrity has been steadfastly maintained even in later interpretations. This Christological model explains that God as Spirit is present in Jesus all throughout his life. Jesus is anointed with God as Spirit. His whole life has been animated by the Spirit of God which determines his inner identity. His uniqueness can be construed in terms of his vocation, mission and appointment by God as the firstborn of many. Jesus was empowered by God's Spirit all throughout his life, death, and resurrection. Because Jesus was empowered by God as Spirit, his existence is fulfilled and not replaced. According to Haight, this is ontological presence, because where God acts, God is. The Chalcedonian formula of one person and two natures, if not conceived in a static and abstract way, can also be explained by this Spirit-motivated Christology. This Christological model claims that Jesus is one person with an integral human nature in whom not less than God, and thus a divine nature is at work (Haight 1999:461).

The Spirit-motivated christological model contends that its understanding of Jesus is an experience-oriented type of Christology. Schoonenberg (1991:47–59) explains that the spirit Christology stresses that Jesus is *of* God while the *Logos* Christology emphasizes that Jesus *is* God. According to him, the Spirit Christology shuns ontological abstraction which characterizes traditional Christological dogmas based on *Logos* Christology, and averts fixation of symbols and symbolic titles into ontological entities that are insignificant and incomprehensible to contemporary peoples and situations. Haight (1999:447ff) says that in order to address contemporary questions related to Christology, one can only make a credible discourse about Jesus by appealing not only to tradition but more importantly to human experience.[5] Haight makes use of the analogy between the symbol of God as Spirit and

---

[5] Haight (1999:446ff) points to a number of authors who deals with the experiential character of Spirit Christology. He shows for instance how Schleiermacher uses the language of the Spirit to explain how the 'experience of absolute dependence' may correspond to the perfect indwelling of the Supreme Being in Jesus' unique being and His inmost self; Matthew speaks of the 'resident spirit' who dwells in Jesus; Tillich points to Jesus' *possession by the divine Spirit* (God was in him); Moltmann (1997; 2000) indicates that Jesus was filled with God as Spirit from the very beginning of his existence; Dunn (1992; 1998) demonstrates that the experience of God as Spirit is the

the language of grace in order to explain the experiential relevance of Spirit-motivated Christology. He explains that there are some basic human experiences like for instance, the fundamental trust in life, the resistance to death, or any other human experiences which demonstrate man's fundamental valuing of the inner ground of existence, which demonstrate how the human spirit is able to open up to a possible experience of an encounter with God as Spirit. Also within the Christian tradition, one is able to point out varieties of experiences wherein God is experienced within the self or within the world which reveals a conception of grace or God's spiritual presence. Haight (1999:452) asserts: "One finds theological resources for a Spirit Christology at every juncture of the Christian tradition: in its prehistory and its theology of the saving influence of the risen Jesus, and in the tradition of the theology of the Spirit that has been carried by the theology of grace right up to the present." Furthermore, he notes that there are several instances in Christian life which demonstrate the effects of grace of the movement of God as Spirit in human lives. One important effect of grace is the empowerment by the Spirit, which according to Haight (1999:454), is the best metaphor to express Spirit Christology. The Spirit empowers Christian life on the ground of the continuity between Jesus and his followers. Because there is continuity with Jesus and his disciples, Christians today can be inspired and empowered to imitate him as well. The presence of God in the person dynamically empowers human freedom. It does not overpower but activate and enhanced human freedom.

Authors favouring a Spirit-motivated Christology argue that a pneumatocentric Christology yields a more positive rendering of other religions than the *Logos* Christology. They propose that it is a possible substitute for the logocentric model. They claim that a pneumatocentric Christology can explain the universal active presence both of the Word of God and the Spirit of God in the world and history. The Spirit of God has been universally present throughout human history and remains active outside Christianity. In contrast to the economy of the Christ-event as presented by a logocentric model, which is unavoidably limited by the particularity of history, the Spirit is not bounded by time and space and may therefore 'blow where it wills' (Jn. 3:8).

---

source of Jesus' conviction and self-understanding, his authority and of his powerful actions; Hick speaks of Jesus as 'inspired man'.

The Holy Spirit is God's 'point of entry' into the life of people and of peoples. The immanent presence of the Holy Spirit is responsible for the reality of God's saving grace both inside and outside the Church. Haight explains that Spirit-motivated Christology accounts for the normativity of Jesus for all human beings. Jesus, who is empowered by God's Spirit, offers universal salvation. Moreover, Spirit Christology affirms that the salvific activity of God's Spirit has been at work in the world already from the beginning because the Spirit is not only the Spirit of Jesus but above all the Spirit of God. The Spirit-motivated Jesus model acknowledges that the Spirit is operative outside the Christian sphere and is open to other mediations of God. "The Spirit is spread abroad, and it is not necessary to think that God as spirit can be incarnated only once in history" (Haight 1999:456). It is the interest of this study to investigate to what extent this Spirit-motivated model has influenced the religious consciousness of the contemporary Dutch believers.

3.1.2.5. *Secular worldview oriented Jesus*
In the 60's, representatives of so-called secular theology responded to the Christological questions raised by the growing secularised temperament prevalent at that time (which extends to date) in most of the western world. The problem for these theologians was how to speak of God and Jesus in the midst of a secularized culture. They reacted against a 'Christology from above' which according to them is irrelevant and archaic. Van Buren describes his conviction as he deals with his theological problematic: 'being a Christian' does not deny one's involvement in the secular world and its way of thinking (Van Buren 1963:18). Given this context, Van Buren develops his concept of God and the relation between God and Jesus on the basis of the text in John 10:39 which reads: "the Father is in me and I am in the Father". He sets off to interpret this text in terms of the covenantal theology which is embodied in both the Old and New Testaments, particularly in the historical Jesus whom he stressed was a Jew. He emphasized the 'call-response' relationship between Yahweh and Israel which characterized this covenantal theology. Van Buren explains that 'Being in the Father' and 'being the Son of the Father' mean being commissioned by God and his covenant and being responsive to both commission and covenant. He juxtaposes the call-response relationship between Israel and Yahweh with that of the call-response rapport between Jesus and his Father. YHWH calls Israel to enter into a relationship of love and

solidarity, and through this relationship be a light to other nations. The Jews responded to this call in love and solidarity, and by living for the sake of others. Jesus manifested his response to this covenantal call of the Father in perfect love for others. It was a response of complete freedom in loving and caring service for his neighbours, even to the cost of his life by dying on the cross. Through his perfect love, Jesus becomes the ultimate example of human love. He is the pre-eminent example of caring for our neighbour. His death was a consequence of this freedom and complete love and solidarity which threatens people who are themselves unfree. It was a death interpreted as death 'for us', death 'for our sins' (Van Buren 1963:150–151). It was a response in complete freedom by Jesus and a freedom that unshackle the fears and 'chains' of other people as well. And through this response, God manifests himself: "this is how Jesus is the full and adequate revelation of God" (Van Buren 1963:146). This revelation of God in Jesus was a revelation of God's action in history. It is God's decisive act of love for this world. Moreover, as Van Buren (1963:148) states, this God who is present in the suffering and death of Jesus implies that God is also weak and shares in the contingent and the sordid dimension of humanity.

Van Buren moves away from the exultative and transcendental characterization of God as in the classical and scholastic terms. He disparages the use of metaphysical and mythological categories in explaining who Jesus is in the secular context. He favours an ethical approach to Christology rather than the speculative and purely sacrosanct image of Jesus. He tries to argue that God's power is the power of impotence, of weakness, of kenosis, which relinquishes everything, sacrifices itself totally in order to exist wholly for others—as Bonhoeffer puts it movingly; as if God did not exist: *"etsi Deus non daretur"* (Van Buren 1968:70–71). He contends: "When Easter is in the center of the picture, however, we can say that the meaning of the gospel is to be found in the areas of the historical and the ethical, not in the metaphysical or the religious" (Van Buren 1966:197). The historical Jesus is a man remarkable in his freedom, in his love, and in the sincerity and creativity of his life. This kind of life was 'contagious' and helped transform Jesus' erstwhile non-believing disciples (Van Buren 1963:103;155; Thompson 1985:57). Van Buren expounds this idea by arguing that Christians are meant for others: for their neighbour, distant friends, the anonymous poor, the indigent stranger. For as Christians they live, so to speak, *without God* (construed as omnipotent, omniscient, omnipresent God, as Bonhoeffer would describe it), and also without the (*deus ex machina*) God of religion, 'religion' taken in its typical Protestant sense. Van Buren highlights the theme of human love, solidarity with other human beings in a sturdily horizontal perspective. This secular-worldview oriented Jesus underscores human relations of people on a 'horizontal' perspective. If asked whether his idea is some sort of humanism, Van Buren would say: "It does, but a gospel-based humanism, inspired by the example of him who saw it as reflecting the love and solidarity of God" (Van Buren 1968:81).

3.1.3. *Humanistic Jesus*

In the course of the development of Christology after the Enlightenment, some models which are considered 'non-religious' in character, have also emerged. Jesus is portrayed on a purely humanistic terms devoid of any reference to his transcendent or divine nature. Arguably, these non-religious models can be seen as the ultimate outcome of the Enlightenment. Hence, it is often doubted whether this notion can be regarded as 'Christology', or 'Christian', if compared to other approaches spelled out earlier. To the least, one can ascribe to it a character of a humanist jesuology. We deemed it necessary to include this model in so far as it brings in a certain reading of Jesus in the context of secularization. Moreover, it is important to look at this model and see how far it played a role in shaping the attitudes of our respondents towards Jesus.

This 'humanistic' interpretation of Jesus accuses traditional and also (to a certain extent) hermeneutic-oriented Christologies to have a penchant of clothing this man Jesus with divinity. According to this model, Jesus has to be radically de-divinized and de-supernaturalized. Jesus is portrayed as a good man and nothing more. He is also compared to Buddha, to Confucius, to Mohammed, and to other religious figures who are regarded as great figures of history. Like most of these religious personalities, a historical movement has been attributed to him. In general, most humanists see Jesus as a good moral teacher whose followers exaggerated his claims and messages until things got way out of hand and people began to fabricate God-myths about him and stories of miracles. Although, most humanist scholars doubt the historical account of Jesus based on the scriptures and extra-testamental documents, they agree that Jesus did exist as a historical figure who lived in Palestine in the first century A.D. He was a wandering teacher or preacher who challenged many of the traditions of the Jewish hierarchy and who acquired a following. His moral teachings were generally humanistic and were concerned with human relations and with the daily practice of social virtues. His death in Jerusalem was probably ordered by the high priests of the Temple. It is likely that Jesus was a charismatic teacher, but not 'god on earth'. He preached love, kindness, and forgiveness. Although humanists do not attribute divinity to Jesus or other religious leaders, they accept that one can discover inspiration in their lives and teachings. They believe that the ways of life taught by Jesus, Mohammed, and Buddha have been obscured by creeds and rituals.

Reimarus (d. 1768) is frequently recognized for being the first to engage in this new critical thinking through his work, *Fragments*. In this book, he interprets religion as a pursuit of high moral ideals which is in line with the 'ideals' of the Enlightenment. He presents Jesus as a 'moral enlightener' or a guru of morality. He explains that the nature and aim of the teachings of Jesus is "nothing other than moral teachings and duties intended to improve man inwardly and with all his heart" (Reimarus 1970:69–70). This idea of Reimarus was later picked up by some other Enlightenment thinkers who maintained that we could know very little of the actual historical life of Jesus because of the lack of reliable records. In *The Life of Jesus Critically Examined*, Strauss (1835/1860) endeavors to strip off any supernatural elements from the gospel by indulging it like any other historical material. He tries to apply the 'myth theory' to the life of Jesus. According to him, the books of the gospel have no historical value and nothing in it can be inferred about the historical Jesus. They are but poetic casing for religious thoughts in order to 'prove' the messiahship of Jesus. Strauss however underscored that Jesus is the first man to realize in himself the idea of humanity. Other 19th century German thinkers like Schenkel and Bauer, among others, argued that Jesus was just a Jewish nice guy whose perfect moral standards and teachings are to be followed. Most of them agree that only a very critical research of the Gospels, after banning anything supernatural, would lead to an acceptable result. This type of attitude was also present among the 19th century Dutch Radicalist thinkers like Hoekstra, Loman, Bolland, van Eysinga, etcetera. Hoekstra, for instance, demonstrated that Mark's gospel does not tell anything of the biography of Jesus. The synoptics are simply symbolic poetry and not a historical account of Jesus. Likewise, Pierson (1879) argues that the Sermon on the Mount is a collection of aphorisms of Jewish wisdom constructed after 70 A.D. and was simply put into the mouth of Jesus. Loman (1882) contends that all New Testament texts are 2nd century constructs. According to him, these texts are contradictory and unreliable, and thus utterly worthless for historical statements about certain early first century persons. There may have been some 'Jesus', but its role is left completely in the dark and can't be reconstructed by scripture or any other extant ancient testimony. The Jesus of scripture is an ideal person, symbolizing the essence of the people of Israel that sacrificed itself in the wars against the Romans, and was revived spiritually in the shape of the Christian community.

Erich Fromm tries to explicate a humanistic 'christology' using the ideas of Freud and Marx in *The Dogma of Christ* (1963). He argues that the hopelessness of realizing the dreams of the early Christians for liberation from Roman oppressors led them "to formulate the same wishes in fantasy" (Fromm 1963:49). Fromm seeks to identify the nature of this fantasy using the Freudian notion of the 'oedipal complex'. According to him, our belief in God comes from our need to project our father's protection and care into a cosmic form: God becomes a father projection. However, this father projection also entails a hidden hostility towards the cosmic father. And it is from this hidden hostility that we derive our 'Christ fantasy'. Fromm explains that Christ is "a symbol of man's unconscious hostility to God the Father, for if a man could become God, the latter was deprived of his privileged fatherly position of being unique and unreachable" (Fromm 1963:54). But this 'Christ fantasy' transformed when Christianity ceased to be a religion of the oppressed and became a religion of the ruling class. Jesus, as it were, was not only thought to have become God, rather, he was always God (Fromm 1963:68). This development saw the perversion of the human element found in the basic postulates of the founder. The history and the evolution of Christendom saw first that the early followers tried to live like its founder, that is, according to his commandments of love, peace and solidarity. But now we know that that message was totally distorted by the Christian church to become a way to dominate and oppress the masses. Fromm however admits that the Jesus of history is different from the 'Christ of dogma', which for him is a distortion. According to Fromm, the teaching of Jesus, for instance, that 'the kingdom of God is within you', results in respect for the dignity of man and avoids the authoritarianism of the dehumanizing forms of religion. For Fromm, religion is any system of thought and action shared by a group which gives the individual a frame of orientation and an object of devotion. This description tried to broaden the concept of religion to include not only classic and theological systems like Judeo-Christianism, Islamism, Confucionism, etcetera, or primitive religions with blood and annihilation rites, but also biophilic philosophies like Zen Budhism, ancient Greek Humanism or European Renaissance, Sartre's existentialism and, also, political ideologies like authoritarian Fascism or Stalinism. He also considers pathological behaviors like masochism and sadism, the craving for success, money, and the like as religious.

Fromm distinguishes between an authoritarian religion and a humanistic type of religion. He describes the authoritarian type as a religion which presumes the reality of a higher power which takes control over a human being. This type of religion demands submission to a transcendent being or power. This attitude of submission often comes with a twofold feeling of personal misery and a feeling of being protected. According to Fromm, by surrendering to this transcending power, one loses one's independence and integrity. That is why, in turn, one feels that it is important to resort to the transcending being. Humanistic religion, on the other hand, has no dimension of a transcendent divine being. It is centered on man and his own strength. It presupposes the autonomy of each human being. Man must develop his own capacity, his own power of reason in order to understand himself. He is responsible to find his position in the universe. He is accountable for his relationship towards his fellow men. In contrast to the authoritarian religion, the goal of man in humanistic religion is to achieve the greatest strength, not the greatest powerlessness; virtue is self-realization, not obedience. Faith is not an assent to a set of propositions but as certitude of conviction anchored on one's own experience of thought and feeling. In this sense, the idea of being overwhelmed, or absolute dependence, or obedience are foreign to this type of religious experience. Humanistic religious experience can accept the concept of God or gods, but only in the sense that ideas of God or gods are no more than another way of expressing a higher part of human being. This distinction between authoritarian and humanistic religious experience, according to Fromm, is found both in theistic and non-theistic religions. This humanistic type of religious attitude according to Fromm is what we assumed to be the frame of reference for the instrument with the help of which we assessed this humanistic jesuology.

Scheme 3.1. Images of Jesus from a Theoretical Perspective

Tradition-bound Jesus
  1. Classical
  2. Neo-classical

Hermeneutic-oriented Jesus
  3. Individual-related
  4. Community-related
  5. Society-related
  6. Spirit-motivated
  7. Secular-worldview oriented

Humanistic Jesus
  8. Humanistic

It is interesting to see how far the contemporary Dutch believers are influenced by this humanistic model in relation to their attitude towards Jesus. Does the humanistic model bring a better resonance of the belief of peoples in a vastly secular situation? Is it possible at all for a believer to claim for a totally human Jesus and still recognize oneself as a 'believer'?

Thus far, we have made an overview of the various attitudes towards Jesus represented by the various Christological and/or jesuological approaches which we assume to be present among our group of Dutch Catholics. We have presented eight Jesus images which we classified as classical, neo-classical, individual-related, community-related, society-related, Spirit-motivated Jesus, secular-worldview related Jesus, and the humanistic Jesus models. The scheme above (Scheme 3.1.) illustrates a summary of the images of Jesus from a theoretical point of view.

3.2. *Images of Jesus from an empirical perspective*

In the previous section, we gather a total of eight conceptual models of the images of Jesus to constitute the theoretical domain of our investigation. These conceptual models have been operationalized based on the instrument constructed by Van der Ven & Biemans (1994: 89–93) who worked on the 28-item list for the seven conceptual models (i.e. classical, dialectical, liberal, jesuological, liberational, secular, and humanistic). In this work, we add the Spirit-motivated Christology and constructed four items in order to operationalize it. And after a try-out among church members, we inserted them into the questionnaire. The respondents were presented with a list of 32 items in total, representing the eight conceptual models (see: Appendix 1, Table 3, Part 2).

The scores on the 32–item list were subjected to factor analysis. We first subjected the scores on Jesus images to free factor solution analysis (mineigen = 1). However, the factors extracted from this free factor solution analysis yielded non-interpretable factors, being theoretically meaningless. Then a forced factor solution analysis was conducted which resulted into six well interpretable factors, with all the factors showing a number of adequate loadings, whereby the community-related items have been erased for statistical reasons, and whereby the individual-related and secular-worldview oriented Jesus images grouped together into one factor which are labeled as interpersonal Jesus image. The six factor solution is explaining 67% of the variance (see: Appendix 3, Table 1). This factor analysis resulted into the following models: classical, neo-classical, interpersonal-oriented, society-related, Spirit-motivated, and humanistic Jesus images. The scales were subjected to a reliability of scales test (see: Table 3.1. below). Based on the results of our empirical investigation and analysis, there is an obvious disparity between the theoretical and the empirical domains. The table below (Table 3.1) gives us a summary of the result of our empirical investigation on the images of Jesus.

Table 3.1. Images of Jesus from an Empirical Perspective

Empirical Model	Mean	Standard Deviation	Pearson Correlation (r)	Reliability of Scales (Cronbach's Alpha)	Valid Cases
I. Classical (Theoretical model 1)	3.6	1.03		.89	401
II. Neo-Classical (Theoretical model 2)	2.7	1.16	.59		409
III. Interpersonal-oriented (Theoretical model 3 & 7)	4.1	.71		.93	397
IV. Society-related (Theoretical model 5)	3.6	.90		.82	410
V. Spirit-motivated (Theoretical model 6)	3.7	.93		.86	406
VI. Humanistic (Theoretical model 8)	2.4	.98		.85	403

If we examine the mean scores of each Christological model, we can gather the following images that are positively accepted by our respondents: interpersonal-oriented Jesus (mean: 4.1), Spirit-motivated (mean: 3.7), classical (mean: 3.6), and the society-related (mean: 3.6) models. The neo-classical image is met with negative ambivalent feelings (mean: 2.7) and the humanistic (mean: 2.4) image is rejected by our respondents. What is also notable from this result is that the 'interpersonal-oriented' Jesus receives the highest score and is even better accepted by our respondents than the classical model which is normally presumed to be highly valued by the ordinary catholic believers. While the classical model is accepted, the neo-classical model is rejected. The three representatives of hermeneutic-oriented christologies, i.e. interpersonal-oriented, society-related, and Spirit-motivated Jesus, are accepted by this group of Catholic believers.

3.3. *Social location of the attitudes towards Jesus*

Earlier, in the previous chapter, we identified certain demographic, social, and religious characteristics to refer to the social locations which we deemed to be relevant for our investigation of the religious attitudes of our respondents. We shall be investigating these same characteristics (i.e. age, gender, education, country of origin, localistic authoritarianism, subjectively-perceived threat, conformism, anomie, church involvement, and religious salience) in relation to their attitudes towards Jesus. We employ variance analysis, Scheffé test, and correlation coefficient (r) to look for significant associations between these categories vis-à-vis the different images of Jesus The table below (Table 3.2) illustrates the result of the analysis.

Some interesting results of the analysis can be indicated here as shown on Table 3.2. If we sum up the columns representing the various images of Jesus in relation to the different characteristics, there are three images which generate the highest number of significant statistical associations in relation to the different characteristics, namely: classical, neo-classical, and Spirit-motivated images. A summary of the rows may likewise be worth noting. The most important demographic characteristics that yield significant associations are age and education (both are associated to five out of six models). Age is associated to all Jesus images except the humanistic image. Members of the third age

Table 3.2. Social location of the attitudes toward Jesus *(eta & rho)*

	Classical	Neo-classical	Interpersonal-oriented	Society-related	Spirit-motivated	Humanistic
DEMOGRAPHIC CHARACTERISTICS						
Age *(eta)*	.19**	.25*	.16*	.15*	.21**	—
Gender *(eta)*	—	.17**	—	—	—	—
Education *(eta)*	.33**	.18**	—	.20**	.24**	.17*
Country of origin *(eta)*	.14**	—	—	—	.11*	—
SOCIAL CHARACTERISTICS						
Localistic authoritarianism *(rho)*	.22**	.21**	.16**	.13**	.24**	.26**
Subjectively-perceived threat *(rho)*	.14**	—	—	—	—	.13**
Conformism *(rho)*	.26**	.28**	.23**	.23**	.26**	.15**
Anomie *(rho)*	.25**	.21**	.15**	.14**	.17**	.16**
RELIGIOUS CHARACTERISTICS						
Church involvement *(eta)*	.31**	.27*	.36**	.33**	.31**	.18**
Religious salience *(rho)*	.43**	.32**	.52**	.48**	.33**	−.30**

** $p < .01$; * $p < .05$ (two-tailed).

group (69 years and older) score higher on classical Jesus, society-related Jesus, and Spirit-motivated Jesus than those of the first age group (57 years and younger) (see: Appendix 3, Table 3). The youngest age group demonstrates clear rejection of the neo-classical Jesus compared to the older age-groups. Education is associated to classical, neo-classical, society-related, spirit-motivated, and humanistic Jesus images. Respondents with a lower education (primary education and/or lower secondary education) score higher on classical Jesus, neo-classical Jesus, society-related, and Spirit-motivated Jesus than those with a higher education (higher secondary education and/or tertiary education) (see: Appendix 3, Table 3). Country of origin is correlated to classical Jesus and Spirit-motivated Jesus. Dutch respondents tend to score lower on classical Jesus and Spirit-motivated Jesus than the non-Dutch respondents. Three of the social characteristics, that is, localistic authoritarianism, conformism, and anomie, are correlated to all of the attitudes toward Jesus. Subjectively-perceived threat, however, is significantly correlated only to classical and humanistic Jesus images (see: Appendix 3, Table 4). Both of the religious characteristics, i.e. church involvement and religious salience, manifest significant associations to all of the images on varying degrees. The active church members score higher on classical Jesus, neo-classical Jesus, interpersonal-oriented Jesus, society-related Jesus, and Spirit-motivated Jesus than the inactive ones. They score lower on the humanistic images. We also notice that the humanistic Jesus is negatively associated to religious salience (see: Appendix 3, Table 3).

Summary

This chapter discusses the second religious theme which is about the images of Jesus. The first part deals with the various conceptual models which are assumed to be theoretically present among the research population. We identify eight Christological models to constitute the images of Jesus from the theoretical perspective, namely: classical, neo-classical, individual-related, community-related, society-related, Spirit-motivated, secular-worldview related, and humanistic Jesus images. These concepts are tested using scales in the survey questionnaire. The results of which are subjected to some statistical data analysis. From the data reduction analysis, the eight conceptual models are reduced to only six. The community-related model is eliminated due to insufficient loadings, and the items of individual-related and the secular-worldview related Jesus images merge into one factor, which is now called as 'interpersonal-oriented' Jesus. There are six Christological attitudes that are manifested in the empirical part of our study, namely: classical, neo-classical, interpersonal-oriented, society-related, Spirit-motivated, and humanistic Jesus attitudes. While all hermeneutic-oriented Jesus images are accepted by our respondents, this group of believers rejects neo-classical and humanistic Jesus images. Results of the correlation analysis and the variance analysis disclose some striking relationships between the population characteristics of our population vis-à-vis their attitudes towards Jesus. Age, education, localistic authoritarianism, conformism, anomie, church involvement, and religious salience, are the most important population characteristics that have significant association and correlation with the attitudes toward Jesus. Age is associated to all Jesus images except the humanistic image. The oldest age group score higher on classical Jesus, society-related Jesus, and Spirit-motivated Jesus than those of the first age group (57 years and younger). The youngest age group plainly rejects the neo-classical Jesus than the older age-groups. Furthermore, we are able to find out that respondents with a lower education (primary education and/or lower secondary education) score higher on classical Jesus, neo-classical Jesus, society-related, and Spirit-motivated Jesus than those with a higher education (higher secondary education and/or tertiary education). Both of the religious characteristics, namely, church involvement and religious salience, manifest significant associations to all of the images on varying degrees. The active church members score higher on classical Jesus, neo-classical Jesus, interpersonal-oriented Jesus, society-related Jesus, and Spirit-motivated Jesus than the inactive ones. They score lower on the humanistic images. We also note that the humanistic Jesus is negatively correlated to religious salience.

CHAPTER FOUR

ATTITUDES TOWARD THE SPIRIT

In the contemporary context of cultural and religious pluralism, the turn to the Spirit has become an emerging trend in theology (cf. Karkkainen 2002; Hinze & Dabney 2001; Houston 1993). Already in the first half of the 20th century, Paul Tillich (1966) heralded the need for theology to give importance to religion of the concrete spirit. Rahner (1988) likewise observes that the shift of emphasis from Christology to pneumatology is a timely theological task in the light of the universal salvific will of God and in legitimate respect for all the major world religions outside of Christianity. He said that it is proper to speak of the Spirit as a "teaching of the inmost divinizing gift of grace for all human beings" (Rahner 1988:97). Ecumenical consultations among churches speak of the centrality of the Spirit in their endeavours to unify themselves, not only to repair the long-standing strained relationship between the Christian east and west over the insertion of the *filioque* clause in the Nicene Creed, but also to forge a better relationship and dialogue with the Pentecostals and other charismatic groups. Hodgson (1994) also reveals that the Spirit is more and more seen as an acceptable religious category when relating with other religions, even more acceptable than the 'Christ' symbol, partly because it is a religious representation that is readily available in one form or another in other religions. Moreover, Hinze and Dabney (2001:21) observe that a "host of new voices: from psychologists, biologists, physicists, and philosophers to pop commentators and gurus have themselves turned to the language of 'spirit' as that which speaks of something more and something other. For that reason, the language of Spirit has become available for discourse, Christian and otherwise, in a way that has not always been the case in the history of the West". They attribute the increasing attention to the Spirit in recent decades to at least three factors, namely: (1) the emergence of new forms of Christianity which emphasize pneumatology to a greater extent than has often been the case in the West (e.g. the emergence of Pentecostal and Charismatic movements), (2) the development of the theological conversation itself among the traditionally dominant churches in which pneumatology has been discovered anew as a theological resource, and (3) changes in contemporary culture which make the language of spirit more readily available for theological use in worship and witness. These points simply demonstrate the fact that in recent theological discourse, the so-called 'orphan doctrine in Christian theology', i.e. the doctrine of the Holy Spirit, has regained its significance for our contemporary times.

While it is true that the turn to the spirit in most contemporary Christian theologies are attempts to build a bridge with other religions and cultures, it has not often been the case that these beliefs necessarily yielded a positive attitude towards the 'them' in the "We-Them" divide. Given the contemporary religious consciousness of the Dutch believers, we can perhaps ask: does this turn to the spirit result into tolerance towards the 'outsider', or perhaps, to bigotry? Does one's attitude to the Spirit have any influence at all to one's regard to the so-called 'other', or does it simply yield an attitude of indifference and/or intolerance? The recognition of the 'spirit' in contemporary theology is indeed a question that we must probe empirically, particularly on how far these diverse pneumatological beliefs truly affect one's attitude towards minorities.

In this chapter, we shall investigate the attitudes of our population towards the Spirit. We intend to answer the question: What are the attitudes of church members toward the Spirit, and what is the social location of these attitudes? This chapter shall proceed by first examining the theoretical structure of the Spirit (section 4.1), then present the result of the analysis of the data based on the empirical investigation (4.2); and lastly, take a look at the social location of these attitudes among our respondents (4.3).

4.1. *Images of the Spirit from a theoretical perspective*

At the outset, it may seem that we are heading into a formidable task in our attempt to integrate conceptually the copious images of the Spirit. There are immense varieties of ways of representing and of addressing the Spirit. However, some sort of structure is inevitable in order to understand how our notions of the Spirit will have some influence in our lives. McIntyre suggests to employ designatory titles that can operate both as shorthand and later as an identifying indicator which could help one to see how the images are composed and related to one another (McIntyre 1997:21). These designatory titles can serve as some sort of a 'model' that can help deduce, at least theoretically, the attitudes of our constituents towards the Spirit.[1] Through these models, we can determine whether these attitudes which we presume to be present among our population, is cogent enough as reflected through the empirical data collected through our investigation. Of course, in real world, these models are often if not always, interlocked with one another. Nonetheless, for heuristic reasons, analytical distinctions are indispensable. Only by abstracting from the complexities of the real world can we set up a conceptual representation that can illuminate it. Thus by distinguishing these images analytically, by exposing their distinctive logic, and by assigning them certain theoretical categories, we aim to clarify certain attitudes of our respondents towards the Spirit.

For the purpose of gathering a broad range of attitudes toward the Spirit, we shall take into account the images that are based not only on the two traditional sources of pneumatological reflection, namely the bible and the doctrine of the Trinity, but also those discourses that are founded on human experience in the broad sense of the term. We call the former the Spirit 'from above' and the latter the Spirit 'from below'. The Spirit 'from above' underscore the biblical and the Trinitarian doctrine as the main source of theological discourse, while the Spirit 'from below' draws their reflection from the sources of the human experience. The Spirit 'from above' (4.1.1.) consists of the pre-Trinitarian Spirit images, the Trinity-related Spirit, and the Jesus-related Spirit. The second group which is categorized as Spirit 'from below' (4.1.2.) is composed of the following: the individual-related Spirit and the society-related spirit.

4.1.1. *Spirit 'from above'*

The Spirit 'from above' models draw their reflections mainly on the scripture and the doctrine of the Trinity as stipulated in the early periods of Christianity. These Spirit 'from above' models rely on the scriptures and appeals to tradition as the principal source of theological explications. Their treatises underscore the nature of the Spirit portrayed either in the biblical image of a pre-Trinitarian Spirit, or as

---

[1] A 'model' is defined by McIntyre (1997:22) as "a generic concept, idea or image, which comprises economically a given class of description of the person and work of the Holy Spirit. It can be seen as a wider framework of interpretation that synthesizes and integrates divergent experiences into harmonious whole."

one of the divine persons of the Trinity. Pneumatology 'from above' flows in a deductive manner from the eternal deity of the Spirit "above", to Jesus' human nature, and to humanity or creatures here 'below'. Furthermore, these 'from above' pneumatological models presupposes that the Spirit is essentially and absolutely a divine being. They stress the divinity of the Spirit, thus they are often characterized as having an essentialist or immanent-Trinitarian conception of the Spirit.

In what follows, we shall expound on the three representatives of the Spirit 'from above', namely: the pre-Trinitarian (4.1.1.1), Trinitarian (4.1.1.2.), and Jesus-related Spirit (4.1.1.3).

4.1.1.1. *Pre-Trinitarian Spirit*
The pre-Trinitarian model describes the Spirit in a fairly non-conceptualized or non-structured form. Its main source in depicting the Spirit is essentially the scripture. Although this model shows a direct relationship between God and Spirit through the biblical tradition, it does not start and rely on human experience or human life in general to represent the Spirit.

According to this pre-Trinitarian model, one can find a variety of symbols of the Spirit in the bible. And yet, despite the pluralism of images of the Spirit in the bible, these varied biblical images of the Spirit neither negate nor efface each other, despite the fact that some of them are not mutually compatible. Most theologians agree that the biblical account of the Spirit, or more specifically its pre-Trinitarian account, is symbolical and not conceptual as in the case of the doctrine of the Trinity in the 4th century.

Gross (1992:232–236) spells out seven characteristics of the Spirit in relation to the world as they are construed in the bible. (1) The Spirit is used as a category to designate God's presence in the world. It is a symbol that is used to indicate the traces or 'footprints' of God in the world. Throughout the Old Testament, the Spirit represents the divine validation of the work of Israel's prophets, leaders, and the community itself. Furthermore, the Spirit has been thematically associated in the Hebrew scripture with creation (Gen. 1:2; Gen. 2:7, Ps. 104:30), ecstatic phenomena (1Sam. 10:10, Mic. 3:8, Neh. 9:30), and wisdom (Wisdom of Sol. 9:17). In case a contrast is made between divine and human spirit, the divine spirit is signified by the term Holy Spirit (Is. 63:10f, Isa. 31:3). In the New Testament, the Spirit is the validating category for God's presence in the world which undergirds the messiah's appearance and the Christian community that emerged; (2) The

Spirit is portrayed not spatially outside the created order but within it. The Spirit is present not only and essentially at Pentecost, but from the first stirrings of creation. LaCugna (1985) argues that the language of the Bible, of early Christian creeds, and of Greek and Latin theology prior to the 4th century is 'economic' (*oikonomia*, divine management of earthly affairs). It is oriented to the concrete history of creation and redemption; (3) Spirit provides a basis for understanding the God-world relation. God is the source and meaning of the work of the Spirit. The world is the location or arena of the Spirit; (4) the work of the Spirit is connected to God's purpose for the created order. Biblical traditions tend to relate the Hebrew and Greek words for the Spirit, *ruach*, and *pneuma*, to energy in speaking of God's purposes. Therefore, the Spirit as intrinsic to God's purposes is linked to understanding or intelligibility as well as to eschatology; (5) The Spirit as the basis of divine love and faithfulness; (6) In the New Testament, the Spirit is closely connected with the resurrected Lord, thus emphasizing the saving aspect of God's work in the world; lastly, (7) The Spirit is active in nature and in history and life. In this respect, the contributions of Teilhard de Chardin and Wolfhart Pannenberg are of major import because both tried to work on a comprehensive idea of the Spirit and its relationship to nature which are in harmony with the biblical account and the vital attributes of nature. Teilhard de Chardin maintains that Spirit and matter are indivisible. The Spirit is neither something that is superimposed on human being nor is it a by-product of the cosmos. The Spirit rather signifies the higher state assumed in and outside of humans by what he calls the 'stuff of the universe'. Pannenberg likewise contends that the Spirit is the origin of all living matter that transcends living beings. Every organism lives beyond itself. Therefore, he defines the Spirit on the basis of the self-transcending tendency of all organic life (Gross 1992:235).

Some contemporary theologians who opt to detract from the Trinitarian model prefer to go back to the pre-Trinitarian model. Some of them choose to regard the Spirit not as one of the 'persons' of the Trinity but as an attribute of God just like the way Paul talks of Jesus as the 'power of God and the wisdom of God' (1Cor. 1:24). For them, the pre-Trinitarian model is preferable because of its openness to employ imagination and variety of symbols in order to describe the Spirit. We will try to find out whether this model permeates the consciousness of our Dutch respondents.

4.1.1.2. *Trinity-related Spirit*

We can assume that the Trinity-related Spirit may have robustly influenced the present-day Dutch believers. This may be partly attributed to the 'orthodoxy' that is often associated to this type of pneumatology, and which church members normally learned from catechism and other sorts of religious education and socialization. We will try to find out in our empirical investigation the extent of influence of this type of Spirit model on our respondents.

From the 60's, there are two main strands of discourses on the Spirit in relation to the Trinitarian-tradition: one is the Spirit that is related to the economic Trinity, and the other, the Spirit that is related to the immanent or ontological Trinity. While the shift in approach towards the economic Trinity has been the trend in most contemporary theological discourses, the immanent or the ontological Trinitarian view has been relentlessly coming back and has been influential among many ordinary believers. For this reason, we shall refer only to the 'ontological Trinity' when talking about a 'Trinity-related pneumatology'.

A Trinity-related pneumatology derives its doctrine on the Spirit from the Trinitarian formulation of Chalcedon (451 A.D.). This Trinity-related Spirit model is a logical offshoot of the doctrine of the Trinity which grew within the context of the Greco-Roman culture. Amidst heresies and controversies, theologians by the end of the fourth century shifted their reflection from the scriptures and also beyond liturgical and creedal expressions of the Trinitarian faith to the ontological Trinity of co-equal persons 'within' God. The shift in this approach goes from function to ontology; from the economic Trinity (that is, the Father, Son, and Spirit in relation to us) to the immanent or essential Trinity (that is, the Father Son, and Spirit in relation to each other). It was prompted by the belief in the divinity of Christ and later in the divinity of the Spirit. The apologists of the *Logos* Christology correlate the pre-existent Christ of Johanine theology with the *logos* (word) of Greek philosophy. Justin Martyr and other church fathers utilize the distinction made by the Stoics between the immanent word (*logos endiathetos*) and the expressed word (*logos prophorikos*) in order to account for the pre-existence of Christ as the immanent word in the Father's mind and then became incarnate in time. In the Council of Nicea (325 A.D.), the famous *homoousius* doctrine defined that Jesus is of 'the same being or substance of the Father'. In this same council, the credal phrase, 'we believe in the Holy Spirit', also appeared. Athanasius, the protagonist of this doctrine, argues that it is only God who could establish salvation. If Christ is not God, then we have no sure access to this salvation. He extended this vision to the Spirit in his later writings saying that the Spirit is also of the 'same substance' of God. The Spirit who works for the salvation of men cannot be other than God who is the blessed source and goal of all things (cf. Imbelli 1987). In the second half of the 4th century, the Cappadocian Fathers (Basil of Caesarea, Gregory of Nazianzus, and Gregory of Nyssa) were confronted with the question: If the Spirit is not only the sanctifying gift bestowed by God upon the creature called to share the divine life, but is itself intrinsic to the Giver, then should not the Spirit be confessed as God, thus explicating yet more clearly the God of Christian faith and experience as fully Trinitarian? In his treatise, *On the Holy Spirit*, Basil argued that the Spirit indeed should be worshipped and glorified just like the Father and the Son. Following the argument of his friend Basil, Gregory of Nazianzus posits that if the Spirit is truly worshipped in the liturgy, if it renders salvation through baptism, and if it bestows grace, then the Spirit cannot be other than God, proceeding from the Father's bounty. Gregory of Nyssa provides a terminological clarification by claiming that 'the Father, Son, and Spirit' are one in being of substance (*ousia*), but three in subsistence (*hypostasis*, or *persona* in Latin). The Cappadocian fathers helped in standardizing Trinitarian language and clarifying conceptual distinctions. These significant contributions of the Cappadocian fathers were formalized in the Council of Constantinople (381 A.D.) which enhanced the creed of Nicea stating that the Spirit is "the Lord the Giver of life, who together with the Father and Son is adored and glorified, who spoke through the prophets." In the succeeding years, this creed becomes the source of the normative Trinitarian doctrine and creed of Western Christianity. The formulation of the creed and the doctrine of the immanent Trinity clinched the Trinitarian controversy but also put in place the 'substructure of a tripartite creed' (Haight 1999:477). Augustine is known to have elaborated on the doctrine of the Trinity in the western tradition. He tried to systematically expound on this doctrine by using it as a starting point to reflect on the divine life itself and by looking for analogy in order to find intelligibility in this internal, three-fold differentiation (Haight 1999:477). He links the doctrine of the Holy Spirit with the mutual love of the Father and the Son. It is this inner Trinitarian quality of the Spirit which enables the Spirit to act out its salvific function and serves as the unifying bond of love among human beings. Following this lead, pneumatological treatises made by other theologians, especially those from the west, revolved around the 'immanent' or pre-existent nature of the Spirit in relation to the doctrine of the Trinity which serves as the 'centering' doctrine for their reflections. Most of these theological discourses indicate the fundamental principle and the logic underlying all Trinitarian theology, i.e. one can make assertions about God on the basis of encounters with God in Jesus and the Spirit (Haight 1999:486).

The doctrine of the Immanent Trinity as it evolved in the western tradition depicts the inner reality of God as differentiated. In this differentiated character of the Trinity, the Spirit is esteemed as the third member. It is conceived as the immaterial, unearthly, and wholly transcendental person of the divine Trinity. Its nature is viewed as unchangeable, supernatural, and purely transcendent. It assumes a pre-existent nature, detached from the world and human existence (cf. Lampe 1977:120ff). In this sense, one may also refer to this pneumatological model as the 'pre-existent Spirit'. The human response to the Spirit is a purely subjective, passive, powerless, and submissive response (Gross 1992:233). The doctrine of the Trinity has been commonly associated with the 'ontological' perspective, and so does the Trinity-related pneumatology. In which case, the 'Spirit is seen as one of the persons of the divine Trinity', that is to say that the Spirit has always existed as part of the Trinity, or that the Spirit is the fruit of the union between the Father and the Son.

4.1.1.3. *Jesus-related Spirit*

Another type of Spirit 'from above' model is the so-called Jesus-related Spirit. Some authors anchor their pneumatological discourse on the Spirit of Jesus. According to this model, one can speak of the Spirit as a way of talking about the creative intervention of God in human history in the person of Jesus Christ (McGrath 1993a:450). Jesus becomes the centering principle when talking about the nature and action of the Spirit. The experience of salvation in Jesus becomes the foundational Christian principle which generated the Trinitarian doctrines and the subsequent elaboration of the doctrines of the Spirit. According to this view, the Spirit is the on-going presence of Jesus in our midst. It is through the operative experience of salvation through Jesus in the here and now that the Spirit manifests itself. The Spirit is the Spirit of Jesus who continues to be present among people. It is the presence of Jesus which people sense in their midst.

In the Old Testament, the Jews acknowledge the presence of the Spirit of God among chosen individuals like for instance the prophets. People who prophecy in God's name are looked upon by the Jews as being filled with the Spirit of God. This view was picked up by the New Testament writers who wrote about God at work in the world for the salvation of men through his son, Jesus. Furthermore, it is most likely that Jesus also regarded himself as the indwelling of God's Spirit which implies that he considered himself to be a man of God and a prophet. According to Dunn (1997:54), "[Jesus'] awareness of being uniquely possessed and used by the divine Spirit was the mainspring of his mission and the key to its effectiveness". However, after the resurrection of Jesus and the Pentecost event, many followers of Jesus started to conceive of the Spirit as the Spirit of Jesus himself, and not only as the Spirit of God present in Jesus. This idea was strengthened by St. Paul, who despite having no intention of showing that belief in Jesus is mightier than belief in God, breaks away from the Old Testament tradition where the Spirit is continuously perceived as the spirit of God manifested in the life of a person. St. Paul preached to the early Christians (Jews and Greeks) who were converted to Christianity on account of the continued presence of the Spirit in the resurrected Christ. To these people, Paul proclaimed that the Spirit is not only the spirit of God present in Jesus but that the Spirit is the Spirit of Jesus himself (Dunn 1998).

Despite the immense influence of the Jesus-related model in most pneumatological discourses, McDonnell (1982) articulates the protests of several authors against the subordination and the making of pneumatology only as an extension of Christology in an unhealthy modalist sense. He says that there is a tendency to portray the Spirit as essentially inferior to Christ, and therefore not as important as Christ. It is often portrayed as an extra or an addendum in order to render symmetry and balance to a theological treatise. Rosato (1983:2623ff) likewise observes that contemporary theologians react against an exclusively christocentric approach to pneumatology. According to him, although such approach to the Spirit may be pedagogically valid and may be considered to be vital from the Christian perspective, however, this Jesus-related pneumatology overlooks the primary lifegiving and sanctifying activities of the Spirit in the world and in other religions. Rosato (1983:263–269) points out that in recent times, it is imperative that Christian faith should be able to lead modern man to the credibility and practicality of faith in God as Spirit in dialogue with the world, by being keen at looking at the presence of divine spirit in human society itself, and by placing pneumatology in a global and communitarian context from the outset.

This comment seems to echo the critical voices among theologians and among some secularists who confront the Christian believers regarding their attitude towards the Spirit. They observe that a Jesus-related pneumatology does not take into account the full integrity of the Spirit who is present in every facets of human life, society, and cosmic universe in general. Moreover, a Jesus-related Spirit seems to be ineffective in the context of dialogue with other non-Christian religions. It fails to recognize the Spirit who is present in other religions without using Christ as a reference point or as a centering principle. Attempts to answer these questions were carried out by some authors by transposing the concept of the Spirit 'from above' to the idea of the Spirit 'from below'. We shall now turn to explicate this shift in pneumatology as we turn to some models which we classify as 'from below' pneumatologies.

4.1.2. *Spirit 'from below'*

All our theological thoughts that moves 'from below' toward God proceeds on the basis of religious experience and symbolic language (Haight 1999:471). This is based on the idea that all our thinking moves from the world to God, and not the other way around. One cannot know God unless somehow God is actually present within the knower.[2] In this sense, revelation may be understood as the experienced self-communication of God in human history, which thereby becomes the history of salvation. These insights support the idea behind the shift in some approaches to pneumatology that moves from the Spirit 'from above' to the Spirit 'from below'. This pneumatological approach 'from below' attempts to refute the dualistic character inherent in most pre-Enlightenment notions which conceives of the spirit as immaterial, unearthly, and wholly transcendent, and the human response to the Spirit as purely subjective, powerless, passive, and submissive (cf. Gross 1992:236). With these suppositions in mind, contemporary authors attempt to reformulate the notion of the

---

[2] This reminds us of the old scholastic saying: "*quid quid recipitur ad modum recipientis recipitur*" (Whatever is received is received in conformity with the modality of the receiver).

Spirit in order to provide a conceptual matrix of meaning and purpose which are impervious to dualism. Most of them aim at looking at the Spirit to be intrinsically related to the natural and human processes. The Spirit 'from below' models assume that the Spirit can be validly explicated as a universal structural feature of human consciousness. Spirit is conceived as an existential reality because it is a phenomenon embedded in the experience of human consciousness. Although one can trace the influence of the ideas of the Enlightenment in some of these models, one could not find a purely immanent interpretation of the spirit. Some authors have tried to relate the Holy Spirit with the human spirit (cf. Hendry 1959:96–117; Come 1959; Barclay 1962: 13–16; Berkhof 1979). They tried to locate the indwelling of the Spirit in human actions and experiences (cf. McDonnell 1982). It is a way of discerning the 'traces' of the Spirit within the human processes which, according to St. Bonaventure, is the *itinerarium ad mentis deum*. Spirit 'from below' holds that an anthropological approach to the reality of the Spirit is central to the thought process of the scriptures (Rosato 1983:263–269). The Spirit is perceived as an entity that evolves within the natural processes, but at the same time, it transcends nature and guides the world to its final destiny. It sees its function as a microcosm of an evolving macrocosm of universal spiritual consciousness that is the God-world relation itself (Gross 1992:236).

Recent trends in theology, however, show two diverse forms of emphasizing the prior place of the indwelling and abiding of the Holy Spirit (McIntyre 1997:227). One form stresses the indwelling of the Spirit in the individual, while the other underscores the indwelling of the Spirit in the society. In what follows, we will describe these two representatives of the Spirit 'from below' which are: the individual-related Spirit (4.1.2.1), and the society-related Spirit (4.1.2.2).

4.1.2.1. *Individual-related Spirit*
The individual-related Spirit asserts that the Spirit resides or dwells in the individual person. It upholds that the individual is the starting point of the Spirit's action. The Spirit is to be found within the "holiness of the heart's affections, and the truth of the imagination" (Keats, cited by McGrath 2001:97). Human subjectivity and inwardness is seen as a mirror of the infinite. Human processes could lead men to the infinite and eternal and provides the key to the higher realms. It is within the inner processes of the individual person where the Spirit indwells. However, in the pneumatological reflections of the indwelling

of the Spirit within human subjectivity and inwardness, there are two models that have developed. We shall make a distinction between the models of cognition-related Spirit (4.1.2.1.1.) and the affection-related Spirit (4.1.2.1.2.).

4.1.2.1.1. Cognition-related Spirit
The cognition-related Spirit highlights the indwelling of the Spirit in the human processes of thinking and imagination within the individual person. The Spirit is manifested through the plurality of cognitive processes in humans from where they transcend the here and now. Through the human cognitive processes like for instance, receptiveness, awareness, focused attention, remembering of past events, narrations, convergent and divergent thinking, processing, imagining evaluating, internal communications, internal speech, internal voice, etcetera, human beings are confronted with the ultimate spiritual questions about origin, destiny, and the goal of life (cf. Van der Ven 2007). This model assumes that it is within these cognitive processes that the Spirit works. Human beings interpret these cognitive processes as a gift of the spirit, as its inspiration, as its inner word, or as being infused by it. The Spirit working in these cognitive processes involves the ability of human beings to transcend oneself which is stimulated by the Spirit's transcendent moving and grasping within the human person.

While the Spirit 'from above' models assume that divine inspiration is mediated through the bible, traditions, religious hierarchies, or from an outside authority, modern man looks at the experience which occurs inside, especially the inner voice of reason. Modern man needs to reflect upon the reasons for his own actions, even for the reasons of his own reasons, the goals behind his or her goals and anchor them not on some external mediation but on the inner resource of one's being. This is also true in the way the Spirit is conceived according to the model of the cognition-related Spirit. The Spirit is discerned in the process of cognition, in the experience of consciousness (Rockmore 1997). It is signified as an image of human creativity which represents the inner life of man's cognitive processes. It is represented as the highest level of human imagination, or the expression of man's deepest human desire. The mystery of the Spirit is disclosed through the power of reason, unveiled through rational self-autonomy *qua* thinking-faith (Olson 1992). Furthermore, the cognition-related Spirit is also revealed through the human processes of imagination. Imagination, as the English poet William Wordsworth orates, "Is but another name for absolute power, and clearest insight, amplitude of mind, and Reason in her most exalted mood" (cited in McGrath 2001:97). Human imagination is the transcending limitation of human reason, and reaching beyond its bounds to sample the infinite through the finite. It is by turning towards oneself, into man's self-consciousness, that one may be able to conceive of the Spirit. However, this focus on the cognitive processes within the human being does not exclude giving attention to the tradition through which the Spirit works, because the effect of the workings of the Spirit is reflected into the individual and collective memory of believers.

We assume that this cognition-related Spirit model may also be present in the consciousness of the contemporary Dutch believers. We will find out how far this Spirit model has been empirically present in the awareness of this group of church members.

4.1.2.1.2. Affection-related Spirit
Another type of individual-related 'spirit from below' is the 'affection-related spirit'. This model of the Spirit claims that the Spirit works in the plurality of affective or emotional processes of the individual person. These affective processes may take the form of 'actual affections' and 'higher affections'. Actual affections of individuals can either be positive (e.g. joy, thankfulness, optimism, etcetera), negative (e.g. anger, depression, disappointment, etcetera), self-related (e.g. pride, autonomy, independence, mastery, etcetera), or other-related (e.g. concern, sympathy, empathy, worry, etcetera). The higher affections may include self-regard, other-related, compassion, love, agape, sacrifice, etcetera. Within these pluralities of affective processes, individuals relate with the ultimate spiritual questions about the origin and aim of human life. It is within these processing of emotions where one locates the arena where the Spirit works. Human beings interpret these affective processes as revelatory *locus* of the Spirit which moves them. This spiritual processing of emotions entails the dialectics between contingency and absoluteness, between finitude and infinity (Van der Ven 2007:22).

In several evangelical circles, the presence of the Spirit in the emotions is deemed significant. Eckman, for instance, believes that the Spirit directly involves our inner life; it involves our emotions. It is through our understanding of our emotions that leads us to a deeper understanding of the spiritual life (Eckman 2005:204). The experience of the emotions is, according to Eckman, the doorway to the inner life. In order to understand and appreciate the place of the Spirit in the emotions, he said, we have to recognize that human beings are an analogy of the divine. The reason that we have emotions is because God also has emotions. Eckman (2005:206) asserts: "We are made in the image of God, an image that includes a key component of emotions—in short, his emotional image." Our capacity to feel comes from our being created in God's image. The emotions within us follow the pattern of the emotions of God. However, he said, whenever we talk of God as having emotions, we are not using anthropopathic language. We do not necessarily make God in our image, but rather, "we are in his; therefore, we feel and want" (Eckman 2005:206). However, Eckman asserts that God is more than emotions: God is the infinitely deep love and relationships shared among the Father, the Son, and the Spirit. Furthermore, he explains that emotions are not meant to authenticate truth. It does however authenticate our understanding of the truth. "A happy heart is the greatest evidence of the apprehension of spiritual truth," says Eckman (2005:205).

Unlike the images of the Spirit from above which locate the Spirit from traditions or from an outside authority, the affection-related Spirit conceives of the Spirit as a reality within the natural processes, but at the same time transcends it. It differs however from the cognition-related Spirit in the sense that the affective-related Spirt underscores the presence of the Spirit within the affective rather than the cognitive processes of the individual person. This does not mean, however, that the cognitive and the affective processes are separated from one another. On the one hand, the cognitive processes are embedded in the emotional processes and stimulated by them. On the other hand, the emotional processes are cognitively structured and fed. They are oriented and directed by the cognitive process. Both processes can be distinguished, not separated. They can only be given focused or attention to. We will try to find out how far our respondents adhere to this type of Spirit model.

4.1.2.2. *Society-related Spirit*
In both Protestantism and Catholicism, pneumatology has been associated mostly with private and individual experiences. The social or the public experiences have often been overlooked. In Protestantism, for instance, the interest in pneumatology has been largely in pietism which serves as a function of interiority and inwardness. In Roman Catholicism, its dominant expression has been in books on spirituality

or on the charismatic renewal, or when speaking of the structural elements of the church (McDonnell 1982). With the advent of political theology in the 60's and 70's, and subsequently, the birth of liberation theology and other contextual theologies like the Black, Asian, feminist, and ecological theologies, the social dimension of the Spirit has been accentuated. They contend that the activity of the Spirit should not be limited to the individual person alone but should also embrace the important structural and cultural dimensions as well. They react against an inward-looking, individualistic, and a-social approach to the Spirit. The Spirit does not take place solely in the secret of the heart or in some a-socio or a-cultural location, as *Redemptoris Missio*, no. 28 declares. The world is the arena or the location of the workings of the Spirit. It has been crucial for western church to acknowledge the continuing activity of the spirit after incarnation and Pentecost, not only in relation to charity and grace, but also in relation to nature, to moral, cultural, and political life of people. Otherwise, the Spirit becomes too sacralized, too tied to holy objects and events.

The 'society-related Spirit' believes that the spirit is present in the ebb and flow of history. The Spirit is the transforming and liberating spirit of Jesus who finds solidarity with the oppressed and the marginalized in their struggle for emancipation and freedom in society. The action of the Spirit is not restricted to any one person, institution, epoch, culture or religion. All human question for truth, beauty, and community, and all humanizing and liberating discoveries and inventions, originate in the promptings of the Spirit abiding deep within (Rayan 2000:98–101). Feminist theologians also underscore the social aspect of the spirit. McFague (1996:146–147) underscores three significant characteristics to highlight the social dimension of the Spirit as perceived by most feminist theologians. First is the emphasis on the immanent character of the Spirit in contrast to the transcendent notion of the Spirit; second is the transforming and liberating power of the Spirit; and third is the scope which encompasses both the natural and the human world. Feminist theologians insist that the Spirit should be conceived as source of creative and transformative energy in society and in the entire cosmos. We suppose that this society-related Spirit is also present in the hearts and minds of our respondents.

Thus far, we have attempted to formulate and compile a broad-spectrum of the concepts regarding the Spirit which we reckon to exist among our respondents based on theoretical grounds. We have made

Scheme 4.1. Images of the Spirit from a theoretical perspective

Spirit 'from above'
  1. Pre-Trinitarian Spirit
  2. Trinity-Related Spirit
  3. Jesus-Related Spirit

Spirit 'from below'
  4. Cognition-related Spirit
  5. Affection-related Spirit
  6. Society-related Spirit

two major classifications, namely: the Spirit 'from above' and the Spirit 'from below'. Under the Spirit 'from above', we identified three sub-categories, namely: the Pre-Trinitarian Spirit, the Trinity-related Spirit, and the Jesus-related Spirit. In the Spirit 'from below', we name two categories, namely: the individual-related Spirit, and the society-related Spirit. The scheme above (Scheme 4.1.) shows us the summary of our theoretical models.

4.2. *Images of the Spirit from an empirical perspective*

In the theoretical section of this chapter, we gathered six conceptual models which have been consolidated into two main categories: the Spirit 'from above' and the Spirit 'from below'. The six models consist of the Pre-Trinitarian Spirit, the Trinity-related Spirit, Jesus-related Spirit, the cognition-related, affection-related, and the society-related Spirit. In order to operationalize these models, we formulated four items to represent each of these Spirit models. A total of 24 items were incorporated in this Spirit-instrument (see: Appendix 1, Table 3, Part 2). It should be noted that these items have been newly constructed for the purpose of this explorative investigation. Again, a five-point Likert scales have been employed.

The scores on all the Spirit images were first subjected to a free factor solution analysis (mineigen = 1). Because of the non-interpretability of the result, we conducted a forced factor solution analysis, which resulted into five factors instead of the six conceptual pneumatic models as presumed in the theoretical section, namely: Trinity-related Spirit, Jesus-related Spirit, cognition-related Spirit, affection-related Spirit, and society-related Spirit. The pre-Trinitarian model was eliminated due to statistical reasons. Furthermore, it is important to note

Table 4.1. Images of the Spirit from an Empirical Perspective

Empirical Model	Mean	Standard Deviation	Pearson Correlation (r)	Valid Cases
Spirit 'from above'				
I. Trinity-related (Theoretical model 2)	3.7	1.12	.79	406
II. Jesus-related (Theoretical model 3)	3.6	1.01	.66	398
Spirit 'from below'				
III. Cognition-related (Theoretical model 4)	3.4	1.05	.62	397
IV. Affection-related (Theoretical model 5)	3.6	.93	.67	407
V. Society-related (Theoretical model 6)	3.9	.88	.65	406

that while we used 4 items to operationalize each Spirit model (see: Appendix 1, Table 3, Part 2), there were only 2 items per model that were left from the factor analysis for statistical reasons (see: Appendix 4, Table 1). This is inevitable due to the fact that these Spirit items have been newly constructed. On the basis of the result of the factor analysis, we constructed five scales. The table above (Table 4.1.) presents a summary of the images of the Spirit from an empirical perspective.

The figures in the table above reveal that our respondents generally agree with all pneumatological models. The society-related Spirit yielded the highest score (mean: 3.9). It is quite revealing to see that our respondents also assent to a Trinity-related pneumatology, garnering quite a relatively high score (mean: 3.7). The Jesus-related (mean: 3.6) and the affection-related Spirit (mean: 3.6) are also accepted by our respondents. The cognition-related Spirit scored the lowest, albeit still positive (mean: 3.4).

4.3. *Social location of the attitudes towards the Spirit*

Similar to what we carried out in the previous chapters, we also investigate the social location of the attitudes towards the Spirit. The table below (Table 4.2.) summarizes the result of the variance analysis and correlation coefficient which will help us to highlight significant associations or correlations between these attitudes with the cross-section of our respondent's socio-demographic and religious characteristics.

Table 4.2. Social location of the attitudes toward the Spirit *(eta & rho)*

	Trinity-Related	Jesus-Related	Cognition-related	Affection-related	Society-related
DEMOGRAPHIC CHARACTERISTICS					
Age *(eta)*	.14*	.18**	—	—	.14*
Gender *(eta)*	—	—	—	—	—
Education *(eta)*	.18**	.23**	.15*	.16*	—
Country of origin *(eta)*	.11*	.17**	.13*	.13**	.13**
SOCIAL CHARACTERISTICS					
Localistic authoritarianism *(rho)*	.20**	.23**	.15**	.19**	.17**
Subjectively-perceived threat *(rho)*	—	—	—	—	—
Conformism *(rho)*	.22**	.28**	.19**	.24**	.25**
Anomie *(rho)*	.15**	.18**	—	—	.15**
RELIGIOUS CHARACTERISTICS					
Church Involvement *(eta)*	.28**	.35**	.16**	.25**	.32**
Religious Salience *(rho)*	.44**	.42**	—	.42**	.47**

** p < .01; * p < .05 (2-tailed)

From Table 4.2 some general observations may be brought forth as a result of the analysis. Age is only relatively significant since it is associated to three Spirit attitudes, namely: Trinity-related, Jesus-related, and society-related Spirit. In these three images, there is a significant difference of attitudes between the older age group and the youngest age group (see: Appendix 4, Table 3). Gender does not play a role in the Spirit attitudes of our respondents. Education demonstrates certain associations to some Spirit images, namely: Trinity-related, Jesus-related, cognition-related, and affection-related Spirit images. However, it does not show significant association with the society-related Spirit. We also notice that respondents with higher education (higher secondary education and/or tertiary education), score lower on Trinity-related and Jesus-related Spirit than those with a lower education (primary education and/or lower secondary education (see: Appendix 4, Table 3). The demographic characteristic that is associated to all the pneumatological models is country of origin. The non-Dutch respondents scored higher on all the Spirit attitudes than the Dutch ones.

Two of the social characteristics, i.e. localistic authoritarianism and conformism, are significantly correlated to all the images of the Spirit. Anomie is correlated to two Spirit images, that is, Trinity-related and the Jesus-related Spirit images. It is interesting to observe that subjectively-perceived threat is not correlated to any Spirit images. Like in the previous chapters, the religious characteristics of our respondents have so far consistently manifested significant associations with most, if not all, of the pneumatological models. Church involvement is associated to all Spirit images. Compared to the non-active members, the active church members score higher on all the Spirit models (see: Appendix 4, Table 3). Religious salience is correlated with all of the Spirit images, except cognition-related Spirit.

Summary

In the theoretical part of this chapter, we assume that our respondents will have six Spirit-attitudes which we categorize into Spirit 'from above' (i.e. Pre-Trinitarian, Trinity-related, and Jesus-related Spirit), and the Spirit 'from below', which we sub-categorized into individual-related Spirit (i.e. cognition-related and affection-related) and the society-related Spirit. As a result of our empirical analysis, we are able to gather five Spirit images, namely: Trinity-related Spirit, Jesus-related Spirit, Cognition-related Spirit, Affection-related Spirit, and Society-related Spirit. The items of the pre-Trinitarian image are eliminated for statistical reasons. All the Spirit images are accepted by our Dutch respondents. In terms of age, we discover that there is a significant difference of attitudes between the older age group and the youngest age group on their scores on Trinity-related Spirit, Jesus-related Spirit, and society-related Spirit. The results of our analysis also show that respondents with higher education (higher secondary education and/ or tertiary education) score lower on Trinity-related and Jesus-related Spirit than those with a lower education (primary education and/or lower secondary education). The country of origin is associated to all the Spirit images. Localistic authoritarianism and conformism are significantly correlated to all the Spirit images. Anomie is correlated to Trinity-related Spirit and Jesus-related Spirit. Church involvement and religious salience play an important role on the attitudes of our respondents toward the Spirit.

CHAPTER FIVE

ATTITUDES TOWARD SALVATION

Like other religions, Christianity teaches universal love, brotherhood/sisterhood, equality, and solidarity of peoples. This discourse is very well taken up by the Christian theme of salvation. Salvation as a Christian concept offers an ideal for binding peoples together in overcoming division and enmity among groups of peoples. However, it is also ironic (but true, nonetheless) that this same theme has been used to justify discrimination, animosities, and hatred towards the so-called 'other'. History abounds with examples to bear out this poignant truth. One can look back at the bloody religious wars that happened in the Netherlands and elsewhere. Several studies have corroborated this point proving that religion is or has been a catalyst for prejudice, social distance, anti-semitism, intolerance, ultra-nationalism, racism, and ethnocentrism (Duriez et al. 1999:5–27). Therefore, it can be said that some of the Christian notions of salvation may, on one hand, exhibit a positive influence towards a negative attitude towards ethnic minorities, but on the other hand, there are also other ideas of salvation that may unmake prejudice or discrimination. Hence, it is interesting to investigate how far one's notion of salvation influence the attitude of believers towards the so-called 'other' in this increasingly pluralistic Dutch society. Which image(s) of salvation 'make' or 'unmake' negative attitude towards ethnic minorities? But in order to answer these questions, we will first try to discover the attitudes of our respondents towards salvation.

In this chapter, we will investigate the type of soteriological images that exist among representatives of the contemporary Dutch believers. More specifically, we shall ask the question: What are the attitudes of church members toward salvation, and what is the social location of these attitudes? We shall structure this chapter in the following: in section 5.1. we shall spell out the soteriological theoretical framework; then in 5.2., we will present the empirical result of the investigation; and lastly, in 5.3., we shall put forward the results of the social location of these soteriological attitudes.

5.1. *Images of salvation from a theoretical perspective*

The word 'soteriology' comes from the Greek term *soter* or *soteria*, meaning 'savior', 'deliverer'; or *sozein*, meaning 'to save'. These are the same words that are used in Christian theology to interpret the saving work of Jesus Christ. In general, one can say that the concept of salvation is a very slippery notion (Jantzen 1984:580). The word 'salvation itself is laden with nuances. It implies that there is something to be saved from. What this is varies according to context. A person might be saved from drowning, bankruptcy, starvation, embarassment, etcetera. One can even speak of saving a person from himself. In religious context, the notion of salvation takes on a more specific contour, though even here it remains highly amorphous. While it is true that the content of salvation varies in accordance with need, it also varies in method: the way to save a drowning child is not the same as saving a student from failure. And if that from which one is saved and the method of salvation vary, the goal—what is obtained by obtaining salvation—varies as well: life, health, solvency, good grades, social equilibrium, etcetera. Certainly there are manifold and diverse interpretations and images wielded throughout the history of Christianity to refer to salvation. Until now, the church has not given any official sanction to specifically understand the saving works of Jesus Christ. Faced with the plurality of concepts of salvation, Jantzen (1984:580) warns us: "we ought not to assume without investigation a monolithic concept of salvation, either in its antecedent condition (from what we are saved), its method (how we are saved), or its goal (to what we are saved)." Added to these concerns is the primary question raised by several religious adherents in terms of 'who is going to be saved?'. These are some of the key questions that are being raised in the contemporary pluralistic and multicultural society. We cannot suppose that all religions or cultures have a concept of salvation at all, let alone that they all mean the same thing by it or offer the same way to obtain it. Apparently, these questions awaken us with the fact that any study of soteriology will have to be confronted with the whole gamut of concepts surrounding this theme. There is no single, universal understanding of salvation, not even in the Judeo-Christian tradition. This is important to bear in mind as we investigate the soteriological attitude of our respondents. We therefore have to formulate a broad theoretical frame of reference in order to investigate the attitudes of our respondents in relation to the theme of salvation.

In order to capture the whole range of salvation images among our respondents, we will structure our investigation of these images according to three dimensions, namely: the dimension of transcendence, the dimension of time (or temporal dimension), and the dimension of space. In what follows, we will explain the three-dimensional soteriological images which we presume to characterize the salvation images present among our respondents, at least theoretically. The dimension of transcendence of salvation will be presented in section 5.1.1.; the temporal dimension will be explained in section 5.1.2.; and the dimension of space, which will be represented by two main categories, namely: the scope of salvation and the realms of salvation, will be elucidated on sections 5.1.3. and 5.1.4., respectively.

5.1.1. *Dimension of transcendence in salvation*

The dimension of transcendence defines the characteristics of salvation within the tension between transcendence and immanence. Transcendence implies a condition or state of being which surpasses physical existence or is independent of it. It is often contrasted to the notion of immanence—the condition or state of being that exist exclusively in the physical, psychic, social order, or is even identical to it. However, some theologians and philosophers believe that these binary contrasting concepts are not mutually exclusive because transcendence can also be located in its immanence. In other words, salvation is both within and beyond the universe, in it but not of it, simultaneously pervading it and surpassing it.

In what follows, we shall elaborate on the three types of salvation models within this dimension, namely: absolute transcendence (5.1.1.1.), immanent transcendence (5.1.1.2.), and absolute immanence (5.1.1.3.).

5.1.1.1. *Absolute transcendence*

The absolute transcendence model of salvation views transcendence as a supernatural cause of reality, and the revelation of transcendence is conceived as a totality of added, new and super-rational truths. Salvation is totally considered as an absolute gift, an absolute grace from above. This notion of absolute transcendent salvation implies that human efforts do not merit at all, except through his/her passive 'fiat'. Human action contributes nothing but merely constitutes the material for God's action, a view held by some orthodox and neo-orthodox circles. Absolute transcendence emphasizes the redemptive

God who, prior to and independent of human action, brings salvation which people, through their innocent and culpable fallibility, cannot accomplish for themselves, even though they are themselves responsible for the plight in which they find themselves and the harm that they have done. It underscores the exclusive action of a divine being who transcends human grasp. Salvation is something that is beyond human reach but only comes to man through divine intervention and initiative. Deliverance is the gracious working out of God's own salvific purpose for his people and does not depend upon the merits of the people. It underscores the totally 'gratuitous' nature of salvation coming from God. As this notion suggests, salvation is the Kingdom of God that is given to human beings. It is like a paradise created by God for humanity. This notion of salvation is exemplified by the idea of salvation by God's grace alone as can be gleaned in Ephesians 2:8–9: "For it is by grace you have been saved, through faith—and this not from yourselves, it is the gift of God; not by works, so that no one can boast."

5.1.1.2. *Immanent transcendence*

The idea of an absolute transcendent salvation has been contested by several theologians. They claim that transcendence is not the negation of immanence nor its opposite. Transcendence is not a contradiction of immanence, nor are they mutually exclusive. Transcendence arises in immanence and goes beyond it. Transcendence reveals itself in immanence, but at the same time also exceeds it. From a hermeneutical-theological perspective, immanent transcendence refers to the interpretation of religious experience of transcendence as the manifestation of a transcendent meaning in the dimension of our historical horizon of experience. The transcendence permeates the core of all that exists more deeply than the core itself permeates all that exists. Experience is considered as the source of revelation of transcendence. Schillebeeckx (1979), for instance, contends that there can be no revelation without experience. Many contemporary models of salvation agree that salvation is rooted in experience, in the context of people's lives, within social and cultural patterns. Salvation can be spoken of in ordinary language, the language of dialogue with people, and of experiences of specific liberating events of well-being, happiness, peace, relief, justice, freedom, etcetera. These are concrete human experiences interpreted in faith as gifts of God because ultimately, they are brought about by God. While Christian salvation cannot simply be identified with the human experience of well-being, wholeness or liberation, it points beyond the experience itself to the presence of God, to a gift, and as such to God's project of total human salvation which radically surpasses the historical process and is therefore eschatological. Yet salvation is already a part of the concrete historical experiences of well-being and wholeness, anticipations, albeit fragments of the fullness of salvation. These fragments of the fullness of salvation exactly allow human beings to hope and to speak about the mystery of a gracious God who is human salvation (Jantzen 1984). For a Christian believer, history is always related to a God who is known as the ground and the dynamic of creation and salvation. It is important to see the soteriological significance of everything that happens in history. This salvation model puts accent on the immanent nature of the transcendent aspect of salvation. In relation to God-talk, immanent transcendence stresses that God is in everything; God's presence by and for the world. From the perspective of immanent transcendence model, salvation history is viewed as a task, a project that one has to build according to God's plan or in view of the reign Kingdom of God. Salvation is something that is achieved by doing something to this world and shaping it according to God's will.

5.1.1.3. *Absolute Immanence*

Salvation according to the absolute immanent model is attributed to purely material, psychic, or social structure of the world and rejects any reference to transcendence. The content of this concept consists of non-religious, purely worldly immanentism. This absolute immanent soteriological model is a result of what can be called as the second wave of the Enlightenment during the so-called 'cultural revolution' of the sixties and the seventies of the past century (although it can be argued that this model has already existed and persisted since the time of the Enlightenment), when religious verticalism was reduced to horizontalism. In terms of God talk, it refers to a God who does not exist above the world, but only in the world, above all in human relations of mutual care and love. Salvation serves nothing more than as function of human existence. Ninian Smart indicates that secular ideologies may likewise have some notions or analogues to the religious doctrine of salvation, e.g. the idea of a millenium when humans live in harmony and glory on earth, a communist society which had overcome class distinction or alienation, or Hitler's 1000 year Reich which is millenarian but tribal in orientation, or the notion of progress (though without a clear idea of ultimate state of satisfaction) of democratic capitalism; existentialism speaks of salvation when an individual can live authentically in the face of, and conscious of, his own death and thus in a sense overcome death from within a finite existence. These concepts are generally based on a community-oriented, this-worldly, or the idea of a renewed blissful or blessed state. The world is perceived to be totally left to human beings to create and re-create in order to achieve the optimum level of human flourishing. Divine action contributes nothing and the word 'God' can be replaced by any fictional, literary, poetic and hence social or individual therapeutic strategy, a view encountered among proponents of a liberal kind of cultural Christianity (Van der Ven 2003:58–59).

5.1.2. *Temporal dimension of salvation*

The integrity of the three dimensions of time, namely: past, present and future, is a genuine attribute of Christian soteriology. This coherence can be demonstrated through the biblical concepts of God's covenant and steadfastness. Israel figured out its own history as a divine promise when it reflected on its history from the point of view of the present, and through which it was able to recognize the steadfastness of God. This divine steadfastness is fundamentally an expectation of a future filled with salvation. Paul Ricoeur, in his book *Time and Narrative* (1984), posits an insightful reflection on time. He depicts both a negative and positive definition of time. He says: time *is* and time *is not*. He explains that time *is not* in the sense that the past is no longer, the present does not remain, and the future is not yet. On the other hand, time *is* because the past is about the things that were, the present is about things that are passing away, and the future is about things that will be. Ricoeur makes a distinction between objective perspective of cosmological time and the subjective perspective of phenomenological time. Both perspectives can be read from the vantage point of the now. The 'now' from the objective perspective is an instant, that has a 'before' and an 'after', and time is the interval between two instants. From the subjective perspective, the 'now' is interpreted as 'presence' whereby I bear with time the memory of the past and the expectation of the future. It signifies the distended-ness of the mind (*distentio animi*) over present, past and future. Ricoeur (1984:60ff) shows the unity and plurality of the temporal structure of the past, present and the future by referring to Book XI of Augustine's *Confessions*. The aporia of the unity and plurality of time can be understood in terms of the present. Hence, the past is interpreted as the present of past (memory), the present as the present of the present (attention or focused awareness), and the future is the present of future (expectation). This constitutes the so-called thesis of the threefold-present. This integral perspective of time according to Ricoeur, which underscores the presence, will serve as the background of the distinction between past, present, and future salvation. This Ricoerian emphasis on the presence is implied in my wording when we discuss the temporal dimension of time as past-oriented, present-oriented, and future-oriented salvation.

Let us now take a short survey of how salvation has been expressed in the various temporal structures of past-oriented (5.1.2.1.), present-oriented (5.1.2.2.), and future-oriented salvation (5.1.2.3.).

5.1.2.1. Past-oriented salvation

Following the thesis of the three-fold present, we shall try to present the temporal notion of salvation as 'present of the past' or memory. This idea is echoed by the remarks of Ellie Wiesel (1990:201), saying: "Salvation can be found only in memory." But the conception of salvation as memory, at least in the sense of 'the present of the past', has a dynamic meaning. Volf (2006:21) explains, "when we remember the past, it is not only past; it breaks into the present and gains a new lease on life." In the Christian tradition, the notion of salvation as 'memory' can be illustrated by the way in which the sacrament of the Eucharist is construed as a 'memory' of Christ's saving event. The Eucharist retells, or better, 'remembers' the story of Jesus' paschal mystery in such a way that believers could share in Christ's death and resurrection every time the sacrament of the Eucharist is celebrated. Atkins (2004:95) explains that the Eucharist is a meal of 'remembering'. Here, 'remembering' is construed in two ways: First, it can be understood in a causative sense, that is, this object or idea will cause you to remember that one. And secondly, it can be construed in a way that one is able to connect past, present and future in a single fold. One can make the past present, imagine the future now, while at the same time remaining aware of the 'history' of the past, and the 'image' of the future. So in liturgy, the call 'to remember' at the time of thanksgiving for the bread and wine at the Eucharist can cause the mind to recall the presence of Christ for this moment of time while also recognizing that Jesus is part of history and that his presence now foreshadows the coming again of Christ in future glory (Atkins 2004:xi).

Salvation as 'present of the past' is also replicating. It allows one to relive past events in the present and gives opportunity for a 'second enjoyment'. The *praeterita* (things that have gone by) has a 'plural adjective' (*praesentia*); it admits internal multiplicity. It allows therefore salvific memory to have a multiplying effect. Memory multiplies pleasure because it re-presents the original experience. Salvation, in other words, involves 'recounting' of things of the past and making them present as they are' in one and several ways. Salvation understood as 'present of the past', whereby events, things, etcetera transpired in the chronological past is perceived as dynamic and multifold, as they unfold and recounted in the present. However if memory reproduce pleasure, it also replicates pain endured in the past. It may also repeat and revive original pain. Thus part of its multiplying nature, salvation as 'present of the past' also involves the ability to re-shape the past, whereby the future becomes more open. One is no longer held captive by the temptation to act out individual and collective memories.[1] As Elliot (1995:201) remarks: "we are free—not with license to do as we like, but with the memory of Jesus to show us the shape of the future." Through this dynamic understanding of salvation, one sees the value of retaining memory, for instance by relating the pain that one suffers and the pain caused to others with the paschal mystery of Jesus.

5.1.2.2. *Present-oriented salvation*

We mentioned earlier that the *present* is not just an instant, a mere dividing line between past and future, but that the present opens onto a future on the basis of the past. Ricoeur (2004:353) appeals for a polysemic reading of the notion of the present: "the present cannot be reduced to presence in something like the optical, sensorial, or cognitive sense of the term; it is also the present of suffering and enjoyment, and all the more so, the present of initiative." Ricoeur prefers to call the present of the present as intuition, as focused attention, or as attentive consciousness of the here and now. This temporal understanding of salvation implies the mindfulness of the now. This dynamic concep-

---

[1] Memory is also essential to achieve the salvation that lies outside of memory. Here, memory is construed as a 'means' to salvation. Atkin (2004) identifies four ways of making memory as 'means' of salvation: (a) by relating it to personal healing (for example, by healing psychological wounds, traumas, etcetera); (b) by unqualified acknowledgement of the truth through remembrances; (c) by generating solidarity with victims; and (d) by serving to protect victims from further violence.

tion of the present prompts us to the Christian notion signs of the times. This concept of signs of the times is actually based on Matthew 16:4 and has been repeatedly employed in the more recent encyclicals and social teachings of the Catholic church. The signs of the times represent the revelation or the 'traces' God in human history working to bring about salvation of peoples and the fuller realization of the Reign of God. Reading or scrutinizing the signs of the times entails prayerful discernment within the Christian community and in dialogue with all people of good will. The criteria for this discernment involve the coherence of the contemporary signs of the times with the gospels, the Christian understanding of human nature, and the common good (Henriot et al. 2003). Salvation as focused awareness also implies being engaged in the unfolding history. Salvation happens within history, in the here and now. Both in the Old and New Testament, salvation has been epitomized by various representations like deliverance from death, disaster, demons, sickness, forgiveness of sins, liberation from the law, and divine acceptance. Soteriology with a focused awareness in the present holds that the temporal locus of the *eschaton* lies not in the future but in the here and now. Salvific actions that transpire in the present, however, are derived from the past and are directed to some goals to the future. Actions in the here and now are interpreted by referring to the experience of God's saving action in the past, and in the promise of God's eschatological saving actions in the future.

5.1.2.3. *Future-oriented salvation*
The future-oriented salvation connotes expectation. It highlights the continuity between the inner-worldly history and the eschatological completion of the world. The continuity between the present world and the eschatological New World implies a relationship between human actions aimed at the future and the eschatological actions of God. However, expectation of the future may also pertain to the concept of salvation or eschatology in a discontinuous form. Salvation is realized neither in this world, nor by human actions; it will come about after this world and independent of human actions. It stresses the surpassing and transcending character of the completion of the world, thereby rendering contemporary history and secular achievements as trivial or unimportant. In the prophetic and apocalyptic literatures, God's salvation was increasingly projected into the future. The hope for an age of salvation to begin and a new temple and all nations bringing tribute to Israel (Isa. 49; Zech. 2). Yet Haggai and

Malachi indicate that the restoration of the people of Israel and the rebuilding of the temple led to disappointment and disillusionment. Therefore, the final saving acts of God were placed in the future with even more radical metaphors of salvation: a new heaven and a new earth (Isa. 65). While previous prophets had seen God's salvation as a future event within history (Hos. 2), the biblical writings after the restoration move toward apocalyptic imagery until finally salvation will be fully expressed in the arena of eternity after the resurrection of the dead (Dan. 12; Isa. 26:19). Salvation is also mentioned in the Letter to the Romans (13:11) which speaks of the future event, in which God will judge the world, destroy the wicked and establish his final kingdom on earth.[2]

5.1.3. *Scope of salvation*

The scope of salvation involves the matrix of exclusivism, inclusivism, and pluralism. In this discussion, we shall be keen on investigating how soteriological images embrace the so-called 'other' in their view of salvation. The scope of salvation involves the range of one's perceptions, thoughts, or actions in relation to who will be saved and to what extent this message of salvation is operative. When we refer to the scope of salvation, we consider the soteriological 'elbowroom' whereby believers discern through their soteriological categories who will be rejected or accepted within one's ambit of salvific discourse. It should be noted, however, that these three categories have but an indicative value and may not be taken rigidly. They are not meant to be an exhaustive classification of the scope of salvation in this study. We acknowledge that many contemporary views do not fit neatly into any one of them (cf. Ogden 1992; Merrigan 2000; D'Costa 2000; DiNoia 1990; Sterkens 2001). The pluralism of perspectives of salvation among religious traditions extends beyond the three-fold classification. Van der Ven et al. (2004:541), for instance, suggest to investigate one's position towards other religion by distinguishing between 'participant' perspectives from an 'observer' perspective. In that way, one can solve a 'false dilemma' whereby one is inclined to reject exclusivism and inclusivism for being excessively particularistic, and also to reject pluralism for being too relativistic. When all the nuances are considered,

---

[2] Similar texts in the New Testament also prove this understanding like in Rom. 9:9ff, 1 Thes. 5:8; Phil. 3:20f; Mark 10:23–26.

there are as many options as there are theological perspectives. Thus by using these three categories, we have to leave room for many shades of opinion among peoples, theologians, and religious scholars. Taken rigidly, they would become misleading as they would freeze theological opinions into the straight-jacket labels. Unfortunately, we do not have the occasion to survey all the other variations in relation to these three primary views. We therefore have to limit our investigation to only three main categories. These three categories nevertheless have the merit of demonstrating clearly that the universality of the mediatorship of Jesus Christ in the order of salvation is at the centre of the debate among Christians (Dupuis 1990). Moreover, these three main categories have been extensively used in several theological debates in relation to the religious attitudes of Christians towards other religions. They are still helpful categories to investigate the basic understanding of salvation among our constituents in relation to peoples of other faiths. Let us now trace our thread through these three scopes of salvation, namely: exclusivism (5.1.3.1.), inclusivism (5.1.3.2.), and pluralism (5.1.3.3.).

5.1.3.1. *Exclusivism*
Exclusivism implies that all salvation requires an explicit faith in Jesus Christ. Salvation, according to this soteriological model, is obtained only in Christ and nobody will be saved outside of Him (cf. McGrath 2001). Therefore, followers of other religious persuasions other than the way preached by Christ cannot be saved. Aside from the explicit belief in Jesus Christ, exclusivists also maintains that membership of the Church is required for salvation. It upholds the axiom *extra ecclesiam nulla salus* in its rigid interpretation (cf. Sullivan 1992). In the Council of Florence (1438–45), it states that "no one remaining outside the Catholic church, not just pagans, but also Jews or heretics or schismatics, can become partakers of eternal life; but they will go to the everlasting fire which was prepared for the devil and his angels, unless before the end of life they are joined to the church" (Hick 1999:328). Jesus Christ and the Church are the necessary way to salvation. No faiths apart from Christianity will lead to salvation. Another characterization of this exclusivist soteriological attitude is the idea that the Word of God, in written or spoken form, is absolutely essential for the salvation of anyone. It also supports the position that all knowledge must be filtered through scripture and the teachings of the church. Exclusivism maintains that there cannot be two or more

competing truth claims that are simultaneously true. Many religions have specific truth claims that are in direct opposition to truth claims made in Christianity, like for instance the belief in incarnation which is central to Christian faith. The significance of hearing and believing the gospel is incommensurate with everything else.

5.1.3.2. *Inclusivism*
Inclusivism, at least in its Christian form, believes on the one hand that salvation of all peoples depends solely on the salvific sacrifice of Jesus on the Cross, yet on the other hand, it admits that salvation is available not only to Christians but to all human beings. Even non-Christians are therefore included in the range of Christian message of salvation. This is reflected for instance in the papal encyclical, *Redemptor Hominis* (1979), which states: "every human person without exception has been redeemed by Christ." Rahner (1978:312) also underscores the notion that Jesus Christ is the saviour of all people. He rejects the idea that God condemns those who have no real opportunity to believe the gospel. He popularized the idea that even the so-called 'anonymous Christians' have a place in the the universal plan of God's salvation. He teaches that even those who do not identify with the light of Jesus Christ but respond to His message according to the values of the Kingdom of God may also be saved. The term 'anonymous Christian', however, has been perceived to be offensive to many non-Christians, who ask whether Christians would like to be called 'anonymous Muslims or anonymous Buddhists'. Justin the Martyr (c. 100–c. 165) argued that traces of Christian truth were to be found in the great pagan writers. He then propounds the notion of *logos spermatikos* which allowed him to affirm that God had prepared the way for his final revelation in Christ through hints of its truth in classical philosophy (McGrath 1998:24–25). Inclusivists recognize that some belief systems of other religions may occasion or prepare other believers to receive the gospel. Inclusivists believe that the grace of God cannot be limited to only the believers.

Inclusivism tries to combine the twofold New Testament affirmations of the concrete and universal salvific will of God, on the one hand, and of the finality of Jesus Christ as universal Saviour, on the other. It affirms that the mystery of Jesus Christ and of his Spirit is present and operative outside the boundaries of the Church, both in the life of individual persons and in the religious traditions to which they belong and which they sincerely practice. Jesus Christ is the way of all. Together with the exclusivist, they hold that all salvation is found through faith in Jesus Christ. The basic difference between exclusivism and inclusivism is related to the nature and content of 'saving faith'. While the exclusivists stress the explicit faith, the inclusivists refers to an implicit faith. This salvation model has been recently the commonly held position among theologians and church leaders for the reason that it upholds the unique centrality and normativeness of the Christian gospel but does not condemn the non-members to eternal perdition.

5.1.3.3. *Pluralism*

Pluralism holds that God has manifested and revealed himself in various ways to different peoples in their respective situations. It maintains that God saves people through their own tradition even as he saves Christians through Jesus Christ. Jesus Christ is the way for Christians while the respective traditions constitute the way for the others. To ascribe a uniquely salvific role to Jesus Christ would constitute a denial of the salvific role of other religious founders (like Buddha and Muhammad), and thus would be an affront to their communities. Salvation is conceived as the fundamental transformation of our human existence. This transformation is available through all the great religious traditions (e.g. eternal life in heaven for the Christians, annihilation of the illusion of separateness for Theravada Buddhism, etcetera). Authors like John Hick (1997) and Paul Knitter (1985) claim that the great religious traditions all mediate full salvation to their believers. According to Hick (1997:124–128), salvation is transformation from centeredness in the self to centeredness in Ultimate Reality or the noumenal 'Real'. He believes that all religions are in essence teaching the same thing and have the same goal at the end. He maintains therefore that Christianity does not have exclusive claims to salvation. Because all great religious traditions mediate salvation, no one is in the position to judge between them. One has to accept the fact that there are several paths to salvation, and should not impose this path on others to follow. He argues that the gratuitous love of God cannot exclude anyone from salvation. He rejects the exclusivists idea that truth claims must necessarily be filtered through the Christian sacred scriptures, rather he believes that all absolute religious claims must be filtered through the historical and cultural contexts where they arise, and should not be imposed as an absolute truth for everyone. Pluralism differs from exclusivism for it claims that non-Christians can be saved. Pluralists are distinguished from the inclusivists for its assertion that not all salvation is in and through Christ.

5.1.4. *Realms of salvation*

Salvation is a 'process of humanization', or the search for the mystery of the *humanum* (Schillebeeckx 1979;1981).[3] This understanding of salvation emphasizes that salvation is a process that transpires in the human being and in human history when human freedom is inaugurated and allowed to develop, when rational deliberation and choice are involved, and when truth and value is discovered which could bring about creative or transformative action. However, this search for the mystery of the *humanum* is not a finished project. "Definitive salvation", Schillebeeckx underscores (1981:837), "remains an indefinable horizon in our history in which both the hidden God and the sought-for, yet hidden, humanum disappear." Nevertheless, although Christian salvation cannot be reduced to sheer human well-being and liberation, one's experience of it already "points to the presence of God, to a gift, and as such to God's project of total human salvation which radically surpasses the historical process and is therefore, eschatological" (De Mesa & Wostyn 1989:32).

Schillebeeckx explains that this process of salvation as the search for the *humanum* can be grasped through negative-contrast experience. When one looks at the absurdity of suffering (negative), what results is a commitment to do something about it. This negative dialectic contains the added capacity to define something about salvation: i.e. minimaly salvation implies the humanization of the world by the elimination of suffering. Our contrast experiences give us a clearer view of the world and drive us towards transformative actions. In the scriptures, the experience of salvation has been specifically defined as to how the believers feel themselves to be freed from (negative experiences) and for what they know themselves to be freed. These negative experiences or the antecendent condition (salvation from) occasions the disclosure of the vision for a better future or the ultimate aim or goal (salvation for). The idea that people need to be saved from

---

[3] Rahner (1994:121) also states similar idea saying that God, "does not originally cause and produce something different from himself in the creature, but rather that he communicates his own divine nature and makes it a constitutive element in the fulfilment of the creature".

entails that a 'defective or unfortunate' situation is deemed ubiquitous according to the perception of the individual or group. Furthermore, perceptions and concrete experiences of peoples as to the root of these antecedent conditions (salvation from) varies, in the same way one's vision of what one is saved for (salvation for) also differs.

In numerous theological traditions in modern western world, the understanding of salvation as the search for the humanum involves what Schillebeeckx calls anthropological constants (1981:733). According to him, these anthropological constants are a system of coordinates which involves permanent human impulses and orientations, values operating in several spheres of value. This system of coordinates, even in the ideal of a perfect synthesis, establish conditions for the flourishing of the humanum. However, they do not provide us with directly specific norms or ethical imperatives because we do not have a pre-existing definition of humanity (Schillebeeckx 1981). These anthropological constants themselves have an eschalogical cast. They reveal that there is something absolute at the core of the human search for salvation. These anthropological constants include the following: relationship with human corporeality, nature and the natural environment; relationship with other humans; relationship with society, institutions and structures; conditioning by culture; relationship between theory and practice; religious awareness; and finally a synthesis of all of these. In this study, we want to make an adaptation of these seven anthropological constants by choosing a number of constants which are relevant for this chapter. Thus, from these seven anthropological constants, we include the bodily, the relationship with other humans (interpersonal), and relationship with society, institutions and structures (structural). We made a separate category for the ecological aspect due to its pressing relevance in contemporary debates concerning environmental issues. Some anthropological constants like the 'conditioning by culture' and 'religious awareness' have already been discussed and investigated in earlier chapters, and therefore will not be repeated in this chapter. In what follows, we will explicate five aspects within the realms of our humanity, namely: bodily salvation (5.1.4.1.), personal salvation (5.1.4.2.), interpersonal salvation (5.1.4.3.), structural salvation (5.1.4.4.), and ecological salvation (5.1.4.5.).

5.1.4.1. *Bodily salvation*
The integrity of the human person cannot discount the importance of the corporeal aspect of a human person. A nondualistic or a holistic

notion of salvation embraces the human body as the locus of salvation. This means that the body is taken seriously as occasion for revelation. St. Paul acknowledges the presence of God in the body of a person. He preached to the Corinthian community by saying: 'Do you not know that you are God's temple and that God's Spirit dwells in you?...Or do you not know that your body is a temple of the Holy Spirit within you?' (1Corinthians 3:16; 6:19). The dualistic worldview in the past which splits us into the war of spirit against the body has created fundamental and enduring problem which is felt even at present. Nelson (1992:9–10) mentions a few of the implications of this dualistic view which denigrates the body: "This alienating dualism manifests itself in a variety of ways. It is clearly present in our sexism and in our homophobia and heterosexism. It is present in the distorted and often violent meanings of our cultural masculinity. It is also the basic problem that confuses us in our struggle to use modern medical technologies in the service of human wholeness rather than in its fragmentation."

Human being's relationship with his body allows him to relate with the wider sphere of nature and her own ecological environment. The corporeal aspect of the human person reflects his/her values that works for life and survival. As Schillebeeckx (1981:734) explains, our relationship with our body "opens up the formal norm of respecting the inescapable limits of our corporeality and of nature—limits which are manifested in the individual and collective protest and resistance that arise spontaneously when human beings feel that their basic needs are not being satisfied and of altering nature by means of instrumental reason in order to create an appropriate human environment". Salvation in bodily terms implies freedom from bodily alienation and suppression, from sickness, hunger, and all sorts of bodily pain. It means achieving good physical well being, having good health, or fulfilling one's basic physiological needs. Bodily salvation also includes the feeling of being at home or being reconciled with one's own body, and being befriended with it.

5.1.4.2. *Personal salvation*
Salvation also relates to the salvation of the individual person. The Old Testament gives some evidence of a shift in emphasis from the collective nature of salvation to personal salvation, which was maintained even in the New Testament. This shift seemed to be accelerated by the experience of the exile. Ezekiel (Ez. 18:20) and Jeremiah (Jer. 31:29), for

instance, emphasize the personal nature of sin and judgment and the individual nature of repentance and forgiveness. Although these texts do not deny the communal nature of faith, they intend to insure that individuals recognize their personal responsibility rather than blaming others. There are also some references to personal salvation from enemies but not from eternal damnation (1Sam. 19:11; 2Sam. 22:4). In the New Testament, one can also gather some texts which highlight salvation of the individual persons, for example, Rom. 1:16, 17; 3:21-28; 7:7-25. Some other texts also indicate personal responsibility towards salvation showing that each person is accountable before God for his own life (James 1:23-25; 2Cor. 5:10; Rom. 14:12; Rom. 2:6-10; Acts 2:38; 2Pet. 3:9). Paul's concern was with the salvation of the individual, and not just with questions of a more collective nature (Burnett 2001). The church fathers (ca. 100-450 A.D.) have also highlighted personal salvation through their notions of salvation which is characterized by these three main characteristics: (1) salvation conceived as revelation of truth and removal of ignorance, (2) forgiveness of sins and justification, and (3) immortality and deification (Jantzen 1984). They preached about the idea of personal salvation in an afterlife which will be offered to those conformed to the hierarchical authorities of the church—specifically, through the acceptance of written creeds and dogmas, the practice of sacraments, etcetera. The sacraments are considered means to salvation administered by the church. Salvation has become more identified with consequences for the future life- heaven and hell. The Council of Trent also highlights salvation on the personal level. Trent underscores that man really cooperates in his personal salvation from sin; and that by justification, man is really made just. Before Vatican II, soteriological concepts emphasize the individual's relations with God in a vertical, one-to-one basis, so that individual salvation was seen as a private affair of piety and charity. But this understanding of 'personal salvation' has changed in lieu of the modern understanding of the 'self' which indicates autonomy, uniqueness, freedom, and independence, over and against the dominating influence of authority, tradition, and other social structures. The autonomy of the individual, as Kant (1986:47) describes it, is the capacity that persons have in formulating their own rules and determining their own destiny. It underscores the capacity of individuals to reflect on his or her behavior—i.e. to be self-conscious. Self-consciousness implies that individuals are active, creative agents, who are far from powerless in the face of society and culture. Culture and structures and contexts of public social behavior do not impose meaning on individuals; rather it offers a framework, in which individuals operate in an interpretive and pro-active manner. Although individuals work within the framework that is given in society, they are not totally determined by it. The self is not constructed by their social membership, rather the self has primacy. Self-consciousness is and always has been the essence of humanness and is always the primary determinant of behavior (Cohen 1994:114). Giddens (1991:35) takes into account the reflexive awareness that is characteristics of all human action and admits that "to be human is to know, virtually all of the time, in terms of some description or other, both what one is doing and why one is doing it." With the growing assertion of the individual in modern society, theologians employ personalistic and existential categories to conceptualize salvation which accentuate the doctrine of grace and sanctification by putting premium value on human subjectivity through authenticity and self-understanding. Salvation is then conceived as a movement from inauthenticity to faith (Bultmann), from estrangement to centeredness (Tillich), from guilt to freedom (Rahner), from *hamartia* to the restoration of vision (R. Niebuhr), from passivity to self-affirmation (feminist theology). The Second Vatican Council also acknowledges the value of the individual, for instance in the document *Dignitatis Humanae* (1965, no. 1) which states: "Contemporary man is becoming increasingly conscious of the dignity of the human person; more and more people are demanding that men should exercise fully their own judgment and a responsible freedom in their actions and should not be subject to the pressure of coercion but be inspired by a sense of duty." The (post-) Vatican teachings which underscores personal salvation differs from the pre-Vatican discourses in that the former reject the individualistic verticalization of the human being's relationship to God to a new appreciation of existential freedom of the individual.

Personal salvation hightlights the notion of salvation as freedom from estrangement from self and repression of the self. It underscores personal authenticity, the freedom to pursue one's happiness, and man's personal responsibility to shape his or her own life.

5.1.4.3. *Interpersonal salvation*
Salvation has also an interpersonal component. It includes what Hodgson (1994:215–216) refers to as inter-human or inter-subjective relationship. Interpersonal salvation consists of relating, interacting, or engaging intersubjectively with the 'other' aside from oneself. It entails

nurturing right intersubjective relationship. It consists of achieving salvation in relationship with other people within a shared world of consciousness.

Salvation never occurs in isolation. It involves what is called an interpersonal *koinonia*. It entails an element of being together, of having contact with other fellow human beings, through which we share ourselves with others and even be confirmed in our existence and personhood by others. It opens up the formal norm of accepting others intersubjectively as they are, in their otherness and in their freedom, for it is precisely by lovingly affirming the other as a person, that is, as an end and not simply as a means that human beings overcome the limitations of their own individuality and arrive at personal identity (Ricoeur 1995a). In our interaction with the other, we also take a glimpse of ourselves; the 'other' whom we ought to acknowledge as the 'other' and whose experience we can never immediately experience ourselves. According to Hodgson (1994:203), "this strange elusiveness of the other constitutes the fact of alterity, which is the precondition of all genuine relationships." The 'other' is the 'face', as Levinas calls it, who appeals for both compassion (suffering with the other) and obligation (suffering for the other). Whenever a person responds with compassion and sympathy for the other in a relationship of mutuality and inclusion, then freedom is experienced in the realm of the interpersonal. Freedom here implies not only the presence to oneself but also presence with and for others (Hodgson 1994) This freedom allows the possibility for an authentic communion of free and equal persons where mutual recognition of the other for the sake of the other can be forged. It is an ideal of a new interpersonal relationship marked by mutual service and wide mercy. It is within this ideal where God shall establish one new humanity consisting of a reconciled people (Eph. 2:14–19). It shall break away alienation between humans, and God will direct his saving action toward the healing of interpersonal relationships. Salvation in this sense, implies that the human salvific activities in which God's actions are embodied are enacted in our interaction with our fellow human beings. God's salvific activities occur in and via activities which people perform in inter-human relations. This is the underlying message of Jesus' version of the 'Golden Rule' which states: "Whatever you want men to do to you, do also to them for this is the Law and the prophets" (Mt. 7:12; Lk. 6:31). The evangelists wrote several teachings of Jesus which summons his followers to do good to others (Mt. 5:20–48). It is the basis from which everyone shall be vindicated in the Last Judgment (Mt. 25:31–46).[4] Therefore, in the Christian teaching, there is no salvation without relating to one's neighbors. Salvation entails being free from social isolation and division within the community. It implies human fellowship and having good mutual relationship based on respect for each other. It strives towards a community united in love and care for each other.

5.1.4.4. *Structural salvation*

Structural salvation emphasises the ocurrence of God's salvific action in the institutional relations of love and justice which each individual person maintains with others. This structural aspect of salvation may take a macro-level, the relationship with the 'we' within the social structures and institutions which protect these relationships and make them possible. This aspect opens up the formal norm of establishing certain measures of social consensus which is supported by structures that make human freedom and the realization of values possible. However, salvation in its structural dimension also calls for the concrete norm of changing specific social structures when, as a result of new circumstances, they have come to enslave and debase human beings rather than liberate and protect them. It appeals to transform the oppresive and unjust political, economic, and the cultural systems. In several developing countries, the structural aspect of salvation implies being liberated from internationally caused poverty and exploitation, and being free to equal distribution of power and wealth, to social justice, and equality. According to Gutierrez (1983:29), liberation means that "we see [the ongoing development of humanity] as a process of human emancipation, aiming toward a society where men and women are truly free from servitude, and where they are active shapers of their own destiny." Gutierrez explains that salvation understood as liberation should be construed as an all-embracing, comprehensive, and integral concept. Salvation understood as liberation from oppressive structures involves the aspiration of the oppressed peoples and social classes, emphasizing the conflictual aspects of the economic, social and political process which puts them at odds with wealthy nations and oppressive classes. In the West, the structural dimension

---

[4] Several texts in the scriptures exhorts man to do good to others (e.g. Gal. 6:1–2; 7–10; Lk. 10:25–37; Rom. 13:8–10; 1Jn 3:16–19; James 2:14–19; Titus 3:13–14; Col. 3:12–17).

of salvation can also be mirrored through the continuing struggle for social reforms within its welfare systems, from exclusion of migrants and ethnocentric tendencies, from marginalization of sub-sectors like women, homos, etcetera. Structural salvation in the western hemisphere also implies solidarity with the rest of the world in forging a just and social world order, emancipation of poorer and marginalized sectors in the society.

5.1.4.5. *Ecological salvation*
Over the past decades, the world has come to the awareness of the indispensable relationship between man and their environment. Contemporary scholars tried to define ecology as the "interdependence of all the living and non-living systems of the earth and the whole cosmos" (cf. Hodgson 1994:92). All things are internally interconnected in a very delicate web of living and non-living systems. This conception of ecology educes new insights into the Christian understanding of faith, more specifically to the Christian notion of salvation. The new ecological awareness brings back the 'religious' notion of a cosmic presence of indigenous religions, but also to the more mystical level of religious awareness of God's presence in nature and environment. Feminist theologians bring in a powerful metaphor of God as a divine mother in creation who gives birth to life and who nurtures it with love. The late Pope John Paul II, in his message for the *World Day of Peace* in 1990, enjoins all believers to care for all of creation. He said (1989): "The commitment of believers to a healthy environment for everyone stems directly from their belief in God the Creator, from their recognition of the effects of original and personal sin, and from the certainty of having been redeemed by Christ. Respect for life and for the dignity of the human person extends also to the rest of creation, which is called to join man in praising God (cf. Ps 148:96)."

Against this backdrop of intensifying ecological awareness comes also the shift in worldview from an anthropocentric to a cosmocentric perspective, a shift from a mechanical/substantial understanding of nature to an ecological/relational one (Hodgson 1994:94). Boff (1997:22–26; 31–34) for instance represents reality as a complex web of relationships anchored on a 'holographic principle'. This principle simply means that the whole is in the parts and the parts are in the whole. This holographic perspective embraces an open system that allows not only order but also disorder, antagonism, contradiction and competition.[5] Boff relates this interplay of relationships with the dialogical or perichoretic logic. Everything interacts dialogically with everything at all points and under all circumstances. The Greek term *perichoresis* (i.e. the interpenetration or circularity and inclusion in all relationships and of all related beings) aptly expresses this ecological proposition. It is the same term used to describe the mutual presence and interpenetrating communion of the Christian teaching of the Trinity.

The new shift towards a cosmocentric worldview also entails changes in man's attitude towards nature. Kockelkoren (1995:99–115) explains that our fundamental attitude towards the world and nature configures our interpretation of reality. He distinguishes four basic attitudes towards nature, namely: dominating, stewardship, partnership and participation. A dominating attitude believes that nature is at his disposal in support for the continued existence of the human race. Nature is something that one has to conquer and control. This attitude seeks maximum utility and profit from nature. The stewardship attitude assumes that human beings take responsibility for the use of nature but not its consumption. Human interests prevail over the vital interests of animals and plants, but the vital interests of plants and animals may not be sacrificed to purely economic interest. The partnership attitude sees life forms other than man as potential allies. This attitude presupposes animals and plants have their own input in the interaction with humans. Mankind may exploit nature, so understood, by means of technological designs and interventions up to a certain extent, so long as it does not involve unnatural forcing of the life forms involved. Mankind distinguishes itself from other life forms in that it not only participates biologically in nature, but also in addition, has a relationship with nature. Finally, the participant attitude believes that nature represents the totality of interdependent and interwoven life forms. Humankind is an integral part of this nature. The first two

---

[5] Boff spells out the current paradigm shift brought about by ecological awareness: wholeness/diversity (totality composed of organically interconnected diversities); interdependence, connectedness/relative autonomy; relationship/force fields; complexity/interiority; complementarity/reciprocity/chaos; arrow of time/entropy; shared destiny/personal destiny; cosmic common good/particular common good; creativity/destructiveness; holistic ecological stance/rejection of anthropomorphism (Boff 1997:31–34).

orientations, the dominating and stewardship attitudes represent the anthropocentric orientation, while the partnership and participant attitudes represent a cosmocentric attitude.

These insights bring us to the understanding of ecological salvation which exhorts us to take responsibility for the salvation not only of human beings but of all creations. It implies a great degree of caring for God's creation and all God's creatures. The right relationship is embodied in the everlasting covenant between God and His/Her creation. There can be no justice without right relationships of creatures with one another and with all of creation. Eco-justice is the vision of the garden in Genesis—the realm and the reality of right relationship. It reminds us that the world-as-a-whole and the universal history is the actual locus of divine activity. Salvation constitutes not only the salvation of human beings but also of the whole of creation. It involves the transformation of the world into a new heaven and a new earth in which righteousness dwells (2Pet. 3:13). The fullness of time "shall be when all things are united in Him, all things in heaven and things on earth" (Eph. 1:9–10).

Let us now sum up all the images of salvation we discussed above to constitute the theoretical framework of this chapter. We divided the soteriological concepts into three dimensions, namely: the dimension of transcendence, the temporal dimension, and the space dimension, which we developed into two categories: the scope of salvation, and the realms of salvation. The transcendence dimension includes three salvation images: the absolute transcendent salvation, the immanent transcendence salvation, and the absolute immanent salvation. The temporal dimension consists of three salvation images which are the past-oriented salvation, the present-oriented salvation, and the future-oriented salvation. For the scope of salvation, we included three images, namely: exclusivism, inclusivism, and pluralism. Finally, we discuss about the realms of salvation which we sub-divided into two categories: salvation from and salvation for. Within each of these categories, we distinguished five aspects in the realms of salvation, namely: bodily, personal, interpersonal, structural, and ecological salvation. The scheme below (Scheme 5.1.) illustrates the images of salvation from a theoretical perspective.

Scheme 5.1. Images of Salvation from a Theoretical Perspective

---

Dimension of transcendence in salvation
    1. absolute transcendence
    2. immanent transcendence
    3. absolute immanence
Temporal dimension of salvation
      4. past-oriented salvation
      5. present-oriented salvation
      6. future-oriented salvation
Scope of salvation
      7. exclusivism
      8. inclusivism
      9. pluralism
Realms of salvation
  Salvation from:
    10. bodily salvation
    11. personal salvation
    12. interpersonal salvation
    13. structural salvation
    14. ecological salvation
  Salvation for:
    15. bodily salvation
    16. personal salvation
    17. interpersonal salvation
    18. structural salvation
    19. ecological salvation

5.2. *Images of salvation from an empirical perspective*

In the previous section, we presented all the theoretical images of salvation. We gathered nineteen conceptual images of salvation in total. These images have been operationalized into three items per conceptual model (see: Appendix 1, Table 3, Part 2). Most of the items used in this salvation instruments are newly constructed for the purpose of this study. Some items, however, are modified versions taken from instruments in earlier studies. The items on the dimension of transcendence are modified versions of the scales of Jeurissen (1993). We differentiate some of the items in Jeurissen's instrument by separating those which signify immanent transcendence qualities and those with temporal indicators. We rework these items and create our distinct instruments for both dimension of transcendence and the temporal dimension. The measuring instruments for the scope of salvation and the realms of salvation are both developed by the author for the purpose of this research. These items have been tried out among church members before their final inclusion in the complete questionnaire.

For reasons of adequate data reduction, we conducted various factor analyses. We made a separate factor analysis of the items on each topic of salvation. Items on the dimension of transcendence were first subjected to a free factor solution analysis (mineigen=1). But this resulted into a non-interpretable outcome. So we conducted a factor analysis with a forced three factor solution. This resulted into three soteriological models as conceived in the theoretical part of this chapter, namely: absolute transcendent, immanent-transcendent, and absolute immanent. The explained variance of this three factor solution analysis is 71% (see: Appendix 5, Table 1a). Next, because a free factor solution analysis on the scores on the temporal dimension did not result into adequately interpretable factors, they were also subjected to a forced three factor solution. The three factors are: past-oriented, present-oriented, and future-oriented salvation attitudes. They explained 58% of the variance (see: Appendix 5, Table 1b). Then, we also subjected the scores on the scope of salvation to a free-factor solution (mineigen = 1). The result was a three-factorial solution, which correspond to the three concepts in the theoretical domain, namely: exclusivism, inclusivism, and pluralism. The explained variance of these factors is 66% (see: Appendix 5, Table 1c). Finally, the scores on the realms of salvation were also put into a free-factor solution (mineigen = 1). The result of the analysis showed that the distinction we made earlier between 'salvation from' and 'salvation for' in the theoretical section for the realms of salvation did not return in the empirical output. The items in 'salvation from' and 'salvation for' were combined to form one factor in every realm of salvation. So what resulted was one factor to represent every realm of salvation. Moreover, the items of the interpersonal and structural salvation were combined into one factor which we now call 'social' salvation. This free-factor solution resulted into four factors, which are: bodily salvation, personal salvation, social salvation, and ecological salvation. The factors yielded a 68% explained variance (see: Appendix 5, Table 1d). The reliability analyses was also performed. All of them satisfied the criterion alpha $\geq$ .60 or r $\geq$ 60, with the exception of past-oriented salvation (r = .56), inclusivistic salvation (r = .44), and pluralistic salvation (alpha = .56). On the basis

Table 5.1. Images of Salvation from an Empirical Perspective

Empirical Model		Mean	Standard Deviation	Pearson Correlation (r)	Reliability of Scales (Cronbach's Alpha)	Valid Cases
I.	Absolute transcendence (Theoretical Model 1)	3.7	1.10	.79		419
II.	Immanent transcendence (Theoretical Model 2)	3.6	.97		.89	418
III.	Absolute Immanence (Theoretical Model 3)	3.6	.83		.78	416
IV.	Past-Oriented (Theoretical Model 4)	2.9	1.05	.56		408
V.	Present-oriented (Theoretical Model 5)	3.2	.82		.80	406
VI.	Future-oriented (Theoretical Model 6)	3.0	.82		.64	407
VII.	Exclusivism (Theoretical Model 7)	2.1	.95		.89	425
VIII.	Inclusivism (Theoretical Model 8)	3.5	.87	.44		424
IX.	Pluralism (Theoretical Model 9)	3.0	.89		.56	416
X.	Bodily (Theoretical Models 10, 15)	3.5	.98		.95	422
XI.	Personal (Theoretical Models 11, 16)	3.4	.80		.84	417
XII.	Social (Theoretical Models 12, 13, 17, 18)	3.9	.76		.94	424
XIII.	Ecological (Theoretical Models 14, 19)	4.0	.86		.94	425

of the outcome of these four factor analyses, we constructed 13 five point scales. A summary of the empirical findings of the images of salvation is presented on Table 5.1. above.

From Table 5.1., our respondents demonstrate varied responses to each type of salvation models. We can gather the following general observations. In terms of the transcendent dimension (I, II, III), the respondents show agreement to all three models. With regards the temporal dimension (IV, V, VI), the scores indicate that the respondents have an ambivalent feeling concerning all the temporal dimensions of salvation. The respondents are rather negatively ambivalent about past-oriented salvation, purely ambivalent about future-oriented salvation, but positively ambivalent about present-oriented salvation. What is also notable on the scores on the scope of salvation (VII, VIII,

XI) is that our respondents clearly reject exclusivistic image of salvation. They are ambivalent about pluralism, but agree with inclusivism. Our respondents agree with all four models in the realms of salvation (X, XI, XII, XIII).

5.3. Social location of the attitudes towards salvation

In regard to the social location of these soteriological attitudes, we examine whether the demographic characteristics, social characteristics, and the religious characteristics are associated or correlated with the soteriological attitudes of our respondents. We conducted an analysis of variance (*eta*) and correlation analysis (*rho*) to our data. The table below (Table 5.2.) gives an account of the result of our analysis.

If we examine carefully the table above, we notice that two demographic characteristics manifest significant association to several salvation images, namely: age and education. The oldest age group scores statistically higher than the youngest age group on the following salvation attitudes: absolute transcendence, immanent transcendence, exclusivistic, inclusivistic, bodily, personal, social, and ecological salvation (see: Appendix 5, Table 3). In terms of education, the respondents with the lower levels of education (primary and/or lower secondary education) score higher than those with higher level (higher secondary education and/or tertirary education) on absolute transcendence, immanent-transcendence, absolute immanence, past-oriented, future-oriented, exclusivistic, inclusivistic, bodily, social and ecological salvation attitudes. The country of origin has also some association to a number of salvation attitudes. The non-Dutch respondents score higher than the Dutch respondents on absolute transcendence, absolute immanence, past-oriented, future-oriented, and exclusivistic salvation attitudes. In terms of social characteristics, conformism and anomie are significantly correlated to all of the salvation images. Localistic authoritarianism is correlated to all of the salvation images except for the present-oriented salvation image. Subjectively-perceived threat is significantly correlated to absolute immanence, past-, present-, future-oriented salvation, exclusivism, inclusivism, bodily, personal, and ecological salvation. The religious characteristics, which involve church involvement and religious salience, also play a very significant role in relation to a number of soteriological attitudes. Active members score higher than the inactive members on their attitudes towards absolute

Table 5.2. Social location of the attitudes toward Salvation *(eta & rho)*

	ab-trans	imm-trans	ab-imm	past	pres	fut	exclu	inclu	plur	bodily	personal	social	ecol
DEMOGRAPHIC CHARACTERISTICS													
Age *(eta)*	.26**	.28**	—	—	—	—	.21**	.18**	—	.17**	.12*	.23**	.22**
Gender *(eta)*	—	—	—	—	—	—	.10*	—	—	—	—	—	—
Education *(eta)*	.23**	.26**	.18*	.34**	.15*	.27**	.19**	.19**	.15*	.20**	—	.15*	.19**
Country of origin *(eta)*	.10*	—	.11*	.16**	—	.12*	.19**	—	—	—	—	—	—
SOCIAL CHARACTERISTICS													
Localistic authoritarianism *(rho)*	.22**	.28**	.25**	.31**	—	.38**	.31**	.28**	.12*	.39**	.32**	.33**	.33**
Subjectively-perceived threat *(rho)*	—	—	.13**	.18**	-.18**	.29**	.25**	.11*	—	.30**	.17**	—	.15**
Conformism *(rho)*	.26**	.26**	.20**	.29**	.13**	.31**	.28**	.26**	.11*	.20**	.19**	.22**	.21**
Anomie *(rho)*	.17**	.22**	.18**	.22**	-.11*	.36**	.21**	.15**	.12*	.30**	.19**	.23**	.26**
RELIGIOUS CHARACTERISTICS													
Church Involvement *(eta)*	.43**	.43**	—	.12*	.22**	.15**	.18**	.24**	—	—	—	.17**	.13**
Religious Salience *(rho)*	.49**	.48**	—	.31**	.33**	—	.30**	.33**	—	—	—	—	.15**

** $p < .01$; * $p < .05$ (2-tailed)

transcendence, immanent transcendence, past-, present-, future-oriented, exclusivism, inclusivism, social, and ecological salvation attitudes. Religious salience is significantly correlated to absolute transcendence, immanent transcendence, past-oriented, present-oriented, exclusivistic, inclusivistic, and ecological salvation. It is also noteworthy to mention that both church involvement and religious salience have no correlation or association with salvation attitudes such as absolute immanence, pluralistic, bodily, and personal salvation.

Summary

In this chapter, we studied the attitudes of our respondents toward salvation. We tried to answer the question that we set in this chapter: what are the attitudes of church members towards salvation, and what is the social location of these attitudes? In the theoretical part, we said that we aim to capture the soteriological attitudes by using a broad and comprehensive framework. Thus, we used the three dimensions of transcendence, temporal, and space dimensions, in which the latter is sub-divided into the scope of salvation and the realms of salvation. The dimension of transcendence includes absolute transcendent, immanent-transcendent, and absolute immanent images of salvation. The temporal dimension consists of the past-, present-, and future-oriented salvation images. The space dimension is represented by two categories, namely: the scope of salvation and the realms of salvation. The scope of salvation is comprised of exclusivism, inclusivism, and pluralism. The realms of salvation include bodily, personal, interpersonal, structural, and ecological. In each of these realms of salvation, we also made a distinction between 'salvation from' and 'salvation for'. In total, we were able to gather nineteen images of salvation in the theoretical part. We presume that these soteriological images of salvation could capture the attitudes of our respondents towards salvation in the empirical part. Results of the empirical investigation showed that several of these salvation images in the theoretical part of this chapter have been corroborated, with a few exceptions. The distinction between 'salvation from' and 'salvation for' has vanished in the empirical part as a result of factor analysis. The interpersonal and structural images of salvation have been combined to form one attitude which is called 'social' salvation. We have identified several striking observations regarding the soteriological attitudes of our respondents. Our research population which is comprised of Catholic Church members agrees on all the three scales in the transcendent dimension, but has differential attitudes regarding the temporal dimension, namely: past-oriented, present-oriented, and future-oriented salvation. Our respondents also clearly reject exclusivism. They are ambivalent about pluralism, but agree on inclusivism. They also accept all four aspects in the realms of salvation. We also analyzed the social location of these soteriological attitudes. Age, education, localistic authoritarianism, subjectively-perceived threat, conformism, anomie, church involvement, and religious salience, appear to be the recurring population characteristics that play significant role in the soteriological religious attitudes of our respondents.

CHAPTER SIX

ATTITUDES TOWARD THE CHURCH

In the New Testament, some of Jesus' fervent and most commanding statements are related to the inclusion of all peoples and providing a place to those excluded or marginalized by others in society. Inspired by the teachings of Jesus, the community of believers aspires to emulate these values that were preached and carried out in action by their master. In the course of history, this community of believers has rethought and reshaped her self-understanding, her organization, and her tasks in the world, in view of proclaiming the message of Jesus through the changing situations of the times. Diverse images of the church cropped up, images that relate to her identity, mission, structure, and tasks. Church members commit themselves to this church image that carry certain values and goals which may have subsequent effects on church members toward their engagement or disengagement in society, most specifically their attitudes towards minorities in their society. In this chapter, we want to find out the attitudes of church members towards the church. We want to answer the question: what are the attitudes of church members towards the church, and what is the social location of these attitudes? In what follows, we shall first take a look at some theoretical framework that captures these images in section 6.1. Then in section 6.2, we shall present the empirical findings of the attitude towards the church. In the last section, section 6.3, we shall look into the social location of these ecclesiastic attitudes.

6.1. *Images of the church from a theoretical perspective*

In what follows, we shall consider theoretically the diverse attitudes of our respondents toward the church by looking at their attitudes toward the mission of the church (6.1.1.), church structures (6.1.2.), and the tasks of the church (6.1.3.).

6.1.1. *Mission of the church*

The mission of the church refers to the relation of the church to the world in terms of fulfilling her task of proclaiming the message of

Jesus and realizing the plan of God for the world. But before we are going to speak about the mission of the church, we will first discuss the identity of the church.

Identity of the Church

The identity of the church refers to the reflection on the nature of the church, her distinct character internal to her self-understanding. According to Küng (1967:236–259), one can draw two strands of interpretations in the New Testament which can roughly portray the identity of the church, namely: the 'body of Christ' model and the 'Christ as head' model.

The first strand of interpretation is based on Rm. 12:4–5 and 1Cor. 12:12–27, which underscores the mutual relations in the church community based on baptism and eucharist. This is called the 'body of Christ' model. The symbolism of the 'body' is used to portray the church as an organ with a head and members. Each member has his or her specific function within the church as a whole, and they are kept in harmonious unity by the church hierarchy (Koffeman 1986). This 'body of Christ' model has been reflected and re-interpreted in later church documents. For instance, in *Lumen Gentium*, the idea of the church as a 'people of God' has been highlighted. The church is conceived as the new people of God, on pilgrimage in history, heading towards the kingdom. The church as a 'people of God' is conceived as a participatory community, a fellowship of life, charity and truth, sent into the world as a light, and as a sign of salvation. Another image that reflects the orientation of the 'body of Christ' interpretation is the notion of the church as 'communion'. This idea of the church suggests that the church is a community that stems from and is aimed at Jesus himself rather than in the community that forms itself. Participation in Christ is the foundation and the aim of communality and connectedness in the church. The church as *communio* implies that pluralism in the church can be accepted and recognized. It does not shy away from diversity but rather rejoices at its presence in mutual exchange and dialogue. It strives for consensus in order to cultivate harmony in the community. Another image that reflects the 'body of Christ' orientation is the idea of the church as a mystery. Pope Paul VI, in his opening address to the second session of the Second Vatican council said: "The church is mystery. It is a reality imbued with the hidden presence of God. It lies therefore within the very nature of the

Church to be always open to new and even greater exploration" (Pope Paul VI 1964:15). According to this understanding, one cannot totally define the church according to its organization nor to its authority. One can only talk of the church in symbols and images since one cannot fully exhaust this reality. It is a mystery because it is understood as part of God's gracious involvement in the history of human beings, an involvement which was fully manifested in Christ.

The second strand of interpretation is called 'Christ as head' model. It is based on Eph. 1:22–23; 4:15–16; 5:23; & Col. 1:18; 2:19, and lays emphasis on the idea of Jesus as the head of the body. Three significant ideas emerge as a consequence of this interpretation (Bromiley 1995:531). The first idea puts emphasis on the spiritual aspects of Christ as head. It holds that Christ as head is the source and the sustenance of the body. Christ being the head has been given the church as His body (Eph. 1:22ff), and that He has all the spiritual gifts at His disposal (Eph. 5:23; Col 1:18; 2:19). The second idea emphasizes His rule over all rule and authority and power and dominion. The headship of Christ is portrayed in Eph. 5:21–22, which exalts the Lordship of the risen Christ who is far above all rule and authority and power and dominion over the whole world in this age and the age to come. 'Christ as head' underscores the primacy of Christ as the Head of creation and the Church which requires the conformity of the members with the Head. The third idea comes as a consequence of the second, claiming that Christ as the Lord of lords, implies that His rule comes in and through His presence in the world through His body, the church. Just as Christ manifests His works in the world, so does He work through the church. Just as Jesus gave His body for the world, so does the body (the church) continue His redemptive works in the world. These ideas underlying the 'Christ as head' interpretation are mirrored in the understanding of the church as hierarchy and as perfect society. Dulles (1987:38) points to the hierarchical orientation in Vatican I (1869–1870) when it declares that the Church of Christ is not a community of equals where all the faithful have the same rights. It is a society of unequals in that some is given to sanctify, teach, and govern, and to others not. Moreover, the church according to Vatican I has all the marks of a perfect society (*societas perfecta*). As a perfect society, the church is distinct from all human societies and has her own nature and characteristics. Hence, the church is not part nor member of any other society. Christ himself determined the existence and the constitution of the church before He left this world.

The period between the French Revolution and before Vatican II saw the intensification of the 'Christ as head' conception of the church.

These two interpretations, the 'body of Christ' and 'Christ as the head' models spawned debates and disagreements in the church. For instance in *Mystici Corporis* (1943), both symbols have been employed to speak exclusively about the Roman Catholic Church. The church as body has been identified with the Roman Catholic Church, including its juridical order (head) and sacramental structure (baptism, Eucharist, and priesthood). Hence, the church is called the 'Mystical Body of Christ' (*Mystici Corporis*, no. 13).[1] Vatican II does not use the term *Corpus Christi Mysticum* in the Latin text, especially in *Lumen Gentium*, no. 7 where it explicitly discusses about the church as 'body of Christ', although in no. 8 as well as in no. 23, the term *mysticum Christi corpus* appears. It is apparent that in *Lumen Gentium*, these two orientations have both been employed.

At the end of the first session of the Second Vatican Council, Cardinal Suenens invited the assembly to look beyond the church's own sense of identity and consciousness, but to give attention to the church's relationship to the contemporary world. His intervention gave birth to a new document called *Gaudium et Spes*. This document brings out "the perspective of an open, dynamic servant church within the one history of humankind, a church committed to the mission for the total well-being of all peoples" (Wostyn 1990:57–58). In *Gaudium et Spes*, no. 40, it states: "through her individual members and her whole community, the Church believes she can contribute greatly toward making the human family and its history more human". The church, according to this document has a mission to the world by fulfilling the command of Jesus to build the Kingdom of God in our midst.

Mission of the church

The mission of the church indicates the context in which the identity of the church has to be realized. It pertains to how the church attunes herself with the societal context either through cultural adaptation or cultural closedness. It deals with the question whether the church has to keep in touch with its cultural environment and engage in fruitful dialogue with what happens in it, or whether it should retreat from

---

[1] It should be noted however that this encyclical tries to harmonize the concept of the church as *societas perfecta* with that of *mystical body of Christ* (Dulles 1974:48).

any critical communication with the emerging cultural developments and simply move on with its own way. In other words, the key question when talking about the mission of the church is: *ecclesia: pro sua vita aut pro mundi vita*? This is the same question asked by Stephen Cardinal Kim during the *Synod on Evangelization in the Modern World* (1974) in which he underscored that the church does not live for herself alone, but for the life of the world. Let us examine two contrasting attitudes toward the mission of the church, namely: 'cultural adaptation' versus 'cultural closedness'.

Cultural adaptation versus cultural closedness

One of the most important features of the *aggiornamento* in the Second Vatican Council is its attitude of openness to cultural realities. In several documents of Vatican II and post-conciliar documents, the church recognizes explicitly the presence of God in cultures. It acknowledges the spiritual qualities and gifts that are embedded in every people of every age. It clearly connects the revelation of God in cultures with the incarnation of the redeemer. It says in *Gaudium et Spes*, no. 58: "For God, revealing Himself to His people to the extent of a full manifestation of Himself in His Incarnate Son, has spoken according to the culture proper to different ages." In this perspective, Christians are taught that respect for culture is imperative for the reason that God himself is the reality that can be disclosed in every culture. Vatican II proclaims that the Church has always the duty of scrutinizing the signs of the times and of interpreting them in the light of the gospel. Thus, in language intelligible to each generation, she can respond to the perennial questions which men/women ask about this present life and the life to come, and about the relationship of the one to the other. *Ad Gentes* (no. 10) states: "in order to be able to offer to all men the mystery of salvation and the life brought by God, the church must become part of [Lat.: *sese inserere debet*] all these groups for the same motive which led Christ to bind Himself, in virtue of His Incarnation, to the definite social and cultural conditions of those human beings among whom He dwelt." In this section, we shall refer to the attitude of openness of the Christian faith to dialogue with culture, particularly to the Dutch modern culture, as cultural adaptation.

Some terms of varying degrees of appropriateness, like translation, adaptation, localization, accommodation, incarnation, acculturation, contextualization, indigenization, inculturation, interculturation, etcetera., have been employed to describe the process of introducing the Christian faith into a local culture and the process by which one may discern the theological significance of this encounter. Despite these terminological profusion (or confusion?) and divergent understanding in contemporary theologies regarding the dialogue between the gospel and culture, some points of agreement, although not a general consensus, may be posited: (1) it is an integral and constitutive dimension of the church's evangelizing mission; (2) it is a double process comprising (a) insertion of the gospel into a particular culture, and (b) introduction of the culture into the gospel; (3) the result is both the transformation of the culture from within the gospel and the enrichment of the gospel by the culture with its new ways of understanding and living it; (4) the gospel, though not to be identified with any culture, is never independent of culture. Consequently, inculturation is necessarily 'interculturation' and must abide by the laws and dynamics of intercultural dialogue; (5) Since religion — a system of beliefs, values and practices — is a constitutive dimension of culture, inculturation is of necessity an interreligious dialogue; (6) it must also go hand in hand with liberation; (7) as a religious process, it is governed by the mysteries of the incarnation, death, resurrection of Jesus, and the descent and active presence of the Holy Spirit; (8) its principal agent is the local church, not the experts and the central authorities; (9) it is comprehensive in scope: it must be carried out in all areas of church life; (10) it must bring about diversity in unity and unity in diversity; (11) it must be guided by a robust theology of the local church which involves contextuality (i.e. faith is reflected in diverse ways in the gospel story and is lived out in various context) and catholicity (i.e. the quality by which the church expresses the fullness, the integrity, and the totality of life in Christ') (Phan 2003:5–10).

Throughout Christian history, it has been noted that Christians have responded to society and culture in different ways. Niebuhr's classic work, *Christ and Culture* (1956), presented five models to describe the interaction between Christians and culture in the past and in the present. He speaks of 'Christ against culture', 'Christ of culture', 'Christ above culture', 'Christ and culture in Paradox', and 'Christ the transformer of culture'. Gallagher (1998:117–124), however, simplifies these five models into three main responses of the church towards culture, namely: tense hostility, innocent acceptance, and discernment and creation of culture. Let us shortly describe these three main responses. A 'tense hostile reaction' is an adverse response or a negative judgment towards contemporary society. This is similar to what Niebuhr describes as 'Christ against culture'. It views contemporary culture as 'simply sick'. According to this view, any attempt to view culture positively would lead only to false compromises. Therefore, Christians ought "to radically be suspicious of the deceptions entrenched in such value-shaping worlds as academic life, international politics, the economic system, or the entertainment industry... Believers have to protect themselves from cultural pollution by maintaining strong church loyalty as a defense against these invading worlds of superficiality" (Gallagher 1998:117). The trouble with this armour-plated reaction is a question of 'roots' and 'fruits'. If the roots lack genuine listening or love for the situation of people, the fruits will be unproductive, and religion can even come to sound like fanaticism (Gallagher 1998:118). The second response is called 'innocent acceptance of culture'. It is a naïve acceptance of a certain culture that is devoid of critical discernment of its dangers or its down side. This tendency can be distinguished into three forms: (1) passive resignation (discarding any attempt to influence the culture or to create alternatives); (2) thoughtless secularization (unreflected 'buying into' the dominant culture; and (3) indiscriminate embracing of pluralism (relinquishes any possibility of evaluating cultures since one culture is as good as the next; it tends towards relativism). The last reaction involves the 'discernment and creation of culture'. It is a critical response marked by listening and identifying seeds of the gospel in each and every cultural encounter. This type of reaction encourages an appreciative awareness in examining the actual data of culture. This of course, does not discount the fact that there are negative aspects of culture as well. But as De Mesa (1987:29) argues, "there has been an overemphasis on the critical elements in theological reflection to the extent that the real wisdom and genius of the culture is not given space to surface. The habit of being critical in theology has led largely to the neglect of the respectful and appreciative modes of thought which are just as valid and legitimate as the critical one." This type of reaction recognizes the intrinsic goodness of cultural values and keenness in discovering the positive, life-giving aspects of a culture. As the letter to the Philippians (4:8) says: "Whatever is true, whatever is honourable, what is just, whatever is pure, whatever is lovely, whatever is gracious, if there is any excellence, if there is anything worthy of praise, think about these things". This appreciative awareness involves also some process of 'unlearning' which implies that one must be able to 'opt out' of the irrelevant models and to let go of the outdated and constraining ways of thinking, speaking and acting in relation to the evangelizing mission of the church. Furthermore, it also involves promoting alternative cultures to the dominant cultures of the times. Alternative culture aims at bringing about a radical change in people's relationships so as to provide conditions where God will be at home among His people. These relationships among peoples and with God are founded on truth animated by compassion and love, and lived according to justice (Labayen 1995:58–59).

Some members, however, are not comfortable and happy with 'change'. Therefore, they assume a 'closed-minded' attitude in relation to the novelties that come in the church and the society. They prefer to cling to what is traditional, to what they are 'used to', because it is there where they can feel secure and certain. Some psychologists try to associate a culturally exclusive attitude to a 'closed-minded' personality structure (Fortmann 1974). Persons with a closed-minded personality structure are unable to absorb new information on change. For them, authority is like a security blanket that renders them security, comfort, and certainty; it dispels their anxiety. Hence, psychologists say that persons who are closed-minded have an authoritarian personality structure, i.e. someone is inwardly un-free over against external authority. In contrast, there is also an open, non-authoritarian personality structure. This type of personality accepts a space for personal freedom of thought and action. Applying this to the church, it may refer to the faithful who do not just accept church statements blindly but either accept or criticize them after independent consideration. An 'open church' is more favourable than the 'closed' church in that, from a sociological perspective, it is attuned with the striving towards individual responsibility in society. Moreover, in modern society, there is also an increasing emphasis on individual freedom and autonomy in making moral decisions (Jeurissen 1993:144). However, a culturally-open church may also take a critical position regarding excessive individualization in society because it puts the community-relatedness of the human being at risk.

A culturally adapted church community is openly engaged in the society, no matter how complex this society is. The complexity of each situation always allows an occasion to learn. Therefore, openness disposes the community to assimilate new things and profit from it. A culturally open church chooses to negotiate, to compromise, to metamorphose internally, and contribute in transforming society. An open church is like an 'adhocracy', one that is constantly making occasional (ad hoc) changes, reforms and reconfigurations because of the ever changing environments. It is a church that is in constant dialogue with the world, hence it is able to adapt to every situation or context in a critical manner in relation to its living tradition. Hence, here is a genuine sense of the church, as in the Latin expression *sentire cum ecclesia* (to think and feel with the living church). It implies that the church is able to 'touch ground' and adapt to what is going on in the living community. A culturally closed church, on the other hand, perceives the church as a pure and uncontaminated community whose truths are valid at all times and at all places. This culturally closed church tends to cut off from emerging ideas and holds fast to old thoughts or paradigms. It chooses to remain insular against change and 'outsiders'.

6.1.2. Structure of the church

After having discussed the identity and mission of the church, we shall now look into the structure of the church. In what follows, we shall distinguish between three types of church structures, namely: hierarchical (6.1.2.1.), centralized (6.1.2.2.), and democratic structures (6.1.2.3.).

6.1.2.1. Hierarchical church

A hierarchical church model can be illustrated by a pyramidal structure which consists of several strata, namely: God, Christ, the Pope, the bishops, priests and deacons; below are the 'non-ordained' religious, and then the 'laity': first the men, and lastly the women and children (Schillebeeckx 1990). In this hierarchical form of polity, a pre-eminent position is rendered to the ordained. Decisions are made from the top of the hierarchy and trickle down to the passive believers who are expected to follow these decisions with unquestioning obedience. In this set-up, women are perceived only as objects of the ministry of a hierarchical and male dominated church structure. It brings forward the idea that the rule of Christ over the entire world is put in the hands of the church hierarchy.

While the New Testament does not give any indication that the historical Jesus deliberately set up any organization like the church, particularly that of a hierarchical structure of the church, proponents of this model however, argue that a hierarchical structure has an origin that is founded by Jesus himself. Biblical texts like Mk 3:13–16, Mt 10:1–4, Lk 6:13–16 are often cited to justify this structure. Matthew

18:18 is also cited to legitimize the church's power to 'bind' and to 'forgive'. They claim that Jesus appointed a small group of twelve to a special position to lead his flock. This group has also been bestowed the power to preside over the Eucharist by virtue of their special status. Other legitimations of this model can be pointed out. One for instance is the emphasis given on the role of the Spirit that is linked with the ministerial succession exclusively for the hierarchy. Another is the significance set on papal infallibility. It insists that the pope is the representative of Christ in this world. As a person, the pope is said to be fallible, but when he speaks *ex cathedra*, his decrees are binding and error free. Schillebeeckx points out the consequences of this development in the organizational structure of the church. He states: "As a consequence of this mysticism of infallibility, a personality cult of the pope overlooks the fact that the Peter or the Petrine function of providing unity or communication involves only one office in the church, and is thus one ministerial service among many other ministries in the church. Moreover, this exaltation of the pope robs all other institutional authorities in the church, both the bishops and the community of faith, of their original Christian authority and authenticity" (Schillebeeckx 1990:199).

Traces of the hierarchical model can still be found in chapter III of *Lumen Gentium*. In the title of chapter III, it is said that the church has a hierarchical structure. In number 20, it is stated that the 'Roman Pontiff has full, supreme, and universal power' (no. 22). To this it can be added that the hierarchical structure is essentially based on divine law (Corecco 1983:19–20).[2] This interpretation goes to the extent of being enshrined into the 1983 Canon Law (Canon 330; see: Coriden et al. 1985) despite its dearth of biblical foundation and patristic backing (Van der Ven, et al. 2004).[3]

However, Chapter III of *Lumen Gentium* mitigates the conferral of absolute power to the supreme pontiff and to the hierarchy in general by introducing new terms such as: local churches, collegiality, co-responsibility, authority as service, etcetera. Vatican II remains in

---

[2] This doctrine only emerged in the juridical thought of church through the influence of Greek thought on the philosophy of law in the west and not in the New Testament. In this sense, theologians argue that this doctrine of the *ius divinum* must be construed in a dynamic way rather than in a static one (Corecco 1983:13).

[3] Canon 330 reads: "Just as, by the decree of the Lord, Saint Peter and the rest of the Apostles form one College, so for a like reason the Roman Pontiff, the successor of Peter, and the Bishops, the successors of the Apostles, are united together in one."

the same perspective as Vatican I by affirming the supreme authority of the pope but extend the supreme authority to the college of bishops (Wostyn 1990:46). The council redefines the universal scope of the Roman Pontiff in *Lumen Gentium*, no. 27 by clarifying that "the supreme and universal power of the Roman Pontiff does not mean that the bishops are to be regarded as vicars of the Roman Pontiff but as vicars or ambassadors of Christ, for they exercise an authority which is proper to them, and are quite correctly called prelates, heads of the people whom they govern. Their power, therefore, is not destroyed by the supreme and universal power."

In this study, we want to know the extent to which our respondents accept the hierarchical structure of the church.

6.1.2.2. *Centralized church*

In the Catholic Church, centralization of power depends on which level one looks at its organization, either on the macro, the meso, and the micro level of the ecclesial organization. Moreover, on each of these levels, one can also distinguish between a centralized-hierarchical structure from a decentralized-hierarchical structure.

On the macro-level, a centralized-hierarchical structure regards the pope as having a 'full, supreme, and universal power' (*Lumen Gentium*, no. 22). It asserts the position of 'papal primacy' which gives the pope authority, as successor of Peter, over the whole Catholic Church. It is characterized by an asymmetrical and non-reciprocal relationship with other members of the church. This tendency in the Catholic Church is manifested in the 1983 Code of Canon Law which states that: "there is neither appeal nor recourse against a decision or decree of the Roman Pontiff" (Canon 333, 3). In this concept, the pope is regarded not only as an ultimate authority but as the only authority. This treats the Church as a monolith where the whole church is dealt with like a single diocese and the pope is the 'superpower' or the 'super-bishop'. On this same level, however, a decentralized-hierarchical structure is characterized by episcopal collegiality and communion. Principles like collegiality, subsidiarity, autonomy of local churches, reception, ecclesiology of communion, may characterize this decentralized-hierarchical structure. Episcopal conferences on the national and regional levels, Synodal assemblies, etcetera, have acquired influence and relative autonomy from Rome after Vatican II (cf. Reese 1989; Rausch 2005). In this case, the pre-Vatican II idea of hierarchy which evolved into autocracy (power is held by a single person) or theocracy (religious legitimation of the power of the monarch/hierarch as *ex iure divino*), have further developed into polycracy (power in the hands of the elite). Vatican II stressed the principle of collegiality in line with its structural reforms. The principle of collegiality means that local churches share responsibility for the whole church; they are co-responsible for and working for, the good of the church, the whole people of God (cf. *Lumen Gentium*, no. 22–23). It means that power and authority belong within the communion of a collegial church (Gleeson 2003). It stressed the idea that authority lies with the college of bishops in union with its head who is the pope. The re-introduction of the notion of episcopal collegiality is based on the idea that the hierarchical church organization is essentially centered on the office of the bishop.

On the meso-level, that is, on the level of the local church or the diocese, a centralized-hierarchical structure may take the form of 'episcopocentrism'. This means that power in the local church is centered on the bishop. In this case, a pre-eminent position is placed on the bishop who acts as a supreme head in the diocese. According to Volf (1998), this understanding is related to the notion of the 'head-members' legitimation where the church needs the bishop in order itself to be concretely capable of acting as a subject. "The bishop acts as *persona Christi* and simultaneously in *persona ecclesiae*. These two are intimately connected as are the head and body in the one organism of Christ which is essential for the church" (Volf 1998:223). This episcopocentric attitude can be reinforced when the bishop invokes his exclusive 'power', according to the Council of Trent, to rule (*potestas juridictionis or potestas regiminis*), to consecrate (*potestas ordinis or potestas ministerii*), and to teach (*potestas magisterii*). On the meso level, the process of decentralization may also take place. In dioceses they form presbyteral councils, diocesan pastoral assemblies, or diocesan pastoral councils, where deliberative consultations regarding planning and decisions regarding the administration of the church on the local level takes place (Hinze 2006).

On the micro-level, centralization may take the form of clericalism. Clericalism is considered to be "a conscious or unconscious concern to promote the particular interests of the clergy and to protect the privileges and power that has traditionally been conceded to those in the clerical state" (Conference of Major Religious Superiors of Men 1983:2; cf. Cozzens 2004:118). Clericalism, as it is said, is manifested by a type of church leadership that is authoritarian and a rigidly hierarchical worldview. It is an attitude where a cleric sees himself as belonging to an 'exclusive, all male, hierarchical, and celibate club', which renders him as part of a system of privilege, esteem and status, especially in traditional societies where the church institution plays an all-encompassing role in society (cf. Frawley-O'Dea 2007). Clericalism believes that the proper role of the laity is to be a docile receiver of grace which can be disposed of or mediated only through the ordained ministers. Aside from clericalism, some forms of centralism may also characterize a centralized structure in the micro-level. It can, for instance, be manifested through the concentration of power in the center of the parish through the parish centered mandated organizations and programs. Decentralization may take the form of small community-based groups or Basic Ecclesial Communities, advocacy groups, charismatic communities, ecclesiastical programs, etcetera. The empowerment of the laity is also a principle that facilitates the decentralization in the micro level. It is important to allow ordinary members to take active and independent participation in the life and work of the church. Theologically speaking, the empowerment and the active and responsible participation of the laity in the life of the church are essentially linked with the identity of the church as people of God.

In this study, we want to know to what extent our respondents agree or disagree about the centralized structure of the church.

6.1.2.3. *Democratic church*

Pesch (1971) articulates the strong urge or impulse among church members to fashion a democratic structure within the church in consonance with the development of democratic structures in society. Greinacher (1971:89) could agree no less with Pesch saying that "if the church wants to be really close to men and women in all different spheres of our highly complicated society, then the forms of the individual church communities in which the church as a whole is realized must above all be flexible, imaginative and adaptable." Schneider (1971:12–47) likewise positively commends the democratic political programme, especially its orientation towards full human realization in freedom and solidarity to be compatible with the Christian ideals. He says that "this basic orientation is rooted in principles which, to say the least are capable of being made a manifestation of the Christian understanding of God, of the world, and of Christianity itself, and therein find a justification and fulfillment which can surely never be surpassed" (Schneider 1971:44). However, we can also ask: if the church seeks to adapt to the democratic principles as forming the basis of modern society, what could be the implications of this for the church in its internal structure? There are two implications. First is the communication of these same principles outwardly, meaning, adherence to the principles of democracy implies prophetically denouncing 'undemocratic' values and systems outside its fold. Second is the recognition of structural reforms inside its organization.

Some authors propose some characteristics that may make up a democratic church: the collegial responsibility of all members of the community in contrast to what is called 'client church' (a client mentality is closely connected with the patriarchal and feudal structures of the church where the participation of the members are minimal). In a democratic structure, all members participate in planning, decision-making and execution of tasks. In this structure, the opinions and perceptions of the faithful are being heard. In theological terms we could say that the *sensus fidelium* has to be taken seriously (Van der Ven & Sonnberger 1985:24.). This structure may also involve the participation of laity and women in the key functions and ministries in the church.

Now the question is: is there any theological legitimation to justify a democratic model of the church? Pesch (1971) argues that although it is difficult to find justification from the New Testament since most of the forms of rule or power therein showed no equivalence with any form of rule or power of the world, one may however point to some foundations of a democratic form of life in the New Testament. He mentions the following aspects from the New Testament that can support some democratic principles: the Christian principle of freedom, the principle of equality, Christian fraternity, service (*diakonia*), collegial 'offices' (based on the principle that service performed in order to build up the Christian community is always official service), and an authority based on love and care in the service of the church. Volf (1998) also points to Phil 1:1 and Thes 5:12 to speak of the exercise of collegiality which is evident in the early church. Various gifts, services and activities are shared by all Christians. Gifts are distributed to all for the benefit of all. Ecclesial persons are interdependent and catholic, albeit autonomous subjects. Members serve one another with their specific gifts of the Spirit in imitation of the Lord and through the power of the Father. There are also some parallelism between gospel values and sociological and political categories that engenders a democratic form of life in society, for instance fraternity, partnership, solidarity, service, renunciation, trust, freedom, dialogue, tolerance, the common good, willingness to compromise, openness, etcetera. Pesch (1971:59) gives however a *proviso* saying that the law of life in the church based on the New Testament should both follow and differ from this secular model, and must be expressed in a contemporary and democratic form of life in the Christian community. This form of life must be able to make the additional freedom, equality, fraternity given to us by God in Jesus Christ visible in the church not only as a prophetic challenge but also as the city set on a hill (Mt. 5:14) or as the lamp on a stand (Mt. 5:15f) which gives light to the world and is above all attractive. In a way, he is saying that Christians must protect the 'eschatological reserve' in relation to any secular or any human-made institutions or structures. Some symbolisms like the church as 'people of God', the 'body of Christ' and the community of the Spirit could also legitimize the democratic principles in the church (Van der Ven 1993; 1996; 2004). Added to this are the possibilities of unearthing significant symbols that are yet existing implicitly in Christian faith and thinking. There is always a 'surplus of meaning' in reading and re-reading the pregnant tradition of Christianity vis-à-vis the ever changing context of the times.

We want to know how far our respondents accept the democratic contribution and involvement of believers in the church. We will, however, restrict our investigation of this broad concept of democracy, into lay people's leadership in liturgy.

6.1.3. *Tasks of the church*

The way the church perceives her identity or self-understanding has some repercussions as to how the church would implement or actualize her responsibility to the world. This responsibility or task of the church can be examined on three different levels, namely: the micro-level task of the church which involves the care for individual persons (6.1.3.1); the meso-level which consists of church praxis that are group-directed in nature (6.1.3.2); and the macro-level which is the task of the church that has a socio-political character (6.1.3.3).

6.1.3.1. *Micro-level: person-directed task of the church*
The primary task of the church on the micro-level is perceived as something that has to be directed to the individual person. This task is conceived as the way for the church to mediate the message of salvation

to each individual. The church views her task as providing services to individual persons in order to cater to their needs for emotional growth and development. They offer emotional help out of compassion and companionship for the weak.

On this micro-level, the church is challenged to address the increasingly individualistic trend in modern Dutch society, especially when the saliency of religion is on the decline (Dekker 1987). Research shows that for many people in secular countries like the Netherlands, religion plays a minimal or entirely insignificant factor in their personal lives. And for those who consider religion to be important, the significance they attach to it is either differential (i.e. role of religion only in private but not in public life) and/or partial (i.e. religion as one factor among other factors and does not play a dominant role among the other aspects of one's life). Van der Ven (1993:241–247) posits three diverse reactions of the church towards the process of individualization, namely: 'amodernization', 'modern adaptation', and 'critical-modern exchange'. The amodern reaction is demonstrated by an attitude of opposition to the process of individualization, and a tendency towards repristination (i.e. restoration of earlier norms) and rehabilitation. It dreams of a relationship and structure that is patterned after the ancient times, particularly in terms of the territorial border and jurisdiction, the central role of the pastor, and the all-embracing influence of the church in the society. This longing is understandable since the church as such is dependent on group and community formation. Without this community, the church has no existence. However, the attempt to restore the church to its glorious past seems to be unrealistic if the conditions and structure of the present society is not taken into consideration. This is particularly true if the features of the urban setting are not considered, like for instance, the intense division of labor, the division between classes and races or ethnic groupings, the radical functionalization, bureaucratization, segregation, and multiculturalization in the cities. These conditions are often ignored or unnoticed because they are beyond the reach and power of intervention of the church in its traditional setting. The second reaction may be called 'modern adaptation'. This reaction is a kind of an uncritical and 'resigned' attitude towards the inevitable process of individualization as society has become modernized. This is a reaction of some who claim that the church cannot do anything structural in urbanized society. It may help people cope in this society but it cannot do anything substantially by challenging its structure through its prophetic role. The role of the church then is limited to support, consolation, and encouragement. For this reason, the primary task of the church is to give religious guidance to individuals, to concentrate its efforts on the rites of passage, and to give consolation and comfort in times of suffering bereavement and funerals (Glock et al. 1965; Bellah et al. 1985). It is interesting how previous research show that most pastors (either Catholic, Netherlands Reformed church, or the Reformed Churches in the Netherlands) spend more time on comfort (i.e. liturgy, pastoral care, church and community development, and visits) and far less time on challenge like for instance, development, mission and diaconal work. It is also noted that most pastors desire to spend their time for liturgy and pastoral care (cf. Van der Ven & Biemans 1992). Hence, this goes to show that the prophetic and critical role of the pastor is relegated to lesser importance than their liturgical and pastoral care tasks. Finally, in the 'critical-modern' exchange approach, there are two approaches that are demonstrated. First, church people criticize the factors in society that lead to gradual isolation and alienation through the process of individualization. They view individualization as a limit and a chance, a risk and a challenge. Second, there are some church people who make alliances with other groups (religious or other non-religious movements) in order to liberate people. Some of these groups of church members try to expand and help develop the possibilities for community formation which the present society offers. They emphasize the formation processes of various groups.

From a theological perspective, one can also make a positive valuation of this so-called 'cult of the person' or 'cult of the individual', as Durkheim (1974) calls it, by bringing in the idea of the emancipation of the individual persons from the tyranny of fatalism, alienation caused by oppressive structures and ideologies, and the culture of silence. The assertion of being subject of one's history and being architect of one's destiny are thoughts that can be regarded as positive Christian ideals which are in tune with the Christian notion of 'human dignity' and 'being made in the image and likeness of God'. One may also bring in the idea of liberating the individual persons from their greed, selfishness, and one's violent nature which produce negative social consequences and subsequently destroy one's own dignity as persons and their relationships with others in society. Herein lies the challenge whereby the church could expand the horizon of the individual, whereby the church can realize her mission effectively and holistically. It is a great challenge and opportunity for the church to efficiently address her task on the level of the individual. However, she has to address and acknowledge the context to which this individual person is situated; without which, she can only regret that in the end, she would fail to realize her task in mediating salvation to the person.

6.1.3.2. *Meso-level: group-directed task of the church*

On the meso-level, the primary task of the church is focused essentially on group or community building. On this level the church functions mainly in doing what the church members regard as their principal tasks namely preaching, liturgy, catechesis, and other churchly activities. The primary attention of this group-directed task is aimed at works related to the institution and its members. It aims to keep the members active by initiating activities that can enhance group fellowship and vigorous participation of members. The importance given to a group-directed task of the church has some theological basis. According to this view, faith tends to form community. The community is the bearer of what you are as believer. The church teaches that faith is substantially communal, not only in its emergence, but in its very structure. This idea also views faith in relation to Jesus Christ who is a corporate personality. It maintains that if you believe, you enter into the corporate personality of new humankind (new Adam). Faith is a gift, it is a gift of the Thou; it is not personal but communal; faith tends to community (Volf 1998).

Sociologists usually employ the theories of Tönnies and Parsons to explicate the formation of the church as a community. Using Tönnies' (1987) distinction between 'community' (*gemeinschaft*) and 'society' (*gesellschaft*), the church is usually identified as a *gemeinschaft* which describes the relationships in the church as affective, spontaneous, expressive, and with genuine solidarity. Unlike in a *gesellschaft* where relationships are mechanical, rationality-based, calculating, and instrumental, relationship in a church community is characterized by an organic unity where people live together based on direct, personal relations and in mutual solidarity. There is also the presence of the 'will of common being'. One may discern a common pattern of values and religious convictions among members of the family and relatives, villages and towns. The pattern of values is viewed as uniform and non-pluriform; the community, as integrating and non-individualizing, as self-evident and non-reflective, as transcendent and non-immanent. This contrast between *gemeinschaft* and *gesellschaft* elicits certain nostalgia for the early community and a certain uncomfortable feeling about the present society. This theory of Tönnies which is used to describe the church as a community may be deemed inapplicable to the modern and urban setting of contemporary society (Van der Ven 1996:255). Parsons (1959) gives another theory about community. He says that all interactions between people, wherever and however it takes place, happen in physical space, a local context, and ecological environments. These interactions can be categorized into: residential (interaction in the family or in a geographically determined neighbourhood or district), professional (interaction related to job or profession), and jurisdictional (interaction that transpires in a legally determined unit where one belongs to, such as, municipality, province or state). According to Parsons, a community refers to this locality (e.g. a family community, a neighbourhood community, school community, hospital community, municipal community, urban community, national community, etcetera). One can also talk about a 'church community' based on this perspective. However, as Van der Ven (1996) points out, this term means no more than that interactions that take place in the physical space of the area that the church covers. Whereas Tönnies theory belongs to the past, Parsons' theory is simply empty. Van der Ven (1996:256–257) proposes a third view, which he calls the church community as network of groups. He states that the church community can be "described proceeding from an angle of the varying density and strength of networks of groups that find themselves in the area that the local church covers...Density has to do with the relationship between the factual and the possible relations between groups. Strength has to do with the multiplicity of these relations: the number of people that bring them about" (Van der Ven 1996:257). He cites as an example the liturgy in basic ecclesial communities. Liturgy can contain an intense community-forming experience which comes from the density and strength of the network of groups from which one participates in this liturgy. In this community-forming experience, there is a high multiplicity: a large number of plural, direct relations between a large number of people in the various groups in the basic community (Van der Ven 1996:260). If we understand the church community as a network of groups, this may broaden the normative understanding of a church community in terms of a 'parish community' in a geographical or jurisdictional sense. A church community as a network of groups may take the forms like a community of small communities in a rural setting, or a single urban parish, but could also be in the form of functional communities in the universities, family groups, or a Christian group consisting of an ethno-linguistic minority, etcetera. The task of building of church community can be more feasible and effective when it can explore possibilities of establishing communities through the network of groups, or forging alliances and linkages with variety of groups (Van der Ven 1996:254–256).

6.1.3.3. Macro-level: socio-political task of the church

The church has time and again affirmed her role in shaping the socio-political landscapes of society. Throughout history, the church's basic attitude towards society either tend towards interaction with society with a view of transforming it, or isolation from society and doing only what it regards as its task like mediating individual salvation, preaching and performing sacramental celebrations. The church however, especially after Vatican II, considers her societal role as her vocation and mission in keeping with the liberational message that is rooted in the words of Jesus himself in bringing about the reign-kingdom of God in our midst. This task is also perceived to be rooted in the 'sacramental nature' of the church. This social role is conceived as one aspect of its task to be present in the world as 'sacrament', as a visible token of God's salvation (Schillebeeckx 1990). The emancipating or liberating praxis of people are manifestations of God's salvation. In the light of this task the church can be characterized as "an eschatological freedom movement, the aim of which is to bring together all men and women in unity and peace: together with one another and all peoples, and with nature. And all this on the basis of unity with the living God" (Schillebeeckx 1989:176). Moreover, on this macro-level, the church assumes a prophetic role and participates in the emancipative and transformative task of changing oppressive and alienating structures of society. The church's intervention on social and political issues has been articulated on the social encyclicals beginning with the publication of *Rerum Novarum* in 1891 by Pope Leo XIII. From then on, official church documents dealing with social issues have recurrently been published. According to the 'spirit' of these social teachings and Vatican II, the "the joys and the hopes, the griefs and the anxieties of the men of this age, especially those who are poor or in any way afflicted, these are the joys and hopes, the griefs and anxieties of the followers of Christ" (*Gaudium et Spes*, no. 1). In the apostolic exhortation *Evangelii Nuntiandi* (1975), the macro-level task of the church has also been keenly acknowledged: "The church considers it to be undoubtedly important to build up structures which are more human, more just, more respectful of the rights of the person and less oppressive and less enslaving" (*Evangelii Nuntiandi*, no. 36). In this respect, the church have also addressed the issues of racism and ethnocentrism in which it states: "any kind of social or cultural discrimination in basic personal rights on the grounds of gender, race, color, social conditions, language or religion, must be curbed and eradicated as incompatible with God's design" (*Gaudium et Spes*, no. 29). The Latin American theologians have brought to the Christian awareness the reality of structural evils and the need for the church to actively participate in social transformation. Liberation theology has articulated the call for the church to be on the side of the victims of oppressive structures and to help in their liberation. It emphasizes that the scope of sin is not limited only to the individual but extends to all aspects of human life and relationships. This affects all people and all relations, both personal and structural. Acknowledging social sin implies: first, that sin should not be reduced to sheer 'spiritual' matters but includes economic, political and cultural dimensions of life; second, the causes and consequences of sin whether committed by an individual or group is not confined to personal relationships but extends beyond the actors who are most directly involved; third, groups and institutions—persons acting corporately-commit sins and can put in place social structures that are unjust (Gutierrez 1984; Hick 2000). The acknowledgment of structural sins also entails a response with a social dimension. Hence, the social task of the church must involve participation in bringing transformation on the economic, political, and cultural sphere of society. This task involves struggle against oppressive 'principalities and powers'.

Contrasting attitudes regarding church's involvement on political and social issues can be posited. These positions reflect either a support for the church's participation in the socio-political affairs in society or one that disapproves of such participation. Those who agree claim that the church should be involved on these issues because such participation is in keeping with the 'utopian' and critical function of the church in society being the eschatological people of God. The church is God's eschatological people when its praxis effectively anticipates the kingdom of God (Schillebeeckx 1989). The praxis of the church must, therefore, also be judged in the light of its consequences. In a church peace praxis which is not effective in the sense that the stated aims are not achieved, God's salvation cannot manifest itself in an immanent transcendent manner (Jeurissen 1993:135). Those who advocate involvement of the church in social issues criticize a privatised and an apolitical way of being church. A church that is not involved in the affairs of society and is simply concerned with religious matters falls short of fulfilling its task of being present in the world as a visible anticipation of God's kingdom of peace and justice. Furthermore, such an a-political attitude may only lend itself to a de facto legitimation of the existing social order (Schillebeeckx 1972). A neutral position does not exonerate the church from taking a political position. By remaining silent one implicitly lends ones authority to an ideological legitimation of existing situations and practices (Metz 1968:99). As long as the church remains a significant factor in society, it has a political function, whether it wants it or not. A politically neutral church does not exist (Moltmann 1984:153). According to Schillebeeckx (1981), the church has its own theological competence regarding issues that are of social or political in nature. Theology is capable to investigate to what extent its social involvement may be perceived as the advent of the kingdom of God. Listening to the 'signs of the times', or to what Schillebeeckx calls 'negative contrast experiences' of people, are already valid source of competence in the field of social questions. The church may however use other non-theological sciences to examine the root causes of these problems. One cannot doubt that the church, in principle, has direct access to these negative contrast experiences. These experiences may compose a source of knowledge for theology on which it can fall back even without the help of other sciences. All that is needed is a listening ear for the stories from people. The church therefore has the acquired competence even if its specific scientific knowledge falls short.

Those who opposed this position claim that such type of attitude of the church is in danger of over-politicisation. The church must spurn the temptation of striving for power which is inherent in all politics (Kuitert 1985). They criticize the tendency in political theologies to put the quality of human life of the individual on the same level as the quality of the social and economic relations. An individual person has an identity that is more than the socio-political situation; politics is not everything. Hence, the primary task of the church is not to pursue social and political ideals but rather to promote a personal relationship between God and man (Kuitert 1985). Furthermore, involvement of the church to politics may lead her to adapt to its rules which are diametrically opposed to the Christian ideals of love, charity, mercy, and truth. According to this view, politics necessarily involve conflict, bigotry, and self-exaltation in view of acquiring and preserving power. The church will inevitably conform to these rules of politics and endanger her Christian identity (cf. Jeurissen 1993:136). Some are apprehensive of the socio-political participation of the church in that it may be instrumental in lending moral and religious legitimation to some political groups. The church might allow itself to be manipulated for the ideological legitimation of political purposes (Kuitert 1985a: 24). This argument is disputed by supporters of the socio-political task of the church by claiming that this may not be the case, especially if one understands politics as a form of exercise of power, in the service of a purposeful design for a future society. In democratic societies political power is committed to a political ethics supported by society, which can correct the Machiavellian tendencies of political action. However, the exercise of political power in a multiform society ought to legitimise itself constantly "in the light of democratic criteria, of the politically liberating relevance of its content and of the burden of suffering and oppression which it can impose on others" (Schillebeeckx 1981:719).

Thus far, we have discussed theoretically the various attitudes of church members in relation to the identity and mission of the church, the church structure, and the various levels of the tasks of the church. We assume that these attitudes that we have elucidated on the theoretical level may find some congruencies with the attitudes of our respondents on the empirical plane. We now summarize the various attitudes towards the church in the scheme below (Scheme 6.1).

Scheme 6.1. Images of the Church: A Theoretical Perspective

Church Mission
　1. Culturally-Adapted church

Church Structure
　2. Hierarchical church
　3. Centralized church
　4. Democratic church

Church Tasks
　5. Micro-level: Person-directed tasks of the church
　6. Meso-level: Group-directed tasks of the church
　7. Macro-level: Socio-political tasks of the church

6.2. Images of the church from an empirical perspective

In the previous section we gathered the following theoretical models of the church: church mission which consists of 'culturally-adapted' church model; the church structure which includes hierarchical, centralized, and democratic church models; and the church tasks which consists of micro-, meso-, and macro-level church tasks. In this section, we investigate to what extent these theoretical church models are actively present among our respondents' consciousness. We examine whether and to what extent these theoretical models of the church can be empirically corroborated by our data. We measure the ecclesiastic attitudes of the respondents using selected items from the instrument developed and employed by Jeurissen (1993:306–307). We operationalize these models by using three items to measure each of the following church images: culturally-adapted, hierarchical, centralized, and democratic. We measure the micro-level task using four items, the meso-level with three items, and the macro-level with five items (see: Appendix 1, Table 3, Part 2).

We conducted two separate factor analyses, one for the items which covered the theoretical models for the church mission and church structures, and the other on the items comprising the tasks of the church. In the first factor analysis, the items on the church mission (culturally-adapted) and church structures (hierarchical, centralized, and democratic) were subjected to a free factor solution analysis (mineigen = 1). This factor analysis resulted into three factors, i.e. the culturally-adapted church, the democratic church, and a third factor that combines the items on the 'centralized' and 'hierarchical' models (see: Appendix 6, Table 1a). Since this last factor contains two items from the hierarchical model with higher loadings than the single item of the centralized model, we label this factor as 'hierarchical-centralized'. It appears that our respondents do not make any distinction between hierarchical and centralized church structure. This result seems to demonstrate that when speaking of church structure, our respondents think of the binary contrast between a hierarchical church structure on the one hand and the democratic church structure on the other. The explained variance of this free-factor solution is 57%. In the second factor analysis, the scores on the items of the tasks of the church were also subjected to factor analysis. The free factor solution analysis (mineigen = 1) resulted in three factors just as they were expected in the theoretical part, namely: micro-level task, meso-level task, and

Table 6.1. Images of the Church: An Empirical Perspective

Empirical Model	Mean	Standard Deviation	Pearson Correlation (r)	Cronbach's Alpha	Valid Cases
I. Cultural adaptation (Theoretical model 1)	3.5	.92	.63	—	438
II. Hierarchical-centralized (Theoretical models 2 & 3)	2.9	.85	—	.68	431
III. Democratic (Theoretical model 4)	3.6	1.06	.71	—	439
IV. Micro-level: Person-directed task (Theoretical model 5)	3.5	.48	—	.81	445
V. Meso-level: Group-directed task (Theoretical model 6)	3.0	.66	.54	—	440
VI. Macro-level: Socio-political task (Theoretical model 7)	2.7	.57	—	.65	441

macro-level task of the church (see: Appendix 6, Table 1b). The factors yielded a 47% explained variance. All the items on the church scales based on the factor analysis were subjected to a reliability of scales test (see: Table 6.1 below). The table above (Table 6.1) gives a summary of the attitudes towards the church from an empirical point of view.

Table 6.1 shows that our respondents are in favour of a culturally-adapted church (mean:3.5) and a democratic church structure (mean: 3.6). The data disclose that church members favour, without any hesitation, a democratic structure, especially in terms of participation of the laity in the liturgical activities of the church. In contrast, however, church members are less inclined to accept a hierarchical-centralized structure. They show a negative ambivalence (mean: 2.9). Concerning the three tasks of the church, one can observe that our respondents agree to a micro-level task of the church (mean: 3.5). They are however ambivalent about the meso-level (mean: 3.0) and even negatively ambivalent on the macro-level tasks of the church (mean: 2.7).

6.3. *Social location of the attitudes toward the church*

In this section, we introduce the differential attitudes of our respondents towards the church. We look at the bivariate relations between the demographic, social, and religious characteristics, and their ecclesiastic attitudes. The table below (Table 6.2) illustrates the social location of the attitudes toward the church.

From this table below, we take notice of the population characteristics that have significant relation with the ecclesial attitudes of our respondents. In Appendix 6, Table 3, one can also observe the variances in the social location of the attitudes towards the church. Age is associated to hierarchical-centralized church, democratic church, meso-level task, and the macro-level task. The oldest age group (69 years and older) scores significantly higher than the youngest age group (57 years and younger) in terms of their attitudes toward hierarchical-centralized church, meso-, and macro-level church attitudes (see: Appendix 6, Table 3). There is however a significant difference between the attitudes of the second age group and the oldest age group on their attitudes toward the hierarchical-centralized church. It is notable that the youngest age group rejects unequivocally the

Table 6.2. Social location of the attitudes toward the Church (eta & rho)

	Culturally-adapted	Hierarchical-centralized	Democratic	Micro-level task	Meso-level task	Macro-level task
DEMOGRAPHIC CHARACTERISTICS						
Age (*eta*)	—	.33**	.14*	—	.14*	.17**
Gender (*eta*)	—	—	—	—	—	—
Education (*eta*)	—	.24**	—	—	.15*	—
Country of origin (*eta*)	.13**	.15**	.18**	—	—	—
SOCIAL CHARACTERISTICS						
Localistic authoritarianism (*rho*)	.19**	.36**	—	—	.15**	.21**
Subjectively-perceived threat (*rho*)	.11*	.31**	—	—	—	—
Conformism (*rho*)	.13**	.20**	—	.10*	.18**	.18**
Anomie (*rho*)	.14**	.29**	—	—	—	—
RELIGIOUS CHARACTERISTICS						
Church Involvement (*eta*)	—	—	.16**	.13**	.35**	.22**
Religious Salience (*rho*)	—	—	—	—	.42**	—

** p < .01; * p < .05 (2-tailed)

hierarchical-centralized model. The second age group (58 to 68 years old) scores significantly higher on democratic church than the youngest age group (see: Appendix 6, Table 3). Gender is not associated to any church models. Education is related to only two church models, namely: hierarchical-centralized church model and meso-level task. Respondents with a lower education (primary education and/or lower secondary education) score higher on these church models than those with a higher education (higher secondary education and/or tertiary education (see: Appendix 6, Table 3). The country of origin is associated to culturally-adapted church, hierarchical-centralized church, and the democratic church. The native Dutch members score higher on culturally-adapted and democratic church attitudes than the non-native Dutch members. However, the non-native respondents score higher on the hierarchical-centralized church structure than the native church members. In terms of social characteristics, we notice that 'localistic authoritarianism' is correlated to culturally-adapted church, hierarchical-centralized church, meso-level task, and the macro-level task. Subjectively-perceived threat is correlated to culturally-adapted church and hierarchical-centralized church. Conformism is correlated to culturally-adapted church, hierarchical-centralized church, micro-, meso-, and macro-level tasks of the church. Anomie plays a role in the culturally-adapted church attitudes and the hierarchical-centralized church attitudes of our respondents. Church involvement is associated to democratic, micro-, meso-, and macro-level tasks of the church. Active church members score higher on these church images than the inactive members. Religious salience is associated only to the meso-level task of the church.

Summary

To sum up, we have indicated in the theoretical part of this chapter that we assume that church members have diverse attitudes toward the church. We make a conceptual distinction of the images of the church in terms of church mission, ecclesial structure, and tasks of the church. We gather seven conceptual models regarding church images which we assume to be present among our respondents. These seven church models include the following: culturally-adapted, hierarchical, centralized, democratic, micro-level task (person-directed), meso-level task (group-directed), macro-level task (socio-political) church models. In the empirical part of this chapter, we indicate six church attitudes, namely: cultural adaptation church, hierarchical-centralized church, democratic church, micro-, meso-, and macro-level tasks of the church. The hierarchical model and the centralized church models form only one factor. We discover that our respondents favour a culturally-adapted church. They support a type of church that adapts to the present day culture and society. Our data also show that church members agree to a democratic structure, especially in terms of participation of the laity in the liturgical activities of the church. They are negatively ambivalent about hierarchical-centralized church structure. Our respondents accept the micro-level task of the church. They are ambivalent about the meso-level task, and negatively ambivalent about the macro-level task of the church. In the third part of this chapter, we examine the social location of the ecclesial attitudes of these church members. We have shown that age, country of origin, localistic authoritarianism, conformism, and church involvement, are the most significant social locators of attitudes toward the church.

CHAPTER SEVEN

ATTITUDES TOWARD MINORITIES

Previous researches have shown that the rising number of ethnic minorities in this country has evoked negative reactions from its native Dutch population. These negative feelings towards minorities are perceived to be coupled with an increasing positive attitude towards their in-group. Sociologists label these complex processes of a positive attitude towards in-groups on the one hand and a negative attitude towards minorities on the other hand as *ethnocentrism*. Previous studies have also pointed out that religious people are more ethnocentric than the non-religious ones. Hence, in this chapter, we shall examine the ethnocentric attitudes of our respondents who are composed mainly of native Dutch church members. The central question that we pose in this chapter is: to what extent are the Dutch church members in our population ethnocentric?, and what is the social location of these attitudes? We shall develop this chapter by first presenting the conceptual structure of the attitudes towards minorities in section 7.1. Then, in section 7.2, we shall give a report of the analysis of these attitudes in the empirical part of this chapter. And finally, we shall investigate the social location of these ethnocentric attitudes in section 7.3.

7.1. Theoretical structure of the attitudes toward minorities

During the past century, the phenomenon of immigration created a dramatic change in the socio-demographic make-up of the Dutch society. An important offshoot of this phenomenon is the rapid increase of ethnic minorities who are now living in the country. Statistics reveal that the proportion of ethnic minorities in the Dutch society has swollen sixfold within one-quarter of a century to nearly 10% of the population and is still increasing rapidly. Between 1971 and 1997, the number of ethnic minorities grew from 200,000 to 1.5 million, or from 1.6% to 9.4% of the entire population.[1] These profound

---

[1] According to recent counts of the Dutch Central Bureau of Statistics (CBS), there are about 1.7 million non-western allochtoon living in the country since the beginning

socio-demographic changes that are happening in this small but densely populated country, the Netherlands, have generated disquieting reactions with alarming social consequences. Studies show that many people belonging to the native Dutch population are unhappy about the presence of immigrants or ethnic minorites in their neighbourhoods.[2] Inevitably, some social problems crop up, like outburst of aggression or violence, segregation, extreme right voting, etcetera. (Hello 2003:2). All these events add up to the increasing tension and antagonism in Dutch society not only between allochtonous and autochtonous groups but also between various groups among the autochtonous. The outburst of aggression and violence can be illustrated for instance by the killing of Pim Fortuyn on May 6, 2003, a politician known for his anti-immigration platform. The issue that he stood for continues to spark debates in various parts of the country. His persuasion even gained influence among the policy makers in some cities. In Rotterdam for instance, a city council member belonging to the party *Leefbaar Rotterdam* commented on the construction of a huge mosque in the city, saying: "There's no reason the minarets have to be that high—it will not be Rotterdam; it will be the Mecca on the [river] Maas". Another instance of this violence was the killing of a controversial film director, Theo van Gogh, on November 2, 2004 by a suspected muslim extremist who accused the latter for his anti-Islam rhetorics. Ethnic segregation can likewise be exemplified, on the one hand, by the presence of neighborhoods comprising of immigrants who live in the older and less prosperous section of the large cities, and on the other hand, by the 'white flight' phenomenon wherein most natives moved to the suburbs in order to flee from the swelling number of immigrants living in their neighborhoods in the cities. What results is that ethnic minorities and the majority Dutch population live highly segregated from each other. This segregation, however, is reported to be different for each ethnic minority group. Turks and Moroccans, for example are found to be considerably more segregated from the native Dutch population than the Surinamese,

---

of 2007. cf. http://www.cbs.nl/nl-NL/menu/themas/bevolking/publicaties/artikelen/archief/2007/2007-2276-wm.htm. [Accessed 7 March 2007].

[2] Hereafter, the native Dutch population will be considered as the 'majority' group, which we define in this case as the dominant ethnic group of this country in terms of political power, economic status, and demographic number. As in most western european countries, these majority group coincides with the indigenous or native ethnic group (Gijsberts et al. 2004:6).

Dutch Antillians, and Southern Europeans. Another problem related to ethnic segregation is the so-called 'ethnic distance', or the tendency to avoid social contact with minorities. Studies show that ethnic distance has been stable between the early 1980's and early 90's. While on the one hand, ethnic Dutch residents are open to contact with ethnic minorities who have, according to them, culturally adjusted, but on the other hand, minority groups who favour more contact with the Dutch, want the Dutch to accept them the way they are. But because they think that the Dutch are not willing to do so, they avoid contact at all (Leeflang 2002:2). Minorities perceive the Dutch majority to have the tendency to label unpleasant events to be caused by their deviant cultures, and attribute the low social-economic position of the minorities to their cultural backgrounds (De Jong & Van de Grinten 1987:64–65). Some studies reveal that there is also what is called a 'minority prejudice' (discordance), which is a prejudice of minority groups against majority. These *ex post facto* judgement are drawn from history of persecution of and discrimination against minorities. Other findings also show that ethnic minorities are only judged negatively by Dutch respondents, if they are not older than the respondent and if their professional status is lower. Dutch residents with a low professional status reject members of ethnic minority groups even if they have a high professional status. They prefer other Dutch people with a low professional status as a neighbor than a minority member (Leeflang 2002: 2). There has also been a wide-ranging tendency among the majority population to support ethnic discrimination. Since 1985, there has been an unremitting increase in the percentages of people who intend to discriminate against ethnic minorities (Scheepers, Schmeets, & Felling 1997:145–159). The rise of right-wing political parties and their influence among the populace has become an alarming trend. Most of them blame immigrants for the social problems like unemployment and criminality. They tend to attack existing immigration policies that grant equal rights to ethnic minorities. Cities like Rotterdam ask the national government for a moratorium of political refugees. Systematic plans were charted to deport illegal immigrants and to end the bringing of spouses by immigrants. In 2004, a policy was passed to return thousands of asylum seekers back to their home country. Some policy makers justify this move as 'pragmatic' and not 'racist' in nature. Ironically, these phenomena seem to run contrary to the popular Dutch approach to social issues, namely: their tolerance (*gedogen*) and liberalism (*vrijzinnigheid*). 'Tolerance' in the Dutch context implies that when society is polarized on a certain issue, various approaches, even some officially illegal ones, are accepted as a way of working toward a solution. Dutch are known to deal with problems through concensus, or the so-called *poldermodel*. This approach has been mirrored invariably by spearheading social policies for the legalization of euthanasia, abortion, drugs, prostitution, and same sex marriage. But should the issue of immigration be treated differently? How far can such tolerance be extended to ethnic minorities? Some pro-immigrant human rights groups warn that these recent developments signal a growing polarization in Holland. According to them, the immigrants should not be made a scapegoat. There is too much *us* and *them* in most of these schemes.

This tension between the majority in-group and minority out-group can be approached in several ways. One can regard this social issue either as a problem of rationalization (which deals with the question: what are the changes that have taken place in a society, and in what direction is a society developing?), as a problem of inequality (do some people have more resources than the others and why is this the case?), or as a problem of cohesion (what keeps people together and what keeps them from struggling with one another?). Although we can approach this issue of ethnic antagonism as a problem of rationalization or inequality, we want to look at it primarily as an issue of social cohesion. The lack of social cohesion in this society can be indicated by the unfavourable attitudes of the majority in-group towards the minority out-group. This of course does not imply that the problem of ethnic conflict and antagonism is not an issue of social or ethnic inequality. In this study, however, the issue of ethnic inequality is treated as part of the overarching problem of social cohesion. Furthermore, the negative out-group attitudes of the in-group are not always directly transmuted into ethnic inequality. In the context of social cohesion, the problem of ethnic inequality can at least be partly explained by the concept of ethnocentrism.

7.1.1. *Ethnocentrism*

Earlier studies show that the unfavourable attitudes of the native Dutch population towards minorities (out-group) are intimately linked to their favourable attitude towards their fellow native Dutch (in-group). This complex of attitudes is called ethnocentrism (Eisinga & Scheepers 1989). Ethnocentrism is defined as a "complex of attitudes, consisting of positive attitudes toward the ethnic in-group and negative attitudes toward ethnic out-groups" (Adorno et al., 1950; Eisinga & Scheepers 1989). The first use of this term is attributed to Sumner (1959) who describes ethnocentrism as a view of things in which one's own group is the centre of everything, and all others are scaled and rated with reference to it. Each group nourishes its own pride and vanity, boasts itself superior, exalts its own divinities, and looks with contempt on outsiders.

One theory that explains ethnocentrism is the so-called social-identity theory (Tajfel & Turner 1979:33–47). According to this theory, human beings tend to categorize other human beings into in-groups (themselves) and out-groups (the others). This distinction between 'us' and 'them' can be made on numerous grounds, for example, on the basis of gender, political preference, religious affiliation, ethnic background, etcetera. People use this distinction in their own social environment in order to attain a positive, or more positive, self-esteem; by ascribing themselves 'positive traits (social identification), and by ascribing others negative traits (social contra-identification), one's self-esteem is boosted twofold. The mental processes of 'social identification' and 'social counter-identification' involve the following phases (Eisinga & Scheepers 1989:239): [1] individuals categorize social reality according to norms derived from the value system of the social group(s) in which they have been socialized; [2] they compare their own social group(s) with others. They are inclined to compare only those characteristics at which their in-group(s) is/are superior to out-groups. In which case, they selectively perceive positively valued cultural characteristics of the in-group(s); and they selectively perceive negatively valued characteristics of several out-groups; [3] from this comparison, they derive a positive social identity: the perceived cultural characteristics are assumed to apply to their own personalities as well.

Another theory that helps explain ethnocentric attitudes is the 'realistic group conflict theory' (Bobo & Smith 1994). This theory states that inter-group competition led to heightened in-group favouritism, in-group solidarity and in-group pride on the one hand, and out-group prejudice and hostility on the other hand. Coenders (2001) distinguishes three theoretical approaches of the realistic group theory. First is the so-called 'narrow interpretation' of realistic group conflict theory. This narrow interpretation of realistic group conflict theory focuses solely on group interests (group threat). In this sense, the in-group members have antagonistic attitudes toward an out-group because the out-group poses a threat to the social position of the in-group. The second approach is called 'self-interest' approach to the realistic group conflict theory because it stresses solely on personal interests (personal threat) (Bobo & Hutchings 1996). The third approach is called the 'broader interpretation' of realistic group conflict theory. This approach claims that nationalistic and ethnic exclusionistic attitudes arise not only because the ethnic out-group is a threat to the social position of the in-group in general (group threat), but also because the ethnic out-group is a stronger threat to specific individual in-group members, given their specific social position. In other words, ethnic out-group members form a threat to the in-group as a whole, because they compete for the same scarce resources, such as status, power, and privileges. Some in-group members, however, have to compete more with out-group members than other in-group members on average, namely, those in-group members who hold similar positions as (the majority of) out-group members in the labour and housing market (Coenders 2001).

These theories form as the theoretical assumptions behind our understanding of ethnocentric attitude in this study. By 'attitude' we mean "a learned predisposition to respond in a consistently favourable or unfavourable manner with respect to a given object" (Fishbein & Ajzen 1975:6). It involves an evaluation of a specific object based on a set of beliefs about this object with some degree of favour or disfavour. These ideas are supposed to guide one's behaviour, or at least one's behavioural intentions (Schuman et al. 1997). Based on this definition of 'attitude', we derive our description of an attitude towards ethnic minorities as "a set of beliefs about people who share certain identifiable ethnic characteristics or are perceived to share these characteristics" (Verberk 1999:3). A positive or favourable attitude means a positive perception of the valued cultural characteristics of the in-group and nationalistic feelings. A negative or unfavourable attitude towards ethnic minorities would mean therefore a disfavorable evaluation of members of ethnic majority groups towards ethnic minorities. It refers to a negative perception of the valued characteristics of several out-groups; also of out-groups with whom actual contacts are highly improbable (Eisinga & Scheepers 1989:239). For the purpose of our study, we shall employ the term 'negative attitudes towards ethnic minorities' to refer to the unfavourable attitude towards minorities in both its latent and blatant form, and ethnocentrism to refer to the combination of positive attitude towards the in-group and negative attitude of a majority group towards the minority. The focal object of our study are the majority position (and therefore not directly the migrant's position). This is due mainly to the fact that the bulk of the Dutch Catholic Church members belong to the majority Dutch natives while the minority groups belong to diverse religious affiliation or simply are non-religious.

7.1.1.1. *Positive attitude towards the in-group*
We explained earlier that ethnocentrism involves positive regard of members of majority to their in-group. This positive attitude towards the in-group may also be represented by a nationalistic attitude. We consider a nationalistic attitude as part of the favourable attitude towards in-group. Here, we apply the label 'nationalist attitudes' as a generic term for favourable attitudes towards in-group and country (Gijsberts et al. 2004).[3] This nationalistic attitude arises from a fundamental human need, which is the need for a positive social identity. Hence, one can expect that individuals would, to some extent, have positive attitude towards the in-group, but also a negative attitude towards the out-group which can be represented by an exclusionist attitude. In general, a nationalistic attitude is a positive perception of the valued cultural characteristics of the in-group. However, since World War II, trends on studies related to 'nationalism' have been more or less focused on its negative consequences, like for instance, nationalism being a cause of war. As Kosterman and Feshbach (1989:259) comments, "the badness of nationalism became the overriding theme for many years to come". They distinguish between nationalistic attitudes as a 'jingoistic cause of war' (i.e. chauvinism) and patriotism as a healthy national concept. A discussion regarding the positiveness or negativeness of national pride as a valued character is still up in the air. Some argue that national pride is an unacceptable attitude because it is associated to prejudice towards ethnic and religious minorities; it views national pride as a fascist ideology. However, some view national pride as a positive and necessary attitude. They contend that certain forms of national pride may have strong positive implications (Gijsberts

---

[3] Note that this concept diverges from another concept of nationalism commonly defined by Bar-Tal (1993; 1997), which is applied as a political-sociological term referring to political claim of a separate, distinct and independent nation-state.

et al. 2004:31). As some would argue, attachment of group members to their group and country of residence are essential conditions for group existence (Bar-Tal 1987; 1990; 1993; 2000). Attachment to national symbols renders a sense of country of origin and integration (Topf et al. 1990); it can also increase social cohesion as long as this pride can transcend boundaries between social classes, religious denominations, and other social groups. Pride in national institutions—especially on democratic institutions- can be seen as significant condition for political stability. Conversely, the absense of pride indicates a deficient attachment to the political democratic system,which in turn implies potential political instability (Gijsberts et al. 2004:31). Hence, Kosterman and Feshbach (1989) make a distinction between two dimensions of a nationalistic attitude, namely: patriotism and chauvinism.[4] Patriotism is described as the feeling of pride based on a critical attachment to one's own country.[5] People feel emotionally proud of their national (majority) group (cf. Bar-Tal & Staub 1997). It somehow reflect a critical understanding rather than a blind attachment to the national group and country (Bar-Tal 1993; Gijsberts et al. 2004:29). Adorno et al. (1969:67) describes a person with a genuine patriotic attitude as someone who can "appreciate the values and ways of other nations, and can be permissive toward much that he cannot personally accept for himself. He is free of rigid conformism; out-group rejection, and imperialistic striving for power". Chauvinism on the other hand refers to feelings of superiority and blind attachment to one's own country and its residents. It views one's country and people as unique and superior. This feeling of superiority is intertwined with a blind, uncritical attachment to one's own national group and country. A more moderate form of nationalism can also be indicated aside from patriotism and chauvinism. We can call this as national identification. People simply identify themselves with their country of origin.

---

[4] There are other refinements of these dimensions. Staub (1997) for instance suggests to distinguish *nationalism*, *blind patriotism*, and *constructive patriotism*. Dekker & Malova (1995) likewise make the following distinctions: national identification, national attachment, and national pride.

[5] This notion is different from Adorno's definition of patriotism as a subscale in his ethnocentric E-scale. However, he and his colleagues acknowledged that their patriotism scale does not mean 'love of country', but a blind attachment to certain national cultural values, uncritical conformity with the prevailing group ways, and rejection of other nations as out-groups. (Adorno et al. 1969:107; Gijsberts et al. 2004:31)

7.1.1.2. Negative attitude towards out-group
Aside from the positive attitude towards the in-group, ethnocentrism also consists of a negative or unfavourable attitude towards the out-group. Earlier studies often associate negative attitudes towards minorities to a number of concepts, like racism, ethnic prejudice, and stereotype. Racism refers to the overt disliking and enmity towards other ethnic groups or race. While the concept racism has been extensively used in several social researches, it has lost sharp conceptual and operational parameters (Verberk 1999:2). Ethnic prejudice refers to a preconceived negative opinion against members of ethnic minority groups. It involves a feeling of antipathy based upon a faulty and inflexible generalization. Stereotype is described as 'the fixed, narrow pictures in our head, generally resistant to easy change'. Traditionally, stereotype is defined as a generalization that was incorrectly learned, rigid, over-generalized, or factually incorrect; it usually carries a pejorative meaning (Duckitt 1991; Tajfel & Turner 1979).

Recent studies reveal that there are not only blatant or overt negative attitudes but also latent or covert negative out-group attitudes. Verberk (1999:55) describes blatant unfavourable out-group attitudes as "the explicit expressions of hostility", and latent unfavourable attitudes refer to "implicit and difficult-to-discern forms of hostility". Blatant forms of negative out-group attitudes are related to biological racism, which is sometimes called as the 'old-fashioned racism' or 'Jim Crow's racism'. These blatant types of negative out-group attitudes are based on the assumption that there is an existence of a biological superiority of ethnic majority groups over and against another ethnic group. It also views minority groups as a biological threat. Pettigrew and Meertens (1995) explain that blatant attitudes consist of two components, namely: the experience of threat from and the rejection of ethnic minorities; second is the opposition to intimate contact with them. Advocates of this biological racism tend to support ethnic segregation and ethnic distance. In the Dutch context, current studies reveal that there is no decline of blatant unfavourable attitudes unlike in the United States (Scheepers, Eisinga & Linssen 1994). Blatant unfavourable attitudes are mainly manifested by the elderly, regular church attenders, the less educated, manual laborers, and self-employed people (Scheepers et al. 1990; 1994). The tendency to avoid social contact with ethnic minorities, or the so-called ethnic distance, have insignificantly changed in the last two decades compared to the 80's and early 90's.

While the support for ethnic discrimination among majority population was declining in the early 80's, new research shows that there is a continual increase of this tendency from 1985 until the end of the 20th century. Furthermore, a strong opposition to policies which aim at establishing ethnic equality in the 90's have also been noted to be increasing (Scheepers, Schmeets, & Felling 1997).

Aside from the blatant forms of negative out-group attitudes, unfavourable attitudes toward minorities may also take a subtle form which is called latent or covert negative out-group attitudes. These latent negative out-group attitudes are identified with various names, like for instance: symbolic racism, aversive racism, laissez-faire racism, new racism, regressive racism, everyday racism, etcetera.

Symbolic racism may be described as the "expression in terms of abstract ideological symbols and symbolic behaviours of the feeling that minorities violate cherished values and make illegitimate demands for changes in the racial status quo" (McConohay & Hough 1976:38). Symbolic racists perceive ethnic minorities to be demanding and receiving more rights than the rest of the population. While they do not deny that majorities and minorities have equal rights, they however believe that emancipation of minorities have gone too far, and that this process has been accompanied by illegal and unfair demands and tactics on the part of minorities. They believe that minorities pose as a threat not so much on their personal self-interest but on the values and principles of the majority group. People express symbolic racism through symbolic acts such as opposition to affirmative action or busing. 'Busing' is an affirmative action program in the US which is intended to promote ethnic integration. Minority children who lived in predominantly minority neighbourhoods were transported by bus to public schools in other areas. This was expected to stimulate contacts between minorities and majorities. Symbolic racists ironically view racism and discrimination as socially undesirable and reprehensible. Therefore, they legitimize their own attitude towards ethnic minorities using ostensibly non-ethnic arguments (McConohay 1986).

Another concept related to subtle form of racism is the so-called aversive racism (Kovel 1970; Gaertner & Dovidio 1986). Aversive racists is said to be rooted on three psychological processes, namely: first, people have the need to categorize the social world around them. This categorization is often based on the characteristics that people first notice about one another. This means that they easily categorize people belonging either to the majority or to minorities. Second, people have a basic need to see the group to which they belong as possessing power and control. Third, socialization processes instill unfavourable attitudes. Aversive racists tend not to discriminate in situations in which they would have to bear overt responsiblitiy for discriminatory behavior.

The concept *laissez-faire* racism holds that ethnic minorities are disadvantaged because of their culture (Bobo & Smith 1994). It maintains that the majority population are not socially responsible for the disadvantage and poor living conditions of many minority communities. *Laissez-faire* advocates tend to actively oppose measures to improve the status of ethnic minorities or to promote ethnic integration. When ethnic discrimination takes place they tend to do nothing. *Laissez-faire* racists believe that minorities are culturally inferior compared to the culture of majority population. Thus, they perceive minorities as a cultural threat.

Another concept is the so-called new racism (Barker 1981). Neo-racists believe that majority culture must be defended against the influence of other cultures. People who belong to different ethnic groups and who are culturally different are considered to be incompatible with the culture of the majority. New racists do not perceive ethnic minorities as threatening in a concrete, personal manner. Rather, they perceive them as a threat to their own way of life, that is, to the customs, values and norms of the majority population. New racism is claimed to be located among the youth of the majority population in the Netherlands. Verkuyten and Masson (1995) found that new racism among Dutch majority youth is correlated with personal self-esteem, collective self-esteem, favourable in-group evaluation, ethnic distance, and the rate of voluntary inter-ethnic contacts. Taguieff (1987) elaborated this concept by claiming that contemporary forms of racism believe that it is not only natural for majority population to defend their way of life against those of other cultures but that they assume that every human being has the right to protect and defend his or her own identity.

Rogers and Prentice-Dunn (1981) speak of regressive racism. They explain that members of the majority usually behave in accordance with egalitarian norms when they interact with ethnic minorities. However, in situations when they get emotionally excited, they tend to discriminate against ethnic minorities.

Some Dutch authors reveal some other forms of subtle unfavourable attitude towards minorities.[6] Essed (1991), for instance, speaks of everyday racism, i.e. the notion that racism manifest itself not only in explicit overt acts of racial intolerance and exclusion, but also in the small, routinized practices of everyday interactions in which the racist motives are more covert. Pettigrew and Meertens (1995) hold that subtle racism includes three components, namely: the defense of traditional values, the exaggeration of cultural differences, and affective prejudice. All these three components involve a socially acceptable rejection of minorities on seemingly non-prejudicial grounds. They conclude that blatant and subtle prejudice although correlated, are empirically distinguishable. Furthermore, they conclude that in the Netherlands, blatant prejudice is less widespread whereas subtle prejudice is more widespread than in other western european countries. They also claim that most western european countries have a norm that prohibit racism and discrimination. This norm is very strong and firmly established. Pettigrew and Meertens explain that people who deny a blatant unfavourable but who do express a subtle one, are acquainted and comply with these social norms. Nevertheless, these people have not internalized these anti-racism norms (Verberk 1999:22).

Despite the nuances among these concepts, studies reveal that unfavourable attitudes towards minorities are recently expressed not so much explicitly or blatantly, but are disguised, covert, subtle, and ostensibly non-ethnic. Furthermore, these subtle forms of negative attitudes are no longer explained by beliefs in biological inferiority but by the assumption of cultural inferiority of minorities.

In sum, we said that ethnocentric attitude consists of two faces, i.e. positive in-group attitude and negative out-group attitude. The positive in-group attitude signifies all representations of a favourable in-group feeling, while the negative out-group attitude involves all representations of unfavourable out-group feeling. In the Dutch context, we explain that a negative out-group attitude can be elaborated through a negative out-group attitude towards specific ethnic

---

[6] See: Essed (1984, 1991), Hagendoorn & Kleinpenning 1991; Kleinpenning 1993; Pettigrew and Meertens 1995; Verkuytand Masson 1995; Meertens and Pettigrew (1997). Studies of these authors conclude that subtle unfavourable attitudes toward minorities prevail in Dutch society.

Scheme 7.1. Ethnocentric Attitudes: A Theoretical Perspective

1. Positive Attitude toward In-group
2. Negative Attitudes toward Ethnic minorities
   a. Negative Attitude towards out-group in General
   b. Negative Attitude towards Specific out-group

groups. The scheme above (Scheme 7.1) gives us an outline of the conceptual framework in our study of the ethnocentric attitudes of our respondents.

7.2. *Attitudes toward minorities from an empirical perspective*

In this section, we report the empirical outcome of our investigation. In order to measure the concept of ethnocentrism, we use previously tested items from the *Social and Cultural Trends in the Netherlands* (SOCON 2000) instruments (cf. Felling et al. 2000; Eisinga et al. 1992; 1999). From the SOCON scales, we draw one set of four items to measure positive attitudes towards the in-group. Some of these items may be indicated, for instance: "We, the Dutch people, are always willing to put our shoulders to the wheel" and "I am proud to be a Dutchman". The SOCON scales also include measurements for the attitudes toward ethnic minorities in general and the attitudes toward specific out-groups. The measurement of the attitudes toward minorities in general consists of six items. Three of these items are stated with positive orientation towards minorities in general. The other three are constructed with a negative orientation. The positive oriented items include the following statements: "most ethnic minorities are friendly"; "most ethnic minorities are decent"; "most ethnic minorities are honest". The negative oriented items include the following statements: "most ethnic minorities are untrustworthy"; "most ethnic minorities are lazy"; "most ethnic minorities are violent". Another set of instrument contains five items which measure negative attitudes towards specific ethnic out-groups. These items refer to specific ethnic groups in the Dutch context, for instance: "Turks have so many children because they are slightly backward" and "With Moroccans, you never know for certain whether they are going to be aggressive or not". All these items have a five-point Likert scale answer format.

The responses to the various measuring scales of ethnocentric attitudes are subjected to factor analyses. First, we conducted a free factor solution analysis on the items measuring the positive in-group attitude. These items formed one factor (see: Appendix 7, Table 1a), resulting to an inter-item reliability of Cronbach's *alpha* .71 (see: Table 7.1 below). Then, we subjected all the items on the out-group attitudes, both the positive and the negative (general and specific) items, to a free factor solution analysis. Based on the outcome of this analysis, we eliminated the positive items on the out-group attitudes for statistical reasons (see: Appendix 1, Table 3, Part 1). Then a free factor solution analysis was again conducted consisting of negative items, both general and specific, out-group attitudes. The outcome of this analysis yielded one factor (see: Appendix 7, Table 1b), a 43% explained variance (Cronbach's *alpha* .85). The positive in-group attitude is correlated with the negative out-group attitude (rho .35) [see: Appendix 7, Table 2].

The respondents agree with the positive in-group attitude (mean: 3.4) but plainly disagree with the negative out-group attitude (mean: 2.3). This outcome is summarized in the table below (Table 7.1.):

Table 7.1. Ethnocentric Attitudes from an Empirical Perspective

Empirical Model	Mean	Standard Deviation	Cronbach's Alpha	Valid Cases
I. Positive in-group (Theoretical model 1)	3.4	.70	.71	443
II. Negative out-group (Theoretical models 2a & 2b)	2.3	.71	.85	439

7.3. Social location of the attitudes toward minorities

In this section we will attempt to find the social location of the ethnocentric attitudes of our respondents. The table below (Table 7.2.) gives us an overview of the results of our variance analysis.

As we can see from table 7.2., there are two demographic characteristics that feature most prominently in both positive in-group and negative out-group attitudes: age and education. We are able to make a comparison between several categories of the population characteristics of our respondents through Scheffé test. In terms of positive in-group attitudes, our findings reveal that there is a significant difference between the mean scores of the oldest generation (mean: 3.5) and the

Table 7.2. Social location of ethnocentric attitudes (*eta & rho*)

	POSITIVE IN-GROUP	NEGATIVE OUT-GROUP
DEMOGRAPHIC CHARACTERISTICS		
Age (*eta*)	.21**	.33**
Gender (*eta*)	—	—
Education (*eta*)	.30**	.40**
Country of origin (*eta*)	—	—
SOCIAL CHARACTERISTICS		
Localistic authoritarianism (*rho*)	.44**	.52**
Conformism (*rho*)	.36**	.30**
Anomie (*rho*)	.30**	.52**
Subjectively-perceived threat (*rho*)	.32**	.68**
RELIGIOUS CHARACTERISTICS		
Church Involvement (*eta*)	.15**	—
Religious salience (*rho*)	.16**	—

** $p < .01$; * $p < .05$ (2-tailed)

youngest age group (mean: 3.2). It reveals that the oldest age-group manifest clear agreement on positive in-group attitude, whereas the youngest generation scores ambivalently. In terms of education, we notice that respondents with lower education (primary education and/or lower secondary education) score higher on positive in-group attitude than those with higher education (higher secondary education and/or tertiary education) (see: Appendix 7, Table 3). All of the four social characteristics are correlated to positive in-group attitude (see: Appendix 7, Table 4). Church involvement and religious salience are associated only to positive in-group attitude (eta .15 and .16), but not to negative out-group attitude.

Looking at the social location of the negative out-group attitude, our findings reveal that age and education associate with negative out-group attitudes. In terms of age, we find out that the older the age group the higher they score on negative out-group (see: Appendix 7, Table 3). In terms of educational level, one notice that the higher the educational level of the respondents, the more they reject the negative out-group attitude (see: Appendix 7, Table 3). All of the four social characteristics are correlated to negative out-group attitudes.

Summary

In sum, we explained in the theoretical portion of this chapter that the positive attitudes toward the in-group and the negative attitudes toward the out-group are the two components of ethnocentrism. We clarified that the social identity theory and the realistic group-conflict theory could aid us in understanding this complex process of ethnocentrism. In the empirical part, we tried to operationalize positive in-group attitude and negative out-group attitude using instruments derived from SOCON. The results of our investigation showed that our respondents who are members of Dutch Catholic church accepted positive in-group attitude, but rejected plainly a negative out-group attitude. Age and education have been revealed as the demographic characteristics that are significant social locators of positive in-group and negative out-group attitudes. All the social characteristics were significantly correlated to both the positive in-group attitude and the negative out-group attitude. We also noticed that church involvement and religious salience were significant social locators of positive in-group attitude but not of negative out-group attitude.

CHAPTER EIGHT

RELIGION AND ETHNOCENTRISM

We mentioned earlier that in this study we aim at exploring relationships that may exist between the religious attitudes of church members and their ethnocentric attitudes. This chapter intends to examine the theoretical and empirical basis of this relationship. We begin here by acknowledging the underlying assumptions with regards the patterns of religious attitudes among our respondents. As we said in chapter 1, this study intends to raise a new question in the whole debate regarding the intricate relationship between religion and ethnocentrism by bringing into the discussion the phenomenon of the Dutch civil religion and the various reactions to it by contemporary Christian believers which we categorized into traditional, contextual, and humanistic reactions. We argue that the problem surrounding this debate can be explicated through an investigation of the religious attitudes within the context of the Dutch civil religion and the various reactions by the Christian believers towards it, which may or may not have an effect on their ethnocentric attitudes. The aim of this chapter is to find out what are the effects of the religious attitudes (which may be distinguished into traditional, contextual, and humanistic reactions to civil religion) on ethnocentrism, while controlling for some population characteristics.

In this chapter, we will describe first in section 8.1 the characteristics of civil religion in the Netherlands. Then, we shall look at the diverse reactions of the present day believers on civil religion in section 8.2. Next, we will discuss our expectations with regard to the effect of religious attitudes on ethnocentrism in section 8.3. And lastly, we will present the empirical impact of religious attitudes on ethnocentrism in section 8.4.

8.1. *Characteristics of Civil Religion in the Netherlands*

At the outset, it has to be recognized that when trying to investigate the religious attitudes of contemporary Dutch believers, one has to reckon with a whole host of religious attitudes among our respondents on the individual level. While we acknowledge the existence of these religious attitudes on the micro level, we are interested in this study to capture the religious attitudes that strongly influence the contemporary believers in the Netherlands on a broad and collective basis. Previous studies revealed that civil religion functions as a strong leverage that impacts the religious attitudes of the present Dutch believers on a collective or on a broad scale (Laeyendecker 1982; 1992; Ter Borg 1990; Van der Ven 1998b).[1] These studies indicate that civil religion is the underlying 'religious core' that lie beneath the foundation of the Dutch's values which is linked to their past tradition, their present identity and their perceived mission for the rest of the world. These common values which are believed to have religious undertones are said to be generally present among all its population. For this reason, we choose the notion of civil religion as the basis of our assumption to describe the religious attitudes of our respondents. We assume that 'civil religion' is a phenomenon that permeates *all* of the Dutch society and shapes the religious landscape of the Dutch believers in general.[2]

The term 'civil religion' is said to be coined by Jean Jacques Rousseau (1712–1778) in his book *Social Contract*.[3] In the 60's, this notion of civil religion was applied by Robert Bellah in the American situation. Like Rousseau, Bellah and other authors believe that civil religion fulfils specialized religious functions which are performed neither by the church nor by the state (Coleman 1970).[4] They argue that civil reli-

---

[1] Objections regarding the existence of civil religion in the Netherlands can also be noted. Some argue that as a modern society, Holland is so *differentiated* that community integration on the basis of religious-value system has become already either impossible if not superfluous. The 'sacred canopy' as Berger (1967) calls it, has been torn down and replaced by a 'mundane-canopy' (Lechner 1989). Others also claim that religion is strongly privatized, and therefore *shared religion* can no longer stand (Luckmann 1967; Fenn 1978). Thus it is no surprise that some writers would claim that the Netherlands do not constitute as a breeding-ground for *civil religion* (Martin 1978).

[2] By making this choice, we do not intend to dismiss the presence of other models of religious attitudes among the Dutch population, neither do we discard other framework to explain their religious attitudes. Civil religion is one vantage point among many others that could serve as a frame of reference to explain the current configuration of Dutch religious attitudes.

[3] St. Augustine in the 4th century used the term *civil theology* in his work *The City of God* by referring to Marcus Terentius Varro (116 B.C.E.–27 B.C.E.), a Roman scholar and writer—known to the Romans as 'the most learned of all the Romans'. The latter made a distinction between three types of religion: the religion of nature, the religion of poetry, and the religion of the state.

[4] Advocates of civil religion argued that civil religion operates as *religion* in that it serves as some kind of a 'superordinate meaning system' to the individual which helps the person to increase his/her social-psychological integration, or to legitimate

gion shares the commonly acknowledged functions of religion which consists of an integrative, a legitimating, and a prophetic role. Furthermore, they also contend that although there are a number of general characteristics of civil religion, one should be aware that civil religion emerged distinctively in each given context in various societies (Bellah & Hammond 1980).[5] According to them, the existence of civil religion differs from one country or nation-state to the other on account of dissimilarities in terms of historical paths and structural conditions of each specific context. Now the question is, how can we describe civil religion in the Netherlands? What could be the shape of civil religion in this highly secularized Dutch society? What are its unique features? Based on our examination of civil religion in the Netherlands, we have identified some of the *ethos*[6] that represent the values beliefs, symbols and rituals—which are regarded by the Dutch people in general as something: that reflects their collective history and destiny; that they can relate with the realm of absolute meaning; that provides them a vision and a principle of unity; that which enables each Dutch individual to identify themselves as 'special' when compared to other nations or communities; and, that they celebrate and ritualized repeatedly and rendered with 'sacred' meaning.[7] Although we can gather several

---

realities within him or herself, or to form a critical position in relation to a certain phenomenon (cf. Roof & Hoge 1980).

[5] In a comparative study of civil religion investigated from several countries, Pierard & Linder (1988) posited five broad characteristics that can be discerned from among a variety of particular context, namely: (1) Civil religion indicates a widespread acceptance by a people of a shared sense of their nation's history and destiny; (2) it prompts people to relate their society to a realm of absolute meaning; (3) it enables them to look at their society and community as in some sense 'special'; (4) it provides a vision which ties the nation together as an integral whole; and lastly, (5) it presents a collection of beliefs, values, rites, ceremonies and symbols which taken together, give sacred meaning to the life of the community and thus provide an overarching sense of unity that transcends internal conflicts and differences.

[6] We shall use the term *ethos* here to mean the distinguishing character, beliefs or moral nature of a person, group, or institution'; it refers to the *esprit d'corps* or spirit of the group; it is the characteristic manner or spirit, either of a community or individual; it indicates a certain attitude or sense of comportment towards others, and generally associated with questions of character or moral selfhood, where character or moral selfhood disclose a bond with others (Random House 2006; Cf. Urban 2007).

[7] In our study of the Dutch civil religion, we should be keen to accommodate not only the existence of a pluralism of *'religious'* worldviews but also of *non-religious* ones. In this case, it will help us to consider what scholars of civil religion acknowledged as *general* civil religion which is based not necessarily on some reference to a 'transcendent being' but to some *universal values* which are considered by the society as a necessary pre-requisite for political and social order. These universal values may

characteristics of civil religion as they may appear on the individual level, we want to limit our discussion to only four of the most prominent features as they appear on literatures and studies, namely: the enlightenment ethos (8.1.1.), the democratic ethos (8.1.2.), the moral ethos (8.1.3.), and the 'hidden' religious ethos (8.1.4.). Let us explain each of them.

8.1.1. *Enlightenment ethos*

One of the key characteristics of the Dutch civil religion is the strong influence of the Enlightenment in the whole of society, and the idea that this project has yet to be completed. As Bosch (1995) pointed out, enlightenment has made deep inroads into western thinking. The Enlightenment ethos reverberates in the Dutch consciousness and challenges them to take courage to make use of one's own understanding in relation to all aspects of life, most particularly the religious aspect. Religion, according to this Enlightenment ethos, has to be eminently reasonable. Religious institutions have to succumb to the pressure of the Enlightenment in order to make faith rationally plausible. It strives to make religion acceptable to its 'cultured despisers' especially in the midst of a highly secularized context. We would like to highlight two important aspects of this Enlightenment ethos, namely rationality and pragmatism, which we thought to have significant influence in the Dutch consciousness and identity.

Rationality

Rationality implies that assertions of religious and moral beliefs must be based on reason rather than on traditions. This 'fatal attraction' of many Dutch people to critical reasoning has been nourished by its long history of Enlightenment thinkers since the 17th and 18th centuries (cf. Israel 2001). The influence of humanism and socialistic philosophy on the religious beliefs of the people are more likely to be manifested than the traditional religious references. The influences of the ideas of modern and liberal thinkers are more acceptable to the average religious Dutch people than the influence of traditional or classical authors. Debates on all matters under the sun, including reli-

---

provide the basis for the responsible, moral citizenship that leads to an integrated society (Bellah 1976:156).

gion, have to be subjected to the 'court of reason'. Religion has to be presentable and fit for society and for reasoned discussion. Underlying this rationality ethos is the implicit suspicion towards ideology, or at least, 'false ideology' underlying any discourse. Uncritical acceptance of beliefs is a great misgiving. Thus, any explicit statement of belief is normally met with dismay if not rejection. In this rational and intellectual Dutch culture, it is preferable to have a discourse about living 'as if there were no Gods' (*etsi deus non daretur*). There is the 'doubting Thomas' in every Dutch man and woman of today. It has been ingrained in the minds of many Dutch people that to refrain from believing unproven assertions is always an act of intellectual honesty and that to believe them is to throw oneself wide open to the suspicion of obscurantism (cf. Bosch 1995:48). Indeed, the legacy of the Enlightenment has permeated many Dutch people of today, especially on the people's partiality towards a rational behavior.

Pragmatism

Dutch people are notably pragmatic in their approaches to life situations. This pragmatic ethos in dealing with various life situations are certainly characteristic of the Dutch values that has been honed by history and its natural environment. For many Dutch people, what is important is to effectively work things out and apply ideas into practice. There is the predilection for practical reasoning or a reasoned action over and against purely metaphysical abstraction and impracticable ideas. Extravagance of abstraction is not something that is appreciated by many Dutch people especially if it does not bring any useful effect in settling conflicts and dilemmas in real life situations (cf. Middendorp 2004; Copeland & Griggs 1986:244; Mitchell 2007; Leuw & Marshall 1994). They prefer to have a 'down-to-earth' settlement of things, at times bordering into instrumental thinking of means to an end. This 'calculated reasoning' is part of the entrepreneurial tradition for which many Dutch were known for historically (cf. Price 1998). Thus, part of this pragmatic approach to life situations is the propensity of the Dutch for meetings, for organizing and planning things. This somehow cultivated a democratic culture and the Dutch's passion for egalitarianism. This pragmatic mode of thought is concerned basically on the contributions of ideas to action and their effects on further experiences. Religious ideas are likewise rendered the same valuations. Religious people assess the significance of any religious concept on the basis of how these religious or theological constructions could provide a useful guide to action. It is for this reason that an average Dutch believer may be disinterested with sheer abstract, dogmatic, or purely transcendental religious construal than with practical, concrete, and immanent ones. There is always the interest to create some impact of religion to society.

8.1.2. *Democratic ethos*

Dutch people in general bestow premium value on democratic ideals and principles. They render democracy a special place in defining both their individual and collective identity (Felling et al. 1986; Thomassen 1991). This democratic *ethos* has been instilled among its people and has become part of their collective consciousness. It has shaped its national history and has become more or less a 'second nature' to each member of the Dutch society. This democratic principle has also been a critical criterion engendered by many Dutch people for reckoning, accepting, suspecting, or isolating any 'religious' body in the Dutch society. It has often been the underlying essential factor behind the questions raised to any group of religious communities—Muslim, Hindu, Buddhist, Evangelicals, Protestants, and Catholics, whether inside or outside the country—related to issues like women's emancipation, lay empowerment, caste system, homosexuality, human rights, etcetera. It has also been the socio-political principle behind the social welfare state policy or the basis of the Dutch people's protest against apartheid policy in South Africa. It is for this reason that Dutch people, both religious and non-religious, are critical towards authority 'from above'. Participation in decision-making is highly favored above authoritarian leadership. This democratic ethos is also perceived to be the source of motivation among many church members to take an active and independent role in the life and work of the church (Van der Ven 1998b:35–36). A more decentralized structure of institutions are preferred than centralized one. Although each individual Dutch person may have their own interpretation of the concept of democracy (Thomassen 1991: 34ff; Ter Borg 1990:165–184), they somehow agree on two of its significant features namely: autonomy and religious tolerance.

Autonomy

Autonomy is said to be one of the main features of democratic ethos which most Dutch people find greater consensus with (Thomassen

1991:165–186). Dutch people prefer to choose their own values and set up their own life projects. Inglehart & Baker (2000:19–51) identify the Netherlands as one of the countries in the west that scores very high on the post-materialist values which includes freedom, self-expression, and subjective well being. Dutch sociologists like Felling et al. (1991:98) maintain that the autonomy of the Dutch people is linked to their 'secular and radical complex' whose elements include critical attitude to social order and authority, the relativising of rules and permissiveness, participation, individual autonomy, and a free choice in alternative primary relations. Autonomy accentuates greater freedom of the individual for self-realization and to fashion one's own life destiny. Individual freedom is more emphasized than authority based on tradition when speaking about worldviews, lifestyles, and religion. Felling et al. (1991:98) explain that autonomy may not only mean that "one is free from the old bond of collectivism and get to enjoy freedom in their choice of social relations, but it also means that the traditional value system is relativised and is divested of dogma, that people are relieved from the pressure of social norms and that they can choose their own values in accordance with their own interests and insights." Thus, individual choice in matters of religion is valued and upheld. This means that each person is conceived as the bearer of one's own religion. This emphasis on autonomy among many Dutch people may even explain why there is an increasing trend towards 'de-ecclesiasticalization' or 'deconfessionalization' particularly among the younger generation (Van der Ven 1996: 342), or the growing number of groups in the population who classify themselves as 'believing but not belonging' (Davie 1994:93ff; 2002; Davie et al. 2008) to any traditional religious institutions or churches. For this reason, sociologists would classify the Netherlands as one of the countries belonging to the *région laïque*, together with Belgium and France, which has a sizeable sector of the population who recognize no religious label (Davie 2000:12). This phenomenon, however, does not imply that religion exerts no influence on the individual person at all. Rather, as Van der Ven (1998b:37) explains: "what the individual does with these influences—the choices he or she makes based on his or her own biography and the way in which he or she constructs or reconstructs these influences—is not reducible to the influence *per se*." Therefore, religion on the individual level has become more and more a product of self-construction, a product of the individual him/herself and not just coming from a ready-made patterns, contents, and forms that has been systematically developed and executed from an outside authority, whether the church or any predetermined social institution. Individuals tend to 'pick and choose' for themselves what to believe, and select their preferred religious practices and ethical options. Individuals tend to mix elements, a patchwork from various religious and non religious sources and incorporate them into their own personal religious outlook. Luckmann (1979:127–138) also refers to this as a phenomenon of *religion à la carte* or a *bricolage*. Aside from this tendency to mix elements from various religious sources, Van der Ven explains that one must be able to distinguish between a 'differential' and a 'partial' influence of religion in the individual's life: 'differential' in the sense that "religion play a role in the private life, for themselves or their significant others, but play little or no role in public matters such as politics; 'partial' because in the areas where religion does play a role, it is not the main factor, but simply one factor among others" (Van der Ven 1998b:40).

Religious tolerance

Another important facet of the Dutch democratic *ethos* is 'religious tolerance'. Tolerance (*verdraagzaamheid*) is said to be 'the' great feature of the Dutch society (Jacobs 2000:123; Zahn 1989; Van Thijn 1997).[8] It is even considered to be the most costly cultural possession that touches deeply the sensibilities of every Dutch man and woman (Van Thijn 1997). For this reason, tolerance occupies a sacrosanct status among many Dutch people. This value of tolerance has been historically the sustaining factor for national unity amidst religious pluralism since the time of the establishment of the Dutch Republic (Berkvens-Stevelinck et al. 1997). This has also been clearly the case during the time of a pillarized society in the previous decades. The value of tolerance has been significantly underscored in consensus forming (*poldermodel*) in order to keep the pillars together. In the national political arena, it has proven that tolerance through pragmatic consensus is essential for harmonious living together of people amidst diversity and religious pluralism. Hence, diversity in the Dutch setting is not only tolerated but also positively valued. The challenge for civil religion in the contemporary setting is how far this religious tolerance can be applied as a cultural tolerance in an increasingly multicultural setting

---

[8] Some studies however reveal that the Dutch are not as tolerant towards aliens as many people would usually think (Bronkhorst 1999).

of this country. The test or challenge for the Dutch tolerance now is on how this value of tolerance can be applied to the increasing number of minorities who bring with them in this majority Christian and secular country—their own non-Christian religion, their own cultural lifestyle or worldview, and their own language.

8.1.3. *Moral ethos*

Another major characteristic of civil religion in the Netherlands is the so-called Dutch moral ethos, which in this study is primarily attributed to Calvinism. Despite the declining role, authority, and influence of denominational churches in contemporary Dutch societies, the historical impact of religion continues to linger on in the consciousness of its people. Religious traditions of a particular society have historically shaped their national culture and have become part of the cultural heritage of the nation. Authors like Goudsblom (1979:20) and Groenhuis (1977:81) believe that some of the elements gathered to form the national identity of the Dutch people can be traced back during the time of the free Batavians and Fries and linked with the present political, cultural, and economic themes. They indicate some of the historical elements such as—the victory against Spain, the language and trade, and the Calvinist religion (whereby some Dutch folks considered themselves as the 'New Israel'),—to be some of the significant foundations of the formation of the Dutch national identity. The impact of the Calvinist religion has been transmitted mainly through nationwide institutions, to the population of the Dutch society as a whole—even to those who have little or no contact with religious institutions. Thus as these authors would claim, we can reasonably suppose that in the Netherlands, there is a widespread fusion of the general Dutch value-system and the Calvinist tradition which are specifically manifested by their idea of the 'elect' and the 'Calvinist work-ethics'.[9]

Concept of the elect

One of the significant Calvinist influence is the idea of the 'elect' or the feeling of being 'chosen by God'.[10] This ethos enkindles the feeling

---

[9] This is not to deny the existing regional differences between northern and southern Catholics. The northern Catholics are said to have been more influenced by Calvinism than the southern Catholics (Peters 1990).

[10] This is not to deny that some authors disagree on the Calvinistic influence among the Dutch people in general. Dutch historians like Smitskamp (1947) and Kossman

of being the 'light for the whole world' in order to lead the rest of the world in pursuit of certain ideals. In his book *De eeuw van mijn vader*, the author Mak (1999) recognizes that one of the main characteristics of the Dutch identity is the sense of a national missionary drive.[11] This missionary drive fostered by the feeling of being light of the world is expressed in the secular version of the feeling that the Dutch people shall set an example for the whole world, or that the Netherlands is an 'exemplary nation'. It is the feeling that what the Dutch people do, the whole world will follow. Many see the dramatic profile of secularization in their own country as portent for future development of other societies. Contemporary indicators of this feeling is the idea that the rest of the world will follow with regards its 'liberal position' on issues like the legalization of euthanasia, abortion, same-sex marriage, etcetera. This is also true with regards the feeling of many Dutch people regarding their 'social welfare' policies, which can be marked by the slogan: "In Social Welfare, We trust!" It is said that the national pride of Holland rests on its exemplary social welfare policy (Ter Borg 1990:174). This *ethos* is also shared by the Catholics demonstrated for instance by the prevailing *élan* during the Dutch Pastoral Council in the 60's which gave the impression that this council will set as an example for the whole Catholic world (Goddijn 1989). There is also an underlying paternalistic and patronizing tendency that is produced from this Calvinist ethos.

Work ethics

Another significant feature of the moral ethos is the so-called Dutch work ethics. On the one hand, Calvinist ethos emphasizes industry, piety and successful life, but on the other hand, it underscores self-denial, sobriety, thriftiness, and efficiency. Dutch people like to see themselves as hard-working people. They take pride on being generally industrious and assiduous worker, thus the saying: 'God created the world, but the Dutch created the Netherlands." For them, laziness is loathsome. As the old Dutch adage states: "Laziness is the devil's

---

(1963) both disagree with the idea that there is such a presence of the notion of *chosen people*. Kossmann argues that the Calvinists did not have the conviction that Holland is the new Israel nor did they conceive of a messianic conviction about themselves in relation to other religions.

[11] Quoted in *De Volkskrant*, 28 April 2006.

pillow" (*Luiheid is des duivels oorkussen*); or, "Work makes noble" (*arbeid adelt*). The Dutch sociologist, Hofstede (1987) portrays the Dutch to play the role of a 'farmer's wife', having to depict him/herself as someone who has a 'no-nonsense, no esthetics, and hardworking nature'. For many a Dutchman or woman, one's daily endeavor counts and success in one's worldly endeavors is valued. One's 'salvation' is a product of one's sweat and personal endeavor. As many Dutch people would say: 'If you want anything in life, you have to work for it'. Each person is responsible for one's own action. Religiously speaking, this Calvinist work ethics emphasizes individual's responsibility before God. Each individual has the responsibility to live a good, productive and moral life before God. Furthermore, many Dutch people are noted to be very conscientious about 'doing the right thing'. This kind of work ethics accounts for the Dutch's record as having one of the highest labor outputs worldwide (Vossestein 2004). While many Dutch people value work as a way to achieve success in life, indulgence to worldly prosperity is perceived to be inauspicious, if not an embarrassment as the book of Schama (1987) would indicate. Thus, simple living, thriftiness and sobriety should accompany success through hard work and diligence. This Calvinist ethos, as Weber would say, could result to a high production and low consumption, creating a surplus that cannot be consumed, which is instead invested for the greater glory of God. Prosperity was not only a sign of God's blessing but also a temptation to worldliness; the more successful one was, the harder one had to work at being godly. This was done not by fleeing from the world but by attacking it head on. This temptation to worldliness can be overcome by taking concern for the needy, to ameliorate with ease the sufferings of the unfortunate. The work of charity or concern for social issues is even more valued than spending wealth through worldly indulgence. As the great Dutch poet Constantijn Huygens (1596–1687) states: "There is a pro-active solution for the rich person of conscience: Give where the need requires; unbolt your hand. In this way, the excess from your table enable a life to live upon your crumb" (cited in: MacCants 1997:15). This type of Dutch ideal may have some repercussions with regards the way the Dutch people may relate to the so-called 'other' in the society. Acceptance of an 'out-group' member to the 'in-group' in the Dutch society may be judged according to these ideals. A person who is active, austere, and hard-working is more acceptable than a person who is indifferent and manifest idleness.

8.1.4. 'Hidden' religious ethos

Civil religion in the Netherlands touches on some underlying 'hidden religiosity' which encompasses Dutch people in general.[12] We call this religiosity 'hidden' in the sense that its manifestations are not easily detectable in the contemporary context of secularism in Holland. This 'latent' religiosity may account for the religious attitudes that break denominational barriers and somehow accounts for the integration of different groups within the Dutch society. This religious ethos may also be attributed as the repository of the people's identity and continues to play a role in their cultural identity. It serves as a 'chain of memory' which influences the worldview of every Dutch men and women in one way or the other. Although there are multifarious facets of this 'hidden' religiosity, we shall identify only two, namely: the Dutch 'representation of religiosity' and a 'ritualized' civil religiosity.

Dutch representation of religiosity

The representation of religiosity of an average Dutch person may be characterized by a pragmatic, democratic, tolerant and rational religiosity. Certainly, one can spell out manifold descriptions of the Dutch religiosity. However, there is a notable levelling off on certain religiosity whereby Dutch people tend to latch on and generally agree with. While it is true that traditional theistic belief have declined in the Netherlands, there is however a strong religious tendency towards immanent transcendence or perhaps even to absolute immanent beliefs in general (Van der Ven 1998). This means that Dutch people tend to find God's immanence in the world's events and in nature so much stronger than the theistic belief in absolute transcendence. This 'immanent-oriented' type of religiosity has become more apparent than the transcendent-oriented type of religiosity (Peters & Schreuder 1987). This type of

---

[12] In investigating civil religion, one has to be keen in finding its peculiar shape, its 'secret presence', as Martin (2005:11) states, and its mutation into unusual variant, sometimes under misleading name (perhaps, even labeled with non-religious appellations). As one author would say, "Christian sources of contemporary mentalities are overlooked because they are no longer identified by their Christian name" (Martin 2005:8). One should also be aware that some of these 'secular values' that form part of the meaning-giving system in a modern society have been mutations, inflections, and deflections from this society's historical religious source. On the part of the Christian believer, one should also be aware of the presence of what Donald Davie calls as the 'Christian oxymoron' which refers to the adaptation of Christianity to worldly contexts (Martin 2005).

religious orientation drives the Dutch people to be concerned for a more humanistic way of dealing with issues which underscores commitment to people and to the society. The 'this worldly-concern' is such characteristics of the Dutch religiosity that at times it becomes indistinguishable from those of secular movements or groups, except for an 'overlay' of religious language attributed by the believer. This might be the reason why Dutch secularists or humanists on the one side and the religionists on the other side can forge solidarity when issues like peace, political freedom, human rights, etcetera. are at stake. This belief is also tied up to the pragmatic ethos of the Dutch whereby the concern for practical import and reasonable action play a significant role in their belief system. The rationalistic tendency of many Dutch people allows for a greater internalization and intellectualization of religion. Thus as Herbert (2003:25) explains, this tendency may be considered as a sort of a 'discursive religion' which according to him is "less tied to traditional legitimating institutions and more characterized by personal conviction" (Herbert 2003:25). Moreover, the religious consciousness of the Dutch people in general is inclined to favor a democratic structure or institution in their religious discourses. Consensus building, participation, and subsidiarity are normative values that embrace the Dutch consciousness. Toleration in terms of religious convictions has been a very strong attribute of the Dutch religiosity. Respect for other's faith claims and non-religious persuasions mark the Dutch religious ethos. Thus, with these characteristics of the Dutch religiosity which is typified by their democratic, tolerant, rationalistic, and pragmatic religiosity, one can assume that claiming otherwise would mean the rejection of such type of religiosity.

Ritualized civil religiosity

These religious ethos of the civil religion have been ritually manifested for instance on certain festivities like the celebration of Christmas day on Dec. 25, on Good Friday during the celebration of Matthean Passion, or on the Dutch secular version of 'holy week' which begins on April 30 (Queen's Day) and ends on May 5 (Liberation Day). In the celebration of the National Memorial Day (May 4) for instance, the core values of the people are not only perceptible but are also used frequently as a source of inspiration and as identification point of the Dutch people (Ter Borg 1990:170). The devastation wrought by World

War II have become a rallying point for them to come together as a nation and ritually swear that things that happened during the war shall never happen again. These are rare occasions during the year that Catholics, Protestants, secularists, etcetera come together and celebrate as a nation. There are also some of the so-called 'holy books' that have been identified as elements or expressions of civil religion, for instance: the Diary of Anne Frank, the Writings of Etty Hillesum, *Het bittere kruid* by Minco, *Ondergang* by Presser, *Het koninkrijk der Nederlanden in de Tweede Wereldoorlog* by de Jong and *De aanslag* by Mulisch (Ter Borg 1990:171). These 'holy books' function to make recognizable these faith propositions of civil religion and stimulates emotional feeling of unity among the people. Amidst a pluralistic and a much differentiated (co-)existence of the Dutch people, this so-called civil religion becomes a binding force for its people.

8.2. *Reactions to civil religion among Dutch Catholics*

The previous section shows us the phenomenon of civil religion which we assume to pervade the entire Dutch society. We endeavor to identify some of the significant elements that characterize the specific makeup of the Dutch civil religion. We make the assumption that the existence of civil religion in the Netherlands may account extensively for the way our respondents interpret the diverse religious beliefs that confront them like for instance the five Judeo-Christian themes that we discussed in the foregoing chapters, namely, God, Jesus, Spirit, Salvation, and Church. And yet, as we try to look back at our explications of these themes, we realized that our Judeo-Christian tradition do not have a monomorphic way of interpretation but rather a polymorphic one. Thus, we decided to include in our conceptualization and operationalization a wide array of approaches and interpretations of these themes which we deemed to have influenced to a certain degree the Dutch believers (Van der Ven et al. 2004:318). Now the question is, to what extent do the religious attitudes of the Dutch Catholics succumb to the pervasive influence of civil religion in the Dutch society? Our hunch is that our respondents have diverse reactions towards civil religion. Although we may assume that civil religion pervades the whole of the Dutch society, this does not however imply that all Dutch believers embrace civil religion as such. There are diverse reactions that can be posited from them. Some would respond negatively to civil religion by rejecting it or by refusing to dialogue with it. This is what we call the traditional reaction to civil religion. Some would also respond positively to it through an authentic endeavor to interpret civil religion critically and constructively in the light of the Christian tradition and vice versa. This type of reaction is what we call the contextual reaction to civil religion. And still, some would respond by totally conforming to civil religion and dismiss the significance of the Christian faith. This is called the humanistic reaction to civil religion.[13]

In order to help us structure all the religious attitudes according to the three reactions to civil religion, we shall use the analogical categories of the three-dimensional coordinates of height, width, and length. This three-dimensional structure can facilitate an easy overview of all the religious attitudes that are categorized according to the three reactions to civil religion.[14] Moreover, this structure is also meant to help us in the implementation of our analysis of the relation between religion and ethnocentrism. Let us describe briefly these three dimensions of height, length, and breadth.

The height dimension of the religious themes involves the tension between transcendence and immanence, of which the extremes function as the upper and lower limits of the religious attitudes respectively. When talking about height dimension of religious attitudes, it is important to speak of limits because there is no absolute in transcendence and immanence. As Van der Ven (2004:323) comments, there is always a "tension between the two, in such a way that their interrelationship appears to vary from one era of Christian history to the next." The length dimension of the religious themes indicates the temporal aspects of religious beliefs which are related to the past, the present, and the future. The religious attitudes of our respondents may be presumed to be permeated by the time orientation which abounds in the Judeo-Christian tradition. This tradition has an elaborate explication

---

[13] I owe this distinction from Berger's (1980) differentiation of deductive, inductive, and reductive religion which I translated into traditional, contextual, and humanistic reactions to civil religion.

[14] This three-dimensional structure has been employed to show the effect of some themes of Christian religion. Schillebeeckx (1981:731) used this three dimensional characterization of religious attitude when he speaks about the 'height, and breadth and depth of human salvation'. Van der Ven et al. (2005:322–325) employed the concepts of Wierbicka on several religious attitudes in their study of human rights and religion in South Africa. I employed the same distinction of height, length and width on the religious attitudes based on the linguistic concepts of Wierbicka.

of the past which involves a primordial beginning like the stories of creation, or a series of new beginnings like the covenant, exodus, exile, return, etcetera. It also underscores the present as a pivotal moment by which things or events are perceived and interpreted. It consists of an attitude that values the 'now' or the present moment in defining other realities. Aside from the past and the present, the Judeo-Christian tradition also emphasizes the future. It involves a vision of the ultimate future that could have been proclaimed in the past and anticipated in the present, and will be inaugurated in the end time in its completeness. Although, we have tried to operationalize them in such a way that some form of analytical differentiation and distinguishability of their temporal nature can be identified in their staccato sequence or in their seeming 'absoluteness' like an absolute past, an absolute present, and an absolute future, we ought to recognize that in the Judeo-Christian tradition, time is not only perceived in their sequential or chronological terms but also in their qualitative form, like for instance a kairos moment, or the inter-signification of events, etcetera. The width dimension concerns the domain in which each individual reaches out to other domains other than him/herself. It involves the expanding ambit of one's relation to the immediate 'other' in the family, neighbourhood, workplace, religious group, country, and natural environment. It is also the sphere in which 'embrace and exclusion' may take place. It is within this realm where we can locate answers to the question broached by the 'lawyer' in the *Story of the Good Samaritan* who asked: "Who is my neighbour?" (Luke 10:29). The religious attitudes of Christians are permeated by concerns that often challenge them to expand their perspective towards the neighbour out there in the personal, social and ecological domains. By using these three-dimensional coordinates of height, width, and length, we hope to capture an elaborate description of the three reactions to civil religion.

In what follows we shall clarify the division of religious attitudes towards God, Jesus, the Spirit, salvation and church into the three reactions on civil religion, namely, traditional (8.2.1.), contextual (8.2.2.) and humanistic reactions (8.2.3.). We are doing this in order to offer a logical and reasonable structure in our presentation. The ultimate aim, as it has been said in question 7 in 1.2, is to try to answer the question whether and to what extent the impact of traditional, contextual and humanistic religious attitudes on ethnocentrism, divided into positive in-group and negative out-group attitudes, vary.

8.2.1. Traditional reaction to civil religion

Despite the compelling influence of civil religion in the Dutch society, there is one type of religious attitude that refuses to engage or simply ignores civil religion. It tends to stick or conserve tradition without any innovation. This type of reaction to civil religion is represented by what we may call as the traditional religious attitude. Let us describe this attitude according to its three dimensional structure.

Height Dimension. One of the underlying reasons why traditional religious attitudes react negatively to the Dutch civil religion can be grasped by examining its position in the tension between transcendence and immanence. Traditional religious attitudes tend to emphasize the transcendence or the vertical aspects of the belief system. They attach absolute meaning to the transcendent reality and to its truth claims. They presuppose that one can have a privileged access to a divine and universal set of truths which becomes an unambiguous and exclusive possession of their community or religious institution. They maintain that by embracing a particular set of religious doctrines, one has thereby become possessor and guardian of the exclusive and absolute truth about the human situation. Traditional religious attitudes also have a dualistic worldview in which reality is dichotomized into the spiritual and the material plane, the former regarded as good and the latter evil, or at least neutral. This highly transcendental nature of traditional religious attitude is bolstered by its notion of revelation by which God is believed to have directly communicated eternal truths from above and that believers have only to 'passively receive the divine truths for eternal salvation beyond all fleeing subjective human experience' (De Mesa & Wostyn 1990:17). In this manner, traditional religious attitudes tend to downplay the mediation of critical rationality and human experience. They tend to stand apart from the on-going development of society and refuse to get involved with the challenges posed by the modern Dutch society.

Length Dimension. Traditional reaction to the Dutch civil religion can also be represented by religious beliefs that have either a *past* or a *future* religious orientation. Traditional religious attitudes underscore a temporal religious orientation that is fixated to a particular symbolic structure of the past, more specifically, to the classical symbolic structure in western Christianity both in its major Catholic and

Protestant forms. Because of this tendency, traditional religious attitudes emphasize doctrinal orthodoxy based on classical tenets, texts or symbolic structures formulated in the earlier period. Furthermore, traditional religious attitudes also believe that final and definitive salvation had already transpired in the past. The tendency to idealize the past makes it hard for traditional religious attitude to adjust to the on-going events of the present, which in this case, implies difficulty in making any headway in establishing dialogue with the Dutch civil religion. Another temporal manifestation of a traditional religious attitude is its future orientation. This religious attitude believes that salvation is something that will happen in the future. It is something that awaits us in the future. In Christianity, this future orientation of traditional religious may be interpreted according to either the apocalyptic eschatology or the prophetic eschatology. Apocalyptic eschatology views the present history of human existence as irredeemable and hopeless. God will destroy this present age and inaugurate a 'new heaven and a new earth'. Salvation therefore will happen in the future but outside human history. The future and 'a-historical' character of the apocalyptic eschaton and its negative view of the present may prompt believers of this apocalyptic future to be suspicious and critical to the state of affairs that represents the society. The pessimistic view of the present engendered by believers of an apocalyptic future tend to denigrate all of society's affairs, its 'distorted' political, economic, social systems and degenerated values and moralities, etcetera, which they expect to be soon facing its doom. Another way of interpreting the future orientation of traditional religious attitudes is through prophetic eschatology. Prophetic eschatology views evil to lie internally among the people of God and that God will accomplish his work in the future but within human history. Prophetic eschatology tends to be critical and dissatisfied with the present state of affairs, not because it is hopeless and doomed, but because it is 'incomplete' and will find fulfillment and completion in the future within human history. The sense of 'incompleteness' of the state of affairs allows believers of the future to relativize and even criticize the present in favor of a benevolent future, which is represented, for instance, by the Kingdom of God. Although, these two interpretations of the future are available in Christian religion, traditional religious attitudes tend to emphasize only the a-historical character of the future orientation according to the apocalyptic eschatology.

Width Dimension. Traditional religious attitudes display a 'proximate' or a 'near' religious orientation. Their scope of concern is limited to the individual or to its *own* religion or *own* church group. They have an exclusivistic disposition and tends to be isolated from the on-going development of society and culture. When speaking about the church structure, traditional religious attitudes tend to emphasize a monocentric structure and highlights hierarchical and centralized authority. They are not able to accommodate the plurality of voices within its group nor is it able to accept other voices aside from its own. It is no wonder that traditional religious attitudes react negatively to the Dutch civil religion which emphasizes democracy, autonomy, tolerance, etcetera. They are incapable of forging dialogue with the values characterizing modernity. In the midst of religious pluralism, traditional religious attitudes tend to be exclusivistic. These types of religious attitudes resonate well with the church's old axiom: *extra ecclesiam nulla salus*.

Offhand, one can have reasons to say that this type of religious attitude can no longer be the prominent model to describe most of the Dutch religiosity in the increasingly secularized context. As Luckman (1967) pointed out, traditional religiosity has become a marginal phenomenon in modern society. Since the 19th century and the first half of the 20th century, the almost exclusive role of tradition gradually declined in western culture which is partly due to Enlightenment. Furthermore, the 'out-of-this-world', or simply the non-engaging character of this religious attitude disallows it, if not shirks itself, to fully deal with the questions that are raised in society. However, despite the pervasiveness of civil religion, this type of religious attitude continues to influence the religiosity of a certain portion of the Dutch population. Its influence among a group of the Dutch population can be attributed to certain contributions of tradition in the development of human community, like for instance: it provides resources for identity, and serves as a communication system that provides cohesion and continuity in the community (Schreiter 1985:105). For these reasons, one can say that traditional religion endures to exist amidst civil religion. Despite the secularization process in most European countries, it may still be the case that, generally, the link with tradition still tends to be stronger than is commonly assumed, and perhaps even stronger than is the tendency to discard them. "Despite all sorts of signs of erosion of 'religious memory' (religious amnesia), the imprint that Christian and church history have left on the collective memory of humankind, and are still making and reinforcing, is not easily erased and its influence cannot simply be undone" (Van der Ven 2004:336).

8.2.2. *Contextual reaction to civil religion*

The second type of reaction to the Dutch civil religion is what we call the contextual reaction. This contextual reaction is represented by religious attitudes that demonstrate a positive or a constructive but critical engagement with civil religion. Furthermore, in contrast to traditional religion where tradition is upheld without innovation, contextual religion uses tradition in a dynamic way. Let us further examine the contextual religious attitude according to its three dimensional structure.

<u>Height Dimension</u>. There are several characteristics that can illustrate the height dimension of contextual religious attitude. One of them is its immanent-transcendent orientation. Schoonenberg (1991:131) describes immanent-transcendent religious attitude in this way: "God's presence in relation to his creation surely has a twofold form: He is at the same time present *in* and present *by* or *for* his creation." Immanent-transcendent religious orientation emphasizes that God is present in the world but transcends the world. This immanent-transcendent orientation of contextual religious attitude is an attempt to strike a balance between immanence and transcendence (Van der Ven 1998:161). Another characteristic of contextual religious attitude in relation to its height dimension is its effort to comprehend the Christian faith not only on the basis of Scripture and tradition but also on the basis of concrete culturally conditioned human experience. It takes into account the context or the *locus* of the gospel proclamation.[15] In the Netherlands, positively engaging with the context implies that the Judeo-Christian tradition has to be in dialogue with modernity and the challenges it poses to Christianity (cf. Van der Ven 1993). This impetus for positive engagement with modernity has been reflected also in

---

[15] *Context*, as defined in Webster dictionary, refers to "the whole situation, the background or the environment relevant to a particular event, personality, creation, etcetera." It is the environment in which something is or occurs. It has temporal and spatial dimensions within which all kinds of factors (economic, political, social, cultural, etcetera.) are influential. Contexts are vitally important because they control, influence, and affect everything within them.

the official teachings of the Catholic church, particularly in *Gaudium et Spes*. This document exhibited the challenge posed by Pope John XXIII when he convened the Second Vatican Council "to take a new look at the world in which the church now lived, to offer an evaluation of its strengths and needs, to examine the appropriateness to this world of its pastoral attitudes, strategies, and institutions, to reform what was no longer appropriate, and to be willing at once to learn from the world, even as it sought to teach it" (Komonchak 2000:88). The Catholic Church reiterated during the council her commitment to re-root the gospel to the present culture and experiences of peoples. She declared for instance, that theological investigation must necessarily be stirred up in each major socio-cultural area (*Ad Gentes*, no. 22) if cultural rooted-ness of the Gospel and of the church is to be achieved (De Mesa 1991:2). In *Evangelii Nuntiandi* (1974), the church emphasizes once again the process of incarnating the Gospel in the context of the local churches. It stresses that the socio-cultural integration of the local church involves translating the gospel into verbal forms meaningful to people in particular existential situations.[16] Another characteristic of this contextual attitude is the manner in which it relates with the humanistic and liberal ideas of the Enlightenment, both learning from it and at the same time conveying its criticism to it. Contextual religious attitude tries to present the this-worldly and human side of religious beliefs, without necessarily reducing it to sheer immanence. It accepts the role of human beings as subjects of human happiness and authors of a better world. It also favors a horizontal, anthropocentric and historical worldview in which truth is secured by reason in the world of the phenomena itself. Human beings are characterized as a free subject who realizes his or her freedom in context, in the very historical process of interaction with his/her environment.

<u>Length Dimension</u>. Contextual religious attitude is temporally oriented to the present. They perceive the present events as salvific. They harbor sanguine attitude towards the current situation, and engage with

---

[16] We have to acknowledge however that even classical theologies are *contextual* during their formation stage. Creative moments in theology have emerged as a form of response of the church to new challenges in a given historical context. They carry the cultural and social imprints of the time. The theology of St. Thomas Aquinas, for instance, was a response to the questions and issues raised by Aristotelian philosophy, and the hierarchical structure of medieval society which greatly influenced the Thomist system of theology.

it critically and yet constructively. They affirm that the Christian core symbol of Kingdom of God has significant implications to our present life, to the worldly well-being of peoples. Salvation, according to these contextual attitudes, happens now! Heaven is what we make of it in the present. Because of the optimistic regard of contextual attitude to the 'present' time, it is able to engage into dialogue with the Dutch civil religion. However, the present orientation of the contextual religious attitude also has a prophetic and critical element in it. Religious attitudes are not completely riveted to the present as they where that they can no longer transform the present situation nor do something better out of it. Present-oriented religious attitudes are prone to make the present a quality present, so to speak. Earlier we mentioned about Ricoeur's 'thesis of the threefold-present' (1984) wherein he speaks of the 'present of the past', the 'present of the present', and the 'present of the future'. In these three instances, the present becomes the vantage point from which history or time is perceived and interpreted.

<u>Width Dimension</u>. Contextual religious attitude displays a far and a mid-far religious orientation. Ever since Vatican II announced the church's *aggiornamento* towards the modern world, several religious discourses have been keen on expanding the horizons that allows Christian faith to connect with other aspects of life, with the society, with modernity and science, with cosmos, with other religious traditions, and also with non-religious persuasions (cf. Gilles 1998; Hodgson 1994). Salvation was no longer contained within the axiom *extra ecclesiam nulla salus*. There is also a shift from an anthropocentric, substantial and mechanistic view of reality to a biocentric/cosmocentric perspective (Hodgson 1994:94). Contextual attitude also acknowledges the merits of democracy both externally (i.e. in modern society) and internally (i.e. within its structure). It accepts *sensus fidei* and *consensus fidelium* as important criteria and sources of the authenticity of the Christian faith and the church. This has been acknowledged in the Catholic Church most significantly during Vatican II. In *Dei Verbum* 10, for instance, it underscores that an 'authentic' (Lt. *authentice* = authoritatively) interpretation of the Word of God is the task of the whole community. Contextual religious attitude differs from traditional religious attitude in that the former recognizes the importance of human experience as a source for reflection on Christian faith and morals. In contrast to traditional attitude which presents revelation as some form of eternal truths that have been handed down to us from

Christ and the Apostles, and that faith is understood to be the intellectual assent to those truths, contextual religious attitude proclaims that revelation is the ongoing act of God's self-disclosure in the personal, interpersonal, social, and cosmic terms. Revelation is the offer of God-self to human beings through concrete actions and symbols in history (Bevans 2002). Faith is conceived as a response of the self as a gift to the personal God. And God's offer of God-self to human beings could be made in ways that is comprehensible in their own contexts.

There is no doubt that contextual religious attitude also characterizes the Dutch religiosity along with the traditional model. Its burgeoning growth in the Dutch context may be attributed to several factors. For one, it has been caused by dissatisfaction to traditional approaches to faith which do not resonate anymore to contemporary experiences. Contextual religious attitude however, relates to the insights of modern philosophies and contemporary science. Its keenness on making its message relevant attracts believers who seriously think about relating one's faith with concrete human experiences.

8.2.3. *Humanistic reaction to civil religion*

Aside from the traditional and contextual reactions to civil religion, we also identify a third type which we call in this study as the humanistic reaction. This type of reaction to civil religion manifests a positive engagement to civil religion and at the same time regards Christian faith and religion in general as inconsequential or even dysfunctional to society's existence. It is a type of reaction which has a non-theistic and non-religious bearing. Modern humanism in the Netherlands blossomed in the 18th century.[17] It was around this time that humanism started to become an alternative discourse to the prominent traditional Christian teaching and served as a substitute for belonging to a religious affiliation. Humanism as a non-Christian worldview appeared around 1857 through the writings of its antagonists such as

---

[17] The phrase 'humanism' is said to have been coined only in the early 19th century based on the Italian word *uminista*, which was used to designate a historical movement in Europe that started in the 14th century with Petrarch and ended in about 1620. This movement is noted to have dedicated themselves to the study of Greek and Roman letters (see: Derckx 1998). In the Netherlands, *humanism* has often been associated with the famous Erasmus of Rotterdam (1469–1536) whose teachings is said to have great impact on the development of the humanistic thinking in modern Dutch society.

the Calvinist leader G. Groen van Prinsterer and Abraham Kuyper, and its protagonists like Allard Pierson, Johannes van Vloten and A. H. Gerhard. In the present Dutch society, humanism has acquired a wide assortment of meanings (cf. Derkx 1998; Duyndam, et al. 2005). Let us examine some aspects of humanistic attitude and the various meanings attached to it. We shall however restrict to the height dimension of the humanistic attitude because in literatures, we do not find peculiar characteristics on the length and width dimensions by which humanistic attitude would distinguish itself from Christian ones. For that reason we decided to leave out the dimensions of length and width in humanistic attitude both in the theoretical and empirical part of this study.

Height Dimension. Humanistic attitude represents the bottom line in the vertical or the height dimension which is immanence. Adherents of this type try to understand and experience human existence and the world meaningfully using purely human terms of reference. God's existence, revelation, and religious practices are judged to be purely human in origin. Social concerns are based on universally accepted human values and avoid reference to any religious dimension. In the Netherlands, humanism is used to refer to a worldview (*levensbeschouwing*, in Dutch) which is characterized as some sort of life philosophy and practice which endorses reason, ethics, and justice, and specifically reject the divine as warrants of moral reflection and decision making.[18] Its basic teachings include the need to test beliefs by reason only; the commitment to reason, evidence, and scientific method; the concern for individual fulfillment, growth and creativity, constant search for truth, arts, and the 'this-worldly' life perspective (cf. Duyndam et al. 2005). Humanism underscores man's responsibility for its own well being. It takes into account the individual person as a primary source of human value (Reichley 1985:41). Humanism maintains that it is up to human beings to find the truth as opposed to seeking it through revelation, mysticism, religious tradition, or anything else that is incompatible with the application of logic to the evidence. Man is the measure of all. He is the maker of history. Humanism ushers the enthronement

---

[18] It is debated whether humanism can be considered as a religion as such by virtue of its totalistic worldview making it a functional equivalent to traditional religious views. Thus it is contested whether its position can be categorized as 'religion' or philosophy.

of man, the individual endowed with rights and autonomy. In many respects, humanism is fairly regarded as the ideology of modernity, or as Comtean's 'religion of humanity'.

If we compare the humanist reaction to civil religion with that of the traditional, one can say that the humanistic attitude serves as the opposite pole of traditional reaction to civil religion in the sense that the humanistic reaction absorbs everything from the civil religion and interprets all that consists of civil religion in purely inner-worldly fashion, whereas the traditional reaction rejects or ignores most, if not all, of that which represents the Dutch civil religion. Compared to contextual reaction, the humanistic reaction can be distinguished for its non-theistic and non-religious life stance. Contextual religious attitude takes a critical correlation approach with regards to civil religion in that it critically and constructively re-interprets civil religion in the light of faith, and it takes a critical and prophetic task in challenging certain aspects of civil religion. Humanistic orientation disengages from anything 'divine', religious or ecclesiastical doctrines, beliefs, and power structures, and extricates itself from anything transcendent. Humanism puts aside or even sometimes discards religion and religious faith in its discourse. Although, it should be noted that humanistic orientation also allow some space for the conception of God but interpreted on a purely immanentist or horizontal way. This can be exemplified for instance by pantheistic or metatheistic God images. Pantheistic and metatheistic God images connect with humanism in terms of their non-personal belief in God. They are critical of beliefs which depend on transcendental beliefs or 'revelations' derived from 'sacred books'. Hartt (1951:38) explains that humanism starts from a frankly human level and may leave some room for defining God concept in terms of pantheism. According to Hartt, pantheism typifies a humanistic attitude in that it believes in an absolutely immanent nature of God. God is an impersonal entity that permeates all things and encompasses all things. God participates in the substance of man and other earthly things, and nothing beyond that. There is no difference between God and the world. God is the structure and totality of the world. Pantheism reflects a humanistic attitude in that it believes that all human beings have inherent value and are worthy of basic respect without any reference to something transcendent (Harrison 2004). Metatheism likewise exemplifies the humanistic attitude in that it negates any personal conception of God and that God radically surpass all forms of human knowing and naming. It transcends all forms of theism of whatever form or character. Metatheism extricates itself from any definite proposition about the divine. That is why, as Van der Ven (1998:111) explains, there is some kind of agnosticism in the metatheistic orientation: "a religious not knowing, a religious shuddering at the forming of a clear thought about God, or speaking explicitly about God." Metatheistic belief reflects the attitudes of many 'agnostics' and perhaps even humanists of today, who do not fundamentally reject every expression about god, but shudder at any attempt to form a proposition, because of their basic uncertainty, or the accurateness of their grasp of the 'unknowable God' (Van der Ven 1998:111–112). This is particularly true if we consider our operationalization of the metatheistic attitude in this study (Appendix I, table 3, part 2, A). This operationalisation may be considered to contain an overlap referring to 'not knowing God' in both Christian 'negative theology' and humanist 'agnosticism'.

It is not impossible to assume that these non-theistic and non-religious characteristics of humanistic attitudes can also be located among the present day Catholic believers. Some religious attitudes of our respondents may have been influenced by humanistic interpretations of religious themes. For this reason, we took them into account in our survey among our Catholic parishioners.

The scheme below (Scheme 8.1) gives us the summary of the religious attitudes in the three-dimensional categories and grouped according to their engagement with civil religion, (i.e. traditional, contextual, and humanistic), and concretize them in terms of the five Judeo-Christian themes which we discussed in the previous chapters: God, Jesus, Spirit, salvation, and church.

Scheme 8.1. Traditional, Contextual, & Humanistic Religious Attitudes in Three Dimensions

Reactions to Civil Religion	HEIGHT DIMENSION			LENGTH DIMENSION			WIDTH DIMENSION		
	Transcendence	Immanent Transcendence	Immanence	Past	Present	Future	Near	Mid-far	Far
Traditional	God - anthropo-morphic theism Jesus - classical - neo-classical Spirit - Trinity-related - Jesus-related Salvation - absolute-transcendent			Salvation - past-oriented		Salvation - future-oriented	Salvation - exclusivism - personal Church - hierarchical-centralized - micro-level - meso-level		
Contextual		God - panentheism Jesus - interpersonal-oriented - society-related - Spirit-motivated Spirit - cognition-related - affection-related Salvation - immanent-transcendent - bodily			Salvation - present-oriented			Jesus - inter-personal - society-related Salvation - inclusivism - social Church - cultural-adaptation - democratic	Spirit - society-related Salvation - pluralism - ecological Church - macro-level
Humanistic			God - pantheism - metatheism Jesus - Humanistic Salvation - absolute-immanent	n.a.*	n.a.	n.a.	n.a.	n.a.	n.a.

* = not applicable.

8.3. *Expected impact of religious attitudes on ethnocentrism*

Earlier, in chapter 7, we touched on the topic about ethnocentrism. We define ethnocentrism as a complex of attitudes involving a positive attitude towards the in-group and a negative or hostile attitude towards the out-group (Eisinga, et al. 1990). Based on the social identity theory (Tajfel and Turner 1979), we learn that the notion of ethnocentrism involves mental processes consisting of 'social identification' (that is, a selective perception of predominantly favourable characteristics among members of the in-group), and 'social contra-identification', (a selective perception of predominantly unfavourable characteristics among members of out-groups). The 'realistic group conflict theory' (Bobo & Smith 1994) also tells us that inter-group competition lead to heightened in-group favouritism, in-group solidarity and in-group pride on the one hand, and out-group prejudice and hostility on the other hand. We also mention that studies in the past have demonstrated that religion has a strong impact on the ethnocentric attitudes of peoples. However, in this study, we want to raise a new question in the whole debate regarding the relationship between religion and ethnocentrism by bringing in the phenomenon of the Dutch civil religion and the various reactions to it among contemporary Christian believers. We argue that the problem surrounding this debate can be explicated through an investigation of the religious attitudes within the context of the Dutch civil religion and the various reactions by the Christian believers towards it, which may or may not have an effect on their ethnocentric attitudes. We raise the question: what are the effects of the religious attitudes, which we distinguish into traditional, contextual, and humanistic reactions to civil religion, on ethnocentrism, while controlling for some population characteristics. In what follows, we shall state some of our expectations in this study regarding the impact of religious attitudes, i.e. traditional, contextual, and humanistic, on both the positive in-group attitude (section 8.3.1.) and the negative out-group attitude (section 8.3.2.) of our respondents.

In general, we can formulate our expectations as follows:

> Expectation 1: Traditional religious attitudes have a negative impact on positive in-group attitude;
> Expectation 2: Contextual religious attitudes have a positive impact on positive in-group attitude;
> Expectation 3: Humanistic attitudes have a positive impact on positive in-group attitude;
> Expectation 4: Traditional religious attitudes have a positive impact on negative out-group attitude;

Expectation 5: Contextual religious attitudes have a negative impact on negative out-group attitude;
Expectation 6: Humanistic attitudes have a negative impact on negative out-group attitude;

A word of caution is needed in regard to the nature of these expectations. These expectations consist of two elements: religious attitudes on the one hand and ethnocentrism, as differentiated into positive in-group and negative out-group attitudes on the other. The first element is derived from chapters 2 to 6 and especially from chapter 8.2, in which the religious attitudes toward God, Jesus, the Spirit, salvation and church have been structured into three groups: religious attitudes as traditional reactions to civil religion, religious attitudes as contextual reactions to civil religion, and attitudes as humanistic reactions to civil religion. The second element is derived from chapter 7 in which the distinction between positive in-group and negative out-group attitudes has been clarified. The expectations are to be seen as indications of the relation between the two elements formulated in terms of impact. The expectations are to be considered as logically and reasonably to be derived and derivable from the previous chapters, and not as a result of a play with preconceived convictions.

Here we intentionally use the methodological term 'expectations' and not 'hypotheses'—the term 'theses' is even *latius hos*—, because we consider the logically and reasonably derived consequences of the previous chapters as an endeavour to approach the relation between religion and ethnocentrism in an adequate way. We stress the words 'endeavour' and 'approach', because there is no robust theory in this area on which we can rely as yet. This makes this study into a new and innovative one. The term 'exploration' is adequately used here because it fits in the aim of this research, which is ultimately descriptive and explorative in character (see: 1.2).

8.3.1. *Expected impact of religious attitudes on positive in-group attitude*

Let us now elucidate further the expectations we have on the differential impact of religious attitudes on the positive in-group.

Expectation 1: Traditional religious attitudes have a negative impact on positive in-group attitude

Based on our examination of its height dimension, we indicated that the *traditional* religious attitudes exhibit a highly transcendent-oriented type of religious attitude. Empirical studies have shown that belief on a purely transcendental religious images have been diminishing among the Dutch respondents (Bernts et al. 2007; Van der Lans 2001:354; Pieper/Van Der Ven 1998; Van der Ven/Biemans 1994). They have become marginal in modern society (cf. Luckmann 1967) and may unlikely be a plausible resource for social-identification among the majority Dutch believers. Moreover, if one examines its width dimension, one can also say that traditional religious attitudes demonstrate a 'narrow' perspective and can be expected to have a negative impact on positive in-group attitude. This prediction can be motivated especially when the particularistic and closed tendencies of this type of religious attitudes run contrary to the democratic, tolerant, and pluralist nature of the Dutch civil religiosity. In relation to their length dimension, traditional religious attitudes portray both past- and future-oriented attitudes. Past-oriented religious attitudes are often related to religious traditionalism and conservatism. Because of their strong orientation to the past, this type of religious attitudes tends to underscore fixed and immutable ideas or values that are firmly anchored on past tradition and are predisposed to preserve customary ways of living and social existence (Felling, Peters & Schreuder 1988). This fixation to the past often comes in conflict with values that characterize modern Dutch culture which underscores liberal values like tolerance, equality, freedom, autonomy, etcetera. For this reason, we can expect that past-oriented religious attitude, like the past salvation attitude, can be expected to have a negative effect on in-group ethnocentrism. Traditional religious attitudes also manifest a strong future orientation, especially the apocalyptic future-orientation. These attitudes have the tendency to relativize or mitigate the past and present state of affairs in view of a definitive and universal salvific event that will transpire in the future. This future-orientation which characterizes traditional reaction to civil religion can be expected to have a negative impact on positive in-group attitude.

Based on our investigation of the traditional religious attitudes according to their three dimensional characteristics, we can plausibly conjecture that traditional religious attitudes towards an anthropomorphic theistic God, classical Jesus, neo-classical Jesus, Trinity-related Spirit, Jesus-related Spirit, absolute transcendent salvation, past-oriented salvation, future-oriented salvation, personal salvation, exclusivistic salvation, hierarchical-centralized church, micro-oriented church, and meso-oriented church, have a negative impact on the positive in-group attitudes of our respondents (see: Scheme 8.2b below).

Expectation 2: Contextual religious attitudes have a positive impact on positive in-group attitude

If we look at contextual religious attitudes based on their height dimension, we can observe that these religious attitudes resonate with the modern 'life orientations' of many Dutch people which put meaning on the inner worldly values and are far positive towards one's engagement to the world (Norris & Inglehart 2004). Contextual religious attitudes express appreciation of the 'world' as a locus of God's revelation. They proclaim that God is in the world albeit not guzzled by it. Religious attitudes which are immanent-transcendent in character are found to be rather the standard religious belief system for many Dutch believers (Van der Ven 1998; Ziebertz 2001; Van der Slik 1994). If we consider their length dimension, we can also indicate that contextual religious attitude exhibits present temporal orientation. This present orientation of contextual religious attitude displays a critical-optimistic regard for the present conditions of life which can be indicated by the level of satisfaction in which Dutch people perceived themselves as a nation. Contextual religious attitude that highlights the present such as the present-oriented salvation, perceives salvation as an affirmation of the well-being that is experienced in the 'now'. This critical-optimistic disposition towards the present state of affairs in the present-oriented salvation can be expected to foster a positive in-group feeling and will be expected to enhance a positive regard for collective identity. In terms of their width dimension, contextual religious attitude demonstrates a far and a mid-far orientation. The far and mid-far orientation of contextual religious attitude directs individuals to reach out to other domains of life aside from his/her own. They engender the attitude of openness and tolerance which can be associated to the tolerance of the Dutch people that has been embedded in its culture ever since the establishment of the Dutch Republic (Shilling 1992:410). This tolerant and open attitude of contextual religious attitude will more likely beget a positive in-group feeling or a sense of belonging in the Dutch society.

After examining the three dimensional characteristics of contextual religious attitude, we can expect that this type of religious attitudes will have a positive impact on positive in-group attitude among our

Dutch respondents. This will be expected from religious attitudes towards a panentheistic God, Spirit-motivated Jesus, society-related Jesus, interpersonal-oriented Jesus, cognition-related Spirit, affection-related Spirit, society-related Spirit, immanent-transcendent salvation, present-oriented salvation, inclusivistic salvation, pluralistic salvation, bodily salvation, social salvation, ecological salvation, culturally-adapted church, democratic church, and macro-oriented church (see: Scheme 8.2a below).

Expectation 3: Humanistic attitudes have a positive impact on positive in-group attitude

In our investigation of the height dimension of the humanistic attitudes, we recognize that these religious attitudes manifest an absolutely immanentist type of faith. They reflect non-theistic and non-religious characteristics which underscore inner-worldly values and beliefs. Many of these inner-worldly values are values that are shared in common by the Dutch people in general, as what previous studies indicated, for instance: the priority attached to their own career, to freedom to enjoy life, to freedom of speech and expression, and to individual freedom in matters of life and death, viz. abortion and euthanasia (Felling et al. 1992:53–69). The horizontalistic orientation of these humanistic attitudes are mirrored in several characteristics of the Dutch civil religion as we described them earlier like for example autonomy, democracy, Enlightenment, pragmatism, etcetera. Several of these characteristics are the underlying moral and political driving force in shaping a just and humane Dutch society (Derkx 2002). These immanentist attitudes reflected through the secular values do mirror some of the most important elements in forging a positive social identification in the present Dutch society. As we mentioned earlier, we restrict our study to the height dimension of the humanistic attitudes. We leave out the length and width dimensions of the humanistic attitudes because they don't really show conceptual difference with those dimensions in the traditional and contextual reactions to civil religion (see: Section 8.2.3). For these stated reasons above, we can therefore expect that humanistic attitudes towards a pantheistic God, metatheistic God, humanistic Jesus, and absolute immanent salvation, will have a positive impact on the positive in-group attitude (see: Scheme 8.2a below).

The schemes below (Scheme 8.2a, Scheme 8.2b., and Scheme 8.3.) summarize the expected effect of religious attitudes on positive in-group attitude.

Scheme 8.2a. Expected Positive Effects of Religious Attitudes on Positive In-Group Attitude

	POSITIVE EFFECTS							
	HEIGHT DIMENSION			LENGTH DIMENSION			WIDTH DIMENSION		
	tran-scendent	*immanent transcendence*	*immanent*	*past*	*present*	*future*	*near*	*mid-far*	*far*
Traditional									
Contextual		God – panentheism Jesus – interpersonal-related – society-related – Spirit-motivated Spirit – cognition-related – affection-related Salvation – immanent-transcendent – bodily			Salvation – present-oriented			Jesus – inter personal-related – society-related Salvation – inclusivism – social Church – cultural adaptation – democratic	Spirit – society-related Salvation – pluralism – ecological Church – macro-level
Humanistic		God – pantheism – meta-theism Jesus – humanistic Salvation – absolute-immanent	n.a.*	n.a.	n.a.	n.a.	n.a.	n.a.	n.a.

* n.a. = not applicable

Scheme 8.2b. Expected Negative Effects of Religious Attitudes on Positive In-Group Attitude

	NEGATIVE EFFECTS							
	HEIGHT DIMENSION			LENGTH DIMENSION			WIDTH DIMENSION		
	tran-scendent	immanent transcendence	immanent	past	present	future	near	mid-far	far
Traditional	God – theism Jesus – classical – neo-classical Spirit – Trinity-related – Jesus-related Salvation – absolute transcendence			Salvation – past-oriented		Salvation – future-oriented	Salvation – exclusivism – personal Church – hierar-chical-centralized – micro-level – meso-level		
Contextual									
Humanistic				n.a.*	n.a.	n.a.	n.a.	n.a.	n.a.

* n.a. = not applicable

Scheme 8.3. Expected General Impacts of Religious Attitudes on Positive In-Group Attitude

	HEIGHT DIMENSION			LENGTH DIMENSION			WIDTH DIMENSION		
	Transc	Imman-transc.	Iman	Past	Present	Future	Near	Mid-far	Far
Traditional	–			–	–	–			
Contextual		+			+			+	+
Humanistic			+	n.a.	n.a.	n.a.	n.a.	n.a.	n.a.

Legend: + = positive effect; – = negative effect; n.a. = not applicable

8.3.2. *Expected impact of religious attitudes on negative out-group attitude*

In this section, we shall try to elucidate on the expected differential impact of religious attitudes on the negative out-group.

Expectation 4: Traditional religious attitudes have a positive impact on negative out-group attitude

We stated earlier that religious attitudes that represent traditional reaction to civil religion exhibit a strong transcendent orientation. These height-oriented religious attitudes are dependent on authority based on traditions and values of the past which runs contrary to the Dutch civil religion that underscores autonomy, rationality and critical thinking. Previous findings (e.g. Eisinga et al. 1990) have also noted that people adhering to traditional and conservative beliefs tend to exhibit prejudice against racial and ethnic out-groups. Glock and Stark (1966:78) for instance argue that orthodox beliefs, such as the traditional religious images, play a causal role in anti-Semitism because they generate particularistic religious orientation, i.e. 'the notion that only one's own religion is true and legitimate and that others are therefore false'. Because of this orientation, traditional religious attitudes have often been considered to be purveyors of intolerance towards other people, especially those who do not subscribe to the 'eternal truths' professed by its adherents (Hughes 2003:2–3).[19] This type of belief system has been associated to confessional-based religion which, according to scholars of civil religion, has been historically responsible for the division and disintegration in society (cf. Bellah 1967; 1985). Likewise, by looking at their length dimension, we realize that traditional reactions to civil religion are characterized by their strong relation to the past and the apocalyptic future. Their strong orientation to the past has been related to conservatism which is linked to ethnocentric attitudes (Adorno et al. 1950; Dahl 1999:93). Naylor (1996:141) also shows that conservatism is linked to ethnocentrism because, according to him, "within cultures, changes and innovations are going to be judged against what is already known and practiced (in the past)". Thus conservatives are often portrayed as restrictive, authoritarian and intolerant (Derber & Ferroggiaro 1995: 147). For these reasons, we can sensibly expect that a 'past-fixated' religious attitude will have a positive effect on negative out-group attitude. We can also conjecture that

---

[19] As Hughes (2003:2–3) contends, "rejection of transcendence in contemporary images is partly due to reaction to religious absolutism, to claims of privileged access to a divine and universal set of truths, claims that lend themselves to self-aggrandizement through oppression, dehumanization, and even slaughter of those without 'the true faith'.

religious images that are absolutely fastened to the future, especially on an apocalyptic future, will have a positive effect on the out-group ethnocentrism. McTernan (2003) states that faith-based antagonism has been motivated by a 'future' conception of salvation whereby those who believe such thought are convinced that when they die defending their faith, they will be immortalized. Furthermore, a lopsided dwelling upon the future construed to be some kind of royal manifesto delivered from the future, can lead to a failure to care for the present (Alves 1975:135). They tend to be oblivious of the inequality, discrimination, inhumanity, and brutality in the present. This can somehow lead to some latent manifestation of out-group ethnocentrism whereby most members of the majority population deny the daily reality of racism and discrimination (Essed 1991). This can take the form, for instance, of marginalization whereby members of the in-group make the out-group feel excluded and unimportant. Moreover, this future oriented attitude can plausibly effect a negative attitude towards the 'outsider' especially when the fear of future insecurity is triggered. When we examine the width dimension of these traditional religious attitudes, we come to realize that this type of religious attitudes have a 'proximate' character in terms scope. Some authors have already pointed out the prejudice-producing potential of these religious images. Previous studies have shown that individualistic beliefs are almost without exception positively correlated with prejudice and authoritarianism (Van der Slik 1994:28). Furthermore, the hierarchical, monocentric, exclusivistic qualities of traditional religious attitudes have also been indicated to be factors that can potentially produce ethnic prejudice.

After examining the traditional religious attitude based on its three dimensional characteristics, we can expect that these type of religious attitudes will have a positive effect on negative out-group attitude among our Dutch respondents. This will be expected on religious attitudes such as the anthropomorphic theistic God, classical Jesus, neo-classical Jesus, Trinity-related Spirit, Jesus-related Spirit, absolute transcendent salvation, past-oriented salvation, future-oriented salvation, exclusivistic salvation, personal salvation, hierarchical-centralized church, micro-level church, and meso-level church (see: Scheme 8.4a below).

Expectation 5: Contextual religious attitudes have a negative impact on negative out-group attitude

By investigating the height dimension, we learned that contextual religious attitudes reveal an immanent-transcendent orientation. Religious attitudes that demonstrate an immanent-transcendent orientation have been related to a positive valuation of autonomy (i.e. the right to live one's life as one wishes), and social autonomy (i.e. egalitarianism, by which the differences between groups in society are reduced) (cf. Van der Ven 1998). This study shows us that people who have an immanent-transcendent religious outlook are mindful in respecting individual rights and social equality. This implies that they will reject racist or aversive attitude towards the out-group. Previous studies have likewise indicated that contextual religious attitudes have a negative impact on negative out-group attitude. For instance, the work of Duriez, Hutsebaut & Roggen (1999) demonstrate that 'second naïveté', which in our study shows conceptual overlap with contextual religious attitude, does inhibit racism or in this case, a negative out-group attitude.[20] When we investigate the length dimension of contextual religious attitudes, we notice that their temporal orientation is bent to the present. This type of religious attitude views salvation as a sense of fulfillment in the present. It gives believers the ability to live the present existence with critical optimistic disposition. A faithful person is one who fully invests his or herself into God. It moves people to connect with his or her daily experience and prods believers to work out his or her salvation in the present time (Phil. 2:12). Since the present is the disclosure of God's saving grace, believers will have to work out salvation effectively in their lives. Believers are motivated to act according to the values of the kingdom in their daily lives. The acting out of these values includes acceptance and hospitality to strangers (Matthew 25:35). For this reason, one may plausibly expect that present-oriented religious attitudes will have a negative effect on negative out-group attitudes. Moreover, contextual attitudes also manifest mid-far and far-reaching extensions of their spheres when speaking about the width dimension. Both the mid-far and far religious attitudes are expected to display a tolerant attitude towards the outsider. The more extended the tolerance of the believer towards the so-called 'other' in the society, the more we can expect that their religious attitudes will have a negative effect on the negative out-group. Furthermore, religious attitudes that demonstrate concern on the socio-political issues in society, issues concerning the ecological environment, and religious and cultural dialogue, can be expected to have a negative

---

[20] Duriez & Husebaut (2000) describe 'second naiveté' as that 'in which one tries to encompass and go beyond all possible reductive interpretations; one which engages the inner life as a whole.

impact on the negative out-group attitudes. Olson (1963) underscores the fact that believers who see the relations of their faith to the issues in the world around them will be less inclined towards prejudice.

Our examination of the three-dimensional structure of contextual religious attitude leads us to the expectation that contextual religious attitude will have a negative impact on negative out-group attitudes of our respondents. This will be expected from religious attitudes such as panentheistic God, interpersonal-related Jesus, society-related Jesus, Spirit-motivated Jesus, cognition-related Spirit, affection-related Spirit, society-related Spirit, immanent-transcendent salvation, present-oriented salvation, inclusivistic salvation, pluralistic salvation, bodily salvation, social salvation, ecological salvation, culturally-adapted church, democratic church, and macro-oriented church (see: Scheme 8.4b below).

Expectation 6: Humanistic attitudes have a negative impact on negative out-group attitude

In our study of the height dimension of the humanistic reaction to civil religion, we found out that this type of reaction have a strong 'immanentist' orientation. The immanentist orientation of humanistic attitudes generally underscores the concern for 'common humanity', for a 'this-worldly' type of salvation and well-being. The humanistic moral or ethical principles and values like for instance, loving all people, tolerance, solidarity, and the conviction that all human beings are fundamentally connected with each other as persons, or that humankind is the highest unity higher than other collectives that might claim the loyalty of peoples—all these qualities strengthen our expectation that this type of attitude will have a negative impact on the out-group ethnocentrism of our respondents. The immanentist character of the pantheistic may bring in the idea of considering the presence of that 'Something higher' among other people, particularly the minorities for this case. Thus, a more respectful disposition may be generated from this type of belief. The metatheistic God image may be able to engender the sense of unity despite the differences in religious affiliations because of its ability to surpass any definite or unshakeable propositions about God which often is the cause of enmity and conflict. As we said earlier, we only expect effects of the height dimension characteristics on ethnocentrism and no peculiar effects of the width and length dimensions (see: Section 8.2.3). Given all these thoughts, we can expect that humanistic attitudes will have a negative impact on out-group ethnocentrism. This expectation holds true to the following images: pantheistic God image, metatheistic God image, humanistic Jesus, and absolute immanent salvation image (see: Scheme 8.4b below).

The schemes below (Scheme 8.4a, Scheme 8.4b, and Scheme 8.5) present the summary of the expected effects of religious attitudes on negative out-group attitude.

Scheme 8.4a. Expected Positive Effects of Religious Attitudes on Negative Out-Group Attitude

	POSITIVE EFFECTS								
	HEIGHT DIMENSION			LENGTH DIMENSION			WIDTH DIMENSION		
	transcendent	*immanent-transcendence*	*immanent*	*past*	*present*	*future*	*near*	*mid-far*	*far*
Traditional	God – theism Jesus – classical – neo-classical Spirit – Trinity-related – Jesus-related Salvation – absolute transcendence			Salvation – past-oriented		Salvation – future-oriented	Salvation – exclusivism – personal Church – hierarchical-centralized – micro-level – meso-level		
Contextual									
Humanistic				n.a.*	n.a.	n.a.	n.a.	n.a.	n.a.

* n.a. = not applicable

218 CHAPTER EIGHT

Scheme 8.4b. Expected Negative Effects of Religious Attitudes on Negative Out-Group Attitude

	POSITIVE EFFECTS							
	HEIGHT DIMENSION			LENGTH DIMENSION			WIDTH DIMENSION		
	tran-scendent	imma-nent-transcend-ence	immanent	past	present	future	near	mid-far	far
Traditional									
Contextual	God – panentheism Jesus – interpersonal-related – society-related – Spirit-motivated Spirit – cognition-related – affection-related Salvation – immanent-transcendent – bodily				Salvation – present-oriented			Jesus – inter personal-related – society-related Salvation – inclu-sivism – social Church – cultural adaptation – democratic	Spirit – society-related Salvation – pluralism – ecological Church – macro-level
Humanistic		God – panthe-ism – meta-theism Jesus – human-istic Salvation – absolute-immanent	n.a.*	n.a.	n.a.	n.a.	n.a.	n.a.	n.a.

* n.a. = not applicable

Scheme 8.5. Expected General Impacts of Religious Attitudes on Negative Out-Group Attitude

	HEIGHT DIMENSION			LENGTH DIMENSION			WIDTH DIMENSION		
	Transc	Imman-transc.	Iman	Past	Present	Future	Near	Mid-far	Far
Traditional	+			+		+	+		
Contextual	–				–			–	–
Humanistic			–	n.a.	n.a.	n.a.	n.a.	n.a.	n.a.

Legend: + = positive effect;— = negative effect; n.a. = not applicable

8.4. *Empirical impact of religious attitudes on ethnocentrism*

After having presented the theoretical expectations on the impact of religious attitudes on ethnocentrism in the previous section, we shall now explore the extent of this relationship from an empirical perspective. This section aims to describe the empirical findings of our analysis. We will proceed first by showing the effects of religious attitudes on the positive in-group attitude (section 8.4.1); and then, we will illustrate the effects of religious attitudes on the negative out-group (section 8.4.2).

The assumptions on which our expectations on the impact of religious attitudes on ethnocentrism are grounded on earlier discussions we made concerning social identity theory which holds that ethnocentrism consists of 'social identification' and 'social contra-identification', and the 'realistic group conflict theory' which holds that inter-group competition leads to heightened in-group favouritism, in-group solidarity and in-group pride on the one hand, and out-group prejudice and hostility on the other hand. This distinction between 'us' and 'them' can be made on numerous grounds, for example, on the basis of gender, political preference, religious affiliation, ethnic background, etcetera. We also assume that religion, on a more specific level, has a strong impact on the ethnocentric attitudes of peoples, as earlier studies reveal. However, we also said that in this study, we want to hoist a new question in the whole debate regarding the relationship between religion and ethnocentrism by bringing in the phenomenon of the Dutch civil religion and the various reactions to it among contemporary Christian believers. We argue that the problem surrounding this debate can be explicated through an investigation of the religious attitudes within the context of the Dutch civil religion and the various reactions by the Christian believers towards it, which may or may not have an effect on their ethnocentric attitudes. We raise the question: what are the effects of the religious attitudes, which we distinguish into traditional, contextual, and humanistic reactions to civil religion, on ethnocentrism, while controlling for some population characteristics. From these assumptions, we expect religious attitudes to have an impact on ethnocentrism, both in regard to the in-group (see: Section 8.3.1) and in regard to the out-group (see: Section 8.3.2).

In order to determine the extent to which religious attitudes influence ethnocentrism, we execute a hierarchical regression analysis on our data. In this analysis, we spell out the independent variables to consist of the religious attitudes. The religious attitudes that are entered in the regression analysis are the following: Attitudes toward God—anthropomorphic theism, anthropomorphic panentheism, non-anthropomorphic pantheism, and the non-anthropomorphic metatheism; Attitudes toward Jesus—classical, neo-classical, interpersonal-related, society-related, Spirit-motivated, and humanistic; Attitudes toward Spirit—Trinity-related, Jesus-related, cognition-related, affection-related, and society-related; Attitudes toward salvation—absolute transcendence, immanent transcendence, absolute immanence, past-oriented, present-oriented, and future-oriented, exclusivism, inclusivism, pluralism, bodily, personal, social, ecological; and, Attitudes toward church—culturally-adapted, hierarchical-centralized, democratic, micro-, meso-, and macro-level tasks of the church.

A number of population characteristics are chosen as controlling variables. These characteristics are noted to have significantly influenced the ethnocentric attitudes of believers, aside from the religious attitudes that we just mentioned. In chapter one, we have argued that each of these population characteristics may have some influence on the ethnocentric attitudes of our respondents. In this study, we identify three main groups of population characteristics, namely: the demographic characteristics (i.e. age, gender, education, and ethnic origin); the social characteristics (i.e. localistic authoritarianism, conformism, anomie, and subjectively-perceived threat); and the religious characteristics (i.e. church involvement and religious saliency).

The dependent variables consist of the two components of ethnocentrism, namely, positive in-group attitude and negative out-group attitude.

In Scheme 8.6, we illustrate the conceptual model for the regression analysis.

Scheme 8.6. Conceptual Model of Expected Predictive Relationships
(*Religious Attitudes & Ethnocentrism*)

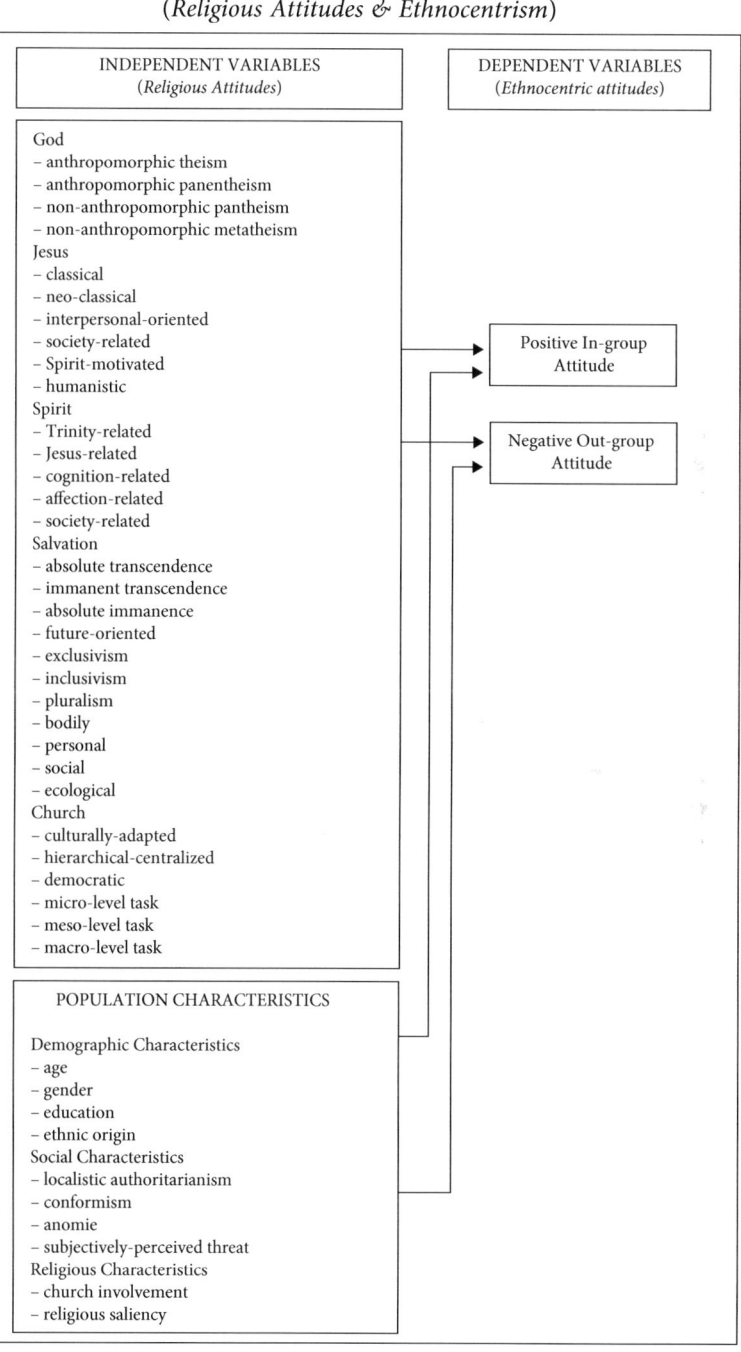

INDEPENDENT VARIABLES
(*Religious Attitudes*)

God
- anthropomorphic theism
- anthropomorphic panentheism
- non-anthropomorphic pantheism
- non-anthropomorphic metatheism

Jesus
- classical
- neo-classical
- interpersonal-oriented
- society-related
- Spirit-motivated
- humanistic

Spirit
- Trinity-related
- Jesus-related
- cognition-related
- affection-related
- society-related

Salvation
- absolute transcendence
- immanent transcendence
- absolute immanence
- future-oriented
- exclusivism
- inclusivism
- pluralism
- bodily
- personal
- social
- ecological

Church
- culturally-adapted
- hierarchical-centralized
- democratic
- micro-level task
- meso-level task
- macro-level task

POPULATION CHARACTERISTICS

Demographic Characteristics
- age
- gender
- education
- ethnic origin

Social Characteristics
- localistic authoritarianism
- conformism
- anomie
- subjectively-perceived threat

Religious Characteristics
- church involvement
- religious saliency

DEPENDENT VARIABLES
(*Ethnocentric attitudes*)

Positive In-group Attitude

Negative Out-group Attitude

8.4.1. *Empirical impact of religious attitudes on positive in-group attitude*

In order to find out whether and to what extent religious attitudes toward God, Jesus, Spirit, salvation and church, predict positive in-group ethnocentrism, we subjected our data to a hierarchical regression analysis whereby the positive in-group attitude is designated as dependent variables, and some selected religious scales (only those with a correlation coefficient of $r \geq .25$) as independent variables in model 1, to which in model 2 the population characteristics have been added as control variables. Table 8.1. presents the result of the regression analysis.

The second column in Table 8.1. contains the beta coefficients which indicate the effects of the religious attitudes on the positive in-group

Table 8.1. Effects of religious attitudes on the positive in-group attitude (beta) (N = 313)

Religious Attitudes	Model 1 Standardized Coefficients (beta)	Model 2 Standardized Coefficients (beta)
God		
Theism	.07	.04
Panentheism	−.03	−.02
Jesus		
Interpersonal	−.06	.00
Spirit-motivated	.03	−.01
Classical	.18*	.15
Society-related	.05	.02
Spirit		
Trinity-related	−.01	.04
Jesus-related	−.01	.01
Salvation		
Immanent transcendence	−.07	−.04
Absolute immanence	.05	.02
Absolute transcendence	.12	.12
Future	−.02	−.09
Past	.14*	.07
Exclusivism	.19**	.13*
Inclusivism	.04	.01
Social	.11	.13
Bodily	.26**	.19**
Ecological	−.21**	−.22**

Table 8.1 (*cont.*)

Religious Attitudes	Model 1 Standardized Coefficients (beta)	Model 2 Standardized Coefficients (beta)
Church		
Culturally-adapted	.34**	.28**
Group-directed (meso)	−.01	.02
Demographic Characteristics		
Age		−.05
Gender		−.04
Education		−.04
Ethnic Origin		−.01
Social Characteristics		
Localistic authoritarianism		.17*
Conformism		.13*
Anomie		−.04
Subjectively-perceived threat		.13*
Religious Characteristics		
Religious Saliency		−.01
Church Involvement		−.01
R Square Change	.40	.07
R Square	.40	.46
R Square Adj.	.36	.41

** $p < .01$; * $p < .05$ (2-tailed)

attitude, without being controlled for the population characteristics (model 1). The third column contains the beta coefficients for the effects of the religious attitudes, while being controlled for their population characteristics, i.e. demographic, social, and religious (model 2).

In model 1, the following religious attitudes have significant positive effects on the positive in-group ethnocentrism: the attitudes to the classical Jesus (.18), past-oriented salvation (.14), exclusivistic salvation (.19), bodily salvation (.26), and culturally-adapted church (.34). There is one religious attitude that acquired a negative beta, which is ecological salvation (−.21). The culturally-adapted church (.34) has the highest positive effect. This goes to show that this type of religious attitude makes the strongest unique contribution to explain the positive in-group attitude of our respondents. This model indicates that the religious attitudes have a strong influence (R^2 adjusted .36).[21]

If we examine the output of this analysis from the perspective of the three reactions to the Dutch civil religion, we can identify three religious attitudes to belong to traditional reactions (i.e. classical Jesus, past-oriented salvation, and exclusivistic salvation) and three attitudes to contextual reactions (i.e. bodily salvation, ecological salvation, and culturally-adapted church). The result also highlights three Christian themes that show important contribution to positive in-group attitude of our respondents, namely: salvation, Jesus, and church. It is also noticeable from the result that most religious variables that have an effect on positive in-group ethnocentrism have something to do with the theme of salvation (four out of six). And, as we said earlier, the ecclesiological variable (cultural adaptation church) has the highest unique effect.

Now we go on with model 2, in which the effects of the religious attitudes are controlled for the population characteristics, namely: age, gender, education, ethnic origin, localistic authoritarianism, conformism, anomie, subjectively-perceived threat, religious saliency, and church involvement. This is an important statistical procedure in order to discover whether or not the effects of religious attitudes on positive in-group attitudes are sheer 'pseudo effects' when some population characteristics may appear to play significant role that may 'explain away' the supposed effects of the religious attitudes.

The third column in Table 8.1. contains the beta coefficients for the effects of the religious attitudes, while being controlled for the population characteristics. This table shows that the attitude toward the classical Jesus shows no significant effect any more (.15). This also applies to the past-oriented salvation attitude (.07). The other four religious attitudes, namely, exclusivistic salvation attitude (.13), bodily salvation attitude (.19), ecological salvation attitude (−22), and culturally adapted church attitude (.28), maintain their significant effect on the in-group ethnocentrism, although all these attitudes weaken their effects, with the exception of the negative effect of the ecological salvation after being controlled for the population characteristics.

The religious attitude that has the highest effect is the culturally-adapted church. There are three population characteristics that have

---

[21] $R^2 < .15$: weak influence; R^2 between .15 and .25: moderate influence; $R^2 \geq .25$: strong influence.

a significant effect on positive in-group attitude, namely, localistic authoritarianism (.17), conformism (.13), and subjectively-perceived threat (.13). This model indicates that the explained variance has increased when the population characteristics have been added (R^2 change .07; R^2 adjusted .41). This result shows that the religious attitudes appear to have a rather strong (albeit lesser) effect on the positive in-group attitudes.

Looking at this result, we notice that there is one religious attitude that belongs to the traditional reaction to civil religion, namely: exclusivistic salvation. There are also three religious attitudes that belong to the contextual reaction, which are: ecological salvation, bodily salvation, and culturally-adapted church. There are only two Christian themes that display an important role on the in-group ethnocentrism of our respondents, namely: salvation and church, and among these two, the attitude towards salvation seems to have a prominent role in defining the positive in-group attitudes of our respondents.

Earlier, we stipulated three expectations concerning the relationship between religious attitudes and positive in-group attitude. Let us now examine whether and to what extent these expectations have been corroborated by the results of the regression analysis undertaken.

Expectation 1: *Traditional religious attitudes have a negative impact on positive in-group attitude.* As far as the exclusivistic attitude is concerned, which is the only significant traditional attitude left in model 2, this expectation is not confirmed.

Expectation 2: *Contextual religious attitudes will have a positive impact on positive in-group attitude.* As far as the bodily salvation attitude and the culturally-adapted church attitude are concerned, this expectation is confirmed. As far as the ecological salvation attitude is concerned, this expectation is not confirmed.

Expectation 3: *Humanistic attitudes have a positive impact on positive in-group attitude.* Model 2 shows that this expectation is not confirmed.

8.4.2. *Empirical impact of religious attitudes on negative out-group attitude*

The same procedure undertaken earlier has been carried out in order to find out how well the measures of religious attitudes predict negative out-group attitudes. We subjected our data to a hierarchical regression analysis whereby the negative out-group attitude is designated as dependent variable, and some selected religious scales (only

Table 8.2. Effects of religious attitudes on negative out-group attitudes controlling for population characteristics (beta) (N = 387)

Religious Attitudes	Model 1 Standardized Coefficients (beta)	Model 2 Standardized Coefficients (beta)
Salvation		
Future	.12*	-.03
Exclusivism	.11	.07
Bodily	.17**	-.01
Church		
Hierarchical-centralized	.24**	.03
Demographic Characteristics		
Age		.08
Gender		-.03
Education		-.01
Ethnic Origin		.02
Social Characteristics		
Localistic autoritarianism		.19**
Conformism		.01
Anomie		.16**
Subjectively-perceived threat		.48**
Religious Characteristics		
Religious saliency		-.03
Church involvement		-.04
R Square Change	.19	.38
R Square	.19	.57
R Square Adj.	.18	.55

** $p < .01$; * $p < .05$ (2-tailed)

those with a correlation coefficient of $r \geq .25$) as independent variables in model 1, to which in model 2 the population characteristics have been added as control variables. Table 8.2. presents the result of the regression analysis.

The second column in Table 8.2. contains the beta coefficients which indicate the effects of the religious attitudes on the negative out-group attitude, without being controlled for the population characteristics (model 1). The third column contains the beta coefficients for the effects of the religious attitudes, while being controlled for their population characteristics, i.e. demographic, social, and religious characteristics (model 2).

In model 1, the following religious attitudes have significant positive effects on the negative out-group ethnocentrism: the attitudes to the future-oriented salvation (.12), bodily salvation (.17), and hierarchical-centralized church (.24). The hierarchical-centralized church has the highest positive effect (.24). This goes to show that this type of religious attitude makes the strongest unique contribution to explain the negative out-group attitude of our respondents. This model indicates that the religious attitudes have moderate influence (R^2 adjusted .18).

If we look at the result of this analysis from the perspective of the three reactions to the Dutch civil religion, we can identify two religious attitudes belonging to the traditional reactions which have a significant unique effect (i.e. future-oriented salvation, and the hierarchical-centralized church), and one attitude belonging to contextual reaction that has also a significant unique effect (i.e. bodily salvation). The result also highlights two Christian themes that showed important contribution to negative out-group attitude of our respondents, namely: salvation and church. It is also noticeable from the result that most religious variables that have an effect on negative out-group ethnocentrism have something to do with the theme of salvation (two out of four).

If we examine model 2, in which the effects of the religious attitudes are controlled for the population characteristics (i.e. age, gender, education, ethnic origin, localistic authoritarianism, conformism, anomie, subjectively-perceived threat, religious saliency, and church involvement), we can observe on the third column that there are no single religious attitude that manifest a significant effect on negative out-group attitude. However, there are three population characteristics that demonstrate significant contribution to negative out-group attitude, namely: localistic authoritarianism (.19), anomie (.16), and subjectively-perceived threat (.48). This result is apparently telling us that negative out-group attitude is facilitated by factors outside religious attitudes, i.e. by the social characteristics of the believers themselves like localistic authoritarianism, anomie, and subjectively-perceived threat. They appear to explain away the earlier effects of the religious attitudes (R^2 change .38; R^2 adjusted .55).

We also mentioned three expectations with regards the relationship between religious attitudes and negative out-group attitude. Let us now try to find out whether these theoretical expectations were substantiated by the results of our analysis.

Expectation 4: *Traditional religious attitudes have a positive impact on negative out-group attitude.* This expectation cannot be substantiated by our findings as far as the result in model 2 is concerned. We can say based on this result that there is no statistical basis to claim that religious attitudes that react negatively to the Dutch civil religion such as the traditional religious attitudes have a reinforcing effect on the negative out-group attitude.

Expectation 5: *Contextual religious attitudes will have a negative impact on negative out-group attitude.* Based on model 2, we cannot ascertain that contextual religious attitudes have a negative effect on negative out-group attitude.

Expectation 6: *Humanistic attitudes will have a negative impact on negative out-group attitude.* We have no way of confirming this expectation as far as the result in model 2 is concerned.

CHAPTER NINE

CONCLUSION

We have gone this far to finally wrap up all the significant learnings we obtained from the explications we carried out in the previous chapters. We made it clear from the beginning of this book that our primary interest in this study is to examine the relations between religion and ethnocentrism, both from the theoretical and empirical points of view. We embark with a two-fold aim: first, to describe both the religious attitudes of our respondents related to the five religious themes, i.e. God, Jesus, Spirit, salvation, and church, especially in regard to the three reactions to civil religion among our catholic population, and their ethnocentric attitude; second, to clarify the relationship between religious attitudes and ethnocentrism from an empirical-theological approach and to come up with hypotheses based on the empirical outcomes of this research.

In section 9.1 of this concluding chapter, we will give a summary of the findings we acquired from previous chapters. In this same section, we will also seek to answer all the specific questions we raised in chapter 1. Next, in section 9.2, we will provide the theological evaluation and reflections based on the analysis we have gained from the preceding chapters. We will also posit some hypotheses drawn from this study. And finally, in section 9.3, we will propose some recommendations for future research on this topic.

9.1. *Summary of findings*

As we mentioned earlier, we have chosen for our research population the Dutch Catholic members who are living in the four big cities in the Netherlands, namely: Amsterdam, The Hague, Rotterdam, and Utrecht. In this study, we ask the key question: What are the effects of religious attitudes on the ethnocentric attitudes of Catholic church members? We examined the religious attitudes on five major Christian themes, namely: God, Jesus, Spirit, Salvation, and Church. We investigated the theological conceptualizations underlying these themes by taking into account the plurality of images in the Christian tradition and the rich experiences, innovative imageries, and religious wisdom which are dialectically implied in them. Then we looked into their positive in-group attitudes and their negative out-group attitudes. And finally, we explored the effect of religious attitudes on ethnocentrism. We spelled out seven specific questions as indicated in the introduction of this book, five of which concerns the attitudes of church members towards a specific religious theme (chapter 2 to chapter 6), one question is concerned about the ethnocentric attitude of our respondents (chapter 7), and the last question pertains to the effects of religious attitudes, as distinguished into traditional, contextual, and humanistic reactions to civil religion, on ethnocentrism (chapter 8). Let us reiterate these seven specific questions:

1. What are the attitudes of church members toward God, and what is the social location of these attitudes? (Chapter 2)
2. What are the attitudes of church members toward Jesus, and what is the social location of these attitudes? (Chapter 3)
3. What are the attitudes of church members toward the Spirit, and what is the social location of these attitudes? (Chapter 4)
4. What are the attitudes of church members toward salvation, and what is the social location of these attitudes? (Chapter 5)
5. What are the attitudes of church members towards the church, and what is the social location of these attitudes? (Chapter 6)
6. What are the ethnocentric attitudes of the church members, and what is the social location of these attitudes? (Chapter 7)
7. What are the effects of these religious attitudes, to be distinguished into traditional, contextual, and humanistic reactions to civil religion, on ethnocentrism, while controlling for some relevant population characteristics? (Chapter 8)

In the Dutch context, we acknowledged that there are several beliefs systems that may have influenced, in one way or the other, the religious attitudes of our respondents. We assumed that civil religion functions as the background in regard to which various groups formulated their own reactions. We depicted the Dutch civil religion to be characterized by the following ethoses, namely: the democratic, the Calvinist, the Enlightenment, and the 'hidden' religious ethos. The democratic ethos involves autonomy and religious tolerance; the Dutch moral ethos includes the concept of election and work ethics; the Enlightenment ethos is comprised of rationalism and pragmatism; and the 'hidden' religious ethos includes the Dutch civil religious perspectives and the Dutch civil religious rituals. Despite the pervasiveness of civil religion in the Dutch society, we realized that church members have diverse reactions towards it. We mentioned three general reactions to civil religion, namely: the traditional, the contextual, and the humanistic religious attitudes. With the presence of these diverse reactions to civil religion, we stated our expectations regarding the relationship between religious attitudes of church members and ethnocentrism:

1. Traditional religious attitudes have a negative impact on positive in-group attitude;
2. Contextual religious attitudes have a positive impact on positive in-group attitude;
3. Humanistic attitudes have a positive impact on positive in-group attitude;
4. Traditional religious attitudes have a positive impact on negative out-group attitude;
5. Contextual religious attitudes have a negative impact on negative out-group attitude;
6. Humanistic attitudes have a negative impact on negative out-group attitude;

We tried to examine the verity of these expectations through the empirical analysis of our data.

In what follows, we will recapitulate our findings from the previous chapters. We shall proceed by answering the specific questions that were stated earlier.

1. What are the attitudes of Dutch Catholic Church members toward God, and what is the social location of these attitudes? (Chapter 2)

In the theoretical part of chapter two, we gathered seven conceptual images of God which we categorized into four levels: iconic versus aniconic, anthropomorphic versus non-anthropomorphic images, transcendent immanence versus immanent transcendence, and the three-fold God-world relations. After subjecting the responses of our respondents to empirical analysis, we discovered that this group of church members exhibited two anthropomorphic God attitudes and two non-anthropomorphic God attitudes. The anthropomorphic God attitudes consist of theism and panentheism, while the non-anthropomorphic God images include pantheism and metatheism. The results of our analysis indicated that our respondents generally agree with all the God images. One can say that panentheism is a plausible characterization of the religious attitudes of the Dutch people we investigated. It is a way of moving over and beyond the traditional theistic God image which characterized pre-modern society, but it can also be interpreted as an indication of a critique against pure immanentism which is represented by the humanistic God image. It is a way of locating the 'divine' within the 'profane', in a non-dualistic or non-dichotomized manner. How can one interpret the agreement of our respondents towards the metatheistic God images? One can argue that this finding seems to indicate the acceptance of church members of the 'religious' character of metatheistic God image, as we explained earlier, which is to be distinguished from the 'non-religious' characteristics of metatheistic God image. The agreement to the pantheistic God image, which is a belief in an absolute immanent God, may be explained by the agreement of believers to some of the inner-worldly values which are shared in common by the Dutch people in general, like autonomy, democracy, pragmatism, etcetera. The acceptance of the notion of the theistic God image reflects the lingering presence of this traditional religious attitude in the consciousness of (even modern day) Christian believers. There are variances of attitudes towards these God images when viewed against the background of the social location of our population. Age, education, localistic authoritarianism, conformism, anomie, church involvement, and religious salience are the most important background characteristics that have significant associations and correlations to several attitudes towards God.

2. What are the attitudes of church members toward Jesus, and what is the social location of these attitudes? (Chapter 3)

In chapter 3, we investigated the attitudes of our respondents toward Jesus. In the theoretical part of this chapter, we discussed eight images of Jesus which we classified into three categories, namely: 'tradition-bound', 'hermeneutic-oriented', and 'humanistic' Jesus images. These 'tradition-bound' images are said to be images of Jesus that are exclusively tethered to the traditional sources of Christian faith, like the bible and the 'deposit of faith'. The 'hermeneutic-oriented' Jesus images consider not only the Judeo-Christian traditions as a vital source of Christological discourse but also the 'human experience' including insights from culture and history, insights coming from varieties of religious experiences and from other religious traditions and secular-worldview. The humanistic type of Jesus image regards solely the 'human experience' as the main source of 'christological' claims. In the empirical part of this chapter, these eight images have been reduced to six. These six attitudes towards Jesus include the following: the classical Jesus, neo-classical Jesus, interpersonal-oriented Jesus, society-related Jesus, Spirit-motivated Jesus, and the humanistic Jesus attitudes. Our respondents accept all the hermeneutic-oriented Jesus images (i.e. interpersonal-oriented Jesus, society-related Jesus, and the Spirit-motivated Jesus). They also accept one 'tradition-bound' Jesus image, that is, the classical image of Jesus. However, they reject the neo-classical and the humanistic Jesus images. It is striking to note that neo-classical Jesus is rejected by this group of Catholic believers, perhaps because of its utterly transcendental orientation and its disregard for other sources of christological reflection, except the bible. Moreover, it can also be that our respondents, who are Catholics, have never been socialized to the discourses of Barth who is the most outspoken representative of orthodox dialectical theology in the Protestant tradition. The rejection of the humanistic Jesus also signifies that believers cannot go as far as interpreting Jesus as 'only' a man like us, and nothing more. We also discussed some striking relationships between the attitudes toward Jesus and the demographic, religious, and social characteristics of our population. The most important population characteristics that exhibited significant associations are age, education, localistic authoritarianism, conformism, anomie, church involvement, and religious salience.

3. *What are the attitudes of the church members toward the Spirit, and what is the social location of these attitudes? (Chapter 4)*

We assume in the theoretical part of this chapter that the attitudes of our respondents toward the Spirit would be represented by the six images of the Spirit which we classify within the framework of the Spirit 'from above' (i.e. Pre-Trinitarian, Trinity-related, and Jesus-related Spirit), and the Spirit 'from below', which we sub-categorized into individual-related Spirit (i.e. cognition-related and affection-related) and the society-related Spirit. The empirical results show that our respondents display only five diverse attitudes towards the Spirit, namely, Trinity-related, Jesus-related, cognition-related, affection-related, and society-related Spirit. They demonstrate agreement to all the Spirit images. Age, education, and country of origin are the demographic characteristics that are significantly associated to all Spirit images. Localistic authoritarianism, conformism, and anomie are the social characteristics that are significantly associated to the attitudes toward the Spirit. Church involvement and religious salience play an important role on the attitudes of our respondents toward the Spirit.

4. *What are the attitudes of the church members toward Salvation, and what is the social location of these attitudes? (Chapter 5)*

In chapter 5, we looked into the theme of salvation through a broad and comprehensive framework using three dimensions: the dimension of transcendence, the dimension of time (or temporal dimension), and the dimension of space. The dimension of transcendence is represented by absolute transcendent, immanent-transcendent, and absolute immanent religious images. The dimension of time (or temporal dimension) is represented by the past-, present-, and future-oriented salvation images. The dimension of space is represented by two categories, namely: the scope of salvation and the realms of salvation. The scope of salvation includes exclusivism, inclusivism, and pluralism. The realms of salvation consist of the bodily, personal, interpersonal, structural, and ecological salvation. We also made a distinction between 'salvation from' and 'salvation for' on each aspect of the realms of salvation. The outcome of the empirical analysis proves that several of these salvation images in the theoretical part have been corroborated by our empirical findings, with a few exceptions, like for instance, the interpersonal and structural images of salvation which were combined into one factor called 'social' salvation. Furthermore, the distinction between 'salvation from' and 'salvation for' was also eliminated. Thus, from empirical perspective, we gathered at least thirteen salvation attitudes namely: absolute transcendence, immanent transcendence, absolute immanence, past, present, future, exclusivism, inclusivism, pluralism, bodily, personal, social, and ecological. The respondents agree with all the salvation images in the dimension of transcendence. Our respondents exhibit a doubtful attitude towards the temporal dimension of salvation. They are negatively ambivalent about past-oriented salvation, purely ambivalent about future-oriented salvation, but positively ambivalent about present-oriented salvation. We also note that exclusivism is rejected by our respondents. They are doubtful about pluralism, but agree with inclusivism. They agree to all the four aspects of the realms of salvation, namely: bodily, personal, social, and ecological. The most important population characteristics that play significant role in the attitudes toward salvation are: age, education, localistic authoritarianism, subjectively-perceived threat, conformism, anomie, church involvement, and religious salience appear to be the recurring population characteristics that play significant role in the soteriological religious attitudes of our respondents. Most of these population characteristics occur persistently as significant social locators of the attitudes toward salvation.

5. *What are the attitudes of the church members towards the church, and what is the social location of these attitudes? (Chapter 6)*

In chapter six, we assumed that the church members have varied attitudes toward the church. In the theoretical part, we examined the mission, the ecclesial structure, and the tasks of the church. We indicated seven conceptual models regarding church images which we assumed to be present among our respondents. These seven church models included: culturally-adapted, hierarchical, centralized, democratic, micro-level task (person-directed), meso-level task (group-directed), and macro-level task (socio-political) church models. In the empirical part, we discovered that our respondents conceived of the hierarchical and centralized church structure as one factor, which we called 'hierarchical-centralized' church structure. As a result of our empirical analysis, we were able to find out that our respondents are in favour of a culturally adapted church. We also discovered that they agree to a democratic church structure, especially in terms of participation of the laity in the liturgical activities of the church. They were rather negatively ambivalent about the hierarchical-centralized church structure. In relation to the tasks of the church, our respondents agreed to a micro-level task, ambivalent about the meso-level task, and negatively ambivalent about the macro-level task of the church. We also found out that age, country of origin, localistic authoritarianism, conformism, and church involvement, are the most significant social locators of attitudes toward the church.

6. *What are the ethnocentric attitudes of the Dutch church members, and what is the social location of these attitudes? (Chapter 7)*

In the theoretical part of chapter 7, we stated that the positive in-group attitudes and the negative out-group attitudes are the two components of ethnocentrism. In the empirical part of this chapter, we discovered that our respondents display a positive in-group attitude, but reject plainly a negative out-group ethnocentrism. Our analysis also showed that age, education, church involvement, localistic authoritarianism, conformism, anomie, and subjectively-perceived threat are the most significant social locators of positive in-group and negative out-group attitudes.

7. *What are the effects of these religious attitudes, to be distinguished into traditional, contextual, and humanistic reactions to civil religion, on ethnocentrism, while controlling for some relevant population characteristics? (Chapter 8)*

The results of the hierarchical regression analysis, as demonstrated by model 1 on Table 8.1., showed that the following religious attitudes have significant positive effects on the positive in-group attitudes: classical Jesus, past-oriented salvation, exclusivistic salvation, bodily salvation, and culturally-adapted church attitudes. The ecological salvation attitude had a negative effect on positive in-group attitude. In model 2, the following religious attitudes maintained their significant effect on the positive in-group ethnocentrism, namely: the exclusivistic salvation attitude, the bodily salvation attitude, the ecological salvation attitude, and the culturally adapted church attitude. The ecological salvation attitude had a negative effect also in the second model. The classical Jesus attitude and the past-oriented salvation attitude did not have a significant effect any more. We also observed that the culturally-adapted church made the strongest unique contribution to positive in-group attitude of our respondents. Three population characteristics indicated significant effect on positive in-group attitude, namely, localistic authoritarianism, subjectively-perceived threat, and conformism. This model (model 2) indicated that the explained variance had increased after the population characteristics having been added. It showed the extent to which some religious variables have been explained away when the population characteristics had been added as control variables.

When we examine these religious attitudes, we notice that one religious attitude belong to the traditional reaction to civil religion, that is, exclusivistic salvation, while the other three belongs to the contextual reaction: bodily salvation, ecological salvation, and culturally-adapted church. We will elaborate more on these points in the next section (section 9.2).

There are only two Christian themes that display an important role on the positive in-group attitude of our respondents, namely: salvation and church, and among these two, the attitudes towards salvation seem to have a prominent role in defining the positive in-group attitudes of our respondents.

We also conducted a hierarchical regression analysis to examine the effects of the religious attitudes on negative out-group attitudes. The results showed that in model 1, as portrayed in Table 8.2., some religious attitudes had significant positive effects on the negative out-group ethnocentrism, namely: future-oriented salvation attitude, bodily salvation attitude, and hierarchical-centralized church attitude. However, when the population characteristics had been added as control variables, as shown in model 2 of Table 8.2., there was no single religious attitude that manifested significant effect on negative out-group ethnocentrism. However, there were three population characteristics that showed significant contribution to a negative out-group attitude, namely: localistic authoritarianism, anomie, and the subjectively-perceived threat. These population characteristics seemed to explain away the earlier effects of the religious attitudes. We concluded based on this result that the negative out-group ethnocentrism is facilitated by factors outside religious attitudes, that is, by the social characteristics of the believers.

9.2. *Theological evaluations, reflections, and statement of hypotheses*

We will present in this section some of the theological evaluations and reflections in relation to the outcomes of our study. We will also deliver some hypotheses based on these reflections.

The previous section showed us a summary of the findings from all the chapters. We noted that our respondents, who are members of the Catholic church, manifest differential attitudes regarding the various religious images.[1] We found out that our respondents exhibited 'agreement' to the following religious images (Scheme 9.1):

- God images—theism, panentheism, pantheism, and metatheism;
- Jesus images—classical Jesus, interpersonal-oriented Jesus, society related, and Spirit-motivated Jesus;
- Spirit images—Trinity-related Spirit, Jesus-related Spirit, cognition-related Spirit, affection-related Spirit, and society-related Spirit;
- Salvation images—absolute transcendence, immanent transcendence, absolute immanence, inclusivism, bodily, personal, social, and ecological salvation;
- Church images—culturally-adapted, democratic church, and individual-directed task of the church.

Our respondents display 'ambivalent' attitudes towards the following religious images:

- Salvation images: pluralistic salvation, past-, present-, and future-oriented salvation;
- Church images: the hierarchical-centralized church structure, the meso-level task, and the macro-level task of the church.

There are also a number of religious images that are unequivocally 'rejected', namely:

- Jesus images: the neo-classical Jesus, the humanistic Jesus;
- Salvation image: exclusivistic salvation.

---

[1] In chapter 1, we interpreted the scores on the attitudinal scales with the help of the following criteria: 1.00–1.79 = I totally disagree; 1.80–2.59 = I disagree; 2.60–3.39 = I feel ambivalent (2.60–2.99 = I feel negatively ambivalent; 3.00–3.39 = I feel positively ambivalent); 3.40–4.19 = I agree; and 4.20–5.00 = I totally agree.

Scheme 9.1. The Religious Attitudes of church members

Agreement	Ambivalence	Disagreement
God images: – theism – panentheism – pantheism – metatheism		
Jesus images: – classical – interpersonal oriented – society related – Spirit-motivated		Jesus images: – neo-classical – humanistic
Spirit images: – Trinity-related – Jesus-related – cognition-related – affection-related – society-related		
Salvation images: – absolute transcendence – immanent transcendence – absolute immanence – inclusivism – bodily – personal – social – ecological	Salvation images: – pluralistic – past-oriented – present-oriented – future-oriented	Salvation image: – exclusivistic
Church images: – culturally-adapted – democratic – micro-level task	Church images: – hierarchical-centralized – meso-level task – macro-level task	

From this synopsis, we can point out some remarkable findings concerning the attitudes of church members toward a number of religious images.

In terms of attitudes toward God, for instance, we notice that church members accept a non-anthropomorphic God image, like the metatheistic God model, which is sometimes suspected to be a 'non-Christian' image of God. From a theoretical perspective, this result may suggest two possible forms of metatheism, namely: a religious metatheistic God image and a non-religious one. It can be the case that our respondents agree on a religious metatheistic type of God image.

We also take note of the way church members reckoned the interpersonal related Jesus as an acceptable image of Jesus. With this agreement on the interpersonal-oriented Jesus image, one may infer that this group of Dutch church members favours a type of Jesus image that has its basis in the interaction among fellow human beings. Moreover, this attitude would also imply that it is within the interaction among fellow human beings, i.e. by loving and caring for one's neighbours, that God through Jesus is revealed. Martin Buber leaves us one interesting insight in this regard: "God is truly present when one man clasps the hand of another. Here alone is the full reality of the Thou...Our relation with other persons is the real simile of our relation with God" (Buber 1970:102–103). However, while church members highly cherish the interpersonal related Jesus, they would not go as far as accepting the humanistic notion of Jesus, which they even reject.

The way the church members accept the Spirit-motivated Jesus is also worth noting. This type of Jesus image has been almost forgotten in the Catholic tradition, which for several centuries had been stressing the 'logos' Christology. Well, this result bolsters the claim by contemporary authors saying that a pneumatological approach to Christology is rather apposite for the modern and post-modern society (Haight 2005; Merrigan 2000).

Concerning the attitudes toward the Spirit, church members accept the images of the 'spirit from above' (Trinity-related Spirit and Jesus-related Spirit) as well as the two representatives of the 'spirit from below' models, namely, affection-related Spirit and society-related Spirit. Here, we notice again the lingering influence of traditional religious images among the consciousness of church members which may have been derived from their previous traditional catechetics, preachings, and religious socialization. This is also understandable due to the high age level of our respondents.

Another notable revelation is the extent to which church members render high appraisal towards the ecological salvation. This appears to be an indication of a consciousness of our population of Dutch church members that moves from anthropocentric conception of salvation towards a more cosmocentric one. It is also remarkable how this group of church members reject outrightly an exclusivistic salvation. However, they take pluralistic salvation ambivalently.

Examining now the result of the attitudes toward the church, it is also surprising that our respondents are negatively inclined towards the hierarchical-centralized church structure. Furthermore, it is also striking to observe that, on the one hand, our respondents agree on the individual task of the church, but on the other hand, they also concur with the society-related Jesus, society-related Spirit, and social salvation. From this outcome, it becomes obvious that individual and society come together in the mindsets of our respondents. This can be seen as a critical comment on the dichotomy that is often projected between 'individual'and 'society'. It may be fair to conclude that 'individual' and 'society'are dialectically related to each other, and this is necessary for a good functioning society. That being said, we also come to realize that when it comes to concrete activities, separately from the society-related attitudes towards Jesus, the Spirit and salvation, the meso-level and the macro-level tasks of the church are met with ambivalence. Here, there seems to be a difference between attitudes regarding theological themes and regarding concrete church activities.

Let us now re-examine these religious attitudes in the light of their reactions to civil religion. The scheme below (Scheme 9.2.) illustrates the attitudes of church members towards the religious attitudes which we categorized into the traditional, contextual, and humanistic religious attitudes.

Scheme 9.2. Agreement, Doubt, and disagreement of Dutch church members toward traditional, contextual, and humanistic religious images

	Agreement	Ambivalence	Disagreement
Traditional	God images: – theism Jesus images: – classical Spirit images: – Trinity-related – Jesus-related Salvation images: – absolute transcendence – personal Church images: – micro-level task	Salvation images: – past-oriented – future-oriented Church images: – hierarchical-centralized – meso-level task	Jesus image: – neo-classical Jesus Salvation image: – exclusivistic salvation
Contextual	God images: – panentheism Jesus images: – interpersonal-oriented – society related – Spirit-motivated Spirit images: – cognition-related – affection-related – society-related Salvation images: – immanent transcendence – inclusivism – bodily – social – ecological Church images: – culturally-adapted – democratic	Salvation images: – pluralistic salvation – present-oriented Church images: – macro-level task	
Humanistic	God images: – metatheism – pantheism Salvation images: – absolute immanence		Jesus image: – humanistic Jesus

If we reflect on our findings in the light of the three reactions to civil religion, we can point out the following observations.

Some traditional religious attitudes are accepted by our church members, namely: theism, classical Jesus, Trinity-related Spirit, Jesus-related Spirit, absolute transcendent salvation, personal salvation, and micro-level task of the church. As we already recognized earlier, traditional religious attitudes left an 'indelible mark' on the religious consciousness of church members that they do not easily disappear despite the pervasive impact of the civil religion in the Dutch society. There are also some traditional religious attitudes that are met with certain ambivalence, namely: past-oriented salvation, future-oriented salvation, hierarchical-centralized structure, and meso-level task church image. There are however two traditional religious attitudes that are outrightly rejected by the church members: the neo-classical Jesus and the exclusivistic notion of salvation.

Church members generally accept contextual religious images, with the exception of pluralistic salvation, present-oriented salvation, and the macro-level task of the church, which are ambivalently received by our respondents. We said earlier that contextual religious attitudes are positively or constructively (but are critically) engaged to the Dutch civil religion. The 'positive' or 'constructive' elements found in contextual religious images are apparently lacking in traditional religious attitudes, especially in the neo-classical Jesus and the exclusivistic salvation, which may explain why it is rejected by these church members. This 'constructive' element found in contextual religious images is perceived by church members to be absent in the humanistic religious attitude like the humanistic Jesus. For this reason, it is rejected by them.

One may however ask why some humanistic religious images, such as metatheism, pantheism, and absolute immanence, are accepted by church members, whereas the humanistic Jesus is discarded by them. If we look at the items of both the metatheistic God image (e.g. "There is Something higher which we cannot name in its totality") and pantheistic God image (e.g. "There is Something higher with which people and the world coincide"), the phrase 'Something higher', is used to represent these two images, while the phrases such as 'only', 'not more than', 'nothing more', are employed to represent the humanistic Jesus models. It might be that the 'restrictive' or 'constraining' connotation of the items representing the humanistic Jesus contributes to its rejection in contrast to the more sinuous connotation of the phrase

'Something higher' for the metatheistic and pantheistic God images. The absolute immanent salvation which our population also agreed with may be accepted most probably due to the eudemonistic vision of good life that resonates with the 'in-worldly' vision of God's Kingdom in the Christian tradition (Richardson 1983:190).

As we noted earlier, we also investigated the respondents' attitudes toward positive in-group and negative out-group attitudes. The respondents are positive about positive in-group ethnocentrism and reject negative out-group ethnocentrism.

From the results of the hierarchical regression analyses, we can also highlight some notable findings concerning significant religious attitudes that are predictors of positive in-group and negative out-group ethnocentric attitudes. The scheme below (Scheme 9.3.) categorizes these religious attitudes according to traditional, contextual, and humanistic religious attitudes, while being controlled for the population characteristics.

Scheme 9.3. Religious Predictors of Ethnocentrism

PREDICTORS OF POSITIVE IN-GROUP ATTITUDE

Traditional	Contextual	Humanistic
– exclusivistic salvation	– bodily salvation – ecological salvation (negative effect) – culturally-adapted church	—

PREDICTOR(S) OF NEGATIVE OUT-GROUP ATTITUDE

| — | — | — |

Scheme 9.3. shows that the religious attitudes that serve as predictors of positive in-group ethnocentrism belong only to the traditional and contextual religious images, whereas there is no single religious image that predicts out-group ethnocentrism. We already stated that although we assume that traditional religious attitudes will have a negative impact on in-group ethnocentrism, there is one religious image that has a positive effect on in-group ethnocentrism, i.e. exclusivistic salvation. The other three are of a contextual character, i.e. bodily salvation, ecological salvation (negative effect), and culturally-adapted church.

We reckon that these religious attitudes reflect the social identification of the present day Dutch believers. In other words, contemporary church members are 'customized' into the traditional (i.e., exclusivistic salvation) and contextual religious images (i.e., bodily salvation, ecological salvation [negative effect], and cultural-adaptation church), which have significant effects on their in-group identification.

Hypotheses

We note that there are some unexpected outcomes from these analyses which are worth our attention. Firstly, in our expectation 1 (sec. 8.3.1), we did not expect the 'exclusivistic salvation' to come out as a positive predictor of positive in-group attitude in the Dutch context. The question is, why is this so? One may say that it is possible to adopt an exclusivist attitude without necessarily being intolerant of others. It does not necessarily imply that one is intolerant of others when you think they are wrong even though you can't convince them, nor demonstrate to them that you are right. DiNoia (1992:33–64) also argues that great religions have diverse visions of life's principle aim, and each of them suggests that their 'aim' is the best, and each of them professes universality and uniqueness in knowing and fostering their aim. Such claims may not necessarily hinder dialogue with other religious communities. According to DiNoia, once we recognize the diversity of soteriological aims of each religious tradition, we may enter into fruitful dialogue. Dialogue may not require as conditions "excluding a priori doctrines, including those with claim to particularist universality, even though any and all doctrines may be modified as a consequence of dialogue" (DiNoia 1992:164). This is to say, from a purely logical perspective that a distinction can be made between a religious attitude which refers to exclusive salvation and an attitude from which one approaches other people, whom he/she thinks are excluded from this salvation, in an unfriendly, indecent, and even hostile way. In other words, exclusivistic salvation may lead to both recognizing religious diversity in a democratic society and rejecting it. Based on these insights, we may state our first hypothesis (hypothesis 1): the extent to which exclusivistic vision on salvation leads to a positive or negative impact on the ethnocentric attitude towards the in-group depends on the recognition of diversity as a democratic orientation in a nation, *in casu*, the Catholics in the Netherlands.

Another unexpected outcome is the 'ecological salvation' which yielded a negative effect on positive in-group attitude. In chapter 8, we identified ecological salvation as one of the representatives of the contextual religious attitude within the framework of the Dutch civil religion. We expected that this type of religious attitude would have a positive effect on the positive in-group attitude of the Dutch believers. A possible explanation can be stated from the ecological model's 'augmented' vision of cosmic identity. The ecological consciousness awakens the understanding of an expanded sense of self which moves from a substantial to a relational view of the self/world, and from anthropocentric to a cosmocentric perspective. Hodgson (1994:93) explains: "An entity is a mode of relating. The ecological model applies to the inorganic as well as the organic, the non-living as well as the living, but in truth there are no sharp boundaries between living and non-living components of the cosmic system." Current ecological consciousness affirms that all creatures exist in relationships, and that each has intrinsic value; that all sentient or non-sentient beings, humans or non-humans, are "co-citizens" of the cosmic world (Rayan 1994: 221ff). The ecological salvation attitude may be a manifestation of a growing consciousness of believers on the interconnected nature of the world and the fact that the responsibilities of citizens extend beyond in-groups or beyond the horizons of the nation to encompass the whole of the cosmic world. This new 'amplified' consciousness of self as propounded by the ecological model enables one to transcend the confines of one's identity within race or national boundaries. As Holmes (2002:16) maintains: "To consider our lives within the scope of a planetary system that is billions of years old would put our race/class/gender scuffles into perspective." For this reason and on the basis of the empirical result of our study, we now state our second hypothesis (hypothesis 2): Ecological salvation attitude has a negative effect on positive in-group attitude.

There are two outcomes of the regression analysis which confirms our expectation as earlier stated on chapter 8. The first one is the 'bodily salvation' which has a positive effect on in-group ethnocentrism. We mentioned in chapter 5 that bodily salvation entails freedom from bodily alienation and suppression, from sickness, hunger, and all kinds of bodily pain. It implies achieving good physical well being, having good health, or fulfilling one's basic physiological needs. This non-dualistic notion of salvation which embraces the body as the locus of salvation characterizes the modern day believers, connects them easily with their fellows in this 'feel-good' perspective and so influences their national in-group identification. For these reasons and on the basis of the empirical result of our study, we want to state our third hypothesis (hypothesis 3): Bodily salvation attitude has a positive effect on in-group ethnocentrism.

Next to bodily salvation, our expectation regarding the positive effect of a culturally adapted church on positive in-group attitude has also been confirmed by our empirical analysis. A culturally-adapted church is keen on adapting to the prevailing culture of the society. It is open to dialogue with modern day culture. It is positively, but also critically, engaged with modernity and the challenges it poses to Christianity. It is able to relate with the humanistic and liberal ideas which characterizes the Enlightenment ethos of the Dutch civil religion, both learning from it and at the same time conveying its criticism to it. It fits into the individual and social identity of today's believers and strengthens their social belonging. For these reasons and on the basis of the empirical result of our study, we want to state our hypothesis (hypothesis 4): Culturally-adapted church attitude has a positive effect on positive in-group attitude.

Lastly, the result of our regression analyses demonstrates that religious attitudes have no effect on negative out-group attitudes. This result runs in contrast with other studies which claim that religion have a positive effect on negative out-group attitudes (Allport 1958; Allport and Kramer 1946; Gorsuch & Aleshire 1974; Batson, Schoenrade & Ventis 1993; Hood et al. 1996; Hood, Spilka, Hunsberger & Gorsuch 1996; Eisinga, Konig and Scheepers 1995; 2000).

So how do we explain this discrepancy? We might offer three reasons. First, we collected the data for our research from the lists of church members of parishes in the four main cities in the Netherlands, i.e. Amsterdam, Rotterdam, The Hague and Utrecht. With the help of those parishes we collected 451 questionnaires which could be considered valid ones (Appendix 1, table 2). All 451 respondents appeared to be church members. This might be one of the explanations of the discrepancy we just indicated, because all sociological studies on the relation between religion and ethnocentrism we know of always include both church members and non-church members. Second, the church members whose attitudes and population characteristics we investigated appeared to be of a relatively high age, as can be seen from the youngest age group we constructed, with the lowest cut-off of 18 years and the highest cut-off of 57 years (36.6% of the research population), the second group between 58 and 68 years old (20.8%) and the oldest group of 69 and older (42.1%) (see: 1.6). This might be a second explanation for the discrepancy I referred to. The third reason might be found in the substantive differences between empirical-sociological and empirical-theological research on the effect of religious attitudes on ethnocentrism. Usually sociological research restricts their measuring of religion to a few, rather globally formulated scales of religion, mostly only church involvement to which is added questions like 'do you believe in God?', and then investigates the effects of those scales on scales of ethnocentrism. In this study however religion is not only measured in terms of church involvement or 'do you believe in God' only, but with the help of 34 attitudinal scales, four about God, six about Jesus, five about the Spirit, thirteen about salvation, six about the church (Appendix 2–6). Because of this substantively richer religious configuration the regression analyses lead to substantively different outcomes.

9.3. *Recommendations for future research*

After examining the summary, the theological evaluations and reflections, and the stated hypotheses above, we are now ready to submit our recommendations for future research on the study of religion and ethnocentrism.

Our first recommendation for future research will have to be the testing of the four hypotheses that was just stipulated in the previous section: (1) the extent to which exclusivistic vision on salvation leads to a positive or negative impact on the ethnocentric attitude towards the in-group depends on the recognition of diversity as a democratic orientation in a nation, *in casu*, the Catholics in the Netherlands; (2) Ecological salvation has a negative effect on in-group ethnocentrism. (3) Bodily salvation has a positive effect on in-group ethnocentrism; and (4) Culturally-adapted church attitude has a positive effect on in-group ethnocentrism. Further research that will carry out the testing of these hypotheses will help facilitate the formulation of a robust theory regarding the relations between religion and ethnocentrism. In regard to the impact of religious attitudes on negative out-group attitude, we decided to leave the expectations formulated in chapter 8 to be explored in future research. These expectations are: (1) traditional religious attitudes have a positive impact on negative out-group attitude; (2) contextual religious attitudes have a negative impact on negative out-group attitude; and, (3) humanistic attitudes have a negative impact on negative out-group attitude.

We also want to recommend a thorough examination of the influence of religious attitudes on the blatant and subtle, overt and covert, or explicit and latent ethnocentric attitudes of church members. Recent ethnocentric studies focus on 'cultural racism' which is manifested subtly or latently by members of the majority (cf. Verberk 1999; see: chapter 7). In nations where democratic or human rights are already firmly institutionalized by the state, there is still a need for a meticulous effort to delve into the latent prejudice of in-group members towards minority out-groups due to the complexity and subtleties of prejudice, too often using 'democratic' principles, like the separation of church and state, as an excuse for ethnocentrism. It may be that some of these 'subtle' ethnic prejudices are wrapped in religious discourses, like the uniqueness of Christianity or the perfection of the social doctrine of the church, or may be directly or indirectly influenced by it. It is therefore a notable contribution to the study of religion and ethnocentrism if future research can penetrate into the recent manifestation of unfavourable attitudes towards minorities which takes covert, subtle, or latent forms.

Since the subject and scope of this study is limited only to church members in the four cities of the Netherlands, it would be a great challenge to investigate the relationship between religion and ethnocentrism through a comparative research on a larger scale, for instance, by including members in the 'rural' and 'urban' areas, a cross-religions, a cross-national study in 'secularized' and 'less secularized' countries, or a comparative study in several countries which have distinct church/state regimes. A large-scale investigation through a cross-national comparative research of the relationships between religion and ethnocentrism could add interesting insights to the results of this empirical theological study.

We also want to recommend a comparative research by taking into account the other two monotheistic religions next to Christianity, i.e. Judaism, and Islam, and also the other major Asian religions like Hinduism and Buddhism. This study will help broaden and deepen the theoretical and empirical foundations of the relationship between religion and ethnocentrism. This would be a significant contribution in contemporary context where inter-religious encounter appears to be inevitable within the context of globalization. Furthermore, findings in this type of research will help in the construal of religious or theological concepts in pursuance of dialogue among religions.

Lastly, it would be interesting to look into the religious attitudes of the minorities themselves, and examine how their religious attitudes affect their social (contra-) identification. How does the in-group identification of these minorities being influenced by religion? What religious attitudes have a positive or negative effect on their integration in the majority in-group? What religious attitudes effect their aversive attitudes toward the majority in-groups? What religious attitudes have a positive or negative effect on their attitudes towards other minority groups? Looking at the relationship between religion and ethnocentrism from the perspective of the 'minority' may broaden our understanding of the intricate relationship of this theme.

APPENDICES & TABLES

APPENDIX 1 (CHAPTER 1: INTRODUCTION)

Table 1. Distribution Per Parish

PARTICIPATING PARISHES	Kanaleneiland Parochie (Utrecht)	Binnenstad parochie (Utrecht)	Overveght Parochie* (Utrecht)	De Graankorrel (Amsterdam)	Gerardus Maella Parochie* (Amsterdam)	Laurentius & Elisabeth (Rotterdam)	Pax Christi (Rotterdam)	Agnes Parochie (The Hague)	Gerardus-Maella (The Hague)	Total
Sample frame	252	1188	1600*	2359	6000*	1634	272	2100	1768	
Distribution	252	476	500	500	500	500	272	500	500	4.000
SILA/Non-SILA users	Non-SILA	SILA	SILA	SILA	SILA	SILA	NON-SILA	SILA	SILA	

* = parishes that made the selection and posting of questionnaires themselves.

Table 2. Distributed and Collected Questionnaires Per City

	Distributed questionnaires	Collected valid questionnaires	Valid in %
Amsterdam	1000	149	14.9
Rotterdam	772	77	10
Utrecht	1,228	181	15
The Hague	1000	44	4
Total	4,000	451	11%

Table 3. Measuring Instruments—Items and Frequencies (The following measuring instruments are the English translation of an originally Dutch questionnaire).[1]

The questions are presented here in three parts:
Part 1 = Ethnocentric attitudes measuring scales
Part 2 = Religious attitudes measuring scales
Part 3 = Population characteristics

Part 1: Ethnocentric Attitudes Measuring Scales

Range of all ethnocentric attitudes scales in the questionnaire: 1 = totally disagree, 2 = disgree, 3 = partly disagree, partly agree, 4 = agree, 5 = fully agree; *miss.* = missing values. For the purpose of presentation in the appendix, the 5-point Likert scale was reduced to three following categories:—= disagreement (scale point 1 and 2); –/+ = ambivalence (scale point 3); + = agreement (scale points 4 and 5).

q 35: The following are some statements about the Netherlands and its citizens. Please indicate the extent to which you agree or disagree with each of the following statements.

Positive attitude towards in-groups

N = 451	–	–/+	+	*miss*
35_1. We. the Dutch people. are always willing to put our shoulders to the wheel.	33.7%	44.1%	20.6%	1.7%
35_2. Generally speaking. the Netherlands is a better country than most other countries.	29%	34.8%	34.8%	1.3%
35_3. Every Dutchman ought to pay honor to our national symbols like the national flag and the national anthem.	8.6%	31.3%	58.5%	1.6%
35_4. I am proud to be a Dutch man.	7.4%	27.7%	63.6%	1.3%

q 34: Please indicate the extent to which you agree or disagree with each of the following statements about ethnic minorities in our society.

---

[1] Items marked with an asterisk (*) have been eliminated due to statistical or interpretability reasons, mentioned in 1.4.

Table 3 (*cont.*)

Negative attitudes towards ethnic minorities in general
N = 451   −   −/+   +   miss

    34_1. Most ethnic minorities are untrustworthy.   72.7%   18.0%   6.6%   2.7%
    34_5. Most ethnic minorities are lazy.   65%   23.3%   9.8%   2.0%
    34_9. Most ethnic minorities are violent.   69.2%   19.7%   8.7%   2.4%
* 34_3. Most ethnic minorities are friendly.   14.6%   40.4%   43.2%   1.8%
* 34_7. Most ethnic minorities are decent.   7.5%   28.6%   62%   1.8%
* 34_11. Most ethnic minorities are honest.   8.6%   35.7%   52.6%   3.1%

Negative attitudes toward specific out-groups
N = 451   −   −/+   +   miss

    34_2. Turks have so many children because they are slightly backward.   64.3%   22.8%   10.2%   2.7%
    34_4. When you do business with Jews. you have to be extra careful.   62.7%   21.1%   13.7%   2.4%
    34_6. With Moroccans. you never know for certain whether they are going to be aggressive or not.   48.4%   29.7%   18.8%   3.1%
    34_8. Most people from Surinam work quite slowly.   37.7%   35.9%   23%   3.3%
    34_10. Gypsies are never to be trusted.   55.9%   31%   9.8%   3.3%

Part 2: Religious Attitudes' Measuring Scales

Range of all religious attitudes scales in the questionnaire: 1 = totally disagree, 2 = disgree, 3 = partly disagree, partly agree, 4 = agree, 5 = fully agree; *miss.* = missing values. For the purpose of presentation in the appendix, the 5-point Likert scale was reduced to three following categories:—= disagreement (scale point 1 and 2); −/+ = ambivalence (scale point 3); + = agreement (scale points 4 and 5).

A. *Attitudes towards God*

q. 24: People think about God in different ways. Below are a number of statements about God.

Anthropomorphic theism
N = 451   −   −/+   +   miss

    24_1. God set the world in motion with the intention that human beings should keep it on the course God established.   14.8%   24.6%   55%   5.5%
    24_5. God got the world going with the intention that human beings would arrange it further.   14%   24.6%   57.5% 4%

Table 3 (*cont.*)

Individual panentheism N = 451	−	−/+	+	*miss*
24_2. God knows and understands me.	11.7%	22.4%	61.5%	4.4%
24_6. I trust God will never abandon me.	8.2%	16.6%	72.7%	2.4%

Social panentheism N = 451	−	−/+	+	*miss*
24_3. When people form friendships, God's love is at work.	11.9%	20.6%	64.5%	2.9%
24_7. When people live in friendship, God's love is present.	8.6%	17.1%	72.3%	2.7%

Cosmic panentheism N = 451	−	−/+	+	*miss*
24_4. I experience God's hand in the beauty of nature.	6.2%	12.8%	77%	4%
24_8. I experience God's goodness in the peace of nature.	9.3%	16%	72.2%	2.4%

q. 25: In certain situations, some people experience the existence of Something higher than themselves, but they think about it in very different ways.

Non-anthropomorphic deism N = 451	−	−/+	+	*miss*
* 25_1. There is Something higher through which everything got into motion.	8.8%	14.9%	69.6%	6.7%
* 25_5. There is Something higher through which the world came to revolve.	13.1%	20.2%	60.7%	6%

Non-anthropomorphic pantheism N = 451	−	−/+	+	*miss*
25_2. There is Something higher with which people and the world coincide.	15.5%	25.9%	51.9%	6.7%
25_4. People and the world together constitute Something higher.	10.2%	22.2%	61%	6.6%

Non-anthropomorphic metatheism N = 451	−	−/+	+	*miss*
25_3. There is Something higher which we cannot name in its totality.	20.6%	18%	56.1%	5.3%
25_6. There is Something higher that completely transcends our imagination.	8.4%	10.2%	78.3%	3.1%

Table 3 (*cont.*)

B. *Attitudes towards Jesus*

q. 26: The following are a number of statements about Jesus Christ. Please indicate the extent to which you agree or disagree with each of them.

Classical Jesus
N = 451

		−	−/+	+	*miss*
26_1.	God sent Jesus, his son, to the earth.	9.5%	19.7%	66.1%	4.7%
26_7.	Before Jesus came to earth, he lived with the Father from the beginning.	22.6%	25.3%	45.4%	6.7%
26_12.	Jesus is the God-man who from the beginning has existed unchangeable with the Father.	21.8%	24.4%	47.3%	6.5%
26_28.	In the same way as his Father, Jesus is a completely divine person.	18.9%	15.3%	59.5%	6.3%

Neo-classical Jesus
N = 451

		−	−/+	+	*miss*
* 26_11.	Jesus Christ puts all human experiences and activities in a critical perspective.	33.5%	32.6%	25.3%	8.6%
26_14.	Jesus Christ faces us with a radical decision: for or against God.	53.7%	18.2%	21.6%	6.5%
* 26_24.	Jesus Christ places us under the definitive judgment of God's words.	24%	28.8%	37.9%	9.3%
26_27.	Jesus Christ confronts us with the radical choice of choosing God or the powers of evil.	41%	19.7%	31.7%	7.6%

Individual-related Jesus
N = 451

		−	−/+	+	*miss*
26_3.	Jesus Christ has shown us through his life how we can believe in God and people.	5.3%	13.1%	77.3%	4.2%
26_8.	Jesus Christ has shown us how people may be touched by God and by their fellow human beings.	5.6%	19.1%	69%	6.3%
26_16.	Jesus Christ leads us in the love of God and of people.	6.4%	10.4%	77.8%	5.4%
* 26_21.	Jesus Christ is the example of our bond with God and people.	7.8%	15.5%	70.7%	6%

Table 3 (*cont.*)

Community-related Jesus
N = 451   −   −/+   +   *miss*

		−	−/+	+	miss
* 26_6.	God expressed his love for the world in the life and work of Jesus.	7.1%	14.6%	73.4%	4.9%
* 26_19.	The appearance of Jesus revealed the care of God for the people.	12.2%	20%	61%	6.8%
* 26_23.	Jesus is the humanity of God in word and deed.	9.6%	11.3%	73.6%	5.5%
* 26_31.	In his words and deeds as a human being, Jesus has brought the loving mercy of God to expression.	6.4%	15.3%	71.8%	6.5%

Society-related Jesus
N = 451

		−	−/+	+	miss
* 26_5.	Jesus supports the oppressed by liberating them from injustice.	8%	20.4%	65.4%	6.2%
26_10.	Jesus guides the oppressed to the land of justice.	14%	29.9%	49.2%	6.9%
26_18.	Jesus continues to live on as a stimulus for the liberation of the oppressed.	11.5%	21.7%	59.6%	7.2%
26_20.	Jesus is present where the oppressed struggle for liberation.	17.3%	30.2%	45.7%	6.9%

Spirit-motivated Jesus
N = 451

		−	−/+	+	miss
26_17.	Jesus is a special human being because God's Spirit directed him	10.7%	17.5%	65%	6.8%
26_22.	Jesus is a unique person because God's Spirit upon him	14.1%	18%	61.2%	6.7%
26_29.	Jesus is a remarkable human being because God's Spirit animated him	20.7%	24.8%	46.1%	8.4%
26_32.	Jesus is a unique human being because God's Spirit inspired him	13.3%	20.8%	59.6%	6.3%

Secular-worldview oriented Jesus
N = 451

		−	−/+	+	miss
26_4.	Jesus is the pre-eminent example of caring for our neighbour.	3.5%	8.9%	83.1%	4.4%
26_13.	At the heart of the symbol of Jesus Christ is the call to love one another.	5.1%	11.3%	78.3%	5.3%

Table 3 (*cont.*)

		−	−/+	+	miss
26_26.	In his words and deeds, Jesus has shown us what it is like to be a good human being.	3.8%	11.8%	78.3%	6.1%
26_30.	In showing us our true humanity, Jesus has shown us how to live in solidarity with others.	2.7%	11.8%	80.1%	5.4%

Humanistic Jesus
N = 451   −   −/+   +   *miss*

		−	−/+	+	miss
26_2.	Jesus is only a good man.	48.6%	14.6%	31%	5.8%
26_9.	Jesus is not more than one of the great figures of history.	62.6%	14%	16.7%	6.7%
26_15.	The only significance of Jesus is that he began an important historical movement.	58.3%	18.8%	15.3%	7.6%
26_25.	Jesus is a special person, nothing more.	61%	14.2%	17.7%	7.1%

C. *Attitudes towards the Spirit*

q. 27: The following are a number of statements about the Holy Spirit. Please indicate the extent to which you agree or disagree with each of them.

Pre-Trinitarian Spirit
N = 451   −   −/+   +   *miss*

			−	−/+	+	miss
*	27_1.	The Spirit is a symbol of God's presence.	10.4%	19.1%	64.7%	5.8%
*	27_7.	The Spirit blows where it wills.	18.6%	19.1%	54.3%	8%
*	27_12.	The Spirit is present in the wisdom of God.	10.2%	16.6%	64.6%	8.6%
*	27_22.	The Spirit is a manifestation of God in the here and now.	14.6%	19.3%	57.2%	8.9%

Trinity-related Spirit
N = 451   −   −/+   +   *miss*

			−	−/+	+	miss
	27_24.	The Spirit is one of the persons of the divine Trinity.	16.6%	20%	55.6%	7.8%
*	27_2.	The Spirit is the bond of love between the Father and the Son.	12.8%	21.5%	58.5%	7.2%
	27_8.	The Spirit has always existed as part of the Trinity.	14.6%	21.7%	54.1%	9.6%
*	27_21.	The Spirit is the fruit of the union between the Father and the Son.	18.7%	21.7%	50.3%	9.3%

Table 3 (*cont.*)

		−	−/+	+	miss
Jesus-related Spirit N = 451					
* 27_20.	The Spirit unfolds in the words and deeds of Jesus.	11.5%	17.1%	62.5%	8.9%
27_3.	The Spirit represents the dynamics of Jesus in the here and now.	13.3%	19.3%	59.2%	8.2%
* 27_9.	The Spirit is the Spirit of Jesus who continues to be present among us.	19.8%	19.7%	53.6%	6.9%
27_19.	The Spirit is the presence of Jesus that people can sense in their midst.	18.4%	26.2%	45%	10.4%
Cognition-related Spirit N = 451		−	−/+	+	miss
* 27_10.	The Spirit is the symbol of the highest forces of the human mind.	19.1%	22.2%	49.5%	9.2%
27_4.	The Spirit is the metaphor of the most precious human creativity.	17.7%	28.4%	43.5%	10.4%
27_13.	The Spirit refers to the highest level of human imagination.	20.4%	24.6%	44.8%	10.2%
* 27_18.	The Spirit is the expression of our deepest human desires.	21.8%	29%	39%	10.2%
Affection-related Spirit N = 451		−	−/+	+	miss
27_16.	The Spirit is active in the hearts of the individual person.	11.3%	22.8%	57.3%	8.6%
* 27_5.	The Spirit works in the hearts of human being.	6%	17.5%	69%	7.5%
* 27_23.	The Spirit turns the hearts of men and women to God.	13.1%	22.6%	56.3%	8%
27_14.	The Spirit dwells in our emotions.	14.2%	26.6%	50.3%	8.9%
Society-related Spirit N = 451		−	−/+	+	miss
* 27_15.	The Spirit engages us to work for transformation in society.	14.2%	27.1%	49.6%	9.1%
27_6.	The Spirit empowers people in their struggle for liberation.	7.3%	21.1%	62.8%	8.8%
* 27_17.	The Spirit motivates us to take social responsibilities.	10.9%	24.8%	55.4%	8.9%
27_11.	The Spirit inspires us to work for justice in the world.	6.2%	17.5%	68.1%	8.2%

APPENDIX 1 (CHAPTER 1: INTRODUCTION)

Table 3 (*cont.*)

D. *Attitudes toward Salvation*

Dimension of Transcendence

q. 30: The salvation granted by God is an important and frequently used expression in the Christian religion. However, it is not always understood in the same way. Please indicate the extent to which you agree or disagree with each of the following statements.

Absolute Transcendence salvation
N = 451   −   −/+   +   *miss*

* 30_1. The paradise on earth which God created for us.   30.6%   29.7%   34.2%   5.5%
  30_4. The Kingdom of God which will be given to us.   13.6%   21.5%   60.7%   4.2%
  30_8. The Kingdom which God will give to us.   17.7%   22.2%   53.6%   6.4%

Immanent Transcendence salvation
N = 451   −   −/+   +   *miss*

  30_6. Our duty to help build God's kingdom.   19.8%   25.9%   48.3%   6%
  30_7. The task given to us by God to look well after the earth.   13%   23.9%   57.3%   5.8%
  30_9. Our working for a world as God wants it to be.   10.6%   21.1%   62.5%   5.8%

Absolute Immanence salvation
N = 451   −   −/+   +   *miss*

  30_2. A certain moment when humans will live in harmony.   8%   26.8%   60.1%   5.1%
  30_3. The ultimate state of satisfaction among humans.   12.2%   27.9%   54.6%   5.3%
  30_5. A blissful state in the hearts of human beings.   13.9%   29.7%   49.5%   6.9%

Temporal Dimension

q. 31: The following statements are about the time in which we believe our salvation will occur. Please indicate the extent to which you agree or disagree with each of the following statements.

Past-oriented salvation
N = 451   −   −/+   +   *miss*

* 31_1. We are already saved.   51.9%   23.9%   15.6%   8.6%
  31_4. Salvation is the ideal state which was established in the beginning. 42.8%   24.2%   24.4%   8.6%
  31_7. Salvation has already taken place in the beginning.   31.1%   29.7%   30.8%   8.4%

Table 3 (cont.)

Present-oriented salvation
N = 451   −   −/+   +   miss
   31_2. Salvation is experienced in our everyday living.   11.1%   38.1%   44.4%   6.4%
   31_5. Salvation is realized here and now.   22.8%   35.1%   33.9%   8.2%
   31_8. Salvation happens now.   23.9%   34.1%   34.5%   7.5%

Future-oriented salvation
N = 451   −   −/+   +   miss
   31_3. Salvation is happiness in the future. 18.6%   32.6%   41.7%   7.1%
   31_6. Salvation is something we are waiting for.   27.9%   27.8%   36.8%   7.5%
   31_9. Salvation is an event that will only happen in the future.   49.6%   23.5%   20%   6.9%

Scope of Salvation
q. 32: Please indicate the extent to which you agree or disagree with each of the following statements about the salvation offered by other religions.

Exclusivistic salvation
N = 451   −   −/+   +   miss
   32_6. Only in my religion do people have access to true religion.   74.7%   12.6%   8.3%   4.4%
   32_7. Only in my religion can people receive true salvation.   78.5%   10.2%   6.4%   4.9%
   32_8. Compared to other religions, my religion contains the supreme salvation.   65%   13.3%   16.4%   5.3%

Inclusivistic salvation
N = 451   −   −/+   +   miss
   32_3. Various religions find their deepest truth in Christ.   10.5%   24.4%   60.7%   4.4%
   32_5. Through Christ, the way of salvation of religions can be completed.   20.2%   29%   45.3%   5.5%
*   32_9. Compared to my religion, other religions contain only part of the truth.   61.9%   20.8%   12%   5.3%

Pluralistic salvation
N = 451   −   −/+   +   miss
   32_1. Religions are mutually equal.   41.7%   28.8%   24.2%   5.3%
   32_2. All religions are equally valuable.   23.1%   31.3%   42.1%   3.5%
   32_4. The hope for salvation is equally embodied in all religions.   27.3%   36.4%   29.7%   6.6%

Table 3 (*cont.*)

Realms of Salvation
q. 33: Please indicate the extent to which you agree or disagree with each of the following statements about the realms of salvation.

Bodily (from) salvation
N = 451

		−	−/+	+	miss
33_1.	being free from sickness;	21.3%	22%	51.4%	5.3%
33_2.	freedom from hunger;	18%	24.8%	51.9%	5.3%
33_3.	being free from pain;	19.7%	23.9%	51.5%	4.9%

Bodily (to) salvation
N = 451

		−	−/+	+	miss
33_4.	achieving good physical well-being;	19.1%	29.9%	44.6%	6.4%
33_5.	fulfilling one's basic physical needs;	22.1%	38.4%	28.9%	10.6%
33_6.	being in good health;	11.1%	22.2%	61.2%	5.5%

Personal (from) salvation
N = 451

		−	−/+	+	miss
33_7.	not simply conforming to authority;	25.2%	33.5%	34%	7.3%
* 33_8.	freedom from personal bondage;	8.5%	16.2%	69.1%	6.2%
33_9.	liberation from being a stranger to myself;	11.5%	27.9%	51.3%	9.3%

Personal (to) salvation
N = 451

		−	−/+	+	miss
33_10.	being responsible for my own life;	7.7%	18.8%	67.5%	6%
33_11.	pursuing personal happiness;	21.2%	32.8%	39.4%	6.4%
33_12.	self-realization;	21.3%	33.7%	37.5%	7.5%

Interpersonal (from) salvation
N = 451

		−	−/+	+	miss
* 33_13.	no misunderstandings among family;	14.8%	27.5%	52.6%	5.1%
* 33_14.	the overcoming of social isolation;	10.6%	23.9%	58.4%	7.1%
33_16.	no more division in the community;	7.1%	25.7%	60.8%	6.4%

Interpersonal (to) salvation
N = 451

		−	−/+	+	miss
33_15.	respect for each other;	3.5%	12.4%	79.4%	4.7%
33_17.	reconciliation in the community;	4.9%	21.3%	67.1%	6.7%
33_18.	unity of the community;	8.4%	23.3%	62.1%	6.2%

Table 3 (*cont.*)

Structural (from) salvation N = 451	−	−/+	+	miss
33_19. freedom from oppressive structures;	5.7%	16.4%	71.5%	6.4%
33_21. freedom from economic inequality;	12.2%	29.3%	51.8%	6.7%
33_23. the overcoming of racism;	5.1%	16.9%	72.5%	5.5%

Structural (to) salvation N = 451	−	−/+	+	miss
33_20. social justice;	3.6%	13.7%	77.2%	5.5%
33_22. having enough jobs for everybody;	10.7%	20.8%	63%	5.5%
33_24. the sharing of power;	14.8%	25.1%	54.3%	5.8%

Ecological (from) salvation N = 451	−	−/+	+	miss
33_25. overcoming environmental devastation;	6.6%	20.8%	66.4%	6.2%
* 33_26. no more natural calamities;	17.5%	22.8%	53.3%	6.4%
33_27. no more exploitation of nature;	7.1%	18.4%	68.7%	5.8%

Ecological (to) salvation N = 451	−	−/+	+	miss
33_28. integrity of nature;	8%	18.6%	67.9%	5.5%
33_29. the wholeness of nature;	6.3%	17.7%	70%	6%
33_30. the beauty of nature;	3.8%	15.5%	75.2%	5.5%

E. *Attitudes toward the Church*

q 28: Please indicate the extent to which you agree or disagree with each of the following statements about the church in general.

Culturally-adapted church N = 451	−	−/+	+	miss
28_5. The church should always keep pace with changing ideas in society.	19.3%	35.7%	42.3%	2.7%
28_12. The church should. as much as possible. keep pace with the new ideas.	11.7%	28.8%	57.9%	1.6%
* 28_15. The church should assume a highly reserved position toward certain ideas in modern society.	34.6%	35.5%	27.3%	2.7%

Table 3 (*cont.*)

Hierarchical church
N = 451

			−	−/+	+	*miss*
*	28_3.	The faithful should be able to make their decisions about what should happen in the church.	22.8%	39.9%	34.2%	3.1%
	28_7.	It is not good that believers have a say in decisions about everything that happens in the church.	39.2%	29.7%	28.4%	2.7%
	28_14.	It is not good when any believer can interfere with any decision in the church.	25%	33.7%	39%	2.3%

Centralized church
N = 451

			−	−/+	+	*miss*
*	28_2.	The church can be best administered by a few authoritative people. who are able to bear the responsibilities.	27.1%	27.5%	42.6%	2.9%
*	28_6.	The responsibility for what happens in the church should not be put into the hands of a small group of administrators.	14.7%	25.3%	57.3%	2.7%
	28_10.	Church policy should only be determined by a small group of responsible administrators.	55.4%	22.8%	18.7%	3.1%

Democratic church
N = 451

			−	−/+	+	*miss*
	28_1.	Lay persons should also have the right to conduct services in the church.	17.3%	23.7%	57%	2%
*	28_9.	Church. services should only be conducted by people who are especially appointed for this.	35.9%	23.7%	38.8%	1.6%
	28_13.	Lay persons should also have the right to conduct religious services.	24.1%	25.7%	47.8%	2.4%

q 29: Please indicate how important the following tasks of the church are to you.[2]

---

[2] Range of scales: 1 = unimportant; 2 = neither important nor unimportant; 3 = important; 4 = very important; miss = missing values.

Table 3 (*cont.*)

Micro-level: person-directed tasks of the church

N = 451		1	2	3	4	*miss*
29_3.	Give religious assistance in cases of illness. impending death or mourning.	.7%	2.4%	39.2%	56.3%	1.3%
29_5.	Give pastoral help to people in mental distress.	.2%	1.1%	37%	60.8%	.9%
29_7.	Give comfort to people who are in trouble.	.4%	2%	47%	48.8%	1.8%
29_10.	Give religious assistance to important events in life.	1.3%	6.9%	45.5%	44.8%	1.6%

Meso-level: group-directed tasks of the church

N = 451		1	2	3	4	*miss*
* 29_4.	See to it that the church is a meeting place of all sorts of active groups of believers.	1.8%	12.2%	47%	37.3%	1.8%
29_8.	Promote the formation of active working groups in the church.	2.9%	17.5%	53%	24.8%	1.8%
29_12.	Promote active groups in the church. operating in the spirit of the gospel.	3.1%	17.7%	49%	28.6%	1.6%

Macro-level: Socio-political tasks of the church

N = 451		1	2	3	4	*miss*
29_1.	Make people aware of societal problems.	4.9%	12%	55.2%	25.5%	2.4%
29_2.	Give material aid to third world countries.	4.2%	14.6%	53%	25.7%	2.4%
29_6.	Give material aid tio people in the Netherlands.	7.1%	29.9%	45.9%	14.4%	2.7%
* 29_9.	Take a critical stand on social issues.	4%	19.5%	51%	23.1%	2.4%
29_11.	Make people politically conscious.	27.1%	40.8%	22.2%	6.9%	3.1%

Part 3: Population Characteristics Scales

A. Age: What is your year of birth? 19____
B. Gender: Please indicate whether you are.... (1) male (2) female
C. Education: Please indicate the highest level of your educational attainment: 1 = primary education; 2 = lower secondary education; 3 = higher secondary education; 4 = tertiary education.

Table 3 (*cont.*)

D. Country of Origin: In what country were you born? (1) In the Netherlands; (2) Others, please specify ____.
E. Authoritarianism, Conformism, Localism, Anomie, Subjectively-perceived threat (cultural, material, power), Subjectively-perceived threat (individual); Range of scales: 1–5; (Possible answers: 1 = totally disagree; 2 = disagree; 3 = partly disagree, partly agree; 4 = agree; 5 = totally agree). For the purpose of presentation in the appendix, the 5-point Likert scale was reduced to three categories:— = disagreement (scale point 1 and 2); –/+ = ambivalence (scale point 3); + = agreement (scale points 4 and 5).

q36: Please indicate the extent to which you agree or disagree with each of the following statements.

Localism
N = 451

			–	–/+	+	miss
*	36_1.	Newspapers generally pay much too little attention to all sorts of local news.	49.2%	30.4%	17.7%	2.7%
	36_7.	It is better to be a member of a local community club than of a nationwide association.	33.9%	33%	27.8%	5.3%
	36_11.	Big cities are important indeed, but the small local community is our country's backbone.	34.1%	36.8%	26.2%	2.9%
*	36_13.	When it comes to choosing someone for a responsible office in my community, I prefer persons who were born and raised here in the Netherlands.*	40.8%	24.6%	31.7%	2.9%
	36_16.	Local News is often more interesting than news about events happening elsewhere.	45.9%	28.4%	23.9%	1.8%
*	36_18.	Big cities are nice for shopping, but not pleasant to live in.	58.1%	22.6%	18.4%	.9%

Authoritarianism
N = 451

			–	–/+	+	miss
*	36_5.	Most of our social problems would be solved if we could somehow get rid of immoral, crooked and feebleminded people.	32.1%	32.2%	34.4%	1.3%
	36_9.	People can be divided into two distinct classes: the weak and the strong.	47.4%	22%	28.4%	2.2%

Table 3 (*cont.*)

		−	−/+	+	*miss*
36_15.	What this country needs most, more than laws and political programs, is a few courageous, fearless, devoted leaders in whom the people can put their faith.	21.7%	27.9%	48.4%	2%

Conformism
N = 451   − | −/+ | + | *miss*

		−	−/+	+	*miss*
36_8.	With respect to my behavior, I try to conform to the behavior of my friends as much as possible.	63.2%	24.6%	10%	2.2%
* 36_12.	I always conform to the rules that hold in my neighbourhood.	7.2%	27.5%	62.9%	2.4%
36_17.	I always conform to the customs of the people in my neighbourhood as much as possible.	28.3%	37.7%	31.8%	2.2%

Anomie
N = 451

		−	−/+	+	*miss*
36_2.	Criticizing the government is useless, because the government simply does what it considers to be proper.	43.9%	31.5%	22.8%	1.8%
36_4.	In spite of what some people keep saying, the lot of the average man is getting worse.	31.3%	35.7%	31.4%	1.6%
36_14.	These days a person does not really know whom he/she can count on.	33.5%	39.7%	24.1%	2.7%

Subjectively-perceived threat (general)
N = 451

		−	−/+	+	*miss*
36_3.	There is much more violence in the streets now than there was 10 years ago.	9.9%	16%	72.9%	1.1%
36_6.	There is much more more tax fraud now than there was 10 years ago.	33.4%	27.9%	30.1%	8.6%
36_10.	There is much more adultery now than there was 10 years ago.	33.4%	27.3%	34.2%	5.1%

F. *Church Involvement*

19a. Do you consider yourself a member of a Christian church or religious community? (1) Yes (go to question 19b); (2) No (go to question 20);

Table 3 (*cont.*)

19b. If yes, of which Christian church or religious community do you consider yourself a member? (1) Catholic Church; (2) Nederlandse Hervormde Kerk; (3) Gereformeerde Kerken in Nederland; (4) other Christian church, namely:___;
20. Do you have a special task or function in your church? (1) Yes; (2) No;
21. Are you an active member of a religious group or association in your church?(1) Yes, namely___; (2) No
22. How often do you attend worship services in a church (not counting funerals, weddings, and so on): (1) about once a week; (2) about once a month; (3) few times a year; (4) (almost) never.

G. *Religious salience*

q23: The following questions are concerned with the importance of Christian faith for your life. To what extent do you agree or disagree with the following statements? (5-point scales: 1 = totally disagree; 2 = disagree; 3 = not sure; 4 = agree; 5 = totally disagree). For the purpose of presentation in the appendix, the 5-point Likert scale was reduced to three categories:—= disagreement (scale point 1 and 2); –/+ = ambivalence (scale point 3); + = agreement (scale points 4 and 5).

N = 451		–	–/+	+	miss
23_1.	My Christian faith has a great influence on my daily life.	14%	15.1%	67.8%	3.1%
23_2.	When I have to make important decisions, my Christian faith plays a major part in my decision making.	19.3%	20.8%	56.1%	3.8%
23_3.	My Christain faith has a great influence on my political attitudes.	31.9%	17.7%	45.1%	5.3%
23_4.	Without my faith, my life would be quite different.	22.7%	18.8%	55%	3.5%
23_5.	I am very interested in my Christian faith.	7.3%	16.4%	73.9%	2.4%

Table 4. Factor Analysis (localistic authoritarianism, anomie, subjectively-perceived threat and conformism)

	Communality	Factor 1	Factor 2	Factor 3	Factor 4	
36_15	.54	.72				localistic authoritarianism
36_11	.39	.61				
36_16	.47	.56				
36_9	.40	.44				
36_7	.31	.39				

Table 4 (*cont.*)

	Communality	Factor 1	Factor 2	Factor 3	Factor 4	
36_4	.43		−.60			anomie
36_2	.45		−.60			
36_14	.41		−.43			
36_10	.69			−.73		subjectively-perceived threat
36_6	.60			−.52		
36_3	.43			−.47		
36_8	.45				.67	conformism
36_17	.38				.47	

Explained Variance = 45.8%

Criteria factors (4); iterate (50); extraction: paf; rotation: oblimin; N= 391

Table 5. Pearson Correlation (r) & Reliability of Scales (localistic authoritarianism, subjectively-perceived threat, conformism, & anomie)

Empirical Model	Mean	Standard Deviation	Reliability of Scales (*Cronbach's Alpha*)	Pearson Correlation (r)	Valid Cases
Localistic authoritarianism	2.95	.77	.77	—	437
Subjectively-perceived threat	2.68	.88	.89	—	437
Conformism	2.71	.77	—	.38	437
Anomie	2.93	.81	.69	—	435

Table 6. Factor Analysis (religious salience)

	Communality	Factor 1
23_2	.78	.89
23_1	.73	.85
23_3	.45	.67
23_5	.45	.67
23_4	.36	.60

Explained Variance = 55.4%

Criteria mineigen (1); iterate (50); extraction: paf; rotation: varimax/ oblimin; N= 414

Table 7. Reliability of Scales (religious salience)

Empirical Model	Mean	Standard Deviation	Reliability of Scales (*Cronbach's Alpha*)	Valid Cases
Religious salience	3.63	.91	.85	414

APPENDIX 2 (CHAPTER 2—GOD)

Table 1. Factor Analysis (Attitudes toward God)

	Communality	Factor 1	Factor 2	Factor 3	Factor 4	
24_1	.56	−.94				Theism
24_5	.91	−.75				
24_7	.79		.94			Panentheism
24_3	.69		.85			
24_8	.67		.82			
24_4	.67		.76			
24_6	.62		.69			
24_2	.61		.64			
25_4	.85			.91		Pantheism
25_2	.71			.70		
25_6	.37				.82	Metatheism
25_3	.67				.58	

Explained Variance = 78%

Criteria factors (4); iterate (50); extraction: paf; rotation: oblimin; N= 379

Table 2. Correlation between Scales (Pearson Correlation)

	panentheïsm	pantheïsm	metatheïsme
theism	.61** (N=419)	.35** (N=400)	.16** (N=408)
panentheism		.36** (N=412)	.17** (N=422)
pantheism			.32** (N=410)

** $p < .01$; * $p < .05$ (2-tailed)

Table 3. Variance Analysis & Scheffé Test

Legend of Categories per Social Location:
1. Age: 1 = 57 years and younger; 2 = 58 to 68 years old; 3 = 69 years and older
2. Gender: 1 = male; 2 = female
3. Education: 1 = primary education; 2 = lower secondary education; 3 = higher secondary education; 4 = tertiary education.
4. Country of origin: 00 = others (non-Dutch); 1 = The Netherlands.
5. Church Involvement: 1 = inactive; 2 = active members

* = significant difference between two categories;
r = Pearson's correlation
N = Cases; Sig.=observed significance (P)

Theism

Age:
N = 419; Eta = .27; Sig. = .00

		2	1	3
3.22	2			
3.27	1			
3.82	3	*	*	

Education:
N = 415; Eta = .25; Sig. = .00

		3	4	2	1
3.26	3				
3.39	4				
3.80	2	*	*		
4.25	1	*	*		

Church Involvement:
N = 422; Eta = .29; Sig. = .00

| 3.16 | 1 |
| 3.81 | 2 |

Panentheism

Age:
N = 434; Eta = .13; Sig. = .02

		1	2	3
3.80	1			
3.83	2			
4.07	3	*		

Education:
N = 430; Eta = .21; Sig. = .00

		3	4	2	1
3.60	3				
3.89	4				
4.10	2	*			
4.29	1	*			

Country of origin
N = 436; Eta = .10; Sig. = .04

| 3.56 | 1 |
| 3.81 | 2 |

Church Involvement
N = 437; Eta = .38; Sig. = .00

| 3.48 | 1 |
| 4.20 | 2 |

Pantheism

Gender:
N = 410; Eta = .12; Sig. = .01

| 3.50 | 1 |
| 3.75 | 2 |

Education:
N = 409; Eta = .14; Sig. = .04

		4	1	3	2
3.48	4				
3.50	1				
3.63	3				
3.78	2	*			

Table 3 (cont.)

Metatheism
Age:
N = 422;   Eta = .17;   Sig. = .00

		2	1	3
3.63	2			
3.82	1			*
3.99	3			

Table 4. Pearson Correlation—Social Characteristics And Attitudes Toward God

	theism	panentheism	pantheism	metatheism
localistic autoritarianism	.26** (N= 413)	.24**(N=429)	.13** (N=407)	.10* (N=418)
subjectively-perceived threat	.15**(N=412)	.09 (N=426)	.08 (N=403)	.05 (N=413)
conformism	.25** (N=413)	.25**(N=427)	.14**(N=407)	.12*(N=416)
anomie	.23**(N=409)	.17** (N=425)	.09 (N=402)	.04 (N=413)

** p < .01; * p < .05 (2-tailed)

APPENDIX 3 (CHAPTER 3—JESUS)

Table 1. Factor Analysis

	Communality	Factor 1	Factor 2	Factor 3	Factor 4	Factor 5	Factor 6	
26_26	.65	.80						Interpersonal
26_3	.73	.77						
26_4	.64	.75						
26_30	.70	.72						
26_13	.63	.70						
26_16	.74	.62						
26_8	.65	.54						
26_25	.67		.80					Humanistic
26_9	.64		.78					
26_2	.54		.75					
26_15	.58		.73					
26_14	.99			1.04				Neo–classical
26_27	.43			.50				
26_32	.76				−.87			Spirit–motivated
26_29	.58				−.70			
26_17	.65				−.55			
26_22	.72				−.53			
26_7	.71					.84		Classical
26_12	.72					.80		
26_1	.70					.72		
26_28	.67					.69		
26_20	.71						.75	Society–related
26_18	.65						.64	
26_10	.58						.45	

Explained Variance: 67%

Criteria factors (6); iterate (77); extraction: paf; rotation: varimax; N = 348

Table 2. Correlation between Scales (Pearson Correlation)

	neo–classical	interpersonal	society–related	spirit–motivated	humanistic
classical	.42**(N=404)	.64**(N=417)	.55**(N=409)	.43**(N=414)	−.33**(N=411)
neo-classical		.33**(N=406)	.38**(N=398)	.30**(N=404)	−.003(N=403)
interpersonal			.66**(N=408)	.58**(N=415)	−.29**(N=413)
society-related				.55**(N=407)	−.19**(N=404)
spirit-motivated					.01 (N=410)

** p < .01; * p < .05 (2-tailed)

Table 3. Variance Analysis & Scheffé Test

Classical Jesus
Age:
N = 422; Eta = .19; Sig. = .00

		1	2	3
3.37	1			
3.75	2	*		
3.77	3	*		

Education:
N = 418; Eta = .33; Sig. = .00

		4	3	2	1
3.19	4				
3.66	3	*			
3.88	2	*			
4.09	1	*			

Country of origin:
N = 424; Eta = .14; Sig. = .00

| 3.93 | 00 |
| 3.55 | 1 |

Church Involvement:
N = 425; Eta = .31; Sig. = .00

| 3.83 | 2 |
| 3.14 | 1 |

Neo-classical Jesus
Age:
N = 406; Eta = .25; Sig. = .06

		1	2	3
2.40	1			
2.64	2			
3.05	3	*	*	

Gender:
N = 406; Eta = .17; Sig. = .00

| 2.90 | 1 |
| 2.52 | 2 |

Education:
N = 403; Eta = .18; Sig. = .00

		3	4	2	1
2.49	3				
2.49	4				
2.89	2	*			
3.04	1				

Church Involvement::
N = 409; Eta = .27; Sig. = .07

| 2.26 | 1 |
| 2.92 | 2 |

Table 3 (*cont.*)

Interpersonal-oriented Jesus

Age:
N = 420;   Eta = .16;   Sig. = .03

		1	2	3
4.00	1			
4.12	2			
4.26	3	*		

Church Involvement:
N = 423;   Eta = .36;   Sig. = .00

| 3.76 | 1 |
| 4.31 | 2 |

Society-related Jesus

Age:
N = 407;   Eta = .15;   Sig. = .01

		1	2	3
3.40	1			
3.62	2			
3.70	3	*		

Education:
N = 403;   Eta = .20;   Sig. = .00

		3	4	2	1
3.31	3				
3.43	4				
3.71	2			*	*
3.91	1				

Church Involvement:
N = 410;   Eta = .33;   Sig. = .00

| 3.14 | 1 |
| 3.77 | 2 |

Spirit-motivated Jesus

Age:
N = 416;   Eta = .21;   Sig. = .00

		1	2	3
3.43	1			
3.77	2	*		
3.85	3	*		

Education:
N = 412;   Eta = .24;   Sig. = .00

		3	4	2	1
3.39	3				
3.47	4				
3.87	2			*	*
4.05	1			*	*

Country of origin:
N = 418;   Eta = .10;   Sig. = .03

| 3.87 | 00 |
| 3.62 | 1 |

Church Involvement:
N = 419;   Eta = .31;   Sig. = .00

| 3.26 | 1 |
| 3.86 | 2 |

Humanistic Jesus

Education:
N = 410;   Eta = .17;   Sig. = .03

		2	4	3	1
2.37	2				
2.37	4				
2.45	3				
3.11	1			*	*

Church Involvement:
N = 416;   Eta = .18;   Sig. = .00

| 2.29 | 2 |
| 2.67 | 1 |

Table 4. Pearson Correlation—Social Characteristics and Attitudes toward Jesus

	classical Jesus	neo-classical Jesus	interpersonal-oriented Jesus	society-related Jesus	spirit-motivated Jesus	humanistic Jesus
localistic autoritarianism	.22**(N=416)	.21** (N=402)	.16**(N=416)	.13**(N=403)	.24**(N=410)	.26**(N=409)
subjectively-perceived threat	.14**(N=414)	.09 (N=399)	.02 (N=412)	-.04 (N=399)	.02 (N=407)	.13**(N=405)
conformism	.26**(N=414)	.28**(N=403)	.23**(N=415)	.23**(N=404)	.26**(N=410)	.15**(N=409)
anomie	.25**(N=412)	.21**(N=398)	.15**(N=411)	.14**(N=399)	.17**(N=407)	.16**(N=404)

** p < .01; * p < .05 (2-tailed)

APPENDIX 4 (CHAPTER 4—SPIRIT)

Table 1. Factor Analysis

	Communalities	Factor 1	Factor 2	Factor 3	Factor 4	Factor 5	
27_14	.86	.74					Affection-related
27_16	.87	.81					
27_24	.90		.96				Trinity-related
27_8	.89		.91				
27_13	.88			.83			Cognition-related
27_4	.81			.59			
27_3	.83				−.64		Jesus-related
27_19	.80				−.68		
27_6	.91					.85	Society-related
27_11	.83					.52	

Explained Variance: 86%

Criteria factors (5); iterate (16); extraction: pca; rotation: oblimin; N = 374

Table 2. Correlation between Scales (Pearson Correlation)

	Jesus-related	Cognition-related	Affection-related	Society-related
Trinity-related	.62**(N=390)	.36**(N=389)	.54**(N=396)	.55**(N=395)
Jesus-related		.64**(N=387)	.70**(N=393)	.71**(N=394)
Cognition-related			.65**(N=394)	.55**(N=392)
Affection-related				.73**(N=399)

** $p < .01$; * $p < .05$ (2-tailed)

Table 3. Variance Analysis & Scheffé Test

Trinity-related
Age:
N = 403;   Eta = .14;   Sig. = .02

		1	2	3
3.47	1			
3.78	2			
3.81	3	*		

Education
N = 400;   Eta = .18;   Sig. = .00

		4	3	2	1
3.41	4				
3.73	3				
3.81	2	*			
4.08	1				

Table 3 (cont.)

Country of origin
N = 405; Eta = .11; Sig. = .03

3.60   1
3.92   00

Jesus-related
Age:
N = 395; Eta = .18; Sig. = .00

		1	2	3
3.32	1			
3.68	2		*	
3.71	3		*	

Country of origin
N = 397; Eta = .17; Sig. = .00

3.46   1
3.90   00

Cognition-related
Education
N = 390; Eta = .15; Sig. = .04

3.24   4
3.27   3
3.53   2
3.71   1

– No two groups are significantly different at the .050 level;

Church Involvement
N= 397; Eta = .16; Sig. = .00

3.16   1
3.51   2

Affection-related
Education
N = 400; Eta = .16; Sig. = .02

3.35   3
3.50   4
3.71   2
3.91   1

– No two groups are significantly different at the .05 level;

Church Involvement
N = 407; Eta = .25; Sig. = .00

3.27   1
3.76   2

Church Involvement:
N = 406; Eta = .28; Sig. = .00

3.22   1
3.87   2

Education
N = 392; Eta = .23; Sig. = .00

		4	3	2	1
3.30	4				
3.43	3				
3.74	2			*	
4.00	1			*	

Church Involvement
N=398; Eta = .35; Sig. = .00

3.03   1
3.80   2

Country of origin
N = 396; Eta = .13; Sig. = .01

3.33   1
3.67   00

Country of origin
N = 406; Eta = .13; Sig. = .01

3.53   1
3.85   00

Table 3 (*cont.*)

Society-related
Age:
N = 403;   Eta = .14;   Sig. = 02

	1	3	2
3.73	1		
3.98	3	*	
4.00	2		

Country of origin
N = 405;   Eta = .13;   Sig. = .01

3.83	1
4.12	00

Church Involvement
N = 406;   Eta = .32;   Sig. = .00

3.49	1
4.07	2

Table 4. Correlation—Social Characteristics and Attitudes toward the Spirit

	Trinity-related	Jesus-related	Cognition-related	Affection-related	Society-related
localistic autoritariansm	.20**(N=401)	.23**(N=393)	.15**(N=392)	.19**(N=402)	.17**(N=401)
subjectively-perceived threat	.07 (N=399)	.04 (N=389)	.02 (N=389)	.06 (N=398)	−.03 (N=397)
conformism	.22**(N=399)	.28**(N=392)	.19**(N=391)	.25**(N=401)	.25**(N=399)
anomie	.15**(N=399)	.18**(N=390)	.09 (N=389)	.10 (N=400)	.15**(N=398)

** $p < .01$; * $p < .05$ (2-tailed)

APPENDIX 5 (CHAPTER 5—SALVATION)

Table 1. Factor Analysis

Table 1a. Dimension of Transcendence in Salvation

	Communality	Factor 1	Factor 2	Factor 3	
30_7	.77	.90			immanent transcendence
30_6	.77	.76			
30_9	.69	.72			
30_3	.73		.91		absolute immanence
30_2	.62		.71		
30_5	.41		.55		
30_4	.91			.97	absolute transcendence
30_8	.73			.61	

Explained variance: 71%

Criteria factors (3); iterate (50); extraction: pca; rotation: varimax/oblimin; N = 409

Table 1b. Temporal Dimension

	Communality	Factor 1	Factor 2	Factor 3	
31_5	.59	.77			present
31_2	.59	.75			
31_8	.62	.75			
31_6	.49		.65		future
31_3	.42		.62		
31_9	.48		.60		
31_7	1.0			−.99	past
31_4	.45			−.48	

Explained variance: 58 %

Criteria factors (3); iterate (45); extraction: pca; rotation: varimax/oblimin; N = 391

Table 1c. Scope of Salvation

	Communality	Factor 1	Factor 2	Factor 3	
32_7	.90	.99			exclusivism
32_6	.87	.94			
32_8	.63	.69			
32_1	.60		.79		pluralism
32_2	.54		.72		
32_4	.51		.66		
32_3	.22			−.41	
Explained variance: 66%					

Criteria mineigen (1); iterate (66); extraction: pca; rotation: varimax/oblimin; N = 407

Table 1d. Realms of Salvation

	Communality	Factor 1	Factor 2	Factor 3	Factor 4	
33_17	.68	.82				social
33_16	.65	.80				
33_20	.79	.80				
33_18	.59	.79				
33_21	.61	.72				
33_19	.69	.71				
33_23	.69	.68				
33_22	.62	.58				
33_15	.60	.53				
33_24	.50	.47				
33_3	.91		.96			bodily
33_2	.89		.94			
33_1	.84		.92			
33_4	.75		.79			
33_6	.72		.74			
33_5	.53		.55			
33_12	.67			.84		personal
33_11	.65			.72		
33_9	.54			.63		
33_10	.59			.59		
33_7	.41			.43		
33_28	.87				.95	ecological
33_29	.81				.91	
33_30	.74				.79	
33_27	.78				.73	
33_25	.67				.47	
68% explained variance						

Criteria mineigen (1); iterate (150); extraction: paf; rotation: oblimin; N= 360

Table 2. Correlation between Scales (Pearson Correlation)

	transcendent immanence	absolute immanence	past	present	future	exclusivism	inclusivism	pluralism	bodily	individual	social	ecological
absolute transcendence	.71**(N=412)	.40**(N=412)	.44**(N=400)	.20**(N=397)	.44**(N=398)	.35**(N=408)	.46**(N=410)	-.12*(N=403)	.09 (N=407)	.05 (N=403)	.30**(N=410)	.32**(N=409)
transcendent immanence		.50**(N=412)	.45**(N=402)	.29**(N=399)	.37**(N=400)	.31**(N=410)	.48**(N=410)	.09 (N=405)	.20**(N=409)	.25**(N=406)	.47**(N=411)	.45**(N=412)
absolute immanence			.40**(N=400)	.24**(N=398)	.30**(N=398)	.16**(N=408)	.27**(N=409)	.17**(N=403)	.35**(N=408)	.31**(N=405)	.36**(N=410)	.39**(N=410)
past				.27**(N=397)	.39**(N=400)	.36**(N=403)	.43**(N=404)	.13*(N=397)	.22**(N=401)	.17**(N=400)	.27**(N=403)	.32**(N=403)
present					.04 (N=398)	.11*(N=401)	.30**(N=401)	.11*(N=398)	.02 (N=399)	.28**(N=396)	.23**(N=402)	.15**(N=402)
future						.39**(N=402)	.33**(N=404)	.06 (N=399)	.31**(N=400)	.22**(N=397)	.32**(N=403)	.36**(N=403)
exclusivism							.29**(N=418)	-.21**(N=411)	.12*(N=413)	.10 (N=409)	.14**(N=414)	.17**(N=414)
inclusivism								.18**(N=412)	.16**(N=413)	.18**(N=409)	.31**(N=415)	.29**(N=415)
pluralism									.18**(N=407)	.20**(N=404)	.19**(N=409)	.14**(N=410)
bodily										.58**(N=415)	.51**(N=418)	.50**(N=421)
individual											.64**(N=415)	.52**(N=417)
social												.78**(N=422)

** p < .01; * p < .05 (2-tailed)

Table 3. Variance Analysis & Scheffé Test

Absolute transcendence
Age:
N = 416; Eta = .26; Sig. = .00

		1	2	3
3.33	1			
3.78	2	*		
3.96	3	*		

Education:
N = 413; Eta = .23; Sig. = .00

		4	3	2	1
3.43	4				
3.45	3				
3.89	2			*	
4.14	1			*	

Country of origin:
N = 418; Eta = .10; Sig. = .04

| 3.93 | 1 |
| 3.64 | 00 |

Church Involvement:
N= 419; Eta = .43; Sig. = .00

| 3.00 | 1 |
| 4.01 | 2 |

Immanent transcendence
Age:
N = 415; Eta = .28; Sig. = .00

		1	2	3
3.29	1			
3.76	2	*		
3.89	3	*		

Education:
N = 411; Eta = .26; Sig. = .00

		3	4	2	1
3.33	3				
3.40	4				
3.86	2			*	*
4.01	1			*	*

Church Involvement:
N = 418; Eta = .43; Sig. = .00

| 3.02 | 1 |
| 3.92 | 2 |

Absolute Immanence
Education:
N = 410; Eta = .18; Sig. = .00

		4	3	2	1
3.42	4				
3.51	3				
3.73	2	*			
3.82	1				

Country of origin:
N = 415; Eta = .11; Sig. = 02

| 3.55 | 1 |
| 3.79 | 00 |

Past
Education:
N = 401; Eta = .34; Sig. = .00

		4	3	2	1
2.50	4				
2.68	3				
3.18	2	*	*		
3.62	1	*	*		

Country of origin:
N = 407; Eta = .16; Sig. = .00

| 2.81 | 1 |
| 3.23 | 00 |

APPENDIX 5 (CHAPTER 5—SALVATION)

Table 3 (*cont.*)

Church Involvement:
N= 408; Eta = .12; Sig. = .01

2.69   1
2.97   2

Present
Education:
N = 399; Eta = .15; Sig. = .03

3.08   3
3.15   2
3.37   4
3.40   1

Church Involvement:
N = 406; Eta = .22; Sig. = .00

2.98   1
3.36   2

- No two groups are significantly different at the .050 level;

Future
Education:
N = 400; Eta = .27; Sig. = .00

		4	3	2	1
2.74	4				
2.90	3				
3.12	2	*			
3.57	1	*	*		

Country of origin:
N = 406; Eta = .12; Sig.= .01

2.93   1
3.19   00

Church Involvement:
N = 407; Eta = .15; Sig. = .00

2.81   1
3.06   2

Exclusivism
Age:
N = 422; Eta = .21; Sig. = .00

		1	2	3
1.85	1			
2.03	2			
2.30	3		*	

Gender:
N = 422; Eta = .10; Sig. = .03

1.97   2
2.17   1

Education:
N = 418; Eta = .19; Sig. = .00

		4	3	2	1
1.89	4				
1.93	3				
2.19	2	*			
2.50	1	*			

Country of origin:
N = 424; Eta = .19; Sig. = .00

1.98   1
2.46   00

Table 3 (*cont.*)

Church Involvement:
N = 425; Eta = .18; Sig. = .00

1.82	1
2.18	2

Inclusivism
Age:
N = 421; Eta = .18; Sig. = .00

		1	2	3
3.34	1			
3.58	2			
3.69	3	*		

Education:
N = 417; Eta = .19; Sig. = .00

		3	4	1	2
3.29	3				
3.40	4				
3.68	1				
3.69	2			*	*

Church Involvement:
N = 424; Eta = .24; Sig. = .00

3.23	1
3.67	2

Pluralism
Education:
N = 409; Eta = .15; Sig. = .03

2.88	4
3.11	2
3.12	3
3.33	1

No two groups are significantly different at the .050 level;

Bodily
Age:
N = 419; Eta = .17; Sig. = .00

		1	2	3
3.30	1			
3.35	2			
3.66	3	*		

Education:
N = 415; Eta = .20; Sig. = .00

		4	3	2	1
3.24	4				
3.48	3				
3.57	2	*			
3.93	1	*			

Table 3 (*cont.*)

Personal

Age:
N = 414; Eta = .12; Sig. = .04

		1	2	3
3.32	1			
3.43	2			
3.54	3	*		

Social

Age:
N = 421; Eta = .23; Sig. = .00

		1	2	3
3.65	1			
3.90	2	*		
4.04	3	*		

Education:
N = 417; Eta = .15; Sig. = .02

		4	3	2	1
3.72	4				
3.87	3				
3.96	2	*			
4.05	1				

No two groups are significantly different at the .050 level;

Church Involvement:
N = 424; Eta = .17; Sig. = .00

| 3.69 | 1 |
| 3.95 | 2 |

Ecological

Age:
N = 422; Eta = .22; Sig. = .00

		1	2	3
3.75	1			
4.05	2	*		
4.16	3	*		

Education:
N = 418; Eta = .19; Sig. = .00

		4	3	2	1
3.80	4				
3.93	3				
4.11	2	*			
4.35	1	*			

Church Involvement:
N = 425; Eta = .13; Sig. = .01

| 3.82 | 1 |
| 4.06 | 2 |

Table 4a. Correlation—Social Characteristics and Attitudes toward Salvation (Dimensions of Transcendent & Temporal)

	absolute transcendence	Transcendent immanence	absolute immanence	past	present	future
localistic autoritarianism	.22**(N=412)	.28**(N=413)	.25**(N=411)	.31**(N=404)	.05 (N=403)	.38**(N=404)
subjectively-perceived threat	.05 (N=409)	.08 (N=410)	.13**(N=407)	.18**(N=401)	-.18**(N=399)	.29**(N=400)
conformism	.26**(N=412)	.26**(N=411)	.20**(N=410)	.30**(N=403)	.13**(N=401)	.31**(N=402)
anomie	.17** (N=411)	.22**(N=410)	.18**(N=409)	.22**(N=401)	-.11**(N=399)	.36**(N=401)

** p < .01; * p < .05 (2-tailed)

Table 4b. Correlation—Social Characteristics and Attitudes toward Salvation (Scope & Realms of Salvation)

	exclusivism	pluralism	inclusivism	bodily	personal	social	ecological
localistic autoritarianism	.31**(N=420)	.12*(N=413)	.28**(N=419)	.39**(N=416)	.32**(N=413)	.33**(N=419)	.33**(N=420)
subjectively-perceived threat	.25**(N=415)	.00 (N=407)	.11*(N=414)	.30**(N=413)	.17**(N=409)	.07 (N=416)	.15**(N=417)
conformism	.28**(N=418)	.11*(N=411)	.26**(N=417)	.20**(N=416)	.19**(N=411)	.22**(N=419)	.21**(N=419)
anomie	.21**(N=417)	.12*(N=409)	.15**(N=)	.30**(N=416)	.19**(N=411)	.23**(N=418)	.26**(N=419)

** p < .01; * p < .05 (2-tailed)

APPENDIX 6 (CHAPTER 6—CHURCH)

Table 1a. Factor Analysis

	Communality	Factor 1	Factor 2	Factor 3	
28_1	.71	.85			democratic
28_13	.74	.84			
28_7	.58		.78		hierarchical-centralized
28_14	.43		.67		
28_10	.27		.46		
28_5	.63			−.80	culturally-adapted
28_12	.64			−.78	

Explained variance: 57%

Criteria mineigen (1); iterate (150); extraction: paf; rotation: varimax/oblimin; N = 424

Table 1b. Factor Analysis (Tasks of the Church)

	Communality	Factor 1	Factor 2	Factor 3	
29_5	.67	.80			micro-level
29_3	.50	.69			
29_7	.47	.64			
29_10	.48	.60			
29_2	.50		.70		macro-level
29_6	.37		.58		
29_1	.29		.50		
29_11	.32		.41		
29_12	.66			−.79	meso-level
29_8	.47			−.60	

Explained variance: 47 %

Criteria mineigen (1); iterate (50); extraction: paf; rotation: varimax/oblimin; N = 414

Table 2a. Correlation between Scales (Pearson Correlation)

	hierarchical-centralized	democratic
cultural adaptation	−.10* (N=427)	.37** (N=433)
hierarchical-centralized		−.25** (N=428)

** p < .01; * p < .05 (2-tailed)

Table 2b. Correlation between Scales (Pearson Correlation)

	Meso-level	Macro-level
Micro-level	.32**(N=440)	.41**(N=439)
Meso-level		.38**(N=436)

** $p < .01$; * $p < .05$ (2-tailed)

Table 3. Variance Analysis & Scheffé Test

CULTURALLY-ADAPTED CHURCH
Country of origin:
N = 437; Eta = .13; Sig.=.0069

| 3.56 | 1 |
| 3.25 | 00 |

HIERARCHICAL-CENTRALIZED CHURCH

Age:
N = 428; Eta = .33; Sig. = .00

		1	2	3
2.56	1			
2.75	2			
3.17	3	*	*	

Education:
N = 425; Eta = .24; Sig. = .00

		4	3	1	2
2.60	4				
2.86	3				
2.92	1				
3.05	2	*			

Country of origin:
N = 430; Eta = .15; Sig. = .00

| 2.79 | 1 |
| 3.11 | 00 |

DEMOCRATIC CHURCH

Age:
N = 436; Eta = .14; Sig. = .02

		1	3	2
3.29	1			
3.51	3			
3.67	2	*		

Country of origin:
N = 438; Eta = .18; Sig. = .00

| 3.56 | 1 |
| 3.06 | 00 |

Church Involvement:
N = 439; Eta = .16; Sig. = .00

| 3.21 | 1 |
| 3.58 | 2 |

MICRO-LEVEL TASK OF THE CHURCH
Church involvement:
N = 445; Eta = .13; Sig. = .01

| 3.40 | 1 |
| 3.53 | 2 |

Table 3 (*cont.*)

MESO-LEVEL TASK OF THE CHURCH

Age:
N = 437;   Eta = .14;   Sig. = .01

		1	3	2
2.91	1			
3.10	3	*		
3.10	2			

Education:
N = 433;   Eta = .15;   Sig. = .02

		3	4	2	1
2.78	3				
3.06	4				
3.07	2	*			
3.15	1				

Church involvement:
N = 440;   Eta = .35;   Sig. = .00

| 2.69 | 1 |
| 3.19 | 2 |

MACRO-LEVEL TASK OF THE CHURCH

Age:
N = 438;   Eta = .17;   Sig. = .00

		1	2	3
2.60	1			
2.71	2			
2.81	3	*		

Church involvement:
N = 441;   Eta = .22;   Sig. = .00

| 2.53 | 1 |
| 2.80 | 2 |

Table 4a. Correlation—Social Characteristics and Attitudes toward the church

	culturally-adapted	hierarchical-centralized	democratic
localistic autoritarianism	.19** (N=428)	.36** (N=423)	.08 (N=430)
subjective-perceived threat	.11* (N=428)	.31** (N=422)	−.05 (N=429)
conformism	.13** (N=428)	.20** (N=424)	.03 (N=429)
anomie	.14** (N=425)	.29** (N=419)	−.04 (N=427)

** p < .01; * p < .05 (2-tailed)

Table 4b. Correlation—Social Characteristics and Attitudes toward the church

	micro-level task	meso-level task	macro-level task
localistic autoritarianism	.05 (N=434)	.15** (N=431)	.21** (N=430)
subjective-perceived threat	−.05 (N=433)	−.09 (N=429)	−.01 (N=428)
conformism	.10* (N=435)	.18** (N=431)	.18** (N=430)
anomie	−.00 (N=433)	.06 (N=429)	.06 (N=428)

** p < .01; * p < .05 (2-tailed)

APPENDIX 7 (CHAPTER 7—ETHNOCENTRISM)

Table 1. Factor Analysis

Table 1a. Positive in-group

	Communality	Factor 1	
35_4	.72	.86	positive in-group
35_3	.42	.65	
35_1	.26	.51	
35_2	.25	.50	
Explained variance: 41%			

Criteria mineigen (1); iterate (50); extraction: paf; rotation: varimax/oblimin; N = 443

Table 1b. Negative out-group

	Communality	Factor 1	
34_1	.39	.63	negative out-group
34_2	.28	.53	
34_4	.26	.52	
34_5	.61	.78	
34_6	.54	.73	
34_8	.27	.52	
34_9	.56	.75	
34_10	.54	.73	
Explained variance: 43%			

Criteria mineigen (1); iterate (50); extraction: paf; rotation: varimax/oblimin; N = 439

Table 2. Correlation between Scales (Pearson Correlation)

	negative out-group attitude
positive in-group attitude	.35**(N=436)

** $p < .01$; * $p < .05$ (2-tailed)

Table 3. Variance Analysis & Scheffé Test

POSITIVE IN-GROUP ATTITUDES									
Age:						Education:			
N = 440; Eta = .21; Sig. = .00						N = 436; Eta = .30; Sig.= .00			
		1	2	3			4	3	2	1
3.17	1					3.14	4			
3.36	2					3.22	3			
3.51	3	*				3.48	2	*		
						3.89	1	*	*	*

Church involvement:
N = 443; Eta = .15; Sig. = .00

3.20 1
3.42 2

NEGATIVE OUT-GROUP ATTITUDE									
Age:						Education:			
N = 436; Eta = .33; Sig. = .00						N = 432; Eta = .40; Sig. = .00			
		1	2	3			4	3	2	1
2.05	1					2.01	4			
2.38	2	*				2.31	3	*		
2.58	3	*				2.54	2	*		
						2.93	1	*	*	*

Table 4. Social Characteristics and Ethnocentric Attitudes

	localistic autoritarianism	conformism	anomie	subjectively-perceived threat
positive in-group attitude	.44**(N=432)	.36**(N=433)	.30**(N=431)	.32**(N=433)
negative out-group attitude	.52**(N=431)	.30**(N=431)	.52**(N=429)	.68**(N=429)

** p < .01; * p < .05 (2-tailed)

BIBLIOGRAPHY

Aalders, M. (2003). *Classification of the Population with a Foreign Background in the Netherlands.* Available: http://www.cbs.nl/en/publications/articles/population-society/population/classification-foreign.pdf. [Accessed 14 March 2003].
Adorno, T., Frenkel-Brunswik, E., Levinson, D.J., & Sanford, R.N. (1950; 1969). *The Authoritarian Personality.* New York: Harper (1950), New York: Norton (1969).
Allport, G. (1958). *The Nature of Prejudice.* Abridged. Garden City: Doubleday, 447–457
——. (1966). "Religious Context of Prejudice," in: *Journal for the Scientific Study of Religion,* 5, 447–457.
Allport, G. & Ross, J.M. (1967). "Personal religious orientation and prejudice," in: *Journal of Personality and Social Psychology* 5, 432–443.
Alves, R. (1975). *A Theology of Human Hope.* Indiana: Abbey Press.
Amaladoss, M. (1998). *Beyond Inculturation.* Delhi: Vidyajyoti Education and Welfare Society.
Atkins, P. (2004). *Memory and Liturgy. The Place of Memory in the Composition and Practice of Liturgy.* Hampshire, England: Ashgate Publishing Ltd.
Barclay, W. (1962). *Flesh and Spirit.* Nashville: Abingdon.
Barker, M. (1981). *The New Racism.* London: Junction Books.
Bar-Tal, D. (1987). *Stereotyping and Prejudice: Changing Conceptions.* New York: Springer.
——. (1990). *Group Beliefs: A Conception for Analysing Group Structure, Processes, and Behaviour.* New York: Springer.
——. (2000). *Shared Beliefs in a Society: Social Psychological Analysis.* Thousand Oaks: Sage.
——. (1993). "Patriotism as fundamental beliefs of group members," in: *Politics and the Individual,* 3, 45–62.
Bar-Tal, D., & Staub, E., eds. (1997). *Patriotism in the Lives of Individuals and Nations.* Chicago, Illinois: Nelson-Hall Publishers.
Barth, K. (1963). *Christ and Adam: Man and Humanity in Romans 5.* transl., Smail, T. London: Oliver & Boyd Ltd.
——. (1961/1962). *Church Dogmatics.* Vol. IV/3. Edinburgh: T.&T. Clark.
Barth, K., Gollwitzer, H., Bromiley, G. (1994). *Church Dogmatics.* transl. Bromiley, G. Westminster: John Knox Press.
Batson, C.D. & Ventis, W.L. (1982). *The Religious Experience.* New York/Oxford: Oxford University Press.
Batson, C.D, Schoenrade, P., & Ventis, W.L. (1993). *Religion and the Individual. A Social-Psychological Perspective.* Oxford: University Press.
Beal, J., Coriden, J., & Green, T. eds. (2002). *New Commentary on the Code of Canon Law. Study Edition.* New York: Paulist Press.
Bellah, R. (1967). "Civil Religion in America," in: *Daedalus* 96, 1–21.
——. (1974). "Civil Religion in America," in: Richey, R. & Jones, D. eds., *American Civil Religion.* New York: Harper and Row, 24–41.
——. (1976). "Response to the Panel on Civil Religion," in: *Sociological Analysis* 37, 153–159.
Bellah, R. & Hammond, P. (1980). *Varieties of Civil Religion.* San Francisco: Cambridge: Harper & Row.

Bellah, R., Madsen, R., Sullivan, W., Swidler, A., & Tipton, S. (1985/2007). *Habits of the Heart, Individualism and Commitment in American Life.* Berkeley, CA: University of California Press.
Berger, P. (1967). *The Sacred Canopy.* Garden City, N.Y.: Doubleday.
———. (1980). *Heretical Imperative.* Garden City, N.Y.: Doubleday.
Berkhof, H. (1979). *Christian Faith.* transl., Woudstra, S. Grand Rapids, MI:: Wm. B. Eerdmans.
Berkvens-Stevelinck, C., Israel, J. & Meyhes, G., eds. (1997). *The Emergence of tolerance in the Dutch Republic.* Leiden: Brill.
Bernts, A., Dekker, G., & De Hart, J. (2007). *God in Nederland, 1996-2006.* Kampen: Ten Have.
Berry, B. (1995). *Fundamental Liberationist Ethics: The Contribution of the Later Theology of Edward Schillebeeckx.* Dissertation. Boston College.
Berry, T. & Clark, T. (1991). *Befriending the Earth.* Mystic, CT: Twenty-Third Publications.
Bevans, S. (2002). *Models of Contextual Theology.* New York, Maryknoll: Orbis Books.
Beyer, P.F. (1990). "Privatization and the Global Influence of Religion in Global Society," in: Featherstone, M.ed., *Global Culture.* London: Sage, 373-396.
Biehl, J. & Staudenmaier, P. (1995). *Ecofascism: Lessons from the German Experience.* Oakland, CA: AK Press.
Billiet, J. (1995). "Church Involvement, Ethnocentrism, and Voting for a Radical Right Wing Party: Diverging Behavioral Outcomes of Equal Attitudinal Dispositions," in: *Sociology of Religion,* 1995, Vol. 56, No. 3, 303-326.
Blank, T. & Schmidt, P. (2003). "National Identity in a United Germany: Nationalism or Patriotism? An Empirical Test with Representative Data," in: *Political Psychology* Vol. 24, No. 2, 289-312.
Bobo, L. & Hutchings, V.L. (1996). "Perceptions of Racial Group Competition: Extending Blumer's Theory of Group Position to a Multiracial Social Context," in: *American Sociological Review* 61, 951-972.
Bobo, L. & Smith, R.A. (1994). *From Jim Crow racism to laissez faire racism. An essay on the transformation of racial attitudes in America.* Paper presented at the Annual Meeting of the Sociological Association, L.A.
Boeve, L. (2003). *Interrupting Tradition.* Louvain: Peeters Press.
Boff, L. & Boff, C. (1979). *Salvation and Liberation.* transl. Barr, R. Maryknoll, New York: Orbis Books.
Boff, L. (1978/1980). *Jesus Christ Liberator.* transl. Hughes, P. Maryknoll, New York: Orbis;/London: SPCK.
———. (1997). *Cry of the Earth, Cry of the Poor.* transl. Berryman, P. Maryknoll, New York: Orbis Books.
Borgman, E. & Valkenberg, P., eds. (2005). *Islam and Enlightenment: New Issues.* London: SCM Press.
Bosch, D. (1991). *Tranforming Mission.* Maryknoll, New York: Orbis Books.
———. (1995). *Believing in the Future.* Harrisburg, Pennsylvania: Trinity Press International.
Brandon, S.G.F. (1963). *The Saviour God. Comparative Studies in the Concept of Salvation.* Manchester: Manchester University Press.
Bromiley, G. (1995). *International Standard Bible Encyclopedia.* Cambridge: Wm. B. Eerdmans Publishing.
Bronkhorst, D. (1999). "Een eeuw vluchtelingen in Nederland. De balans opgemaakt," in: *Contouren Vol.5,* 14-19.
Brooks, S., ed. (2002). *Challenge of Cultural Pluralism.* Westport, CT: Greenwood Publishing Group, Inc.

Brown, L. (1966). "The Structure of Religious Belief," in: *Journal for the Scientific Study of Religion.* Vol 5, No. 2, 259-272.
Buber, M. (1970). *I and Thou.* transl. Kaufmann, W. New York: Charles Scribner's Sons.
Burnett, G. (2001). *Paul and the Salvation of the Individual.* Leiden: Brill.
Buruma, I. (2006). "The Dutch redefine tolerance," in: *International Herald Tribune.* Available: http://www.iht.com/articles/2006/09/08/opinion/idlede9.php. [Accessed 8 Sept. 2006].
Bussmann, C. (1985). *Who do you say? Jesus Christ in American Theology.* transl. Barr, R. Maryknoll, New York: Orbis Books.
Cassanova, J. (1994). *Public Religions in the Modern World.* Chicago: University of Chicago Press.
CBS. (2003). Available: http://www.cbs.nl/en/publications/articles/population-society/population/classification-foreign.pdf. [Accessed 6 December 2003].
——. (2003b). *Allochtonen in 2002.* Voorburg: CBS.
Charry, E. et al. (1998). *A Passion for God's Reign.* Grand Rapids, MI: Wm. B. Eerdmans.
Clements, K.W. (1987). *Friedrich Schleiermacher: Pioneer of Modern Theology.* Fortress Press: Minneapolis.
Cobb, J. (1990). "Beyond Pluralism," in: DÇosta, G. ed. *Christian Uniqueness Reconsidered.* Maryknoll, New York: Orbis Books, 81-95.
——. (1975). *Christ in a Pluralistic Age.* Philadelphia: The Westminster Press.
Coenders, M. (2001). *Nationalistic Attitudes and Ethnic Exclusionism in a Comparative Perspective.* Dissertation. Nijmegen: KUN.
Coenders, M. & Scheepers, P. (2003). "The Effect of Education on Nationalism and Ethnic Exclusionism, an International Comparison, in: Political Psychology 24 (2), 13-343.
Cohen, A. (1994). Self Consciousness. *An Alternative Anthropology of Identity.* London: Routledge.
Cole, W. & Hammond, P. (1974). "Religious Pluralism, Legal Development, and Societal Complexity: Rudimentary Forms of Civil Religion," in: *Journal for the Scientific Study of Religion.* Vol.13, No. 2, 177-189.
Coleman, J. (1970). "Civil Religion," in: *Sociological Analysis* 31, 67-77.
Comblin, J. (1988). *Der Heilige Geist.* Düsseldorf: Patmos Verlag.
Come, A. (1959). *Human Spirit and Holy Spirit.* Philadelphia: Westminster Press.
Conference of Major Religious of Men. (1983). *In Solidarity & Service: Reflections on the Problem of clericalism in the Church.* Washington, D.C.: Conference of Major Religious Superiors of Men.
Copeland, L., & Griggs, L. (1986). *Going International: How to Make Friends and Deal Effectively in the Global Marketplace.* London: Plume Publications.
Corecco, E. (1983). "Theologie des Kirchenrechts," in: *Handbuch des katholischen Kirchenrechts.* Regensburg: Pustet.
Coriden, J., Green, T., & Heintschel, D. (1985). *The Code of Canon Law: a text and commentary.* New York: Paulist Press.
Cowdell, S. (1996). *Is Jesus Unique? A Study of Recent Christology.* New York: Paulist Press.
Cozzens, D. (2004). *Sacred Silence: Denial and the Crisis in the Church.* Minnesota: Liturgical Press.
Crollius, A.R. (1978). *What is so new about inculturation?* Rome: Gregorianum 59, 721-738.
Cunningham, L.S., & Barineau, R.M. (1995). "The Breadth and Depth of Religious Experience" in: *The Sacred Quest: An Invitation to the Study of religion.* 4th ed. Prentice Hall, 1ff.
Dahl, G. (1999). *Radical Conservatism and the Future of Politics.* London: Sage Publications Ltd.

Dahl, R. (1965). *Preface to Democratic Theory*. Chicago: University of Chicago Press.
Davie, G. (1994). *Religion in Britain Since 1945: Believing Without Belonging*. Oxford: Blackwell Publishers.
——. (2000). *Religion in Modern Europe: A Memory Mutates*. New York: Oxford University Press.
——. (2002). *Europe: The Exceptional Case: Parameters of Faith in the Modern World*. London: Darton Longman and Todd.
Davie, G., Berger, P., & Fokas, E. (2008). *Religious America, Secular Europe? A Theme and Variation*. Aldershot: Ashgate.
D'Costa, G. (2000). *The Meetings of Religions and the Trinity*. Edinburgh: T&T Clark, Ltd.
De Cruchy, J.W. & Villa-Vicencio, C. eds. (1983). *Apartheid is a Heresy*. Grand Rapids, MI: Wm. B. Eerdmans.
De Jong, W. & Van der Grinten, P. (1987). *Buren van Buiten. Pleidooi voor een pluralistische benadering op wijkniveau*. Utrecht: Vereniging Gamma.
De Mesa, J. (1987/1991). *In Solidarity with Culture*. Quezon City: Maryhill School of Theology,
De Mesa, J. & Wostyn, L. (1989). *Doing Christology*. Quezon City: Claretian Publications.
——. (1982/1990). *Doing Theology*. Quezon City: Claretian Publications.
De Wit, T. (2005). "The Necessary Disillusionment: The Netherlands after the Murder of Theo van Gogh," in: *Concilium*. London: SCM Press, 13–22.
Dekker, G. (1987). *Godsdienst en samenleving. Inleiding tot de studie van de godsdienstsociologie*. Kampen: Kok.
Dekker, G., de Hart, J., & Peters, J. (1997). *God in Nederland 1966–1996*. Amsterdam: Anthos.
Dekker, G. & Malova, (1995). "The concept of nationalism," in: Cross, M. ed., *Nationalism, Ethnic Conflict and Conceptions of Citizenship and Democracy in Western and Eastern Europe*, Volume 1: Theories and concepts, Utrecht: ERCOMER, 15–56.
Depoortere, K. (1994). *A Different God*. Louvain Theological & Pastoral Monographs 17. Louvain: Peeters Press.
Derber, C. & Ferroggiaro, K. (1995). *What's Left? Radical Politics in the Postcommunist Era*. Massachusetts: University of Massachusetts Press.
Derkx, P. (2002). "Modern Humanism in the Netherlands," in: Halsema, A. & Van Houten, D. eds., Available: http://www.xs4all.nl/~pderkx/modhumNeth.pdf. An article based on chapter 3, of *Empowering Humanity: State of the Art in Humanistics.*, Utrecht: De Tijdstroom.
——. (1998). "Het woord 'humanism': opkomst en betekenis," in: Derkx, P., Jansz, U., Molenberg, C., & van Baalen, C. (eds), *Voor menselijkheid of tegen godsdienst? Humanisme in Nederland 1850–1960*. Hilversum: Verloren, 10–33.
DiNoia, J. (1992). *The Diversity of Religions*. Washington, D.C. Catholic University of America Press.
——. (1990). "Varieties of Religious Aims: Beyond Exclusivism, Inclusivism, and Pluralism," in: Marshall, B. ed., *Theology and Dialogue: Essays in Conversation with George Lindbeck*. Notre Dame: University of Notre Dame Press, 249–274.
——. (2000). *Cambridge Companion to Barth*. Cambridge: Cambridge University Press.
Dobbelaere, K. (1981). *Secularization*. London: Sage.
——. (1984). "Secularization Theories and Sociological Paradigms," in: *Social Compass* 31, 199–219.
Doomernik, J. (2005). *The State of Multiculturalism in the Netherlands*. Available: http://www2.fmg.uva.nl/imes/books/doomernik2005.pdf. [Accessed 12 April 2005].
Dorr, D. (2000). *Mission in Today's World*. Maryknoll, New York: Orbis Books.

Dostoyevsky, F. (1999). *The Brothers Karamazov.* transl. Granett, C., Komroff, M., & Bayley, J. New York: Signet Classic.
Duckitt, J. (1991). "The Development and validation of a subtle racism scale in South Africa," in: *South African Journal of Psychology, 21, 233-239.*
Dulles, A. (1974/1987). *Models of the Church.* Garden City, New York: Doubleday & Company, Inc.
Dunn, J. (1992). *Jesus Christ as Universal Saviour in the Theology of Edward Schillebeeckx.* Dissertation. Catholic University of America.
——. (1998). *The Christ and the Spirit.* Vol.2. Cambridge: Wm. B. Eerdmans.
——. (1997). *Jesus and the Spirit: A Study of the Religious and Charismatic experience of Jesus and the First Christians as Reflected in the New Testament.* Cambridge: Wm. B. Eerdmans.
Dupuis, J. (1990). *Religious Plurality and the Christological Debate.* Available: http://www.sedos.org/english/dupuis.htm. [Accessed 25 October 1990].
——. (1991). *Jesus Christ at the Encounter of World Religions.* Maryknoll, New York: Orbis Books.
——. (1997). *Toward a Christian Theology of Religious Pluralism.* Maryknoll, New York: Orbis Books.
Duriez, B., Hutsebaut, D., & Roggen, F. (1999). "Racism and Post-Critical Belief," in: *Journal of Empirical Theology* 12, (1), 5–27.
Duriez, B. and Hutsebaut, D. (2000). "The Relation between Religion and Racism: The role of post-critical Beliefs," in: *Mental Health, Religion, and Culture*, Vol. 3, No. 1, May 2000, 85–102.
Durkheim, E. (1953). *The Division of Labor.* transl., Halls, W.D. Glencoe, Ill.: Free Press.
——. (1961/1972). *Moral Education.* New York: Free Press.
——. (1974). *Sociology and Philosophy.* New York: Free Press.
Dux, G. (1973). "Ursprung, Funkktion und Gehalt der Religion," in: *Internationales Jahrbuch für Religionssoziologie* 8, 7–64.
Duyndam, J. Poorthuis, M., & De Wit, T. (2005). *Humanisme en religie: controverses, bruggen, perspectieven.* Delf: Uitgeverij Eburon.
Eckman, D. (2005). "The Holy Spirit and our Emotions," in: Wallace, D. & Sawyer, J. eds., *Who's afraid of the Holy Spirit?: An Investigation into the Ministry of the Spirit of God Today.* Biblical Studies Press.
Edwards, D. (1986). *What are they Saying about Salvation.* New York: Paulist Press.
Eisinga, R., Felling, A., & Lammers, J. (1994). "Religious Affiliation, Income Stratification and Political Preference in the Netherlands", in: *The Netherlands Journal of Social Sciences* 30, 2, 107–127.
Eisinga, R. & Scheepers, P. (1989). *Etnocentrisme in Nederland. Theoretische en Empirische Modellen.* Dissertation. Nijmegen: KUN.
Eisinga, R., Felling, A., and Peters, J. (1990). "Religious Belief, Church Involvement, and Ethnocentrism in the Netherlands", Journal for the Scientific Study of Religion, Vol.29, No. 1. Mar., 54–75.
——. (1990a). "Church Involvement, Prejudice, and Nationalism," in: *Review of Religious Research.* Vol.31 (4), 417–433.
Eisinga, R., et al. (2000). *Religion in Dutch Society 2000.* Amsterdam: NIWI/Steinmetz Archive.
Elliot, C. (1995). *Memory and Salvation.* London: Darton, Longman and Todd.
Eriksen, T. (1996). "Ethnicity, Race, Class and Nation," in: Hutchinson & Smith eds., *Ethnicity.* Oxford: Oxford University Press, 33–42.
Essed, P. (1991). *Inzicht in alledaags racisme.* transl., Gircour, R. Utrecht: Het Spectrum.
Fabella, V. & Sugirtharaja, R., eds. (2000). *Dictionary of Third World Theologies.* Maryknoll, New York: Orbis Books.

Felling, A., Peters, J., & Schreuder, O. (1981). *Gebroken Identiteit. Een Studie over Christelijk en Onchristelijk Nederland*. Nijmegen: KDC.
——. (1986/1994). *Geloven en Leven*. Zeist: Kerckebosch BV.
——. (1988). "Religion and Politics in the Netherlands: A Causal Analysis," in: *Journal of Empirical Theology* 1, 55–76.
Felling, A., Lammers, J., & Spruit, L. (1992) "Church-Membership, Religion and Attitude towards Abortion in the Netherlands," in: *Journal of Empirical Theology 5*, 53–69.
Fenn, R.K. (1978). *Toward a Theory of Secularization*. Storrs, Conn.: Society for the Scientific Study of Religion.
Finley, J. (1978). *Merton's Palace of Nowhere*. Notre Dame: Ave Maria Press.
Fishbein, M. & Ajzen, I. (1975). *Belief, attitude, intention and behaviour, an introduction to theory and research*. Massachusetts: Addison-Wesley Publishing Company.
Fortmann, H. (1974). *Als ziende de onzienlijke. Een cultuurpsychologische studie over de religieuze waarneming en de zogenaamde religieuze projectie. (Like seeing the invisible. A cultural-psychological study of religious perception and the so-called religious projection.)*, I/II, Hilversum: Gooi en Sticht.
Frawley-O'Dea, M. (2007). *Perversion of Power. Sexual Abuse in the Catholic Church*. Nashville: Vanderbilt University Press.
Freedman, D.N. ed. (2000). *Eerdmans Dictionary of the Bible*. Grand Rapids, MI:: Wm. B. Eerdmans.
Fromm, E. (1963). *The Dogma of Christ and Other Essays on Religion*. New York: Holt, Rinehart and Winston.
——. (1959). *Psychoanalysis and Religion*. New Haven: Yale University Press.
Gabennesch, H. (1972). "Authoritarianism as world view," in: *American Journal of Sociology*. 77(5): 857–875.
Gadamer, H-G. (1975). *Truth and Method*. London: Sheed & Ward.
Gaertner, S.L. & Dovidio, J.F. (1986). "The aversive form of racism," in: *Prejudice, discrimination and racism*. Dovidio, J.F., & Gaertner, S.L. eds., New York: Academic Press, 61–89.
Galema, A., Henkes, B., & Te Velde, H. (1993). *Images of the Nation: Different Meanings of Dutchness 1870–1940*. Amsterdam: Rodopi.
Gallagher, M. (1998). *Clashing symbols: an introduction to faith and culture*. New York: Paulist Press.
Gehrig, G. (1979/1981). "The American Civil Religion Debate," in: *Journal for the Scientific Study of Religion*, Vol.20, No. 1, 51–63.
Gerle, E. (2000). *Contemporary Globalization and its Ethical Challenges*. Ecumenical Review. Available: http://www.Findarticles.com/cf_0/m2065/2_52/64190033/print.jhtml. [Accessed 16 June 2000].
Giddens, A. (1991). *A Modernity and Self-Identity and Society in the Late Modern Age*. Cambridge: Polity Press.
Gijsberts, M., Hagendoorn, L., & Scheepers, P. eds. (2004). *Nationalism & Exclusion of Migrants*. Burlington: Ashgate Publ. Company.
Gillis, C. (1998). *Pluralism: a New Paradigm for Theology*. Leuven: Peeters.
Gleeson, B. (2003). "Power-Sharing in the Catholic Church Today. Making Collegiality Happen," in: *Australian EJournal of Theology*. http://dlibrary.acu.edu.au/research/theology/ejournal/aet_1/BGleeson.htm. [Accessed October 2003].
Glock, C. & Stark, R. (1965). *Religion and Society in Tension*. Chicago: RandMcNally.
——. (1966). *Christian Beliefs and Anti-Semitism*. New York: Harper and Row.
——. (1968). *American Piety: the nature of religious commitment*. Los Angeles: University of California Press.
Goddijn, W. (1989). "Toward a Democratic Ideal of Church Government in the Netherlands, 1966–70: A Sociological Analysis," in: Bianchi, E. & Reuther, R. eds. *A Democratic Catholic Church*. New York: Crossroad.

Goddijn, W. et al. (1967). *Opnieuw: God in Nederland.* Amsterdam: De Tijd.
Goldewijk, B.K. (1993). "Culture and Religion in Context of Integration and exclusion," in: *Liberation from Exclusion.* Schennink & Goldewijk (eds). Oegstgeest: CEBEMO; Nijmegen: Peace Research Center; Utrecht: Pax Christi Netherlands.
Gorsuch, R.L. & Aleshire, D. (1974). "Christian faith and ethnic prejudice: a review and interpretation of research," in: *Journal for the Scientific Study of Religion,* 13, 281-307.
Goudsblom, J. (1979). "De Nederlandse samenleving in ontwikkelingsperspectief," in: *Symposium* 1, 8-27.
Green, G. (2000). *Theology, Hermeneutics, & Imagination.* Cambridge: Cambridge University Press.
Green, L. (1994). *Earth Age.* New York: Paulist Press.
Greene, C. (2003). *Christology in Cultural Perspective: Marking Out of Horizon.* Grand Rapids, MI: Wm. B. Eerdmans.
Greinacher, N. (1971). "A Community Free of Rule," in: Müller, A. ed. *Democratization of the Church.* New York: Herder & Herder/Concilium 63.
Grigg, R. (2000). *Imaginary Christs.* New York: University of New York Press.
Groenhuis, G. (1977). *De Predikanten :de sociale positie van de gereformeerde predikanten in de republiekder Verenigde Nederlanden voor + 1700.* Groningen: Wolters-Noordhoff.
Gross, L. (1992). "Holy Spirit", in: Musser & Price, (eds). *A New Handbook of Christian Theology.* Nashville: Abindon Press, 236-240.
Gutierrez, G. (1974; 1988). *A Theology of Liberation: History, Politics, and Salvation.* transl. Eagleson, J. Maryknoll, New York: Orbis Books.
——. (1983; 1984). *Power of the Poor in History.* transl. Barr, R. London: SCM Press.
——. (1999). "The Task and Content of Liberation Theology," in: Rowland, C. ed. *The Cambridge Companion to Liberation Theology.* Cambridge: Cambridge University Press, 19-38.
Hagendoorn, L. & Kleinpenning, G. (1991). "The Contribution of Domain-specific stereotypes to ethnic social distance," in: *British Journal of Social Psychology.* 30, 63-78.
Haight, R. (1979). *The Experience and Language of Grace.* New York: Paulist Press.
——. (1985). *An Alternative Vision. An Interpretation of Liberation Theology.* New York: Paulist Press.
——. (1999). *Jesus Symbol of God.* Maryknoll, New York: Orbis Books.
——. (2005). *The Future of Christology.* New York/London: Continuum International Publishing Group.
Haleh, A., & Maynard, M. (1994). *The Dynamics of Race and Gender. Some Feminist Intervention.* London: Taylor & Francis.
Halman, L., Heunks, F., Moor, R., & Zanders, H. (1987). *Traditie, secularisatie en individualisering. Een studie naar de warden van de Nederlanders in een Europese context.* Tilburg: Tilburg University Press.
Harrison, P. (2004). *Elements of Pantheism.* Coral Springs, Fla.: Llumina Press.
Harskamp, A. & Musschenga, A. (2001). *The Many Faces of Individualism.* Leuven: Peeters.
Hartshorne, C. (1976). *The Divine Relativity, A Social Conception of God.* London: New Haven.
Hartt, J.N. (1951). *Humanism versus Theism.* Antioch: Antioch Press.
Heim, M. (1995). *Salvations.* Maryknoll, New York: Orbis Books.
Hello, E. (2003). *Educational Attainment and Ethnic Attitudes. How to Explain their Relationship.* Dissertation. Nijmegen: KUN.
Helminiak, D. (1986). *The Same Jesus: A Contemporary Christology.* Chicago: Loyola University Press.
Hendry, G. (1959). "The Holy Spirit and the Human Spirit," in: *The Holy Spirit in Christian Theology.* Philadelphia: Westminster Press, 96-117.

Henriot, P., DeBerri, E., & Schultheis, M. (2003). *Catholic Social Teaching: Our Best Kept Secret*. Maryknoll, New York: Orbis Books.
Herbert, D. (2003). *Religion and Civil Society. Rethinking Public Religion in the Contemporary World*. Hampshire/Burlington: Ashgate.
Heschel, A. (1953). "The Divine Pathos," in: *Judaism: A Quarterly Journal of Jewish Life and Thought*. Vol.2, 61–67.
Hessel, D. & Ruether, R., eds. (2000). *Christianity and Ecology. Seeking the Well-Being of Earth and Humans*. Cambridge, Massachusetts: Harvard University Press.
Hick, D. (2000). *Inequality and Christian Ethics*. Cambridge: Cambridge University Press.
Hick, J. (1999). "A Philosophy of Religious Pluralism," in: Plantinga, R. (ed). *Christianity and Plurality*. Oxford: Blackwell Publisher, 322–346.
——. (1997). "A Christian Theology of Religions: The Rainbows of Faith," in: *International Journal for Philosophy of Religion*. Vol.42, No. 2. Springer Netherlands, 124–128.
Hillman, E. (1989). *Many Paths: A Catholic Approach to Religious Pluralism*. Maryknoll, New York: Orbis Books.
Hinze, B. & Dabney, D. (2001). *Advents of the Spirit An Introduction To The Current Study Of Pneumatology*. Milwaukee Wisconsin: Marquette University Press.
Hinze, B. (2006). *Practices of Dialogue in the Roman Catholic Church*. New York/London: Continuum International Publishing Group.
Hodgson, P. (1994). *The Winds of the Spirit*. London: SCM Press Ltd.
Hofstede, G. (1987). *Gevolgen van het Nederlanderschap: gezondheid, recht, en economie*. Maastricht: Rijksuniversiteit Limburg.
Holmes, B. (2002). *Race & Cosmos*. New York/London: Continuum International Publishing Group.
Holmes, S. (2002a). *Listening to the Past. The Place of Tradition in Theology*. Carlisle: Paternoster Press.
Hood, R., Spilka, B., Hunsberger, B., & Gorsuch, R. (1996). *Psychology of Religion: an empirical approach*. 2nd ed. New York: Guildford Press.
Hooghe, M. Reeskens, T., Stolle, D., & Trappers, A. (2006). "Ethnic Diversity, Trust, and Ethnocentrism and Europe," A paper presented at the 102nd Annual Meeting of the American Political Science Association. Philadelphia, Aug. 31–Sept. 3, 2006. Available: http://soc.kuleuven.be/pol/docs/0608-APSA.pdf.
Houston, J.M. (1993). *The Holy Spirit in Contemporary Spirituality*. Nottingham: Grove Books Ltd.
Hughes, G. (1985). *God of Surprises*. London: Darton, Longman, and Todd, Ltd.
——. (2003). *Transcendence and history: the search for Ultimacy from ancient societies to postmodernity*. Missouri: University of Missouri Press.
Hunsinger, G. (2000). "Karl Barth's Christology: Its Basic Chalcedonian Character," in: *Disruptive Grace*. Grand Rapidss, MI: Wm. B. Eerdmans, 131–147.
Hutchinson, J. and Smith, A. eds. (1996). *Ethnicity*. Oxford: Oxford University Press.
Imbelli, R.I. (1987). "Holy Spirit", in: Komonchak, J. et al. ed. *Dictionary of Theology*, Dublin: Gill & Macmillan, 474–489.
Inglehart, R. & Baker W. (2000). "Modernization, Cultural Change, and the Persistence of Traditional Values," in: *American Sociological Review* Vol. 65, 19–51.
Israel, J. (2001). *Radical Enlightenment: Philosophy and the Making of Modernity 1650-1750*. New York:Oxford University Press.
ISSP. (2002). Available: http://www.gesis.org/en/Data_service/issp/data/list_quest_pdf.htm. [Accessed: 25 November 2002].
Jacobs, D. (2000). "Giving Foreigners the Vote: Ethnocentrism in Dutch and Belgian Political Debates," in: Ter Wal, J. & Verkuyten, M. eds. *Comparative Perspectives on Racism*. Aldershot/Burlington: Ashgate, 117–138.

James, W. (1978). *The Varieties of Religious Experience*. Garden City, N.Y.: Image Books.
Janssen, J. et al. (1994). "Images of God in Adolescence," in: *The International Journal for the Psychology of Religion*. 4, (2), 105-122.
Jantzen, G. (1984). *Human Diversity and Salvation in Christ*. Religious Studies 20. Cambridge: Cambridge University Press.
Jeurissen, R. (1993). *Peace and Religion*. Kampen: Kok Pharos Publishing House.
John Paul II. (1979). *Redemptor Hominis*. Vatican: Libreria Editrice Vaticana.
——. (1984). *Salvifici Doloris*. Vatican: Libreria Editrice Vaticana.
——. (1989). *Peace with God the Creator, Peace with All Creation*. Vatican: Libreria Editrice Vaticana.
Kalbheim & Ziebertz. (2001/2002). "God in Creation? An Empirical Survey among Dutch Adults," in: *Imagining God*. Münster: LIT, 145-157.
Kant, I. (1986). *Foundations of the Metaphysics of Morals*. transl., Beck, L.W. Indianapolis: Macmillan Publishing.
Karkkainen, V. (2002). *Pneumatology: The Holy Spirit in Ecumenical, International, & Contextual Perspective*. Grand Rapids, MI.: Baker Academic.
——. (2002a). *Toward a Pneumatological Theology*. New York: University Press of America.
Kasper, W. (1976). *Jesus the Christ*. transl. Green, V. New York: Paulist Press.
——. (1984). *The God of Jesus Christ*. transl. O'Connell, M. New York: The Crossroad Publ. Company.
Katechismus van de Katholieke Kerk. (1995). Baarn/Kampen:Gooi en Sticht/Intermedium.
Kaufmann, F-X. (1979). *Kirche begreifen. Analysen und Thesen zur gesellschaftlichen Verfassung des Christentums*. Freiburg: Herder.
Kelly, J. (2000). *Early Christian Doctrines*. New York/London: Continuum International Publishing Group.
Kerkhofs, J. (1971). "The Dutch Pastoral Council as a Model for a Democratic Church Assembly" in: Müller, A. ed. *Democratization of the Church*. New York: Herder & Herder/Concilium 63, 135-142.
Kleinpenning, G. (1993). *Structure and content of racis beliefs. An empirical study of ethnice attitudes, stereotypes and ethnic hierarchy*. Utrecht: ISOR.
Knitter, P. & Hick, J., eds. (1987). *The Myth of Christian Uniqueness*. Maryknoll, New York: Orbis Books.
Knitter, P. (1985). *No Other Name?* London: SCM Press.
Kockelkoren, P. (1995). "Ethical Aspects of Plant Biotechnology. Report for the Dutch Government Commission on Ethical Aspects of Biotechnology in Plants," in: Huizer, G. & Verkleij, F., (eds). *Agriculture and Spirituality*. Utrecht: International Books, 99-105.
Koffeman, L. (1986). *Kerk als sacramentum*. Kampen: Van den Berg.
Koenig, J. (1985). *New Testament Hospitality: Partnership with Strangers as Promise and Mission*. Philadelphia: Fortress Press.
Komonchak, J. (2000). "The Significance of Vatican Council II for Ecclesiology," in: Phan, P. & Granfield, P. eds. *The Gift of the Church: A Textbook Ecclesiology in Honor of Patrick Granfield, O.S.B*. Minnesota: Liturgical Press, 69-93.
Komonchak, J., Collins, M. and Lane, D., eds. (1987). *The New Dictionary of Theology*. Dublin: Gill & Macmillan Ltd.
Kossmann, E.H. (1963). *In praise of the Dutch Republic: some seventeenth-century attitudes*. London: Lewis.
Kosterman, R., & Feschback, S. (1989). "Toward a measure of patriotic and nationalistic attitudes," in: *Political Psychology*, 10, 257-274.
Kovel, J. (1970). *White Racism, a psychohistory*. New York: Vintage Press.
Kroeger, D. (1991). *The New Universalism. Foundations for a Global Theology*. Maryknoll, New York: Orbis Books.

Krüger, J.S. (1989). *Metatheism: Early Buddhism and traditional Christian Theism.* Pretoria: Unisa.
Küng, H. (1965). *Structures of the Church.* transl. Attansio, S. London: Burns & Oates.
——. (1967). *The Church.* London: Burns & Oates.
——. (1971). *Infallible? An Inquiry.* transl. Quinn, E. Garden City: Doubleday.
Kuitert, H.M. (1985). *Alles is politiek, maar politiek is niet alles. Een theologisch perspectief op geloof en politiek.* Baarn: Ten Have.
——. (1985a). "Ook een politiek onbelangrijke kerk moet blijven," in: Musschenga, A.W. en de Haan, W. eds. *Moet de kerk zich met politiek bemoeien?.* Amsterdam: VU Uitgeverij, 17–34.
Labayen, J. (1995). *Revolution and the Church of the Poor.* Quezon City: Claretian Publication and Socio-Pastoral Institute.
——. (2001). *Incarnational Spirituality.* Monograph. Quezon City: Socio-Pastoral Institute.
LaCugna, C. (1985) "Re-conceiving the Trinity as the Mystery of Salvation," in: *Scottish Journal of Theology,* 38, 1–23.
——. (1991). *God for us. The Trinity and Christian Life.* New York: HarperCollins.
LaCugna, C. & McDonnell, K. (1988). "Returning from the Far Country: Theses for a Contemporary Trinitarian Theology," in: *Scottish Journal of Theology,* 41, 191–215.
Laeyendecker, L. (1982). "Publieke Godsdienst in Nederland," in: *Sociologische Gids* 29, 346–365.
——. (1992). "Publieke Godsdients: Wat Moeten We Ermee?," in: ten Berge, G. ed. *Voor God en vaderland. Nationalisme en religie.* Kampen: Uitgeversmaatschappij J.H. Kok., 23–31.
Lampe, G.W.H. (1977). *God as Spirit.* Oxford: Clarendon Press.
Lapsley, J. (1972). *Salvation and Health.* Philadelphia: The Westminster Press.
Lechner, F. (1996). "Secularization in Netherlands?", in: *Journal for the Scientific Study of Religion* 35: 252–264.
——. (1991). "The Case against Secularization," in: *Social Forces* 69, 1103–1119.
Leeflang, R. (2002). *Ethnic Stereotypes & Interethnice relations: a Comparative Study of the Emotions and Prejudice of Dutch & Turkish Residents of Mixed Neighborhoods.* Dissertation. University of Tilburg.
Lenski, G. (1954). "Social Correlates of Religious Interest," in: *American Sociological Review.* Vol.18, No. 5, 533–544.
——. (1961). *The Religious Factor. A Sociological Study of Religion's Impact on Politics, Economics, and Family Life.* Westport, Conn.: Greenwood Press.
Leuw, E. & Marshall, I.H. (1994). *Between Prohibition and Legalization: The Dutch Experiment in Drug Policy.* Amsterdam: Kugler Publications.
Lijphart, A. (1968). *Verzuiling, pacificaie en kentering in de Nederlandse politiek.* Amsterdam: De Bussy.
——. (1975). *The Politics of Accommodation: Pluralism and Democracy in the Netherlands.* Berkeley: University of California Press.
Loman, A.D. (1882). "Quaestiones Paulinae," in: *Theologisch Tijdschrift* 16.
Lonergan, B. (1971). *Doctrinal Pluralism.* Milwaukee: Marquette University Press.
——. (1976). *The Way to Nicea.* London: Darton, Longman & Todd.
Luckmann, T. (1967). *The Invisible Religion.* New York: Macmillan.
——. (1979). "The Structural Conditions of Religious Consciousness in Modern Societies," in: *Japanese Journal of Religious Studies* 6, 121–137.
——. (1990). "Shrinking Transcendence, Expanding Religion?" in: *Sociological Analysis* 50, 127–138.
Luhmann, N. (1982). *The Differentiation of Society.* New York: Columbia University Press.

MacCants, A. (1997). *Civic Charity in a Golden Age: Orphan Care in Early Modern Amsterdam*. Urbano & Chicago: University of Illinois Press.
Mackey, J. (1983). *The Christian Experience of God as Trinity*. London: SCM.
Macquarrie, J. (1990). *Jesus Christ in Modern Thought*. London/Philadelphia: SCM Press.
Mahoney, J. (1987). *The Making of Moral theology: A study of the Roman Catholic Tradition*. Oxford: Clarendon.
Martin, D.A. (1978). *A General Theory of Secularization*. Oxford: Blackwell.
——. (2005). *On Secularization: Towards a Revised General Theory*. Hampshire, England: Ashgate Publishing, Ltd.
McBrien, R. (2001). "Dominus Iesus: An Ecclesiological Critique," in: *Bulletin/Centro Pro Unione* No. 59, 14–22.
——. ed. (1995). *Encyclopedia of Catholicism*. New York: The Harper Collins Publichers Inc.
McClave, J. & Sincich, T. (2003). *Statistics*. New Jersey: Prentice Hall.
McConohay, J.B. & Hough, J.C. (1976). "Symbolic Racism," in: *Journal of Social Issues*, 32 (2), 23–45.
McConohay, J.B. (1986). "Modern racism, ambivalence, and the modern racism scale," in: Dovidio, J.F. & Gaertner, S.L. eds., *Prejudice, discrimination, and racism*. New York: Academic Press, 91–125.
McDonald, M. (1996). *Christian Life and Liberation: The Basis for a Christian Spirituality in the Thought of Gustavo Gutierrez*. Washington: Catholic University of America
McDonnell, K. (1982). "The Determinative Doctrine of the Holy Spirit," in: *Theology Today*. Vol.39, No. 2. Available: http://theologytoday.ptsem.edu/jul1982/v39-2-article3.htm#McDonnell. [Accessed 13 October 2005].
McFague, S. (1982). *Metaphorical Theology*. Philadelphia: Fortress Press.
——. (1987). *Models of God: A Theology for an Ecological Nuclear Age*. Philadelphia, PA: Fortress Press.
——. (1996). "Holy Spirit," in: Russell, L. & Clarkson, J.S. eds. *Dictionary of Feminist Theologies*. Louisville, Ken: Westminster John Knox Press, 146–147.
McGrath, A. (1993). *Intellectuals Don't Need God*. Michigan: Zonder Van Publishing House.
——. ed. (1993a). *The Blackwell Encyclopedia of Modern Christian Thought*. Oxford: Blackwell Publishers.
——. (1998). *Historical Theology*. Oxford: Blackwell Publishers.
——. (2001; 2006). *Christian Theology. An Introduction*. Oxford: Blackwell Publishers.
McIntyre, J. (1997). *The Shape of Pneumatology. Studies in the Doctrine of the Holy Spirit*. Edinburgh: T&T Clark, Ltd.
McTernan, O. (2003). *Violence in God's Name*. Maryknoll, New York: Orbis Books.
Merrigan, T. (2000). *The Myriad Christ*. Leuven: Peeters Publishing.
Merton, R.K. (1938). "Social Structure and Anomie," in: *American Sociological Review* 3, 672–682.
——. (1968). Social Theory & Social Structure. 2nd rev. ed. New York: Free Press.
Merton, T. (1961). *A Thomas Merton Reader*. New York: Harcourt, Brace & World, Inc.
Messick, S. (1967). "The psychology of acquiescence: An interpretation of research evidence," in: Berg, I., ed. *Response set in personality assessment*. Chicago: Aldine, 115–145.
Metz, J. (1975). *God and the Evil of this World. Forgotten Unforgettable Theodicy*. Concilium 5, 3–8.
——. (1968). *Zur Theologie der Welt*. München: Mainz/Kaiser.

Middendorp, C. & Meloen, J. (1991). "Authoritarianism in the Netherlands: The Empirical Distribution in the Population and its Relation to Theories of Authoritarianism—1970-1985," in: *Politics and the Individual* 1, 49-72.
Middendorp, J. (2004). *Dutch Type*. Rotterdam: 010 Publishers.
Mitchell, J. (2007). *Understanding Assisted Suicide*. Michigan: University of Michigan Press.
Moltmann, J. (1984). *Politische Theologie, Politische Ethik*. Munchen/Grunewald, Mainz: Kaiser.
——. (1997). *God for a Secular Society*. transl. Kohl, M. London: SCM Press.
——. (2000). *Experiences in Theology*. Minneapolis: Fortress Press.
Moltmann, J., et al. ed. (1998). *A Passion for God's Reign*. Michigan: Wm. B. Eerdmans.
Moser, C.A. & Kalton, G. (1971). *Survey methods in social investigation*. Hampshire, England: Ashgate Publishing Ltd.
Müller, A. ed. (1971). *Democratization of the Church*. New York: Herder & Herder/Concilium 63.
Murphy, N., Brown, W., and Newton, H., eds. (1998). *Whatever Happened to the Soul?* Minneapolis: Fortress Press.
Naess, A. (1989). *Ecology, Community and Lifestyle*. Cambridge: Cambridge University Press.
Naylor, L. (1996). *Culture and Change: an Introduction*. Westport, CT: Greenwood Publishing.
Nelson, J. (1992). *Body Theology*. Westminster: John Knox Press.
Niebuhr, H.R. (1960). *Radical Monotheism & Western Culture*. New York: Harper & Brothers, Publishers.
——. (1956). *Christ and Culture*. New York: Harper.
Nikkel, D.H. (1995). *Panentheism in Hartshorne and Tillich*. New York: Peter Lang Publishing.
Norris, P. and Inglehart, R. (2004). *Sacred and Secular: religion and politics worldwide*. New York: Cambridge University Press.
Novak, M. (1993). *The Catholic Ethic & the Spirit of Capitalism*. New York: The Free Press.
O'Meara, J. (2002). "Salvation: Living Communion with God," in: Hilkert, M. & Schreiter, R. eds. *The Praxis of the Reign of God: An Introduction to the Theology of Edward Schillebeeckx*. Fordham University Press, 97-116.
O'Meara, T. (2007). *God in the World: A Guide to Karl Rahner's Theology*. Minnesota: Liturgical Press.
Ogden, S. (1992). *Is there Only One True Religion or Are there Many?* Dallas: Southern Methodist Univ. Press.
Olson, A.M. (1992). *Hegel and the Spirit. Philosophy as Pneumatology*. Princeton, New Jersey: Princeton University Press.
Olson, B. (1963). *Faith and Prejudice*. New Haven/London: Yale University Press.
Oosthuizen, G.C. (1988). *Religion, Intergroup Relations, And Social Change In South Africa*. New York: Greenwood Press.
Pallant, J. (2001). *SPSS Survival Manual*. Philadelphia: Open University Press.
Panikkar, R. (1973). *The Trinity and the Religious Experience of Man*. Maryknoll, New York: Orbis Books.
——. (1999). *Intrareligious Dialogue*. New Jersey: Paulist Press.
Pannenberg, W. (1968). *Jesus—God and Man*. Philadelphia: Westminster.
——. (1977). *Jesus-God and Man*. 2nd ed. Philadelphia: The Westminster Press.
Parekh, B. (2000). *Rethinking Multiculturalism. Cultural Diversity and Political Theory*. Cambridge, Mass.: Harvard University Press.
Parsons, G. (2002). *Perspectives on Civil Religion*. Hampshire, England: Ashgate.
Parsons, T. (1959). "The Principal Structure of Community," in: Friedrich, C.J. ed. *Community. Nomos*, II. Liberal Arts Press, 152-179.

——. (1971). *The System of Modern Societies*. Engelwood Cliffs: Prentice Hall.
Peirce, C.S. (1985). "Logic as Semiotic. The Theory of Signs," in: Innis, R. ed. *Semiotics: An Introductory Anthology*. Bloomington, Indiana: Indiana University Press, 1–23.
Pesch, R. (1971). "The New Testament Foundations of a Democratic Form of Life in the Church", in: Müller, A. ed. *Democratization of the Church*, New York: Herder & Herder/Concilium 63, 48–86.
Peters, J. & O. Schreuder. (1987). *Katholiek en Protestant. Een historisch en contemporain onderzoek naar confessionele culturen*. Nijmegen: ITS.
Peters, J. (1990). "Religie in Meervoud," in: Schreuder, O., Snippenburg, L. eds. *Religie in de Nederlandse samenleving. De Vergeten Factor*. Baarn: Amboboeken, 42–65.
Pettigrew, T.F., & Meertens, R.W. (1995). "Subtle and blatant prejudice in Western Europe," in: *European Journal of Social Psychology*. 25, 57–75.
Phan, P. (1987). *Theology and Praxis: Epistemological Foundations*. Maryknoll, New York: Orbis Books.
——. (2003). *In Our Own Tongues*. Maryknoll, New York: Orbis Books.
Pieper, J., & Van Der Ven. (1998). "The Inexpressible God," in: *Journal of Empirical Theology* 11(2), 64–80.
Pierard, R. & Linder, R. (1988). *Civil Religion and the Presidency*. Grand Rapids, MI: Academie Books.
Pierson, A. (1879). *De Bergrede en andere synoptische Fragmenten*. Amsterdam: Van Kampen & Zoon.
Pieterse, H., Scheepers, P., & Van Der Ven, J. (1991). "Religious Beliefs And Ethnocentrism," in: *Journal of Empirical Theology* 4 (2), 65–85.
Platinga, A. (2000). "Pluralism: A Defense of Religious Exclusivism," in: Meeker, K. & Quinn, P. (eds). *The Philosophical Challenge of Religious Diversity*. New York: Oxford University Press, 172–192.
Pollefeyt, D. (1999). "Racism and Christian Belief: A Theological Reflection," in: *Journal of Empirical Theology* 12 (1), 28–36.
Pope Paul VI (1964). 'The Task', in: *Council Speeches of Vatican II*. Congar, Y., Küng, H., & O'Hanlon, D. eds., London: Sheed & Ward, 15–17.
Post, H. (1989). *Pillarization: An Analysis of Dutch and Belgian Society*. Avebury/Gower Publishing Company.
Price, J.L. (1998). *The Dutch Republic in the Seventeenth Century*. New York: St. Martin's Press.
Pseudo-Dionysius Areopagita. (ca. 500 A.D./1987). *The Complete Works of Pseudo-Dionysius*. transl. Lubheid, C. New York: Paulist Press.
Raedts, P. "De Nederlandse Katholieken en Hun Vaderland," in: ten Berge, G. ed. *Voor God en Vaderland*., Kampen: Uitgeversmaatschappij J.H. Kok.
Rahner, K. & Thüsing, W. (1980). *A New Christology*. New York: The Seabury Press.
Rahner, K. (1978; 1994). *Foundations of Christian Faith*. London: Darton, Longman & Todd/ New York: Crossroad.
——. (1988). "Aspects of European Theology," in: *Theological Investigations*, Vol. 21, transl. Riley, H. New York: Crossroad.
——. (1997). *The Trinity*. New York: Crossroad.
Random House. (2006). *Random House Webster's Unabridged Dictionary*. Random House, Inc.
Rath, J. (2001). 'Research on immigrant ethnic minorities in the Netherlands', in: Ratcliffe, P. ed. *The Politics of Social Science Research. 'Race', Ethnicity and Social Change*, Hampshire: Palgrave, 137–159.
Rausch, T. (2005). *Towards a Truly Catholic Church. An Ecclesiology for the Third Millenium*. Minnesota: Liturgical Press.
Rayan, S. (1978). *The Holy Spirit:Heart of the Gospel and Christian Hope*. Maryknoll, New York: Orbis Books.

——. (1994) "Theological Perspectives on the Environmental Crisis," in: Sugirtharajah, R.S. ed. *Frontiers in Asian Christian Theology*, Maryknoll, New York: Orbis Books.
——. (2000). "Holy Spirit," in: Fabella, V. & Sugirtharijah, R.S. (eds). *Dictionary of Third World Theologies*. Maryknoll, New York: Orbis Books.
Reese, T. (1989). *Episcopal Conferences: Historical, Canonical, and Theological Studies*. Washington, D.C.: Georgetown University Press.
Reichley, J.A. (1985). *Religion in American Public Life*. Washington, D.C.: Brookings Institution Press.
Reimarus. (1970). *Fragments*. Talbert, C. ed. Philadelphia: Fortress.
Richard, R. (1967). *Secularization Theology*. Herder and Herder.
Richardson, A. & Bowden, J., eds. (1983). *The Westminster Dictionary of Christian Theology*. Philadelphia: The Westminster Press.
Richardson, A. (1983). *A New Dictionary of Christian Theology*. London: SCM-Canterbury Press Ltd.
——. ed. (1983a). *The Westminster Dictionary of Christian Theology*. Philadelphia: Westminster Press.
Ricoeur, P. (1973). "The Critique of Religion," in: *Union Seminary Quarterly Review* 28.
——. (1976). *Interpretation Theory. Discourse and the Surplus of Meaning*. Texas: Texas Christian University Press.
——. (1981). *Hermeneutics and the Human Sciences*. transl. Thempson, J. Cambridge: Cambridge University Press.
——. (1984). *Time and Narrative*. transl. McLaughlin, K. & Pellauer, D. Chicago: University of Chicago Press.
——. (1995). *Figuring the Sacred*. transl. Pellauer, D. Minneapolis: Fortress Press.
——. (1995a). *Oneself as Another*. transl. Blamey, K. Chicago: University of Chicago Press.
——. (2004). *Memory, History, Forgetting*. . transl. Blamey, K. & Pellauer, D. Chicago: University of Chicago Press.
Rockmore, T. (1997). *Cognition. An Introduction to Hegel's Phenomenology of Spirit*. Berkeley: Univ. of California Press.
Rogers, R.W., & Prentice-Dunn, S. (1981). "Deindividuation and anger-mediated interracial aggression: unmasking regressive racism," in: *Journal of Personality and Social Psychology*. 41, 63–73.
Roof, W.C., & Hoge, D. (1980). "Church involvement in America: social factors affecting membership and participation," in: *Review of Religious Research* 21 (4), 405–426.
Rosato, P. (1983). "Holy Spirit," in: Richardson, A. ed. *The Westminster Dictionary of Christian Theology*, Philadelphia: Westminster Press, 262–269.
——. (1981). *The Spirit as Lord: The Pneumatology of Karl Barth*. Edinburgh: T. & T. Clark.
Rousseau, J.J. (2003). *On The Social Contract*. transl. Cole, G. New York: Dover Publications.
Rowland, C. (1999). *The Cambridge Companion to Liberation Theology*. Cambridge: Cambridge University Press.
Ruether, R. (1981). *To Change the World. Christianity and Cultural Criticism*. London: SCM Press.
Russell, L. & Clarkson, J. eds. (1996). *Dictionary of Feminist Theologies*. Louisville, Ken: Westminster John Knox Press.
Sabatier, A. (1897). *Outlines of a Philosophy of Religion Based on Psychology and History*. London: Hodder & Stoughton.
Sacks, J. (2003). *The Dignity of Difference. How to Avoid the Clash of Civilizations*. London/New York: Continuum.

Sartre, J-P. (1976). *Critique of Dialectical Reason*, Vol. 1, *Theory of Practical Ensembles*. transl. Sheridan-Smith, A. London: New Left Books.
Schama, S. (1988). *The Embarassment of Riches. An Interpretation of Dutch culture in the Golden Age*. Berkeley: University of California Press.
Scheepers, P., Felling, A., & Peters, J. (1990). "Social Conditions. Authoritariansim & Ethnocentrism: A Theoretical Model for the Early Framework School Updated and Tested," in: *European Sociological Review*, 6. 15–29.
——. (1992). "Anomie, Authoritarianism, and Ethnocentrism: Update of a Classic Theme & an Empirical Test," in: *Politics and the Individual*, 26, 43–60.
Scheepers, P., Gijsberts, M., & Hello, E. (2002). "The Church's Mission For A Just Society: Tolerance Against Ethnic Minorities Among Religious People" in: Dreyer, J. & Van der Ven, J. eds. *Divine Justice-Human Justice*. Pretoria: Research Institute for Theology and Religion, 235–261.
Scheepers, P., Eisinga, R., & Linssen, E. (1994). "Etnocentrisme in Nederland. Verandering bij kansarme en/of geprivigileerde groepen?," in: *Sociologische Gids*, 41, 185–201.
Scheepers, P., Schmeets, H., & Felling, A. (1997). "Fortress Holland, Support for ethnocentric policies among the 1994 electorate of the Netherlands," in: *Ethnic and Racial Studies*, 20, 145–159.
Schillebeeckx, E. (1966). *Christ. The Sacrament of Encounter with God*. New York: Sheed & Ward.
——. (1969). *God and Man*. New York: Sheed and Ward, Inc.
——. (1971). *World and Church*. transl. Smth, W. London & Sydney: Sheed & Ward.
——. (1972). *Geloofsverstaan. Interpretatie en Kritiek*. Theologische Peilingen V. Bloemendaal: Nelissen.
——. (1973). *The Mission of the Church*. transl. Smith, N. New York: Seabury Press.
——. (1979). *Jesus. An Experiment in Christology*. transl. Hoskins, H. New York: Vintage Books.
——. (1981). *Christ. The Experience of Jesus as Lord*. transl. Bowden, J. New York: The Crossroad Publ. Comp.
——. (1981a). *Interim Report on the Books Jesus and Christ*. transl. Bowden, J. New York: Seabury.
——. (1987). *Jesus in our Western Culture*. transl. Bowden, J. London: SCM Press.
——. (1989). *Mensen als verhaal van God*. Baarn: H. Nelissen.
——. (1989a). *Een democratische kerk*. Nijmegen: De Bazuin.
——. (1990). *Church: The Human Story of God*. transl. Bowden, J. New York: Crossroad.
——. (1995). *The Language of Faith*. Maryknoll, New York: Orbis Books.
Schillebeeckx, E., & Kuitert, H. (1986). *Gesprek Tussen Twee Vuren*. Ten Have/IKON.
Schineller, J. (1976). "Christ and Church: A Spectrum of Views," in: *Theological Studies* 37, 545–566.
Schineller, P. (1996). "Inculturation: a Difficult Task," in: *International Bulletin of Missionary Research 20*, 109–112.
Schleiermacher, F. (1928). *The Christian Faith*. transl. MacKintosh, H. & Stewart, J. Edinburgh: T & T Clark.
——. (1960). *Der christliche Glaube*. Herausgegeben von Maretin Redeker. Bände 1–2. Berlin: De Gruyter.
Schneider, H. (1971). "Democracy," in: Müller, A. ed. *Democratization of the Church*, New York: Herder & Herder/Concilium 63, 12–47.
Schoonenberg, P. (1971). "God's Presence in Jesus: An Exchange of Viewpoints," in: *Theology Digest* 19, 29–38.

———. (1991). *De Geest, het Woord en de Zoon. Theologische overdenkingen over Geest-Christologie, Logos-Christologie en Drieënheidsleer.* Averbode/Kampen: Altiora/Kok.
Schreiter, R. ed. (1984). *The Schillebeeckx Reader.* New York: Crossroad.
———. (1985). *Constructing Local Theologies.* Maryknoll, New York: Orbis Books.
———. (1997). *The New Catholicity. Theology Between The Global and the Local.* Maryknoll, New York: Orbis Books.
Schreuder, O. & Snippenburg, L., eds. (1990). *Religie in de Nederlandse samenleving. De Vergeten Factor.* Baarn: Amboboeken.
Schuman, H., Steeh, C., Bobo, L., & Krysan, M. (1997). *Racial attitudes in America, trends and interpretations.* Massachusetts: Harvard University Press.
Schwienhorst-Schönberger, L. (1995). *Fremder. Lexikon für Theologie und Kirche 4.* Freiburg:Herder.
Sen, A. (2000). *Beyond Identity. Other People.* The New Republic.
Shaw, R. (2000). *Papal Primacy in the Third Millenium.* Indiana: Our Sunday Visitor Press.
Shilling, H. (1992). *Religion, Political Culture and the Emergence of Early Modern Society.* Leiden: Brill.
Shorter, A. (1988). *Toward a Theology of Inculturation.* London: Geoffrey Chapman.
———. (1992). "Inculturation: The Premise of Universality," in: Cornille, C. & Neckebrouck, V. eds. *A Universal Faith?* Louvain: Peeters Press/Wm.B. Eerdmans, 1–19.
Smart, N. (1968*). Secular Education and the Logic of Religion.* London: Faber.
Smith, A.D. (1999). *Myths & Memories of the Nation.* Oxford: Oxford University Press.
———. (1998). *Nationalism and Modernism: a critical survey of recent theories of nations and nationalism.* New York: Routledge.
Smith, M. (2001). *The Origins of Biblical Monotheism.* New York: Oxford University Press.
Smitskamp, H. (1947). *Calvinistisch national besef in Nederland vóór het midden der 17ᵉ eeuw.* 's-Gravenhage: Daamen.
Sniderman, P., Hagendoorn, L., & Prior, M. (2004). "Predisposing Factors and Situational Triggers: Exclusionary reactions to Immigrant Minorities," in: *American Political Science Review* 98, 35–49.
Sniderman, P., Peri, P., De Figueiredo, Jr., & Piazza, T. (2002). *The Outsider.* Princeton: Princeton University Press.
Sobrino, J. (1978). *Christology at the Crossroads.* transl. Drury, J. Maryknoll, New York: Orbis Books.
———. (1993). *Jesus the Liberator. A Historical-Theological View.* Maryknoll, New York: Orbis Books.
SOCON (2000). *Sociaal culturele ontwikkelingen in Nederland.* Nijmegen: ITS.
Sölle, D. (1984). *Suffering.* Philadelphia: Fortress Press.
———. (1984). *The Strength of the Weak.* Philadelphia: The Westminster Press.
Soroka, S., Johnston, R., and Banting, K. (2005). *Ties that Bind- Cohesion and Diversity in Canada.* Paper Presented at the IRPP Conference Diversity and Canada's Future. Montebello.
Sparks, K. (1998). *Ethnicity & Identity in Ancient Israel.* Indiana: Eisenbrauns.
Spilka, B., Reynolds, J.F. (1965). "Religion and prejudice: A factor-analytic study," in: *Review of Religious Research* 6, 163–168.
Srole, L. (1956). "Social Integration and Certain corollaries: an exploratory study," in: *American Sociological Review* 21, 709–716.
Stark, R. & Glock, C. (1969). "Prejudice and Churches," in: Stark, C. & Siegelman, E. eds. *Prejudice U.S.A.* New York: Praeger, 70–95.
Stark, R. & Bainbridge, W. (1985). *The Future of Religion. Secularization, Revival and Cult Formation.* Berkeley: University of California Press.

——. (1987). *A Theory of Religion*. New York: Peter Lang Publishing Inc.
Stark, R. (2001). *One True God. Historical Consequences of Monotheism*. Princeton: Princeton University Press.
——. (2003). *For the Glory of God*. Princeton: Princeton University Press.
Staub, E. (1997). "Blind versus constructive patriotism: Moving from embeddedness in the group to critical loyalty and action," in: Bar-Tal & Staub (eds). *Patriotism in the lives of individuals and nations*. Chicago: Nelson-Hall, 213–228.
Sterkens, C. (2001). *Interreligious Learning*. Leiden: Brill.
Strauss, C.L. (1979). *Le Monde* 21–22 Jan. 1979.
Strauss, D. (1835/1860). *The Life of Jesus Critically Examined*. transl. Evans, M. New York: Calvin Blanchard.
Streib, H. ed. (2007). *Religion inside and outside Traditional Institutions*. Leiden/London: Brill.
Stylianopoulos, T. & Heim, M. eds. (1986). *Spirit of Truth. Ecumenical Perspectives on the Holy Spirit*. Massachusetts: Holy Cross Orthodox Press.
Sullivan, F. (1992). *Salvation Outside the Church?* New York: Paulist Press.
Sumner, W.G. (1959). *Folkways*. New York: Dover Publications.
Swinburne, R. (1977). *The Coherence of Theism*. Oxford: Oxford University Press.
——. (1979). *The Existence of God*. Oxford: The Clarendon Press.
Tae Wha Yoo. (2002). *The Spirit of Liberation: Jürgen Moltmann's Trinitarian Pneumatology*. Dissertation. Amsterdam: Vrije Universiteit.
Taguieff, P.A. (1987). *La force du prejudge: essays sur le racisme et ses doubles*. Paris: Gallimard.
——. (2001). *The Force of Prejudice: On Racism and Its Doubles*. Minnesota: University of Minnesota Press.
Tajfel, H., & Turner, J. (1979). "An integrative theory of intergroup conflict," in: Austin, W.G., & Worchel, S. (eds). *The social psychology of intergroup relations*. Monterrey: Brooks/Cole, 33–47.
Tavernier, J. (1991). "Human or Secular History as a Medium for the History of Salvation or its Opposite: Outside the World there is No Salvation," in: *Concilium* 1991/4, 3–15.
Taylor, C. (1989). *Sources of the Self. The Making of the Mordern Identity*. Harvard: Harvard University Press.
Ter Borg, M.B. (1990). "Publieke Religie in Nederland," in: Schreuder, O., Snippenburg, L., (eds). *Religie in de Nederlandse samenleving. De Vergeten Factor*. Baarn: Amboboeken, 165–184.
Ter Wal, J., Verkuyten, M. (2000). *Comparative Perspectives on Racism*. Aldershot: Ashgate.
Tesser, P., Dugteren, C., Heiweijer, L., & Van der Wouden, H. (1995). *Rapportage Minderheden 1995. Concentratie en segregatie*. Rijkswijk: Sociaal Cultureel Planbureau.
Thomassen, J., ed. (1991). *Hedendaagse Democratie*. Alphen a/d Rijn: Samsom, 165–186.
Thompson, W. (1985). *The Jesus Debate. A Survey and Synthesis*. New York: Paulist Press.
Thung, M. (1980). *Naar een publiek ethos? Godsdienstsociologische kanttekeningen bij de jaren '60 en '70*. Leiden.
Tillich, P. (1966). "The Significance of the History of Religions for the Systematic Theologian," in: Brauer, J. ed. *The Future of Religions*. New York: Harper & Row, 80–94.
——. (1966a). *Systematic Theology*, Vol. 1–3. Chicago:University of ChicagoPress.
Tönnies, F. (1987). *Gemeinschaft und Gesellschaft*. Leipzig: R.Reisland.
Topf, R., Mohler, P., Heath, A., & Trometer, R. (1990). "Nationalstolz in Grossbritannien und der Bundesrepublik Deutschland," in: Mohler, P, & Erbslöh, B., & Wasmer,

M. (eds). *Blickpunkt Gesellschaft. Einstellungen und Verhaltender Bundesbürger.* Opladen: Westdeutscher Verlag, 172–190.
Tracy, D. (1975). *Blessed Rage For Order.* New York: The Seabury Press, Inc.
——. (1968). *A New Catechism: Catholic Faith for Adults.* A Book Review. Theology Today—Vol 25, No. 3.
——. (1988). *Plurality and Ambiguity: hermeneutics, religion, hope.* London: SCM Press.
——. (1990). *Dialogue With the Other. The Inter-Religious Dialogue.* Louvain: Peeters Press.
——. (2002). *Forms and Fragment: The Recovery of the Hidden and Incomprehensible God.* Princeton, New Jersey: Center of Theological Inquiry. CTI Reflections. Vol. 3.
Tschannen, O. (1992). *Les théories de la sécularisation.* Geneva: Librairie Droz.
United Nations (2003). *UN Trends in Total Migrant Stock: The 2003 Revision.* Available: http://www.un.org/esa/population/publications/migstock/2003TrendsMigstock.pdf. [Accessed 14 September 2004].
Urban, T. (2007). *The Struggle of Values in Bio-Ethical Decision Making.* Houston Community College. Available: http://www.texascollaborative.org/Urban_Module/glossary.htm. [Accessed October 2007].
Van Buren, P. (1963/1966). *The Secular Meaning of the Gospel.* New York: Macmillan.
——. (1968). *Theologisch onderzoek.* Dutch translation of *Theological explorations.* Utrecht: Ambo.
Van der Lans, J. (2001). "Empirical Research into the Human Images of God", in: Ziebertz, H-G. ed. *The Human Image of God.* Leiden: Brill, 347–360.
Van Der Slik, F. (1994). "Measuring Christian Beliefs a Review of Two Research Lines and the Introduction of a New Scale," in: *Journal of Empirical Theology* 7 (1), 5–34.
Van Der Veer, P. (1996). *Conversions to Modernities.* London: Routledge.
Van der Ven, J. & Beauregard, A. (1997). "Religious Attitudes And Societal Values," in: *Journal of Empirical Theology* 10 (1), 21–38
Van der Ven, J. & Biemans, B. (1992). *Pastorale professionalisering. Intern rapport vakgroep praktische theologie.* Nijmegen: KUN.
——. (1994). *Religie in Fragmenten.* Kampen: KOK Publishing.
Van der Ven, J. & Sonnberger, K. (1985). "The Structure of the Church," in: *Journal of Empirical Theology* 8, 24–45.
Van der Ven, J. & Vossen, E. (1995). *Suffering: Why For God's Sake.* Kampen: Kok.
Van der Ven, J., Dreyer, J., & Pieterse, H. (2002). "Human rights in the Name of God?", in: Ziebertz, H-G. ed. *Imagining God. Empirical Explorations From An International Perspective.* Münster: LIT., 191–228.
——. (2004). *Is there a God of Human Rights? The Complex Relationship between Human Rights and Religion: A South African Case.* Leiden: Brill.
Van der Ven, J. (1991). "Religieuze variaties: Religie in een geseculariseerde en multiculturele samenleving," in: *Tijdschrift voor Theologie* 31, 163–182.
——. (1993). *Practical Theology.* Kampen: KOK Pharos, 1993.
——. (1995). "Het religieuze bewustzijn van jongeren en de crisis van het jongerenpastoraat," in: *Praktische Theologie* 22, No. 3, 342–364.
——. (1996). *Ecclesiology in Context.* Grand Rapids, MI: Wm. B. Eerdmans.
——. (1998). *God Reinvented.* Leiden: Brill.
——. (1998a). *Formation of the Moral Self.* Grand Rapids, MI: Wm. B. Eerdmans.
——. (1998b). *Education for Reflective Ministry.* Louvain: Peeters Press.
——. (2007). "Three Paradigms for the Study of Religion", in: Streib, H. ed. *Religion Inside and Outside Traditional Institutions.* Leiden/London: Brill, 7–34.

Van Hemert, M. (1991). *Achtergronden van Kerkelijke gedrag. Een onderzoek in zeven rooms-katholiek parochies.* Den Haag: KASKI.
Van Thijn, E. (1997). *Ons kostelijkste cultuurbezit. Over tolerantie, non-discriminatie en diversiteit,* oratie, Leiden: Rijksuniversiteit.
Vellenga, S.J. & Seldenthuis, B.J. (1992). *Normvervaging, de zin en onzin van een maatschappelijke discussie,* Zoetermeer: Meinema.
Verberk, G. (1999). *Attitudes towards Ethnic Minorities.* Dissertation. Nijmegen. University of Nijmegen.
Vergote, A. (1994). "God Beyond the Seduction of Deism," in: Mertens H.-E., Boeve, L. (eds). *Naming God Today.* Leuven: Peeters.
Verkuyten, M. & Masson, M. (1995). "New Racism, self-esteem, and ethnic relations among minority and majority youth in the Netherlands," in: *Social Behavior and Personality,* 23, 137-154.
Volf, M. & J.M. Gundry-Volf. (1997). *A Spacious Heart. Essays on Identity and Belonging.* Pennsylvania: Trinity Press International.
Volf, M. (1996). *Exclusion & Embrace.* Nashville: Abingdon Press.
——. (1998). *After Our Likeness.* Grand Rapids, MI/Cambridge, UK: Wm.B. Eerdmans.
——. (2006). *The End of Memory.* Grand Rapids, MI/Cambridge, UK: Wm. B. Eerdmans.
Vorgrimler, H. (1985). "Van sensus fidei naar consensus fidelium," in: *Concilium* (NL) 23, 4, 16-23.
Vossestein, J. (2004). *Dealing with the Dutch. The Cultural Context of Business and Work in the Netherlands.* Amsterdam: KIT Publication.
Wallace, D. & Sawyer, J., eds. (2005). *Who's afraid of the Holy Spirit?: An Investigation into the Ministry of the Spirit of God Today.* London: Biblical Studies Press.
Wallace, R.A. & Wolf, A. (1991). *Contemporary Sociology Theory, Continuing the Classical Tradition.* Englewood Cliffs: Prentice-Hall Inc.
Ward, K. (1974). *The Concept of God.* Oxford: Basil Blackwell.
Watson, H. (2002). *Towards a Relevant Christology in India Today.* Frankfurt: Peter Lang.
Weber, L. & Dillaway, H. (2001). *Understanding Race, Class, Gender, and Sexuality: Case Studies.* London: McGraw-Hill.
Wessels, A. (1986). *Images of Jesus: How Jesus is perceived and portrayed in Non-European Cultures.* Grand Rapids, MI.: Wm. B. Eerdmans.
Westphal, M. (1993). *Suspicion and Faith: The Religious Uses of Modern Atheism.* Grand Rapids, MI: Wm. B. Eerdmans.
Whitehead, A. (1957). *Symbolism: its meaning and Effect.* New York: Capricorn Book.
Wickeri, P.L., Wickeri, J., & Niles, D., eds. (2000). *Plurality, Power, and Mission: Intercontextual Theological Explorations on the Role of Religion in the New Millenium.* London: The Council for World Mission.
Wiederkehr, D. (1979). *Belief in Redemption.* Atlanta: John Knox Press.
Wiesel, E. (1990:201). *From the Kingdom of Memory: Reminiscences.* New York: Summit Books.
Witte, H. (1999). "De christologie van de katechismus van de katholieke kerk," in: Haers, J. & Merrigan, T. eds. *Christus in veelvoud. Pluraliteit en de vraag naar eenheid in de hedendaagse christologie.* Leuven/Amersfoort:Acco., 243-253.
Williams, D. (1968). *The Spirit and Forms of Love.* New York: Harper & Row.
Wood, R. & Collins, J. (1988). *Civil Religion and Transcendent Experience.* Macon, GA.: Mercer University Press.
Wostyn, L. (1990). *Doing Ecclesiology.* Quezon City: Claretian Publications.
Zack, N, Shrage, L, & Sartwell, C. (1998). *Race, Class, Gender, & Sexuality.* Blackwell Publishing.
Zagorin, P. (2003). *How the Idea of Religious Toleration Came to the West.* Princeton, New Jersey: Princeton University Press.

Zahn, E. (1989). *Regenten, rebellen en reformatoren, een visie op Nederland en de Nederlanders*. Contact, Amsterdam.
Ziebertz, H-G. ed. (2001). *The Human Image of God*. Leiden: Brill.
——. ed. (2002). *Imagining God. Empirical Explorations From An International Perspective*. Münster: LIT.
Zondag, H. (1992). "Religion in Modern Society," in: *Journal of Empirical Theology* 5 (2), 63–73.
Zuidgeest, P. (2001). *The Absence of God*. Leiden: Brill.

INDEX

absolute immanence/immanent, 190, 234
  God, 30, 39, 40, 232
  salvation, 107, 109–110, 127–129, 131, 133, 205, 210, 217, 220, 222, 232, 234, 238–239, 243, 250, 261, 283, 285, 286, 290
absolute transcendence, 53, 190
  God, 30, 39, 40
  salvation, 107–108, 131, 133, 208, 212, 214, 217, 234, 243, 261
actus tradendi, 28
affection-related Spirit, 97–98, 100, 101–103, 205, 216, 220, 233, 238, 239, 240, 242, 260, 279, 280
aggiornamento, 139, 200
agnostic, 30, 204
allochtoon, 3, 163
alternative culture, 142
amodernization, 150
aniconic, 34–36, 43–45, 231
anomie, 14, 15, 17, 24, 46–48, 81–83, 102–103, 131–134, 160, 161, 177, 220–224, 226–227, 232–237, 267, 268, 270, 273, 278, 281, 290, 293, 296
anthropological constants, 119
anthropomorphic, 28, 32, 36–38, 43–48, 208, 214, 220–221, 231, 255
anti-semitic, 8
apocalyptic, 33, 107
  eschatology, 196
  future, 196, 208, 213–214
assylum seekers, 4
attitude
  definition, 11, 168
authoritarianism, 267
  definition, 17
authoritarian religion, 78
autonomy, 41, 55, 60, 78, 96, 97, 121, 126, 142, 145, 184–186, 197, 203, 208, 210, 213, 215, 230, 232
aversive racism, 172

biophilic philosophies, 78
blatant racism, 168, 171–172, 174, 249
bodily salvation, 119–120, 128, 123, 130, 205, 210, 211, 216, 218, 223–227, 236, 237, 243–244, 246, 248

Body of Christ, 136–138, 149
bricolage, 186

Calvinism, 187
centralized church, 143, 145–147, 157, 158, 162, 184, 197, 265
Chalcedon, 53–56, 71, 90
chauvinism, 16, 169–170
Christ as Head, 136, 137–138
Christ fantasy, 77
christian oxymoron, 190
christocentric, 58, 59, 93
christology from above, 73
christology from below, 68
Church
  attendance, 7
  involvement, 14–17, 19, 46–48, 81–84, 102–103, 131, 133–134, 160–162, 177–178, 220, 221, 223–224, 226–227, 233–236, 248, 268
  membership, 6–8
civil religion, 8–15, 26, 32, 170–172, 203, 220, 232, 237
  Dutch, 8–11, 13, 24, 26, 179, 181–182, 192, 195–198, 200, 203, 204, 206, 210, 213, 216, 219, 223, 227–230, 236–237, 241, 245, 246
classical Jesus, 52–55, 82–84, 208, 214, 223–224, 233, 236–238, 241, 257
clericalism, 136, 146–147
cognition-related Spirit, 96–97, 100–101, 103, 205, 210, 216, 220, 221, 233, 239, 242, 260
community-related Jesus, 62–67, 258
conformism, 14, 15, 17, 19, 24, 46–48, 81–83, 102–103, 131, 132, 134, 160, 162, 170, 177, 220–222, 224, 226, 227, 232–237, 268–270, 273, 278, 281, 290, 293, 296
consensus fidelium, 200
consensus, 1, 124, 136, 140, 185, 186, 191
contextual, 10, 11, 12–15, 26, 51, 70, 99, 139, 140, 179, 193, 194, 198–201, 203–207, 209–212, 214–219, 224–228, 230, 231, 236, 237, 241, 242, 243–246, 249

INDEX

control variables, 15, 16, 222, 226, 237
country of origin, 14–16, 19, 24, 46, 47, 81–82, 102, 103, 131–132, 160–162, 170, 177, 233, 235, 267, 272
critical-modern approach, 150, 151
cult of the individual, 151
cultural adaptation, 138–139, 159, 162, 211, 218, 224, 245, 291
  culturally adapted, 142, 157–158, 161, 162, 220–225, 235–239, 242–244, 247, 248, 264, 291–292
cultural closedness, 138–139
cultural racism, 248
culture, 1, 7, 28, 41, 64, 67, 73, 86, 90, 99, 106, 119, 121, 139–142, 151, 162, 165, 173, 182, 183, 187, 197, 199, 208–209, 213, 232, 247
  contemporary, 86, 141
  democratic, 183
  dominant, 7, 141–142
  enlightened, 64
  Greco-roman, 90
  intellectual, 67
  local, 140
  modern, 41, 139
  national, 187
  western, 197
culture of silence, 151
cultured despisers, 182
curvilinear relationship, 7

decentralization, 146–147
deconfessionalization, 185
deism, 31–32, 44–45, 256
democratic, 110, 170
  church, 143, 147–149, 157–162
  ethos, 10, 182, 184, 186, 230
  structure, 143, 147, 148, 159, 162, 191
descriptive aim, 12
differential role of religion, 150, 186
discordance, 165
discrimination, 105, 155, 165, 172–174, 214
discursive religion, 191
doctrine of election, 7

ecological, 42–43, 99, 120, 130, 153, 194, 205, 210–211, 215, 220–222, 223–225, 234, 238, 240–246, 264, 289, 290
  salvation, 119, 125–127, 128, 129, 131, 133, 210, 216–223, 224, 234, 236–240, 244–246, 248
elect
  concept of, 187
endogenous variable, 16

enlightenment, 32, 54, 59, 60, 62, 75, 76, 94, 95, 109, 182–183, 197, 199, 210, 230
ethos, 10, 182, 230, 247
eschatological prophet, 66
ethnic minorities, 3–4, 6, 8, 20–21, 105, 163, 166, 168, 171–173, 175, 254, 255
ethnic prejudice, 6–8, 171, 214
ethnocentrism, 1–2, 5, 6, 8–20, 26, 106, 155, 163, 166–174, 179, 193, 204, 206–208, 213, 214, 216, 217, 219, 220, 222–225, 227, 229–231, 236, 237, 243, 244, 246–250
everyday racism, 172, 174
exclusivism, 114–117, 127–131, 133–134, 205, 212, 217, 220–222, 226, 234, 235, 284, 285, 287, 290
exclusivistic, 5, 131, 133, 197, 208, 214, 223–225, 236–240, 241–245, 248, 262
exogenous variable, 16
extreme right voting, 4, 164
extrinsic religious orientation, 8

feminist, 43, 99, 122, 125
filioque, 85
future-oriented salvation, 111, 113–114, 127–130, 134, 208, 214, 227, 234, 237, 239, 242–243, 262

gemeinschaft, 152, 153
gender, 14–16, 19, 46–47, 81–82, 102, 132, 155, 160–161, 167, 177, 219–222, 224, 226–227, 246, 266, 272
gesellschaft, 152, 153
God as Spirit, 71–73, 93

hermeneutical cycle, 65, 67
hermeneutic-oriented Jesus, 50–51, 62, 67, 79, 83, 232, 233
hermeneutics of suspicion, 68
hidden religious ethos, 10, 182, 190, 230
hierarchical, 137, 214
  authority, 121
  centralized, 158–162, 208, 214, 220, 221, 226–227, 235, 237, 238, 241–243, 291, 292
  church, 143–147, 151, 158, 162, 197, 235, 265
  regression analysis, 20, 219, 220, 225, 236–237, 243
historical Jesus, 56, 63, 64, 66–69, 71, 73, 74, 76, 143
holographic principle, 125
humanistic, 7, 11, 19, 195, 199, 243, 247

Jesus, 50–51, 75–82, 232, 233, 238–240, 243, 259, 275, 277, 278
 reaction, 10, 12–15, 26, 181, 193, 194, 201–204, 205–207, 210–212, 216–219, 225, 227, 230, 231, 236, 241–244, 247, 276
humanum, 118, 119
hypostasis, 54, 91

iconic, 28, 34–36, 43, 44, 231
immanent, 29, 30, 73, 99, 153, 184, 190
 immanentism, 31, 33, 109, 203
 immanent-transcendent, 107, 108–109, 190, 205
 immanent-transcendent God, 34, 38–39, 43, 98
 immanent-transcendent salvation, 108–109, 209, 216
 immanent Trinity, 88, 90–92
immigration, 3, 4, 164–166
 anti-, 164
 immigrants, 1–4, 16, 164–166
inclusivism, 114–117, 127–131, 133–134, 205, 211, 218, 220– 222, 234, 235, 238, 239, 242, 262, 285, 288
inculturation, 139–140
individual
 -related Jesus, 60–62, 257
 -related Spirit, 87, 95–97, 100, 233
 salvation, 121, 154
interpersonal salvation, 119, 122–124
interpersonal-oriented Jesus, 80, 81, 83, 84, 210, 221, 233, 238, 240, 277
intrinsic religious orientation, 8

Jesus-related Spirit, 88, 92–94, 100, 102, 103, 208, 214, 238, 239, 242, 260

laissez-faire racism, 172–173
latent racism, 168, 171, 172, 214, 249
liberalism, 165
liberation, 67, 69, 77, 109, 113, 118, 124, 140, 154, 155, 258, 260, 263
Liberation Theology, 99, 155
Likert scale, 20, 100, 175, 254, 255, 267, 269
localism, 17, 19, 267
localistic authoritarianism, 14, 15, 17, 19, 24, 46–48, 81–83, 102, 103, 131–132, 134, 161–162, 177, 220–225, 224, 227, 232–237, 269, 270
Logos
 anthropos, 53
 prophorikos, 90
 endiathetos, 90

sarx, 53
spermatikos, 116
Logos Christology, 71–72, 90, 240

marginalization, 125, 214
metatheism, 34, 43, 44, 45, 46, 47, 48, 203–205, 211, 216–218, 220–221, 231–232, 238–239, 242–243, 256, 271, 273
mission, 9, 66, 70, 71, 93, 135–136, 138–143, 151, 154, 157, 158, 161, 180, 235
model, definition, 87
multiculturalism, 1
Mystici Corporis, 138
myth theory, 76

nationalism, 105, 169, 170
 nationalistic, 1, 168–170
negative out-group, 13–15, 18, 166, 171–174, 176–178, 194, 206–207, 212–221, 225–228, 230–231, 236–237, 244, 247–249, 295, 296
negative-contrast experience, 118
neo-classical Jesus, 55–59, 82–84, 208, 214–220, 233, 238, 242–243, 257, 276, 278
new racism, 172–173
nihilistic, 30
non-personal God, 30, 32, 37, 38, 203
non-western population, 3–4, 163

old-fashioned racism, 171

panentheism, 30, 33, 35, 38, 39, 44–48, 205, 211, 218, 220, 221–222, 231, 238–239, 242, 256, 271–273
pantheism, 30, 39–40, 44–48, 203, 205, 211, 218, 220–221, 231, 238, 239, 242–243, 256, 271–273
partial, 150, 186
past-oriented salvation, 111, 127–130, 131, 133, 134, 208, 214, 223, 224, 234, 236, 239, 242, 243, 261
patriotism, 16, 169, 170
pentecostal movements, 85–86
People of God, 136, 146, 147, 149, 155, 196
perichoresis, 126
personal God, 30, 31, 201
personal salvation, 119–122, 128–129, 133, 208, 214, 243
philoxenia, 5
pluralism, 50, 62, 70, 86, 88, 114–115, 117–118, 127–131, 133–134, 136, 141,

181, 186, 197, 205, 211, 218, 220–221, 234–235, 284–285, 288, 290
pluralistic, 106, 129, 133, 192, 210, 216, 238–243, 262
plurality, 11, 15, 28, 49, 52, 96–97, 106, 110–111, 197, 229
pneumatology, 85, 88, 90, 92–94, 98, 101
poldermodel, 166, 186
positive in-group attitude, 13–15, 18, 174, 177, 178, 194, 206–212, 219–225, 231, 236–237, 244–247, 295–296
potestas
  juridictionis/regiminis, 146
  ordinis/ministerii, 146
  magisterii, 146
pragmatism, 182, 183, 210, 230, 232
praxis, 63, 65–67, 69–70, 149, 154–155
pre-existent Spirit, 92
preferential option, 69–70
prejudice, 2, 6–8, 16, 32, 105, 165, 167, 169, 171, 174, 206, 213–214, 216, 219, 249
present-oriented salvation, 112, 127–128, 130–131, 209, 210, 215–216, 220, 234, 243, 262
pre-Trinitarian Spirit, 87, 88, 100, 259
prophetic, 86, 113, 148, 149, 151, 154, 181, 196, 200, 203
prophetic eschatology, 196

quantitative method, 12, 18

racism, 105, 155, 171–174, 214–215, 249, 264
racial prejudice, 6
rationality, 57, 152, 182–183, 195, 213
realistic group conflict theory, 167, 168, 178, 206, 219
realms of salvation, 19, 107, 118, 127–129, 131, 133–134, 234, 235, 263, 284, 290
Redemptoris Missio, 99
refugees, 1, 3, 4, 165
région laique, 185
regressive racism, 172–173
religion à la carte, 186
religious beliefs, 6, 10, 51, 182, 192–193, 195, 199
religious experience, 6, 8, 28, 78, 94, 108, 232
religious particularism, 7, 8
religious practice, 6, 7, 186, 202
religious saliency, 6, 18, 20, 220, 221, 223, 224, 226, 227
religious tolerance, 184, 186, 230
research
  aims, 12

method, 2, 18, 25
population, 2, 20, 23, 25, 29, 83, 134, 229, 247
questions, 10–14
ritualized civil religiosity, 190, 191

sampling method, 2, 20, 25
second naïveté, 215
secular(ized), 30, 36, 49, 73, 74, 79, 94, 109, 113, 149, 150, 181, 182, 185, 187, 188, 190, 191, 192, 197, 210, 232, 249
secularization, 10, 27, 29, 51, 75, 141
secular worldview oriented Jesus, 51, 60, 3–75, 79, 80, 83, 258
Secular Theology, 73
segregation, 4, 150, 164, 165, 171
sensus fidei, 200
SILA, 22, 23, 253
social identity theory, 14, 178, 206, 219
societas perfecta, 137–138
society-related Spirit, 82, 83, 87, 95, 98–103, 210, 216, 220, 233, 234, 238, 240–241, 260
soteriology, 106, 110, 113
Spirit from above, 98, 240
Spirit from below, 97, 240
Spirit-motivated, 19, 51, 60, 70–73, 79–84, 205, 210, 216, 220–222, 233, 238–240, 242, 258, 275–276, 277–278
stereotype, 171
structural salvation, 119, 124, 125, 128, 129
subjectively-perceived threat, 14, 15, 17, 19, 24, 46–48, 81, 82, 102–103, 131, 132, 134, 160–161, 177, 220, 221–227, 235, 236, 267–270, 278
symbolic racism, 172

theistic, 11, 30, 39, 43, 78, 190, 208, 214, 232
three-dimension, 107, 193, 194, 204, 216
tolerance, 81, 86, 149, 165–166, 184, 186–187, 197, 208–209, 215–216, 230
traditional
  reaction, 10, 193, 195, 203, 208, 213, 224, 237
  religiosity, 197
tradition-bound Jesus images, 50, 51, 52, 55, 59, 79, 232, 233
traditum, 28, 50
Trinity-related Spirit, 87, 90, 100, 103, 208, 214, 220–222, 233, 238–240, 242–243, 259

weltanschauung, 30
work ethics, 187–189, 230